W9-AYH-504

Rebel on the Road

MICHAEL FROME

Rebel

on the Road

AND WHY I WAS
NEVER NEUTRAL

TRUMAN STATE UNIVERSITY PRESS

Cover photo, Boundary Waters Wilderness, Minnesota 1993. All photographs from author's collection.

Cover design: Teresa Wheeler

Type: Text is Palatino, Copyright © 1992 Linotype Hell/Apple Computer Inc./Type Solutions, Inc..
Printed by: Thomson-Shore, Dexter, Michigan USA

Library of Congress Cataloging-in-Publication Data

Frome, Michael.
Rebel on the road : and why I was never neutral / Michael Frome.
p. cm.
ISBN: 9781931112657 (hardcover : alk. paper)
1. Frome, Michael. 2. Environmentalists—United States—Biography. 3. Conservationists—United States—Biography. 4. Journalists—United States—Biography. 5. Environmental protection—Press coverage. 6. Environmentalism. 7. Conservation of natural resources. I. Title.
GE56.F76F76 2007
333.72092—dc22
[B]

2007009857

To the memory of our parents. They meant the best for us.

It's not where you start,
It's where you finish.
　　　　—Dorothy Fields

CONTENTS

PART ONE
From the Bronx to Bellingham

Thanks to Irving Howe – Growing up in the Bronx – Mothers didn't work outside the home – My parents, for all their hard work, never owned a home – Midtown Manhattan had a kind of desperate sparkle – Many of those people brought with them into maturity the sharp edge of growing up poor

Lincoln Steffens was still on the scene – Journalism seemed immediate, direct, and essential – Dorothy Day asked, "What were we here for?" – CCNY, evening session, was a lively place – Where Kazin taught the power of feeling – Grades did not matter much to us

Pittsburgh, 1937 – With its awesome symbols of corporate industrial America – Where the whole river suddenly lit to a rosy glow – Three Serbians and five eggs – The strike was on – The less people had, the more they shared and cared

Not a single one of our stories was worth publishing – Stavisky liked the camaraderie of the small, dedicated staff – I registered for the draft – Lots of hurrahs, but what was war really all about?

The Air Corps was my home – We learned to salute smartly and recognize authority – Studying astronomy, stars, trigonometry, and angles – She was a loner – "But I can't let you go without seeing you first"

Part Two
When Ortonville Meets the Bronx

PREFACE

I was over eighty when I found myself communicating in a college classroom with twenty- or twenty-one-year-olds, wondering how to bridge the years with something worth listening to and useful to them.

I opened by offering the supposition that it must be hard for them to realize I once was their age, but they should indeed believe that was so; further, that one day they would be my age—but first they would have to live long enough.

I acknowledged that the students could look forward to a lifetime ahead, which I could no longer do. On the other hand, I could look back on a lifetime already lived and the lessons learned from it, which they could not.

I might have impressed them by citing the *Dialogues of Plato*. In the very opening pages, at the house of Cephalus at Piraeus, the aged Cephalus remarks: "The more the pleasures of the body fade away, the greater to me is the pleasure and charm of conversation. " Socrates responds that he likes nothing better than conversing with aged men, "for I regard them as travelers who have gone a journey that I too may have to go, and of whom I ought to enquire, whether the way is smooth and easy or difficult.… Is life harder towards the end, or what report do you give of it?" Cephalus in turn allows that "old age has a great sense of calm and freedom … he who is of a calm and happy nature will hardly feel the pressure of age."

With due respect, I do not agree. My own life is still incomplete, regardless of my age. But in the *Dialogues* I found a theme that repeats itself again and again: "To the good poor man, old age cannot be a light burden, nor can a bad rich man ever have peace with himself." That I feel to be a transcendent truth regarding aging and purpose. Presently I invited the students to ask me whatever they wanted, but first suggested a few guidelines on how to have a fulfilling life and career, based on my own perspective of age and my life. Here they are.

> Everyone comes into the world with love and trust and an innate desire to do good works.
> True success comes only from within. It has little to do with the acquisition of wealth or property or power.

The great use of a life is to create something that outlasts it.

There is no limit to what you can accomplish as long as you don't care who gets the credit.

Avoid, if possible, getting involved in issues of personality, since you will have it tough enough dealing with issues of principle.

Have faith, not necessarily in yourself, but in the goals you have chosen for yourself.

"If you haven't been lost, you haven't navigated." So I was taught on my first day in navigation school early in World War II. That is another way of telling someone to learn from mistakes, to be patient and not to get hung up by them. I advised the students to keep loving themselves, no matter what, especially since they would have to love themselves in order to love others.

Cultivate friends. Make friends on the way up because you will need them on the way down. And if you don't go to your friends' funerals, well, then, they won't go to yours.

Following the class, I found a lot more that should be said in order to make a life worth living. I might have told them about Dietrich Bonhoeffer. He was born to an educated, influential upper-class German family in 1906 and joined the faculty of Berlin University as a theologian in 1930. Three years later he denounced Hitler and Nazism; he wrote against compromise in the church, defining "cheap grace" versus "true grace." Consequently, he was forbidden to write, teach, lecture, or make speeches.

He was arrested in April 1943, but even then pursued his principle, using his prison time for reflection on religious thought and becoming involved, from his jail cell, in the abortive plot to assassinate Hitler in July 1944. After imprisonment in Buchenwald, he was hanged at Flossenbürg April 9, 1945. However, in *Letters and Papers from Prison*, published after his death, Bonhoeffer left challenging words certain to long outlast him:

> Something which puzzles me and seems to puzzle many others as well is, how quickly we forget about a night's bombing. Even a few minutes after the all-clear, everything we were thinking about while the raid was on seems to vanish into thin air. With Luther a flash of lightning was enough to alter the whole course of his life for years to come. What has happened to this kind of memory today? Does it not explain why we sit so lightly to the ties of love

and marriage, of friendship and loyalty? Nothing holds us, nothing is firm. Everything is here today and gone tomorrow. Goodness, beauty, and truth, however, and all great accomplishments need time, permanence, and memory, or else they deteriorate. The man who has no urge to do his duty to the past and to shape the future is a man without a memory, and there seems to me no way of getting hold of such a person and bringing him to his senses.[1]

That is why I am now recounting my life's adventures, and what I've learned from them, and what I have tried to do. I should also mention at this point a message from C. S. Lewis. In *Surprised by Joy*, he wrote that he was blessed while growing up because his father had no car. Although most of his friends were better off and sometimes took him for rides, he himself had not been given what he called the deadly power of rushing about. Consequently he measured distances based on standards of walking on his two feet. He came to believe the truest and most horrible claim for modern transportation is that it conquers and annihilates space. That, of course, is the essential rationale behind planes, trains, and automobiles—the faster the better. But Lewis took another view of mechanized speed.

It annihilates one of the most glorious gifts we have been given. It is a vile inflation which lowers the value of distance, so that a modern boy travels a hundred miles with less sense of liberation and pilgrimage and adventure than his grandfather got from traveling ten. Of course if a man hates space and wants it to be annihilated, that is another matter. Why not creep into his coffin at once? There is little enough space there.[2]

In this same vein, I think of what Thomas Merton, in *Confessions of a Guilty Bystander,* called "The Time of the End," which he described as "the time when everyone is obsessed with lack of time, lack of space, with saving time, conquering space, projecting into time and space the anguish produced within them by the technological furies of size, volume, quantity, speed, number, price, power, and acceleration."

That is civilization in the twenty-first century. It's not only distance, but also sound—or perhaps I should say noise—the noise of motors and machines, and voices on the radio, television, home telephones, and cell phones, in the classroom, and at conferences on how to generate more volume, quantity, power, price, and profit.

It is impossible to escape it, even in the wildest, remotest reaches of nature. I (or C. S. Lewis) might claim nature symbolizes stability in an unstable age, and no one can justify his presence in nature unless he goes there on his own power, for the simple reason that if one enters in a machine, then he relegates himself to being a cog in the machinery. And yet, off-road vehicles and all-terrain vehicles—snowmobiles, dune buggies, motor scooters, motorcycles, airboats, hovercraft—"make the impassable passable." They "go through hell and high water—and everything else in between." They contaminate streams and destroy soils and render an area unsuitable for camping, fishing, and wildlife. The user feels a sense of power, excitement, and control, but the focus is in riding the machine as an end in itself, rather than on nature or scenery. He is unmindful of shattering silence on a wintry day or night, of polluting clean air with exhaust fumes. The presence of the machine signals that nature has lost its defenses. But isn't that the point in the Time of the End?

In this same vein, I opened a speech at the Northwest Wilderness Conference in Seattle on October 8, 1994, with the following words:

> Everything is green. Everything is waiting and still. Slowly things begin to move, to slip into their place. Groups and masses and lines tie themselves together. Colors you had not noticed come out, timidly or boldly. In and out, in and out your eye passes. Nothing is crowded; there is living space for all. Air moves between each leaf. Sunlight plays and dances. Nothing is still now. Life is sweeping through the spaces. Everything is alive. The air is alive. The silence is full of sound. The green is full of color. Light and dark chase each other. Here is a picture, a complete thought, and there another and there…. There are themes everywhere, something sublime, something ridiculous, or joyous, or calm, or mysterious. Tender youthfulness laughing at gnarled oldness. Moss and ferns, and leaves and twigs, light and air, depth and color chattering…. You must be still in order to hear and see.

I was quoting from the journal of Emily Carr, written while sketching and painting her powerful impressionistic portraits and landscapes of totem poles, and of trees, tree trunks, and wild forests of British Columbia. Emily believed the glories she found and felt were derived from spiritual sources. But then, creative persons forever seek the primeval as source material and inspiration. Literature, poetry, and science, as Emerson wrote, all are homage to the unfathomed secrets of nature.

I have asked myself many times how I managed to make the journey, starting as a boy in the crowded, noisy city streets of the Bronx and ranging as far as the wildness of the Northwest, and how I presumed to speak with expertise about silence and Emerson's homage to nature. And yet, wherever I am, when I am still and listen, I hear the chorus of thrushes, thunder of waterfalls, mist rising from a mountain meadow at twilight, and ancient voices riding the breezes of night.

But the transcendence of noise is only one way the world has changed in my lifetime. In 2003, I read that Jessica Lynch would receive an advance of one million dollars for a book about her heroics in Iraq. Jessica was the nineteen-year-old Army private captured when her truck took the wrong turn. That much is true, but the Pentagon wrote the rest of the script, starring Jessica in a daring rescue from her hospital prison. As the world saw on video, U.S. commandos broke down doors, entered with guns drawn, and dramatically carried away the prisoner in the dead of night with helicopter and armored vehicle backup. Then the truth came out: the Iraqi guards had long fled, Jessica was well cared for, the doors were not locked, and the hospital staff did not resist.

That much can be expected of a military machine merchandising a war. It was also accepted that Jessica's book would be "cowritten" by Rick Bragg, who had earlier been suspended by, and then resigned from, the *New York Times* for taking credit for reporting on an assignment an intern did for him. He claimed it was common practice, though the *Times* said he violated a rule appropriately called "dateline integrity."

The worst part of the story, what I find hardest to believe, is that Jessica's book was published by Alfred A. Knopf, a firm that built its reputation on memorable, world-class literature. As it happens, I knew Alfred A. Knopf, the founder and president of the firm. He was courtly, articulate, and good-humored. In his later years, he became interested and involved in conservation work and in the *New York Herald/Tribune* reviewed with kind words my book about national forests.

That was nearly fifty years ago. Between then and now a handful of mammoth private organizations have swallowed up the independent, smaller firms—Knopf included—to dominate the media. Now profit is the primary paradigm. The creed is greed and nothing in our culture seems to be exempt.

Business and politics are the most obviously impacted, but it prevails as well in sports, entertainment, music, news, and in book publishing.

Norman McLean, for example, was trained and gifted, a teacher of writing who sent the manuscript for his book around to New York publishers. They read the first paragraph, thought it was about religion and fly-fishing, and all rejected it. McLean then turned to editors at the University of Chicago Press, who took it on and published *A River Runs Through It*, now well recognized and praised as an American classic.

University presses like Chicago actually do publish and sell books of quality in a wide range of fields, perhaps not in the same volume as the New York houses, but they are staffed with competent and conscientious people. They care about their authors and keep their books in print. I can attest to that, having published seven books with them. Four were written for academic presses; commercial houses first published the other three.

Doubleday, for instance, issued *Strangers in High Places* in 1966. After it received positive reviews and healthy sales, I urged my editors at Doubleday to make it available in paperback. They declined and in 1980 declared it out of print, and the University of Tennessee Press picked it up. Since then, the book has had various editions and printings and still sells well in paperback, forty years after it first appeared. In fact, it is one of the ten all-time best sellers on the University of Tennessee list.

In the final analysis, it depends on one's goals. In 1926, when he declined the Pulitzer Prize, Sinclair Lewis said, "Every compulsion is put upon writers to become safe, polite, obedient, and sterile." Norman McLean didn't write *A River Runs Through It* for commerce; he wrote it for himself, in search of his soul, and as therapy in the process.

It isn't about money. Yes, money matters, but I think the challenge is to write something of meaning, beyond the moment, and of self-fulfillment. In my writing career, I came to believe society needs transformation, a viewpoint of human concern to counter the greed and deceit so transparent in this business today. And I have tried to act on that belief.

Early in 2004 Scot Danforth, the editor of the University of Tennessee Press, wrote to me after reading a draft manuscript of this book:

> I'll speak my piece plainly and without fear of offending, since I trust you to sort through what is valuable in my comments (no matter how small) and ignore what is not (and your judgment, as an author, must have the final say)....

Personally, I'd like to see more reflection on the significance of various career choices, some reflection on what it is to develop the skills of an organizer and a political force (as you have been and are) and more lyrical dwelling on details.

I appreciated his thoughtfulness and the respect he gave my work and me. However, I did not think of myself as "an organizer and a political force." I tried to express my opinion without fear or favor, focusing on accountability and action. If it came to an issue of clearing an area of campers or of bears, I said the bears, or any native species, ought to come first and be safeguarded and the place should be closed to camping. I tried to focus on accountability and action, where others—writers, editors, publishers, and leaders of civic organizations, too—preferred the benign and acceptable.

There is a price to pay. I. F. Stone, the conscience of twentieth-century journalism, was scorned by colleagues in the media, investigated by the FBI, and excoriated on the floor of Congress. He followed a lonely road, ever independent and incorruptible. In summing up, he said:

Philosophically, I believe a man's life reduces itself ultimately to faith—the fundamental is beyond proof—and that faith is a matter of aesthetics, a sense of beauty and harmony. I think every man is his own Pygmalion, and spends his life fashioning himself. And in fashioning himself, for good or evil, he fashions the human race and its future.[3]

One can understand how Stone was drawn to ancient Athens, where democracy and free speech were born. He taught himself Greek and explored Greek thought and civilization.

Zeno believed that freedom and equality would bring out the essential goodness of human nature. In my own way, I've been haunted by Plato's image of the cave from the passage in book 7 of the *Republic,* in which he seeks to show the meaning of enlightenment. He warns that unless we move toward enlightenment, we are destined to remain in the cave of illusion and error, without hope of bringing order into a distracted world. Plato wrote also about the true nature of education: it is not really as some professors claim it to be, since they deny the importance of understanding the soul, substituting their own rules "as if they were putting sight into blind eyes."

Plato and the other Greek philosophers devoted considerable attention to the soul in human life. So did Marcus Aurelius, the ascetic Roman emperor-philosopher, who urged the individual of his time to define his own actions and feelings with critical detachment from those of others:

> Forget not there is a boundary set to thy time, and that if thou use it not to uncloud thy soul it will anon be gone, and thou with it, never to return again.
>
> Let it be thy hourly care to do stoutly what thy hand findeth to do, as becomes a man and a Roman, with carefulness, unaffected dignity, humanity, freedom, and justice. Free thyself from the obsession of all other thoughts; for free thyself thou wilt, if thou but perform every action as though it were the last of thy life, without light-mindedness, without swerving through force of passion from the dictates of reason, without hypocrisy, without self-love, without chafing at destiny.[4]

Maybe, as a bit of ancient history myself, as an octogenarian reflecting on his world, time, and the unclouding of the soul, I feel free to express these ancient, timeless concepts of enlightenment. Maybe the ideas have long been with me, but age and the approaching inescapable end clearly evoke a different perspective. Illness makes it more acute. I had a letter in 2004 from my close friend Brock Evans. He had been active for years, working for the Sierra Club, National Audubon Society, and as head of the Endangered Species Coalition until he was stricken by bone marrow cancer. That disease is very serious, almost always fatal. But Brock was not ready to die and made an amazing comeback. He wrote that he was touched by something I had sent to him about reflection:

> I think I am entering such a period in my own life, with my thought process enhanced by the knowledge of my disease and that I may not live as long as I had hoped. I have a heart full of memories of campaigns and battles to rescue the earth and a basement full of papers. I hope I can find a way to do it in the disciplined way you have done.

Besides his sense of purpose, I think his abundant friendships helped pull him through. He mentioned a communication from my wife: "June wrote me the most wonderful warm letter when I was lying there *in extremis* in those first desperate weeks. It moved me greatly and I have saved it. So all this is just to say how you have enriched my life, and thank you for it, all of it." To me, that letter represents an attainment in itself, accepting the gratitude of my friend, plus the reminder that I have been privy to many wonderful warm letters from June, and still am. Can it be that the best is yet to come?

PART 1

From the Bronx to Bellingham

CHAPTER 1

Thanks to Irving Howe – Growing up in the Bronx – Mothers didn't work outside the home – My parents, for all their hard work, never owned a home – Midtown Manhattan had a kind of desperate sparkle – Many of those people brought with them into maturity the sharp edge of growing up poor

Perhaps I owe this book to Irving Howe. In 2001, I read a review in the *New York Times* of the reissue of his monumental *World of Our Fathers*. The reviewer, Morris Dickstein, called it a classic history and "an elegy for a lost world." He wrote that Howe was born in 1920—the same year as me—and "like most children of immigrants, he worked hard to put the ghetto behind him." So did I, but in a very different way.

That review led me to reflect on my own beginnings. I felt that I must read the book to rediscover and relive my early life and explore the world of our fathers. I bought a copy and plunged into it. Presently I realized I had actually known Irving Howe when his name was Irving Horenstein and mine was Murray Fromm. I knew him as a fellow student at the main center of the City College of New York (CCNY) when he was a socialist and I was a young communist. I recall occasionally riding the subway together and discussing the issues of the day en route to our respective homes in the Bronx. He was a very vigorous person, full of ideas, evocative, anticommunist, and sure that he was right.

His book recounts life on the lower East Side, a cosmos of immigrants who came to escape repression, harassment, humiliation, the fearful Russian pogroms, and hard life under the czar. They had fled the cities and the *shtetls* of eastern Europe, hanging together in the marketplace of the East Side. It was their world, with its abundant shops, booths, tables, stands, butcher blocks, and wooden synagogues. They spoke Yiddish, a distinct eastern European language combining German, Hebrew, and fragments of other languages. Howe described the precise way a chicken must be slaughtered, the singsong in which the Talmud was read, foods served during Sabbath, and Yom Kippur and other services. His book deals with Jews as a spiritual community held together by shared history, culture, and religion, despite the lack of a common homeland.

At first Jews congregated in lower East Side tenements along Division Street and along Canal, Delancey, Hester, Houston, and Rivington streets. But thousands more poured through Ellis Island. Between 1900 and 1910, more than a million Jews arrived from eastern Europe, with the peak in 1906 of more than 153,000. In that period, my father, William Fromm, came from a town named Zaleschiki on the Dniester River in the province of Galicia, a pawn of history and a people without control of their own destiny. In earlier centuries, Galicia had been part of Poland, then in 1772 it passed to Austria and the Austro-Hungarian Empire. At the end of World War I, it reverted to Poland; at the end of World War II, it was ceded to the USSR, and when the Soviet Union collapsed, it was incorporated into the new nation called Ukraine. My father, called Velvel in Yiddish, came as a child with his mother, older brother, Abraham (or Avroom), and three sisters. My mother was born in this country. I know little of her antecedents, except that her name originally was Barnowski or Bronowsky, which the family changed to Marks. Her mother's maiden name was Stirman, which I believe is the name of a family of wine merchants in Washington DC to whom I am related. My mother was born Yetta, which she changed to Henrietta.

By the time I was born in 1920, shortly after the end of the first World War, the Brooklyn Bridge and subways had enabled Jews to spread out from the East Side to Brooklyn and the Bronx, taking their values and culture with them—the Jewish grocery, butcher, restaurant, synagogue (shul), candy store, and Hebrew school. In a sense, they were still living in ghettos. Howe recorded that, on one hand, they were criticized for being clannish, on the other hand, they were often excluded from clubs, universities, medical schools, and honor societies, or at best, subject to quotas. They were considered alien, repugnant, vulgar, unclean, grasping, and money-minded. They were ridiculed as "kikes" and "sheenies." Large segments of the economy were closed to Jews, both immigrant and native-born. Banks, corporations, advertising agencies, and professions such as engineering specified "Christian" in ads in the *New York Times* and other New York papers.

Any Jew has experienced anti-Semitism, just as any black, Asian, Hispanic, or Native American has experienced racism. It was, and is, a defining fact of their lives. In *Jews Without Money*, Michael Gold described his own encounter.

> The very first morning the shipping clerk, a refined Nordic, realized I was a Jew. He politely fired me. They wanted no Jews. In this city of a million Jews, there was much anti-Semitism among business firms. Many of the ads would read "Gentile only." Even Jewish business houses discriminated against Jews. How often did I slink out of factory or office where a foreman said Jews were not wanted.[1]

I could relate to that. One summer as a teenager I was out job hunting with a Gentile friend. I showed him the ads specifying "Christian." "Don't tell them you're a Jew," he said. That gave me the idea I could get away with it. It led also in a few years to the name change. It was not uncommon for Jews to Americanize their names; it made it easier to gain entrance and to get along in the Christian-American society. There was still another reason. In those days, almost all communists used pseudonyms like a secret in a trendy game. That is why I changed my name. Over time I may have believed I was somebody else. I may have misled others, but deep down, no matter how hard I tried, I could never shake off my origins. My roots clung to me in my speech and gestures, in a thousand subtle ways I lived my life and did my work. I knew who I was, but kidded myself that I was fooling others.

Many years later, in 1998, I was visiting in the Seattle home of a good friend, Alfred Runte, historian and author. Runte said, "I didn't know you were Jewish until...." While doing research at the Forest History Society in Durham, North Carolina, he had read the text of an oral history interview with William E. Towell. "He called you 'a little Jew from New York,'" Runte said. "But he did say you were a very good writer." Towell had been executive vice president of the American Forestry Association in 1971, when I was writing a column in the association's monthly magazine, *American Forests*. He had decided that I was writing terribly seditious things criticizing foresters and the way they were managing the nation's forests, and so he fired me. I got a copy of the oral history that Runte had mentioned and found Towell's statement:

> There's a great story about Mike Frome. He's a New York Jewish boy with a great disfigurement over half his face. Enormous birthmark. Small of stature, with a deep ingrained inferiority complex. He was a poor boy and, as I recall, he did not have much

education, but he's one hell of a good writer.[2]

The full story of my experience at *American Forests* follows later in this book. For the present, I was glad and relieved, finally, in my maturity, to quit fooling and get the identity issue behind me.

Learning that I was a Jew—not how to be one, but that I was one—was part of growing up in the Bronx. As a child I dutifully went to the cheder (Hebrew school) but it was all duty and doctrinaire. Walking to synagogue with my parents on the holy days we passed through an Irish Catholic neighborhood, where families on the front stoops jeered and heckled, and blamed me for the crucifixion of Christ. I did not have the foggiest notion of what they were upset about. My brother, who was almost three years older than me, celebrated his bar mitzvah, but when my turn came, I opted to grow into manhood without ritual. Perhaps because it was in the Depression years I got away with it.

I was born with a birthmark over my right eye and lip, which made me a little different from the start. In time I learned to cover the lip part with a mustache, but little kids will still stare and point and ask their mothers, "Hey, ma, what's wrong with him?" To make matters worse, I was born left-handed, but the teachers at school forced me to write with my right hand. They considered that to be progressive education; actually, it was painful and punishing. And, as a child of the Depression, I was obliged to wear my brother's hand-me-downs, while my mother darned socks for us both. That was never any fun. Both of my parents worked hard to raise the family. My father had a fur shop on Burnside Avenue with a sign in the window proclaiming "William Fromm, Furrier."

As a child, I believed I was safe and secure in my family unit. I could not conceive of ever being without both my parents—certainly there was no such thing as divorce and I shuddered at the impossible thought of either of them taking ill and dying. I looked a lot like my father and was called "little Willie" by my aunts and uncles and other Galician landsmen. My father would whistle to announce coming home from work in the evening; we listened for that distinctive song and would run to greet him. My father was attractive, ambitious, and jaunty, with blue eyes and wavy brown hair. He was of middling height—nobody in the family was very tall—but he sometimes wore a derby that enhanced his appearance and height. He made no pretense of being an intellectual, but kept well informed by reading the *New York Times* (as well as *Women's Wear Daily*). He and my mother had a partial subscription to the Metropolitan Opera for about six performances a year. He was not athletic or into sports, but still, on some sunny Sundays, my mother would prepare a picnic lunch and my father, brother, and I would go to watch a doubleheader at the Yankee Stadium. It was a special treat when the Philadelphia Athletics, managed by the legendary Connie Mack, came to town and I could cheer for Lefty Grove, a southpaw like myself, in his daring, dominating pitching against Babe Ruth, Lou Gehrig, and the other Bronx Bombers. On many Saturdays, my brother Marvin and I rode the subway to our aunt's home in the Flatbush section of Brooklyn to visit my grandmother. It was a bit of a duty call, but Grandmother was a gentle and kindly person, and gave me candy or coins. Then we would join our cousins for the matinee at the movies. The talkies were just coming on, but the big attraction was the weekly serial, with its highly improbable hazards and heroics.

My mother was pleasant and good-looking in a quiet way. She did not look Jewish, but never thought of herself as anything else. Her sisters and brothers, all American-born, never spoke Yiddish—they didn't know how. Mother tried, influenced by my father and his circle, but she wasn't especially proficient. She had worked as a bookkeeper before marrying in 1917; after that, she was content to play a womanly, wifely, motherly role. When I was a child, she diligently took me to a clinic for weekly X-ray treatments of my birthmark (that didn't do a bit of good) and to a shoe store for special shoes meant to help my weak arches.

My parents, for all their hard work, never owned a home or had much of a bank account. In the Bronx, we lived in five-story walk-up apartments. Those places sprouted all over New York, housing families by the thousands and tens of thousands. The apartment had a large room in front, kitchen in the back, and two bedrooms in between, one for my parents, the other shared by my brother and me. I suppose they were better than the older tenements in downtown Manhattan and Harlem, but they rose up from the cement pavement like stone forests. They were not nearly as quiet, with assorted noises starting with the milkman early in the day, then tenants going in and out, neighbors playing the radio or simply moving around above us.

We moved almost every two years to qualify for the "concession" (as they called it) of one month rent-free. Years later, my parents moved out of the city to Rockland County, New York, and Bergen County, New Jersey, still relocating about every other year. My brother became an engineer; he and I tried to help our parents. "I hope they can find some peace—they've had so little for so long," my brother wrote to me. But it could always be worse. I remember, in the Depression years, grown men offering apples on street corners for five cents apiece and homeless men clustered in Hoovervilles in Central Park.

Many years later, in the 1960s (after my father's death), Mother moved to an apartment to be near my family—my wife, our two children, and me—in northern Virginia. When she died in 1963, her papers showed that she had received a $55.30 monthly Social Security payment. In addition, my brother and I sent her $65 per month. She also earned $15 to $20 a month babysitting a neighbor's young daughter. That was the extent of her income. On the expense side of the ledger, her apartment rental was $72.50; gas and electric were her only other monthly bills. My brother and I learned that she had saved $62 during 1962, from which she had spent absolutely nothing. Moreover, she had bought nothing for herself, nothing for the apartment. Although she had made close, loving friends in the neighborhood, she never entertained. She detested, resented, and resisted medical and drug bills; we frequently had to buy the drugs to encourage her to take them, and often had to pay the last doctor's bill before she would go again.

My father failed in business (more than once), but I believe he was skilled at his work, a craftsman who fared better when employed by others. He was a furrier in the needle trades—ladies' garments, cloak and suit wear, millinery, and furs—virtually all Jewish industries, with an Italian minority. In the early twentieth century, shops were located close to the East Side so the workers didn't need English. This arrangement was ideal for homework, child labor, and sweatshops until unions were organized, conducting bitter but successful strikes and ultimately establishing a system of living wages and decent conditions for many thousands of skilled workers. By the 1930s, they were laboring in lofts of huge buildings in a city within a city, an area bounded by Times Square on the north, south past Pennsylvania Station and the Hotel Pennsylvania to about 26th Street, Sixth Avenue on the east, and Ninth Avenue on the west. The heart of the fur trade was 29th Street and Seventh Avenue. Throughout the day, streets were clogged with trucks making pickups and deliveries and with hand-hauled carts moving from one shop to another. At noontime, the streets were filled with Yiddish—spoken on every street corner, read in Yiddish newspapers, and tasted in knishes sold by street vendors. Working in the fur market, my father rubbed shoulders with his older brother, Avroom; his nephew, Herman; his brother-in-law, Nathan Intner, and other landsmen of Galicia, all working in the fur market. My father's townspeople belonged to a fraternal order that acquired a cemetery plot in Bergen County, New Jersey. Although no longer Orthodox, they wanted to spend eternity among Jews with whom they had grown up.

New Yorkers rode the subways downtown in the mornings and homeward each evening, passing through stone and brick canyons where shattering noise reverberated off the buildings. Mornings weren't too bad; most people got seats. But the homeward rush hour was chronically on overload, with subway guards packing in the straphangers. The relatives on my father's side all lived in Brooklyn. I'm not sure why we were in the Bronx, but they were two different dominions, with different accents, cheers, jeers, and baseball teams. In Brooklyn, the Dodgers of Ebbets Field were loved as laughable chronic losers (until Branch Rickey arrived to turn the team around and move them to California). In the Bronx, the Yankees played proudly in "the house that Ruth built" and that the Babe still adorned with his presence. Everybody loved the Yankees, except for a few deviants who favored New York's third team, the Giants, who played at the Polo Grounds in uptown Manhattan.

I remember life in the Bronx in the 1920s and '30s. Victrolas were in vogue before the age of radio. The iceman brought a block of ice for the kitchen icebox before the age of the refrigerator. The milkman left heavy glass bottles of milk with cream on top. Trolley cars were vital to getting around; looking back, they were pleasant, too. The Bronx had its share of speakeasies until repeal of the Volstead Act in 1933. Al Smith, governor of New York, "the Happy Warrior," failed as a presidential candidate in 1928 because he was a Catholic and a progressive. Mothers didn't work outside the home. Like my own mother, they darned socks, shopped, kept two sets of dishes, cooked kosher meals, cleaned, and, after school, greeted the children with cookies. Doctors made house calls. Parents were immigrants or second generation Americans who forgot the little Yiddish they had learned from grandparents. Few, if any, in my neighborhood owned automobiles.

Life in the neighborhood revolved around the candy store, which offered penny candies, licorice sticks, gumdrops, Dixie cups of ice cream, comic books, and coloring books. Kids played in the streets. Marbles was a popular sport. Roller-skating and stickball were other street sports. I was never a great athlete but enjoyed skating and softball, and later handball and Ping-Pong, two very Bronx sports. By 1932, *The Goldbergs* were a top radio show, often mixing an Irish pub, a Chinese laundry, and Italian and German elements with affairs of the traditional Jewish family. The fictitious address of Molly Goldberg (played by Gertrude Berg) was 1030 East Tremont Avenue, at the corner of East Tremont and Boston Road, in the East Bronx. Jake, Molly's husband, was a cloak and suit operator. Sammy was the son, Rosalie the daughter. The last radio show ran in 1945; the television version ran from 1949 to 1954. Radio featured live performances for a variety of tastes: *Uncle Don, Jack Armstrong, The All American Boy, The Lone Ranger, The Shadow, The Goldbergs, Just Plain Bill, Ellery Queen,* and performers like Eddie Cantor, Jack Benny, Fred Allen, and Kate Smith, whose theme song, "When the Moon Comes Over the Mountain," everybody in America knew and was able to hum.

Old-line vaudeville yielded as movie houses sprouted along all the major thoroughfares—wide east-west shopping streets (in the West Bronx, where I lived) like Kingsbridge Road, Fordham Road, Tremont Avenue, and Burnside Avenue, and north-south streets like Jerome Avenue. Admission to the movies was ten cents for kids. In the 1930s, Loew's opened its showpiece, the Paradise, on the Grand Concourse, the broad boulevard of boulevards, with majestic make-believe clouds and stars mixed and moving in the ceiling, and its very own organist leading sing-alongs on the Wurlitzer. For one price, the audience got to see a newsreel, a short subject, the main feature, and a live celebrity guest like Eddie Cantor. In midtown Manhattan the Radio City Music Hall charged 99 cents for a movie and a stage presentation featuring the Rockettes. The Paramount Theater, adjacent to the Astor Hotel in Times Square and the Roxy, a few blocks north, featured the latest movies, plus stage shows and live bands led by Glen Miller, Russ Morgan, Shep Fields, or Vaughn Monroe.

Midtown Manhattan in the 1930s had a kind of desperate sparkle to it, different from the contrived stagy displays of today. A rare fragment of New York flourished on 42nd Street between Broadway and 8th Avenue (around the corner from the Paramount Theater), including Minsky's Burlesque, peep shows, and sideshows (where I saw Grover Cleveland Alexander, the great old baseball pitcher, long past his heyday, peddling memories and autographed baseballs), and little movie houses where for a dime or a quarter I saw *Wuthering Heights* when it was new and British drawing room comedies with Rex Harrison. It was easy to get around on the subway and explore the classy endowments of New York, like Central Park, a great green sanctuary, free to all, adjacent to the Metropolitan Museum of Art and the American Museum of Natural History, and the endowments of neighborhoods—Greenwich Village, Harlem, Yorkville, Little Italy, Chinatown, Hell's Kitchen, the Bowery—all different and accessible. I joined the 92nd Street YMHA when it was new and went down once a week to swim and play basketball, while a few blocks away, in Yorkville, storm troopers paraded under the elevated line and shouted, "Sieg heil!"

Looking back to the 1930s is like going to another world as well as another time, really difficult for a young generation to fathom. There were no cell phones, no computers, no televisions, no jet planes, and no black players in big league baseball. New York was a city of Jewish immigrants, who supported three or four Yiddish dailies and live Yiddish theater on Second Avenue. People were poor but appreciated cultural things in life, like Eva LeGalliene's Civic Repertory Theater on 14th Street and Orson Welles's Mercury Theater, a part of the WPA's Federal Theater Project. Artists and writers were on public relief rolls, working for $25 to $35 a week; people like Mark Rothko, William de Kooning, and Jackson Pollock painted posters and murals for post offices, schools, libraries, airports, and other public buildings.

I entered a level of awareness, or consciousness, at the convergence of the Great Depression and the New Deal, at roughly the same time I graduated from junior high school and began as a sophomore at DeWitt Clinton High School. This was a school of ten thousand students, all boys, mostly white and Jewish, spread across the main building and four or five annexes in the Bronx and Manhattan. I was assigned to the main building near the north end of the Bronx. There was no such thing as a school bus: I could either walk about ten blocks from home to the Kingsbridge Road subway station and ride two stations north to the school or walk directly from home, about twice as far. Most students in the neighborhood, including me, walked the long way of two or three miles through all the seasons.

My brother, Marvin, who graduated from high school as I entered, was a much better student than I was. I lacked the focus and discipline. If the rule said do it one way, I wanted to do it another or not do it at all. From early on, I chose to be in rebellion against authority, whether my parents, the school principal, organized religion, or the capitalist system. When prices were raised in the school lunchroom, I helped to call a lunchroom strike. Nobody bought anything until prices were reduced again.

I can't tell where and when I felt that I wanted to write, or exactly what I wanted to write. In one class, I wrote a review of an essay by Helen Keller on what she would do with three days left to live. The teacher wrote "Merveilleuse!" and "This is work of a quality I would expect from a really intelligent and mature person. It is good college work." What I wrote was:

> I fear the picture engraved on her brain of "these vast banks of stone and steel structures such as the gods might build for themselves!" will be sharply disrupted when she takes her eye from the glittering spire of the Empire State Building and casts it down on the streets beneath the object of her admiration where so many forsaken souls are in the gutter.

On one hand, the comment of my teacher, Leon Chutroo, certainly was encouraging. On the other hand, I did not intend to write anything deprecating Helen Keller. While I was in high school she was a prominent personality, a woman who had taught America and the world to respect the blind and deaf. I respected her. She was a socialist and social reformer, a woman who, like First Lady Eleanor Roosevelt, refused to accept a second-class or third-class role in the shadow of society. As Keller wrote: "The public must learn that the blind man is neither genius nor a freak nor an idiot. He has a mind that can be educated, a hand which can be trained, ambitions which it is right for him to strive to realize, and it is the duty of the public to help him make the best of himself so that he can win light through work."[3]

I joined the staff of the high school paper, the *Clinton News*, where I found myself in company with bright, energetic, ambitious people who considered themselves in training for professional careers. In fact, a substantial number of Clinton boys made good: my contemporaries went on to work for the *New York Times, New Yorker, Time/Life,* for book publishers, and radio and television networks. During my last semester, I was the tryout editor, which meant I met regularly with candidates for the staff and led them through prescribed lessons to help them qualify. The last issue of the semester listed the tryouts who made the staff, including Sidney Chayefsky. I confess that I have no recollection of him, but in a few years, as Paddy Chayefsky, he became renowned as a writer of plays, television dramas, and Hollywood films, including the classic *Marty* (1955), an extraordinary love story about the most ordinary of people, and *Network* (1976), about how Hollywood sold its soul for ratings.

I think many of those people brought with them into maturity the sharp edge of growing up poor in the Bronx. In January 2005, I came across the following in *Time* magazine:

> DIED, WILL EISNER, 87, comic book pioneer; in Fort Lauderdale, Fla. The person after whom comics' most prestigious award is named, Eisner helped launch a company in 1937 that created Dollman and *Sheena, Queen of the Jungle*. Later he created the Spirit, a witty antihero with no superpowers who roamed back alleys in search of bad guys, and wrote one of the first graphic novels, about a Bronx, NY, slumlord, *A Contract with God*. "My interest is not the superhero," he said, "but the little man who struggles to survive in the city."

I remembered Will Eisner. He was one or two years ahead of me in high school, ebullient, self-confident, in a hurry to get wherever he was going. Elsewhere I read of him: "Will Eisner was born March 6, 1917, in Brooklyn, NY. The son of Jewish immigrants, his early life and experiences growing up in New York tenements would become the inspiration for much of his graphic novel work. At DeWitt Clinton High School in the Bronx, Eisner's budding interest in art was fostered, and it was in the school newspaper that his first work was published."[4]

About the same time, I learned of a new book called *Native Sons*, about the close friendship of Sol Stein (Clinton '42—six years after me) and James Baldwin (Clinton '41). It included an exchange of letters showing how Stein spurred Baldwin to write *Notes of a Native Son* (1955) and about what it meant to be black and alienated in America. Stein and Baldwin were on staff of *The Magpie*, the high school literary magazine, together with Richard Avedon, then a shy poet and later a famous fashion and portrait photographer. Stein, who became a book publisher and editor, wrote, in *Native Sons*:

> I knew James Baldwin first in our early teenage years, when I was thirteen and he was fifteen. It all began in the tower of DeWitt Clinton High School in the north Bronx at a time when students anywhere in the five boroughs of New York City didn't need to be bused anywhere but could elect to go to a high school of

their choice. Baldwin, known then and since as Jimmy, went the distance by subway, bus and foot from Harlem in Manhattan to DeWitt Clinton at the far northern edge of New York City, an exceptional school where his last formal education took place.[5]

I knew nothing of James Baldwin and Sol Stein. They were after my time and anyway, were on the literary magazine while I was on the newspaper. Still, I wonder if the school was exceptional or if they and others of our period were exceptional, shaped by the times and the world around us. Many years later, James Baldwin was quoted to me in the most surprising manner and place. I was at the Grand Canyon attending a ceremony marking its dedication as a world heritage site. The speaker was an official of the United Nations and a native of a Middle Eastern country. I found the quotation strange but highly appropriate, and soon after, when I was invited to deliver the Wilderness Resource Distinguished Lecture at the University of Idaho on December 1, 1982, I used it myself.

> For you must say Yes to Life wherever it is found, and it is found in some terrible places. But there it is, and if the father can say Yes Lord, then the child can say that most difficult of words, Amen. For the sea does not cease to grind down rock, generations do not cease to be born, and we are responsible to them for we are the only witnesses they have.

To which I ventured to add:

> We *are* responsible to the future and for the present. Our generation is overwhelmed with challenges—of war and peace, overpopulation, energy, food, and the need of each individual to achieve fulfillment in his or her own way. Yet possibly the most critical challenge of our time is to protect the shreds of wilderness that yet remain.

Thus, when asked (as I have been many times) where and how my work in advocacy for nature in the wild began, the plain answer is that it began as a boy in the wilds of the Bronx.

CHAPTER 2

Lincoln Steffens was still on the scene – Journalism seemed immediate, direct, and essential – Dorothy Day asked, "What were we here for?" – CCNY, evening session, was a lively place – Where Kazin taught the power of feeling – Grades did not matter much to us

In high school, I enjoyed English, French, and history and working on the school newspaper, but generally read what I wanted and tuned out the rest. I learned there was another world beyond the Bronx and Broadway through the novels of Sinclair Lewis, who in 1930 became the first American to win the Nobel Prize for Literature. He recorded life in his own native prairie village in Minnesota, which he called "that most Scandinavian part of America." In one of his early books, *The Trail of the Hawk,* he wrote of Carl Ericson, whose father had come from Norway in steerage and Americanized his name—just as Jews did in New York. Lewis pictured the small Scandinavian towns in his incisive and critical way. He disturbed convention by attacking the myth that American villages were noble and happy. His hometown, Sauk Centre, became the fictional Gopher Prairie, and later Zenith, the setting of *Babbitt* and *Elmer Gantry,* stories of conflict between idealistic heroes and heroines versus flag-waving, self-serving entrepreneurs, charlatans, and scoundrels. He showed America the truth about itself—truth it did not want to recognize or admit.

Writers with social conscience awaited and awakened me starting in the 1930s. I also read the works of Upton Sinclair, Jack London, Theodore Dreiser, Frank Norris, Ida Tarbell, and Willa Cather, but I found myself attracted more to journalism than to literature. Journalism seemed more immediate, direct, and essential in the public process of decision making. Yet I've sometimes wondered whether and when journalism can be considered literature as well, with enduring value beyond the newspaper or periodical in which it first appears.

One book that made a lasting impression was the *Autobiography of*

Lincoln Steffens, by the foremost of the early twentieth century investigative journalists called muckrakers. Steffens was aged but still alive when I first read the book, so he was a living inspiration to me. When he died in 1936 at 76, I was already a young communist and read his laudatory obituary in the *Daily Worker,* the organ of the Communist Party. I noted that he left a widow, Ella Winter, who was a writer, and a son, Pete, who was eleven. I thought it must have been quite special for that boy to be fathered and raised by my hero. Lincoln Steffens appealed to me as a journalist's journalist who fearlessly exposed the wrongdoers in society. He had traveled the country and the world, following the trail wherever it led. The *Autobiography* had only lately been published (in 1931), summing up a long and adventurous life. It is for me, even now, the one book in journalism that stands above all others, teaching the student to be resourceful, unafraid, and "to tell it like it is."

Steffens didn't start as a reporter or a journalism major, but as the son of wealth, who, after graduating from the University of California at Berkeley, continued studies in Europe largely for the sake of study. But when he returned from abroad he found a letter waiting from his father: "By now you must know about all there is to know of the theory of life, but there's a practical side as well. It's worth knowing."[1] His father enclosed one hundred dollars, which he hoped would last the young Steffens in New York until he could find a job. Encouraged by the sale of a magazine article, he applied to the newspapers of the city. All turned him down except, at last, for the *Evening Post,* where he started as a freelance, working "on space"—that is, getting paid only for what he produced that made it to print. But he was energetic and imaginative and before long was earning more than anyone on staff. The editor hired him and he became a star reporter. In 1897, he joined a group that took over the *Commercial Advertiser,* the oldest newspaper in New York, at a time when it had lost its influence and circulation was down to 2,500. As city editor, he cleaned house of the old staff committed to reporting "strictly the facts" and proceeded to hire fresh young men and women (who wanted, openly or secretly, to be poets, essayists, or novelists) and attracted a new readership. Then Steffens went on to magazine work with *McClure's* and later *American Magazine,* both distinguished by strong staffs of investigative journalists. Ida Tarbell joined *McClure's* in 1894 and became one of its stars. In November 1902, she began her historic nineteen-installment exposé of Standard Oil, supporting all of her statements with painstaking research and hard evidence. With Theodore Roosevelt in the White House, it was the period of populism and progressivism, marked by the advent of women's suffrage, civil service, municipal home rule, prison reform, and child protection laws. Muckrakers of the media flourished and influenced the course of history, yet the periodicals for which they worked were mostly weeklies, monthlies, and alternative media, rather than mainstream daily newspapers. Steffens expressed his personal ideas. In the foreword to *The Shame of the Cities*, a 1904 collection of powerful articles published the year before in *McClure's*, he wrote:

> But of course the tangible results are few. The real triumph of the year's work was the complete demonstration it has given, in a thousand little ways, that our shamelessness is superficial, that beneath it lies a pride which, being real, may save it yet....
>
> We Americans may have failed. We may be mercenary and selfish. Democracy with us may be impossible and corruption inevitable, but these articles, if they have proven nothing else, have demonstrated beyond doubt that we can stand the truth; that there is pride in American citizenship; and that this pride may be a power in the land.

The message to me was to challenge the system; that I *could* beat city hall if I never quit trying, never quit digging for the truth. That is what journalism is at its truest and best. In this period, I also read a biography of Paul Robeson written by his wife, tracing Robeson's career through Rutgers, where he was a football all-American, to his success in music and his independent views on social issues and world affairs. Robeson and Steffens regarded the Soviet Union with confidence and hope. Both were demeaned in the media as fellow travelers, which meant they were never openly members of the Communist Party but generally followed the party line. So was Heywood Broun, a progressive columnist for the *New York World-Telegram*, who was instrumental in 1935 in founding the American Newspaper Guild, which seemed to me to bring respect to journalism as a profession.

As a teenager I read a variety of periodicals representing the radical cause. Some afternoons I would ride the subway downtown and hang out around Union Square, the heart of radicalism, where poor people listened to soapbox orators and distributed leaflets to other poor people. One publication I picked up was an anarchist journal called *MAN!*—typical of many that did not last long. Another was the *Catholic Worker*, newly established by Dorothy Day and Peter Maurin, which sold for a penny, and which has lasted till now. In her autobiography, *The Long Loneliness,* Dorothy Day wrote that she always felt "the common unity of our humanity." That is what I too wanted to believe. She recorded that while growing up in Chicago she had read about people who amassed fortunes by cornering wheat and exploiting the workers in the stockyards. She had not seen anyone of means taking off his coat and giving it to the poor. She had not seen anyone having a banquet and calling in the lame, the halt, or the blind:

> I wanted life and I wanted the abundant life. I wanted it for others too. I did not want just the few, the missionary-minded people like the Salvation Army, to be kind to the poor, as the poor. I wanted everyone to be kind. I wanted every home to be open to the lame, the halt, and the blind, the way it had been after the San Francisco earthquake [which she had lived through earlier]. Only then did people really live, really love their brothers.[2]

Growing up, I was troubled by the same issues. I asked the same question that Dorothy asked: "What were we here for, what were we doing, what was the meaning of our lives?"[3] But I did not ask the other question: "What is man, that thou are mindful of him, O Lord?" that she asked as she knelt in prayer. I never prayed, not in any religion. I saw only a material world and thus was more inclined and attuned to the *Daily Worker* than the *Catholic Worker.* I felt the communists pursued a militant, activist program for peace, equality, and social justice, and to bring the Depression to an end. On more than one May Day, as a member of the Young Communist League (or YCL), I marched through downtown Manhattan into Union Square with many thousands of others behind bold red banners demanding freedom for Tom Mooney, the labor leader imprisoned in California, and for the nine Scottsboro Boys facing execution in Alabama, and denouncing the fascism in Italy and the rising tide of Nazism in Germany.

When I graduated from high school in January 1936, a career in journalism was little more than a vision on the other side of the moon. I was not yet sixteen. I did not have good grades, but somehow had assembled sufficient credits and was ready to move on, logically to CCNY, like my brother. It was a public institution open to all. However, my grades were a shade too low for admission to the day session; I was advised that I could enroll in the evening session, at a modest fee, and work to bring up my grades. That sounded reasonable, but I didn't want to go to school; I wanted to work, to follow my father's trade—not because I wanted to be a furrier, but to join the union, the International Fur Workers, one of the most militant of the so-called red unions, which ranked alongside the longshoremen of the Pacific Coast for its defiance of employers and the established old guard unions. The president of the fur workers, Ben Gold, who had come through strikes and struggles with gangsterism in the fur market, differed considerably from leaders of other unions in the needle trades. David Dubinsky, of the ladies garment workers, and Sidney Hillman, of the clothing workers, had long been through wars to eliminate sweatshops, and by the 1930s were respectable "labor statesmen," while Gold was a tough advocate for labor's rights and openly a communist. Everybody who worked in the fur trade belonged to the union and benefited in wages and working conditions. As the son of a furrier, I was entitled to follow my father's trade and to join the union.

My father helped me, but was not enthusiastic. Like other immigrant fathers, he wanted his children to stick to school and move out of the needle trades into the professions. We made a deal that if he would help me to become a furrier, I would do my best to gain access to the CCNY day session and become a serious full-time student. Consequently he convinced his boss, George, who owned the company, to take me on as an apprentice. I learned to be an operator, working at a sewing machine, beginning with scrap shavings of fur, sewing until I could make a clean and thin seam. I sat, feet on the pedals, strips of fur in my hands. The hair stuck high, my thumbs kept pushing the hair down, down, down, with my untrained fingers stiff and trembling (especially when somebody watched). I sewed the pieces together, then opened the seams to start anew. With time and practice, my thumbs moved more rhythmically, hands grew steady, working faster, more efficiently. Then one day, the boss handed me a little karakul jacket. I was frightened, fearful of making a mistake. But I did it correctly; soon I lost my fears and began to feel like a professional. I was happy to be my father's coworker and hoped he was pleased with my progress. He and the others, many of them foreign-born, were good, honest, and skilled people. They were, in the sequence of production, the cutter (my father), working from a pattern with small hand-held knife designed for use on skins of fur; the operator, who sewed the skins together; the nailer, who took the product and stretched and nailed it on a board; the finisher, who sewed in the lining; and the floor boy, who kept everything going by providing the others what they needed. Finishers were women; almost all the rest were men. My sweat dripped down onto the fur and my feet grew tired of sitting in one place for seven hours. I took pride in my work, finding it creative in its own way, though I did not care much for George, who kept reminding me of the favor he had done by hiring me. I never thought then of where the skins came from, of the animals slain and slaughtered: the beautiful Persian lambs, silver foxes, karakuls, beaver, musk-rats, minks, martens, and all the rest from places around the world, stacked high in the street-level stores of merchants and traders.

The trouble in keeping the agreement I made with my father—to pursue studies seriously—arose the first evening I attended CCNY. Before my first class, I went to visit the college newspaper, *Main Events*. The office of the paper was perched in a mezzanine above a cavernous basement divided into alcoves. I heard a lot of noise and commotion and saw a tall figure, well over six feet, with a head rather large for the body, sitting at a desk. It was the editor, Howard Silverberg, or "Howie," the friendliest of fellows, who assured me I would be welcome on the staff. Presently, I wrote almost a full column in the first issue, the lead article in the second issue, the lead again in the third. Student writing was a joyous experience, though now I would likely be critical of everything I wrote. "What we all wrote then," as Sol Stein recalled in *Native Sons* of his early high school work with James Baldwin, "is today mostly embarrassing." That certainly was so for us at *Main Events*. As Howie wrote to me many years later:

> I can still remember Bernie Stepensky's submitting a story to me, his first straight news story after covering sports, and my calling it "a nice little story," and Bernie glowing from the compliment for the rest of the evening. I remember the reciprocal glow it gave me. It allayed some of my chagrin at having thoughtlessly lacerated another young writer earlier in the week. I had asked someone else to "show him how to write a decent lead to this story!" I seem to remember having said that quite loudly, probably under the influence of Front Page, or similar infantilism.

Maybe it was the joy of doing things together with friends or of writing uncensored, as freely as we wished. Clearly, working on the paper was my priority—studies took second place. Still, I felt upbeat, at least for a while, working steadily in the day and having school waiting for me in the evening. I studied French and history, two favorite subjects, although I did not do the homework and dozed off in class. History was from 9:20 to 10:15, and the instructor struggled to stay awake along with the students.

CCNY was a lively place on the west side of Manhattan, twenty blocks north of Columbia University and near the western edge of Harlem. It was filled with bright, energetic people. A friend of mine, Ray Fuller, edited a literary magazine called *Pulse* for the Writers Club, one issue of which featured a message from a CCNY alumnus, the literate sports columnist of the *New York Times*, John Kieran, who defied convention by occasionally telling his *Times* readers about birdwatching in Central Park. Now, for the student litterateurs, he wrote:

> The thing that I value most that I received from City College was a firm grounding in the classics. They pounded Latin and English classics into my head, and while it seemed a little hard to take at the time, I have often realized in more recent years how much I owe to the good grounding I received at City College many years ago.
>
> It makes our own language so much more full of meaning when we know the roots from which our own words have sprung. I certainly would recommend a study of literature on a wide basis, if for no other reason than that it is a study that will fit the tastes of old and young, rich and poor, and it is also within the reach of rich and poor. In other words, it is the universal field where the entrance is cheap and the enjoyment deep from youth to old age.[4]

That was a great line: The entrance into the study of literature on a broad scale is cheap and the enjoyment is deep. We were lucky; instructors in the evening session generally were talented people and interested in their students. Abraham Polonsky, who became a prominent screenwriter and director, was advisor to *Pulse*. Philip Foner, later noted as a labor historian, was advisor to *Main Events*. Alfred Kazin, at the start of his teaching career, was among the accessible. Many years later, the Authors Guild honored Kazin with the 1998 Award for Distinguished Service to the Writing Community, calling him "the finest living critic of American literature until his death June 5, at the age of 83." Kazin had been unable to attend the awards dinner in March, but sent a message that included these words: "Above all, I have tried to make the young understand that feeling, not structure or ideas by themselves, is the power that drives all good literature." Those were the kind of teachers we had.

The faculty was one thing, the administration was another. In the mid-1930s, when students demonstrated against the campus visit of several of Mussolini's fascist envoys, the college president, Frederick B. Robinson, denounced them as "guttersnipes—worse than senseless things." This stimulated a *Main Events* staff member, Sam O. Kaylin, writing a column signed SOK, to strike back in verse and song:

High on a bluff
Stands the City College,
Where the guttersnipes go
For knowledge hell bent.
High on a bluff
Stands the City College
BUT THE BIGGEST BLUFF OF ALL
IS ITS PRESIDENT.

In 1940, a new issue arose. After Bertrand Russell was prepared to teach philosophy at the college, the Board of Higher Education, its trustees, withdrew the invitation—not because Russell wasn't qualified, but because of his views on sexuality. I've heard it said that Russell was arrogant and did not really want to teach. If true, he fooled many people: in April after the state supreme court abrogated the appointment, more than 2,000 students cut classes to attend a Great Hall rally in protest. The CCNY campus was alive with activism, and that was thirty years before the eruptions at Berkeley in protest to the war in Vietnam. Evening session students were bright and zestful. Some actually studied and graduated in six or eight years, all at night. They were combative, spirited, and sectarian left-wingers, arguing with each other when they couldn't agree on a common enemy.

I recall Lewisohn Stadium (now long gone), where the New York Philharmonic performed its summer series (and students were admitted for fifty cents), and where the whole place was abuzz one evening when George Gershwin came to oversee a performance of his new show, *Porgy and Bess*. One evening when the concert was rained out and moved to the Great Hall, I was in a classroom, but instead of heeding the instructor, I was busy looking through a transom at the eloquent hands, for only the hands were visible, of the renowned conductor, Leopold Stokowski.

Main Events was like a family. Howard Silverberg wrote a literate column called Hayfoot-Strawfoot, the title of which, he said, referred to the untrained peasant conscriptees in the Czar's army who had to be taught left foot from right in marching by using hay tied to one leg and straw to the other—and Howard was implying that his column was proceeding by just such plodding reasoning. Lou Green, the managing editor, wrote reviews of musical events, which he signed "The Trumpeter," since he played trumpet in a jazz band. In the issue of January 11, 1937, however, Tod Brill's Night Life column reported:

> Clairvoyant: The Trumpeter is at last in his glory. In reviewing the concert of a year ago [of the City College Orchestra], he criticized the timpanist for playing too loud; and was kicked all over! There was no timpanist in the orchestra that time.
>
> But revenge is sweet. There was a timpanist at the last concert, and he played too loud.

We carried stories such as the one headlined "Fight on for Negroes in Baseball," echoing the campaign by the sports editor of the *Daily Worker,* and the report of a campus speech by Joseph P. Lash, national secretary of the American Student Union (later confidant and biographer of Eleanor Roosevelt), on his three-month tour of Spain, which was in the throes of the fascist Franco rebellion against the elected republican government.

Some evening session students actually completed their course work and graduated. David Beiles, a friend at *Main Events* and in later years, was one of them; he went on to graduate work at the Columbia School of Journalism. Ray Friedlander, a later editor of *Main Events,* was bright enough to work during the day, take a full course load at night, and still put the paper together. He worked in a photofinishing shop and lightened our evenings by sharing prints of assorted sexual scenes and poses. Unfortunately, he was killed as an aerial bombardier during World War II. Other stalwarts included Bernard Stepensky (later Stephens), Gordon Spielman, Fred Oberlander, and Abe Kagan, a former editor and our senior statesman. There were women, too, including Madeline Dremel, an editor shortly before my time, and Helen Price, a gorgeous shiksa worth drooling over.

Those willing to stick it out became dear to each other. Grades did not matter much. Howie Silverberg lived in Brooklyn, a long subway ride away, but he became my closest friend. "I never did know how many credits I had," he reminisced years later. "I was chiefly hanging around to work on the paper." Many nights, our little group trooped to the Blue

Diamond Cafeteria, a café at 145th Street and Amsterdam Avenue, staying until midnight before spreading out by subway to our respective homes around the city. "I can still taste the delicious oatmeal I had there," recalled Howie. "At about 11:00 PM I took the IRT [subway line] home to Brooklyn and sleepwalked ten blocks from the subway station to home. Then I got up at six in the morning and went to work and sometimes dozed off standing up." Abe Kagan reported that late one night, he was walking through the park to catch a subway in Harlem when he was accosted by a knife-wielding desperado. "Your money," the man demanded. "I have just five cents for subway fare." "Pass, man."

I lived at home with my parents, dreaming of somehow finding a career in newspaper work. The odds seemed hopelessly against it. *Main Events* was as close as I would come, and I cherished the experience. Meanwhile, things were not going well at work. I didn't like George and did not want to embarrass my father, so I quit. Evidently, I wasn't meant to be a furrier.

I wanted to join the Abraham Lincoln Brigade and go to fight in Spain, as various young communist friends were doing. I wasn't afraid and wanted to go. Support of the Spanish Republican government was a major cause of the communist movement. Over the years since then it became "the forgotten war," scarcely mentioned in textbooks, yet the Spanish Civil War was a defining issue of the twentieth century, and a dress rehearsal for World War II. It brought forth the best and worst in men and women, and the worst in governments too, including our own. Hitler had come into power in Germany in 1933, then two years later, Mussolini invaded Ethiopia. Those two held center stage, intimidating the old western powers, Great Britain and France, and the United States as well. Spain at that time was a young republic, having shed the monarchy in 1931. In February 1936, the Spanish people elected a new democratic government, the Popular Front, causing shock waves among generals in the military establishment and cardinals in the Catholic Church, an establishment of authority and power that controlled education, restricted the rights of women, and allied itself with the wealthy landowning class. The outbreak of violence in Spain in 1936 was not unlike the later military coup in Chile, when Augusto Pinochet in 1973 overthrew the democratically elected government of Salvador Allende, who was leading the way on the "Chilean path to socialism" by nationalizing industries and instituting agrarian land reform. The Pinochet coup might never have succeeded without the active encouragement and military and financial support of the United States. In the case of Spain, the forces of General Francisco Franco were equipped by Germany and Italy with troops, tanks, submarines, and planes. The Republicans were outnumbered and outgunned. Only Mexico and the Soviet Union gave support to the Spanish government. In the United States, the Roosevelt administration was hampered by the Neutrality Act, which forbade it from providing arms to either side, though it could have done much, much more by sending nonmilitary supplies and giving diplomatic aid to a democratic government in confrontation with our ultimate enemies.

Many sympathizers all over the world supported the Spanish Republicans by raising money and sending medical supplies. Members of the fur workers union in New York volunteered to manufacture garments to keep soldiers warm in the trenches, and other unions helped too. I remember stopping at an art gallery on 57th Street to view on display in the window a small version of *Guernica,* one of the world's great paintings. Picasso's powerful interpretation of the Basque holy city reduced to rubble in the aerial bombing of 1937 was a portrait of outrage and despair, of defiance and death. Ernest Hemingway, Theodore Dreiser, John Dos Passos, Langston Hughes, and other prominent authors visited Spain to report on the heroism and tragedy they found there. Andre Malraux organized a squadron of French planes. More than 35,000 volunteers from fifty countries formed international brigades to join with troops loyal to the Republic. These included about 2,800 Americans, who came to be called the Abraham Lincoln Brigade. I wanted to go and was interviewed by a recruiter. The problem was that in order to avoid violating federal laws, I had to be of age or have the permission of my parents and they would not give it to me. They wanted me to go to school, while I wanted to be a communist.

By the time of Franco's ultimate victory in 1939, one million lives had been lost. Of the international volunteers, fully half died; of the Abraham Lincoln Brigade, 750. At least a half dozen of my friends went to Spain—none came back. Hemingway, in 1939, wrote "On the American Dead in Spain," which began, "The dead sleep cold in Spain tonight," and ended, "Those who have entered it honorably, and no men ever entered earth more honorably than those who died in Spain, already have achieved immortality." Langston Hughes wrote a memorable poem, "Hero—International Brigade":

I came
An ocean in between

And half a continent.
Frontiers,
And mountains skyline tall,
And governments that told me
NO,
YOU CANNOT GO!
I came.

That was not the end. In 1938, with the appeasement of the Munich agreement, Britain (and France, too) gave part of Czechoslovakia to Hitler. The following year, Germany seized all of Czechoslovakia, and in September 1939, the Germans invaded Poland, but Stalin signed a nonaggression pact with Hitler, evidently hoping to save the USSR from invasion.

Most of the American media portrayed Franco in a favorable light. To publishers like William Randolph Hearst and Colonel Robert McCormick of the *Chicago Tribune*, Franco was a heroic figure ridding Spain of communism; by the same token, they credited Hitler and Mussolini with controlling and cleaning out the "red menace." Liberal publications that dared criticize Franco or give the viewpoint of the Spanish Republic were hurt by boycotts of the Catholic Church and right-wing organizations like the American First Committee and the Christian Front. Westbrook Pegler in the Scripps-Howard papers, George Sokolsky in the Hearst papers, and Fulton Lewis Jr. on the Mutual Broadcasting System were the Rush Limbaugh and Pat Buchanan of that day. But the most extreme was Father Charles Coughlin of Royal Oak, Michigan, the "radio priest" who defended Hitler and Mussolini and every Sunday night warned his thirty million listeners against "socialism, communism, and kindred fallacious social and economic theories," and against atheism and the Jewish plot to take over everything.

This was not the day of the muckraker. Yet George Seldes endeavored to pick up where Lincoln Steffens (who died in 1936) left off. Seldes was a veteran journalist who had worked overseas for the *Chicago Tribune* and other publications and had written books like *Lords of the Press* (1938). In 1940, he began publishing *Infact*, a bright, peppy weekly newsletter that carried no advertising but was filled with exposés that were hard to find anywhere else. *Infact* went well and reached a circulation of 175,000, but ultimately, the witch hunt brought it down. It was common belief that the FBI under J. Edgar Hoover had compiled lists of subscribers. People were frightened and Seldes quit publishing in 1950. My whole family read and respected *Infact*. When I went into the military service in World War II, my father mailed it to me regularly, which I appreciated as a form of family bonding as well as a way of keeping up on issues.

In 1941, Seldes picked up on scientific studies showing cigarette smoking as a health hazard. While the mass media paid little heed, he hammered away with reports on the power and influence of the tobacco industry. Smoking in those days was common and accepted. There was no such thing as a smoke-free restaurant or smoke-free airplane. Doctors and dentists smoked while examining and treating patients. Magazines were filled with tobacco advertisements, while cigarette companies sponsored some of the most popular network radio shows. I started smoking when I was thirteen or fourteen. It was something kids did, with or without parental consent. Polite women did not smoke in the street, although the manufacturers targeted women with extra long cigarettes that were professed to be chic. A pack cost fifteen or twenty cents, but I remember a brand called Wings that sold for a dime and had the most awful taste. My brother and I bought a little hand-powered gadget to roll our own cigarettes, but the tobacco taste was awful there, too.

Most of us on *Main Events* smoked, just as we thought real newspaper people did, or as Humphrey Bogart did in the movies. At times, working in the office late at night, we would run out of cigarettes and pass around a butt, or the "dincher," as I believe we called it, inhaling deeply, blowing out smoke rings, learning to write and edit, and living in a world that was half-real, half-dream.

CHAPTER 3

Pittsburgh, 1937 – With its awesome symbols of corporate industrial America – Where the whole river suddenly lit to a rosy glow – Three Serbians and five eggs – The strike was on – The less people had, the more they shared and cared

When I was seventeen, John Muir had already lived his life and gone to his reward but I had no idea of who he was or what he stood for. Years later, however, I learned (and wrote) about him in detail. His father was a stern, gloomy Scottish Presbyterian, and John fled his father's home. He studied at the University of Wisconsin, not following the prescribed curriculum, but taking the courses he wanted, including science. Then, after four years, and without a degree, he strode into his future, "leaving one University for another, the Wisconsin University for the University of the Wilderness."[1]

Muir worked as a woodworker until an accident to one eye (in 1867) forced him to quit. Then he began his famous "thousand mile walk to the sea," through Indiana, Kentucky, Tennessee, Georgia, and Florida, then across to Cuba, and from Cuba to California, and his ultimate kingdom in Yosemite. At first, he earned his living by tending sheep. Then he built and operated his own sawmill. His wants were few. He made long foot journeys exploring the Sierra, sleeping out where night found him.

In my case, my father was neither stern nor gloomy, and did his best as a provider, while my mother expressed tender feeling and affection for us all. Nevertheless, like John, I fled, leaving one university for another, not to the wilderness but to the heart of smokestack America. In early March of 1937, two months short of seventeen, I left New York for Pittsburgh. I rode with a fellow I knew who owned a car and was driving there, and made arrangements through communist friends for housing when I arrived.

It took considerably longer back then to drive across the forests of the Allegheny Mountains than it does now over high-speed freeways, but in due course we came into Pittsburgh over the Westinghouse Bridge spanning Turtle Creek. Deep in the valley, hundreds of feet below, on one side, in Braddock, stood the smoky Edgar Thomson Works of United States Steel, employing 5,000 workers, and on the other side, in East Pittsburgh, the Westinghouse plant with 11,000 workers.

Those factories were awesome symbols of the power of corporate industrial America. Yet there was still another side to Pittsburgh that registered with me. I had come here to the western front of the Appalachian mountain range. I mean that nature, although wounded and obscured, nevertheless was present and expressive. Theodore Dreiser, the leading literary figure of the early twentieth century, had come this way one generation earlier as a stranger. That was long before writing his classics, *Sister Carrie* and *An American Tragedy*, and his other novels. He had left Indiana University after one year to work on various newspapers, including one in Pittsburgh. He had spent only spring, summer, and fall in Pittsburgh, but later recollected: "What a city for a realist to work and dream in! ... Certainly no other newspaper work I ever did seemed so pleasant, no other city more interesting."[2] He had not seen mountains before—and neither had I—but he came down through the mountains of western Pennsylvania, winding around the base of one or another of them, following the bed of a stream or turning out into a broad smooth valley, crossing directly at the center of it, or climbing some low ridge with a puff-puff-puff and then clattering almost recklessly down the other slope. He went to the south side of the city, where he rode the incline tram to Grandview Boulevard on Mount Washington, and then later recorded:

> I had the finest view of a city I have ever seen. In later years I looked down upon New York from the heights of the Palisades and the hills of Staten Island; on Rome from the Pincian Gardens; on Florence from San Miniato; and on Pasadena and Los Angeles from the slopes of Mt. Lowe; but never anywhere have I seen a scene which impressed me more than this: the rugged beauty of the mountains, which encircle the city, the three rivers that run as threads of bright metal, dividing it into three parts, the several cities joined as one, their clambering streets presenting a checkered pattern emphasized here and there by the soot-darkened spires of churches and the walls of the taller and newer and cleaner office buildings.[3]

Pittsburgh was all of that, and all of it overlain with the symbols and reminders of industrial power. "The whole river for a mile or more was suddenly lit to a rosy glow," wrote Dreiser, "a glow which, as I saw upon turning, came from the tops of some forty or fifty stacks belching a deep orange-red flame. At the same time an enormous pounding and crackling came from somewhere, as though titans were at work upon subterranean anvils."[4] But there is more. The Point, where the Allegheny and Monongahela Rivers merge to form the Ohio, has long been glorified as "the river-gate through which poured the tide of conquest, of trade and ideas which made America." Power and might were reflected in the stainless steel headquarters of United States Steel Corporation (U.S. Steel) and the innovative design of the aluminum headquarters of the Aluminum Corporation of America (Alcoa), in Mellon Bank, stronghold of Andrew W. Mellon, king of financial kingpins, and in Oakland's Carnegie Institute, the art gallery, library, and museum endowed by Andrew Carnegie, who began the firm that ultimately became U.S. Steel, the largest, most powerful conglomerate of them all.

I arrived in Pittsburgh on March 1, 1937, the day when U.S. Steel startled the country by signing a contract with the United Steel Workers, formerly the Steel Workers Organizing Committee. Wages were raised at once to a five dollar daily minimum, hours were cut to forty a week, and, most important of all, the union was recognized. All this happened due to the initiative of bushy-browed John L. Lewis, president of the United Mine Workers, who considered himself a kingpin in his own right. The year before, he had established the Congress of Industrial Organizations (CIO) as a rival to the old, conservative American Federation of Labor and opened the drive to unionize steelworkers, with his principal lieutenant, Philip Murray, in charge. The union had poured money and dispatched 150 organizers into steel communities; the companies, in turn, had answered by placing hostile advertisements in daily newspapers and sending spies into union ranks.

It was an old routine, recalling dreams, challenges, and the efforts of working men and women to organize and improve their fate that were met with violence and ended in failure. Ever since the industrial revolution that followed the Civil War, workers had tilted at windmills like Don Quixote. Strikes, lockouts, blacklisting, and the use of police and Pinkerton detectives to break strikes with force all marked America's industrial history. Pittsburgh in particular remembered the violent (and unsuccessful) strike in 1892 at the Carnegie Homestead Mill, where an army of Pinkertons battled striking steelworkers in a daylong gun battle that killed three Pinkertons and seven steelworkers and left many more wounded. Pittsburgh also witnessed the bitterness of the general steel strike of 1919. Every strike, according to the newspapers, was an unjust strike. Despite the conviction that their cause was just and their actions valid, strikers always felt defensive, the sense of being in the wrong when on a picket line, and vulnerable. They found themselves set apart by their protest from their communities and the rest of humankind. They were dependent on the support of public opinion, but denied support by the press. And, according to these same papers, every strike failed once again, as though the outcome was inevitable.

But then, in 1937, newspapers reported that United States Steel had come to terms without a strike and without violence. While the organizers felt encouraged, a solid block of corporations, known as Little Steel (composed of Bethlehem Steel, Republic Steel, Jones & Laughlin [J&L], Inland Steel, and Youngstown Sheet and Tube) threatened to go their own way and defy the union. Those firms were giants in their own right. Their leader and spokesman, Tom Girdler, president of Republic, had earlier established his reputation as an official of J&L by making Aliquippa (outside Pittsburgh) into a model company town. Years of exploitation, company unionism, and unsuccessful union campaigns kept the workers cautious. Nevertheless, workers at Republic Steel went on strike May 12, 1937. It reached a bloody climax outside the Republic plant in Chicago in the Memorial Day Massacre, when police fired on a parade of strikers and supporters, killing ten and wounding ninety others.

The Memorial Day Massacre became the subject of an investigation by the Senate Civil Liberties Committee chaired by Senator Robert La Follette of Wisconsin, which ultimately published fourteen volumes of testimony and documents portraying American big business as a lawbreaker through its employment of thugs, use of violence, and denial of civil rights to labor. These pages left little doubt that forces of law and order initiated the violence in Chicago and that police officials lied at the time of the massacre and at the Senate hearing. Nevertheless, the *Chicago Tribune* praised the police for "protecting life and property." In search of a scapegoat, the *Tribune* charged Communists with inspiring the workmen, but that was proven false by the Senate investigation.

In steel-producing communities, police were plainly at the service of the companies, and to a large degree, so were the newspapers. In *Crisis in Bethlehem,* John Strohmeyer, a former editor of the Bethlehem (PA) *Globe-Times,* wrote:

In 1940, the National Labor Relations Board (NLRB), a key agency established under the New Deal, ordered Bethlehem Steel to decertify its Employee Representation Plan. The NLRB ruled, in effect, that the ERP was an arm of the company and not a bona fide union. The Steel Workers Organizing Committee immediately asked that the company enter negotiations toward an NLRB election to select a collective bargaining agent.

Six months later, Strohmeyer continued, after repeated threats to shut down the plant, the steelworkers struck. And then:

During the next four days, I was appalled at the hatred that exploded in Bethlehem. I also became ashamed of the *Globe-Times*, the newspaper that I would someday run as editor. As ugly as the demonstrations were and as much a newcomer as I was to the business, I could sense serious inequities in coverage and was soon convinced that the newspaper had become a willing company partner in a conspiracy to undermine the strikers.

At the behest of Bethlehem Steel, the city sent police in cruisers to protect nonstrikers trying to enter the gates. The cars were pelted with bricks and stones. Police responded by firing tear gas into the crowd. A police car was overturned, and several officers were taken to the hospital.

The *Globe-News* nonetheless featured a company statement on page one that day, proclaiming that all men were working. A companion story ominously pointed out that the strikers were jeopardizing $1 billion in defense contracts at Bethlehem Steel.[5]

It was little wonder, since in those days the might of nations was measured by steel production. An interlocking colossus of steel mills, shipyards, railroads, and coal mines shaped the skylines of cities. Steel was the melting pot for hundreds of thousands of immigrants with willing muscles. While the workers performed the hard labor of building steelmaking empires, the emperors on top were greedy, smug, and shameless. Consider that the process began with iron ore in the famous Mesabi Range of northern Minnesota, once one of the richest deposits in the world. The ore was so plentiful and close to the surface, it could be shoveled out of pits, then shipped and barged to feed the furnaces, where it was mixed with limestone, coal, coke, manganese, and scrap, to make steel. The corporations cared little about the future of natural or human resources. They stripped the Mesabi of the ore until it was cleaned out. Ultimately, instead of updating their aging mills, they shut them down, never to reopen; and the jobs of honest wage earners were lost forever.

In 1937, when I arrived in Pittsburgh, steel was in its heyday. At first I stayed with two young fellows, Jim and Phil, in their little apartment in the Hill district, a cross between Harlem and the lower East Side. The apartment was located in a shadowy, lightless alley, reached by climbing a dark staircase up a steep dirt hill. Soon Jim left to join the Abraham Lincoln Brigade while Phil went to work for Jones & Laughlin in Aliquippa. Then I was invited to move in with Jim Egan, his wife, Joan, and their little daughter, Patsy, who was often ill and needed medical attention. They were cramped, yet made room for me and treated me like a brother. I learned then that the less people have, the more willing they are to share and care.

The Egans were thoroughly proletarian. Jim, a black-haired Irish-American, was a Communist functionary, who the year before had run for mayor of Pittsburgh on the Communist Party ticket. He was by training a plasterer, who missed his old trade, but compensated by analyzing and evaluating plastered walls and ceilings and explaining them to me. Joan was the daughter of a Croatian coal miner, raised in a company town, when almost every rural town in Pennsylvania and Ohio was controlled by an aluminum factory, a coal mine, a steel mill, or a glass works, with the workers living in company housing, shopping at the company store, and indebted to the company like indentured servants. Theodore Dreiser described the scene.

> The sight of sooty-faced miners at certain places, their little oil and tin lamps fastened to their hats, their tin dinner-pails on their arms, impressed me as something new and faintly reminiscent of the one or two small coal mines around Sullivan, Indiana, where I had lived when I was a boy of seven. Along the way, I saw a heavy-faced and heavy-bodied type of peasant woman, with a black or brown or blue or green skirt and a waist of a contrasting color, a headcloth or neckerchief of still another, trailed by a few children of equally solid proportions, hanging up clothes or doing something else about their miserable places. These were the much

maligned hunkies just then being imported by the large manu-
facturing and mining and steelmaking industries of the country
to take the place of the restless and less docile American working
man and woman.... I did not then know of the manufacturers'
foreign labor agent with his lying propaganda among ignorant,
often fairly contented peasants, painting America as a country
rolling in wealth and opportunity, and then bringing them here.[6]

Under Jim's guidance, I started job hunting. I wanted to work in a steel
mill; my sights were on the J&L mill on the South Side, the largest mill in the
city, stretching for more than a mile on both sides of the Monongahela River.
Thus one bright morning I walked through the Hill district and across the
Twenty-second Street Bridge, within close smelling range of dirty black and
brown smoke oozing out of endless stacks, and crossed to the South Side to
the employment office next to the main gate at Twenty-seventh and Carson
Street. A long line of men stretched close to the wall; this was a time when
business was on the upswing, when grown men were returning to work after
years of unemployment, and young men were being hired for the first time
in their lives. A chorus of staccato thumping, hisses, and rhythmic sounds
from the mill made us all on the outside feel ambitious and upbeat, eager
for the chance to get inside. Most young fellows when they came before the
employment clerk said, "Labor." I said it too. The man in shirtsleeves shook
his head—there was more than enough unskilled labor.

I went to the employment office for several days in a row, but it was always
the same story. Then I met a fellow who told me about the free employment
agency operated by J&L downtown, where he was going to see if he could
get an electrician's job. We walked together and there it was, written in white
chalk on a little blackboard in the window: "Chippers, castings (white)." I
had no idea what that meant, but wished my fairy godmother would make
me into a chipper. Later that day, by the best of good fortune, Little Johnny
walked into my life. He was a bricklayer's helper at J&L and wanted to help
me. On Grant Street, in the middle of downtown Pittsburgh, he took a piece of
chalk from his pocket, kneeled on the ground and started drawing. Passersby
stopped to watch, thinking he was doing chalk art. He drew several lines,
explained about a chisel and a chalked line. "The important thing is getting
in," he said. "Once you're on the job it will be easy. Ask one of the other
chippers to help. Tell him you have a family to support and had to bluff your
way in. They're all decent guys."

I asked whom to use for references. "Say you worked for Sun Shipbuilding and Drydock in Chester as a chipper and caulker for two years. Before that you worked for American Steel Castings in Lester, right next to Chester. That's where you were born."

"In Lester?"

"No, Chester. That's where I was born."

Johnny cooked up such a good story, I almost believed it myself. I walked back to the free employment agency. The blackboard in the window looked up at me as large as life, with that word "chipper." For a moment, I lost my breath in fear that my hoax would be exposed. But it wasn't. The clerk handed me a slip and told me to take it to the employment office on the South Side. I did not ride the streetcar as directed; I didn't have any money, yet I flew across town. Brandishing the little white slip, I strode into the employment office. Though it was late in the afternoon, a long line still paraded through. I heard the familiar "Labor," and saw the head shake sidewise, and again, "Armature winder," and the head went the same way. I placed the slip before him. He eyed me carefully, respectfully, then wrote on another slip and told me to take it to the superintendent of the foundry. "Show this slip to the officers where the railroad tracks go into the mill. They will show you where to go."

Two uniformed mill police in a booth next to the railroad tracks directed me. I was in the mill at last, a world of red, orange, and yellow, of flames of every color, of a never-ceasing deafening racket, of overhead giant cranes swinging huge steel bulks like toothpicks, and of men in goggles, indistinguishable, their faces covered with dirt. The superintendent sat at a steel-topped desk in a glassed-in office, separate from the mill. I gave him the slip. He looked me over critically and asked questions. I wanted to tell him that a chipper works with an air-driven chisel, holding it firmly in place on the billet to knock off chips, crust, and dust, but that wasn't enough. I gave the wrong answers and the whole beautiful story of Chester, Lester, shipbuilding, and shipping crumbled and collapsed. The superintendent wrote something on the slip and told me to take it back to the employment office. His handwriting said, "Not needed at present."

Jim Egan shared my disappointment and suggested I canvas a certain area of the city with many small businesses. I followed his advice and was hired almost at once at a dry cleaning plant. After the first day, I returned to the Egans, thanked them for their kindness, and moved to a pleasant furnished room on Fifth Avenue, near the University of Pittsburgh. But on my second day on the job my body started burning. The naphtha set my skin on fire. I couldn't sleep at night and went through torture during the day. One of the bosses noticed my arms were red and gave me salve to apply, which only caused further irritation. I was having hot and cold chills and I couldn't sit or lie down. It was the kind of work a young fellow could walk into right off the street without experience, but I quit after four days.

I yearned to be a chipper and to work in steel. I had come close and did not want to give up. I ate a can of sardines with bread every day while checking the newspaper ads until soon I found a notice about hiring chippers in Alliance, Ohio. That was near enough to make a run for it, which I did at once by thumb. But I was too late—the foreman said they had been running the ad several days and had just finished hiring all the chippers they needed. I turned around and headed back to Pittsburgh the way I had come, disappointed, but disappointment, after all, was nothing new.

Near midnight I stood alone on a dark road in Imperial, a small town in the western corner of Pennsylvania. It was quiet, except for singing from a café half a mile away. Only a few cars passed, and none would stop. It was a cold March night and my leather jacket left my legs open to the wind. When the café closed the town was as still as the wintry open field, and as dark and lonely. My only companions were the high stars, the sound of the wind, and an infrequent car approaching and passing.

I might have stood there all night, trying to thumb a ride at the turn of a road in a mountain village, but I was cold. I walked back and forth, swinging my arms across my chest to keep from growing numb, hoping to find a friendly light. On a street off the highway I did see a light—but a dog chased me off. I found another, knocked at the door, and for a few moments I left the roadside chill for the comfort of a living room fire. My host was a young man, a late night reader, who set down his book and watched me suspiciously as I held my hands to the flame. We hardly talked before I asked, "Is there someplace here in the town where I could spend the night?"

"Yes," he said, "go across the highway and two blocks up the hill. Try the house on the corner." He looked relieved to see me go.

It was an old dark frame house, overhanging a hill, with wooden steps at the side leading to a dimly lit window and door. I knocked and it opened slowly. The man wore denim trousers but no shirt, only heavy winter underwear buttoned down the middle.

"I've been standing down on the road trying to hitchhike a ride, but I haven't been able to, and it's very cold. Somebody said you might let me stay here tonight," I explained.

He stared at me and shrugged. With the half-light cast across his face, I could see he was unshaven and unsmiling. He turned to speak in a foreign language to someone on the inside. Then he spoke to me slowly in broken English, "We got no extra place for you."

I hesitated in the doorway, frightened by the deep, guttural voices coming from the inside and by the appearance of the man who faced me— dark, broad-shouldered, and silent. But if I left here, where could I go?

"No," he said again. "No other place. See, three of us." I looked beyond him and saw there were two other men inside. "Where we put you?" Then he spoke to the others in their own language.

"Could I come in for a little while and get warm?" I asked.

"Okay. Sure. You come in."

Three men lived here, in one room. The wide bed they shared—the widest bed I've ever seen—stood in one corner. In the center was a table, behind it an old black stove. I walked across the room and thawed out.

They studied me and talked their foreign tongue. They were all built lean with thick, strong arms and dark, unshaven faces. One of them put coals in the fire and soon it grew hot.

"You hungry?" he asked.

"No."

"We fix some food. You eat?"

"Yes. I really am hungry."

"Okay, we give you something to eat."

For the first time in a long night, I smiled. And they smiled, looking quite friendly. I felt I had found a haven and they understood that I was only a boy, alone and astray, who needed their help. All three shared in preparing the meal. One brought a huge black frying pan, another a can of lard, and the third a pot of coffee. Crack! A yellow-white egg floated across the frying pan sea. I wrote earlier of learning that the less people have, the more willing they are to share and care, and here was another lesson.

An egg and a cup of coffee, and a loaf of bread on the table. I closed my eyes and smelled, and felt a little dizzy. But then a second egg dropped into the pan, and a third.

And a fourth and a fifth. Five eggs, a pot of coffee, a loaf of bread.

Surely, I thought, they're going to eat, too.

But I was wrong—the five eggs were all for me. "Go ahead, you eat," they said. I took off my jacket, sat down, and cleaned the plate, along with four slices of bread and three cups of coffee. The food was good, but more nourishing was the kindness of men to a stranger, their younger brother. When I was through they passed me tobacco and a cigarette paper and I rolled an awkward cigarette.

We smoked and talked around the table in front of the stove behind the wide bed and window in the old frame house on the hill above the cold highway, the three poor men of Serbia who had come from a small country in middle Europe to work as coal diggers in the Pennsylvania mines, and I, who told them where I came from and whither bound. It was a friendly talk about places in this country and their native faraway land and about the difficulty in learning a new language. They seemed quite pleased that I would listen to them speak in English and tell them how well they sounded.

It was late enough when I arrived. When we finished our cigarettes and conversation it was after one o'clock. My friends said I could sleep on the floor near the stove, and I curled up with my leather jacket for a blanket.

At six in the morning one of the Serbians shook me awake. Under my head were some cloths, which they had evidently rolled into a pillow for me sometime during the night. He was dressed for work, wearing the mark of his trade, the miner's cap, bulging with a small lamp; the others had already left. "I wish we could give you a dollar or something," he apologized, "but here, you take this tobacco." Together we walked down to the highway, where we shook hands and he left me.

I headed east on foot into a bright, clear morning, toward a new misty mountain in the distance ahead. I was not alone—birds flew back and forth across the road, singing and chattering. I could not understand their language, but sensing somehow they might be singing to me, I watched, listened, and whistled back, as close to their key as I could. Magic was in the wind. On returning to my rooming house, I found a message that J&L had called, directing me to get to the South Side right away for a physical examination and start to work.

A group of others also waited to be examined, and the chippers soon got together. They included Charles, a tall, rangy young black from Ohio, who said he had chipped concrete; and an Irishman, Paddy, who called me Red because of my birthmark. None, I suspected, had ever chipped steel;

they had made up stories too. Soon the doctor came, pronounced us fit and sent us to the bar plant at 34th Street, one of the newest parts of the mill, and one of the cleanest, without the smoke and dust of the foundry and blooming mills. The timekeeper said we would work forty hours a week for 67 1/2 cents an hour—the minimum wage then was 65 cents an hour—plus a piecework, or "tonnage," bonus of fifteen cents a ton.

I felt elated. I had been in Pittsburgh one month and now had found what I came for. Although I was to be at the mill at seven the next morning, I was awake and out at six. The South Side was already alive. Men came down its glum streets into the mill, through one gate or another. I went to the bar plant office, where the foreman said a brief word of welcome and handed each of us a pair of goggles. We followed him into a tremendous shed that seemed to stretch more than a mile. There was no flooring, just dark earth, with a giant crane overhead and railroad tracks running through the shed. We came to the chipping bed, divided into four sections, with thick steel girders resting on the ground. The foreman assigned Charles and me to two fellows, Pete and Andy, with instructions to work in a crew with them. There were four crews of four men each.

"Hey, where's your gloves?" Pete, one of the veterans in my gang, demanded.

"I haven't any...."

"Hell, brother, you can't work without gloves! Look around. Maybe you'll find a pair."

He was angry and intimidating. I looked around and finally found a pair of torn gloves.

A giant crane overhead moved a load of steel billets and stopped above our girders. A fellow on the ground flicked directions to the crane operator, supervised the unloading, unhooked a thick chain that had bound the steel, and motioned the crane away. Pete, who had bawled me out, leaped across the steel, which was bound by twisted wire. Dressed in denim work clothes, he was short, and the cap he wore made him look even shorter. But he was built solidly, like a bull, and he plunged into the work full of energy. He swung a long pair of tongs, hitched them into the wire and snapped. The steel billets rolled free across the girders.

The billets were about twenty feet long and an inch around. With a tong, Andy spread them out into a clean single line. Andy took me to work with him.

The air hammer weighed about twenty-five pounds, attached to a long hose, in turn fixed into a valve on the ground nearby. Suddenly the whole shed was pounding with rhythmic *rat-a-tat-tat*. A man sat on a stool sharpening chisels at a large stone wheel and sparks flew. He was the grinder—that was what he did all day.

We worked with goggles over our eyes, gloves on our hands, and chisels in the air hammers. I bent low, swung the hose around, fit in a chisel, pressed the hammer into my right knee and dug unto the steel. Clean shavings slid off onto the ground near Andy. At first I couldn't control the chisel, I couldn't control myself. The hose kept getting in the way. I tried again and started to move smoother, to harmonize with the steel. The foreman watched Charles and me and said, "You'll be okay in a while."

Pete and Andy started making yellow crayon lines on the billets where we had to chip. When he finished one side of a billet Andy would pick up the tongs and turn it over to the next side, with a deft twist of the wrist.

Pete bellowed out for the foreman and we all stood erect. The foreman, now inspector, made a chalk mark. Andy bent low and chipped. Then one side was okayed, and the inspector surveyed the next, and the next.

"OKAY! HEY!"

And we started again. I felt deafened by the racket of sixteen pneumatic hammers, while my own hammer bounced against my knee every time I pressed the trigger and my whole body shook. The pressure pulled my leg muscles and back, contorted, bent in an unnatural position.

Pete was yelling, this time for the crane to take the load away and bring another load. The crane rattled overhead and suddenly I heard a clanking bell. The crane stopped.

"Get the hell outta there!" Pete shouted. Steel billets crashed over each other and the even line across the girders was broken. The chainman and Pete tied wires around the load and away off high into the air it went. The bell sounded as the crane slid along the rails and chippers below moved away. No one is allowed underneath a loaded crane. With a crash, the load was deposited in a railroad car at the side. Then, while we stood idly by or went for new chisels, the crane picked up another load out of another railroad car.

I began to catch onto what I was doing. I saw the steel part into two strips. That was the seam and I was to keep digging until the seam ran out. Sometimes a black line would show up and the seam would open up again and I would dig again until the steel was clean. There would also be slivers, splintery steel bumps on the side of a billet that had to be trimmed off.

The foreman's face was small and smooth. He spoke without vehemence. His entire appearance, his humble stride, seemed like a plea to the men to consider him one of them and not the representative of the company. One day he handed me a ham sandwich, saying he had an extra one. We got twenty minutes for lunch. It was "free time," meaning it was not deducted from our eight hours.

Andy was hardworking, quiet; he spoke as though each time he said something he was apologizing for not saying more. Paddy the Irishman, with streaks of sweat across his ruddy face, had been trying to turn over a billet. The tongs flew out of his hands and he almost fell. Charles wore a red and blue football jersey and looked like a tackle. I had one sandwich, he had three hamburgers and gave me one. He didn't think much of Paddy: "That guy can't work!"

The chipping hammers, the noise of the flying crane, followed us and called us back. A smoky engine passed by. Every time a load was finished meant a few minutes' rest waiting for the inspector, then for the crane to take the load away, then waiting for another load. The load came down and Pete wasted no time clipping the wires. He lifted the tongs over his head and brought them down hammerlike into the wire and split it. Then he split the two other wires binding the load so the billets rolled loose by themselves.

We started to work on this load. Andy didn't make any marks. He directed me to dig in here and there and wherever there was a seam to carry it through and wherever a sliver to knock it off.

There didn't seem to be any seams. The others realized that too. Pete yelled, "Ho, Andy! We get some work done!"

They put Charles and me to one side and told us to chip on five or six billets, while Andy and Pete went to work on the rest of the load. Pete turned the billets over rapidly while Andy climbed over the billets, digging in here and there. The load was done in no time. And another load came bouncing through the air. Pete worked with fury. He walked over to me and said defiantly, "We get paid on tonnage, you know."

At three in the afternoon the next shift drifted in, clean and fresh, strong, husky men in overalls and dungarees. I walked out through the 34th Street gate, picked the card out of the rack, and punched the clock. I felt partly deaf; a streetcar went by and I could barely make out its screeching, but I didn't care. In the days, weeks, and months to follow, I learned to love the work. I loved the men I worked with. They were Bohemians, Hungarians, Slovaks, Poles, Croatians, Serbians, and Lithuanians, the Bohunks, Hunkies, and Polacks, who themselves, or whose parents, had been recruited to come from central or eastern Europe to work along with Germans and Irish in the mines and mills of America. Steelworkers believed their skills set them above and apart, that they had the most demanding jobs. Anyone with muscle can dig coal or make a car, but they figured it takes something special to transform red dirt into molten metal and then into the framework of civilization.

I enjoyed being part of their community. The people lived in unhealthy little houses on the South Side and shopped "on tick" at the Pittsburgh Mercantile, the company store on Carson Street. Workers' wives came to fill shopping bags with food and vegetables, and buy clothing for their families. Their men frequented Emil's Place, on the corner. Emil was a big, barrel-chested Serbian ex-steelworker from whom I learned to drink Green River straight or as a boilermaker—a double shot with a beer chaser for twenty-five cents.

I walked almost everywhere in the mill and outside of it, sometimes at night, when the Bessemer furnace on full blast lit up the sky and made Pittsburgh look, as Dreiser wrote, "like hell with the lid off."

Clouds of smoke rose from the complex of blast furnaces, open hearths, forges, and coke works and never stopped streaming skyward. Days were smoggy and smoky, sometimes nearly as dark as night. Inside the mill, I watched fierce tongues of flame leap out from liquid steel poured into ingot molds. Huge overhead cranes carried ladles of hot metal processed at the blast furnace and poured into the open hearth. The liquid iron was about 2,500 degrees, with huge globs of molten metal leaping above the surface like an active volcano. Then they were cooled by great volumes of water and tested to see if the batch of steel met specifications. If the carbon content was too high, hot metal from the blast furnace would be added. The fuel input could be raised or lowered, and lime or phosphorus added. The coke works was always hot, the air dirty, the noise ear-shattering, and a misstep could be fatal. A man can slip from the open hearth platform into the pit below, filled with slag and jagged metal. Danger was a constant companion and SAFETY and SAFETY FIRST signs were everywhere. These were all physically strong, tough men, but limbs were shattered, and faces burned and disfigured.

Gruesome accidents in steelmaking are reported, but seldom detailed.

We worked, I hustled, the steel was good quality and we didn't have much chipping. It was mainly turning them over with the tongs and scanning the four sides. I tried but the tongs kept sliding off the steel. I asked Andy to show me. He took my hands in his, wrapped them around the handles and made the twist with me. Those billets, the lightest we worked on, weighed one-seventh of a ton each. It took an effort for me to turn one. Every time I did the sweat poured out and drenched my clothes. Because I was keeping up the pace, Pete smiled at me.

"Hey," he asked while we were waiting for a load, "what's your name?"

"Mike."

"Mike? Every third guy around here is named Mike. But you ain't from Pittsburgh, are you, Mike?"

"No, I'm from New York."

"New York! Hey, Andy! Mike's from New York."

Andy nodded. He confessed to coming from Ellsworth, a coal mining patch about thirty miles south.

"I was up to New York once," Pete said. "It's too fast for me. Besides, I can't go running around any more."

"No? How come?" I asked.

"I'm married now. My wife is due to give birth soon. I need to make some money for the kid. Hey, what are you doing down here anyway, Michael?"

I looked at Pete's hands, dark, chunky solid mitts. His fingers were short and bulged at the knuckles. Perhaps he was shy too, like Andy, but in a different way; as gruff as he had been earlier, so friendly was he now.

I told him I had come to look for work.

"Well, you got it! I been here three years and that's all they give."

I didn't have to fear Pete anymore. The steel came in slowly. It was good quality, so everybody was taking it easy. Pete took his twenty minutes out. When he came back he gave me an apple and told me to go eat again. When it got close to eleven and our last half load was inspected, Pete told us to make a little noise because the superintendent might pass through and if we weren't working, the foreman would catch hell. So I went to the toolman to get some new chisels. He always had a smile and a good word.

A few feet away, Andy was standing talking to three or four fellows from the next shift. As I passed by, Andy said, "I hear they're giving out buttons." There could be only one kind of button under discussion. They knew I had heard, looked down at the ground. Andy walked away. None of the chippers wore union buttons on their caps.

Chippers weren't the only ones to punch out at the 34th Street shanty. There were men from the tie plant, the other half of the bar plant, the gang in the number twelve rolling mill across the tracks from us, the welders who built steel barges at the river bank, and others who worked in the yards further up.

On the way to the shanty, I caught sight of a railroader's cap. This wasn't unusual except this cap had a blue union button pinned to it: "I am a member of the Steel Workers Organizing Committee." I recognized the face as Sam Bielich, whom I had met a time or two. He was an everyday steelworker but clearly with courage.

"A strong back and weak mind is what makes a good chipper," Pete had proclaimed during a break. I wouldn't say anything happened to my brain, but muscles in my legs, back, and arms grew taut and solid. My weight went down and I learned to be nimble on my feet. I began to synchronize with the gang. Then one day I came to work with a button pinned on the band of my hat. Nobody said a thing about it. I became the one person in the whole department to show support for the CIO.

Day after day organizers met shifts as they came off, at seven in the morning, three in the afternoon, and eleven at night, spoke to the men individually, showed how pay raises had come because of the union drive, explained that conditions would improve more with a union contract, and then tried to get the worker's signature on a card.

Sign a card, sign a card. A majority must sign before the union can claim representation and recognition of the National Labor Relations Board. Come on, buddy, sign a card. Everybody's signing. Let's stick together and get a chance to live. The card read: "I hereby request and accept membership in the Steel Workers Organizing Committee, and of my own free will authorize it, its agents or representatives to act for me as a collective bargaining agency in all matters pertaining to pay rates, wages, hours of employment and other conditions of employment." Day after day men with blue cards stood in front of gates, walking three miles with a guy to get his signature, while Sam Bielich and a few others worked on collecting signatures on the inside.

Little by little men lost their fear. The number of names recorded at the union headquarters on Sarah Street, one block from the main gate, kept growing, nearing the majority. Workers spoke openly on the job, comparing attitudes of various superintendents toward the union, the number in each department already signed up, and how it was hard to get those farmers in the strip mill to come around.

Steel production nationally was close to 100 percent of capacity. A strike would cause serious disruption, but neither Jones & Laughlin nor any of the other firms was ready to negotiate with the union.

Our chipping crew went on the eleven-to-seven turn. It was like going through seven days of darkness, being awake through the breadth of night. I kept asking, "What time is it, Andy?" a dozen times a night. We were aided by powerful lights on movable poles a few feet overhead, which we would swing around in order to see better, but the lights looked dim. I kept trying to swing the pole closer and hoped that Pete's would be pointed our way. Then I felt a peaceful coolness, as though night and I reached an understanding.

It started to rain in Pittsburgh. It rained when I awoke in the afternoon. It rained when I went to work at eleven and it was raining in the morning when I left. Pittsburgh grew nervous as river levels rose. We can't have a flood this year, people would say, we were all but ruined last St. Patrick's Day. But it rained until the city grew frantic. Rumors ran through the mill that tracks would be flooded and locomotives would not be able to move. One morning when we came out, the gulley between the shanty and Carson Street was filled with water, about four feet deep, and we were taken across in a rowboat.

Later in 1937, I was still living in Oakland. Returning home one evening I saw a crowd nearby and learned that Andrew W. Mellon was on hand to officially open the Mellon Institute for Industrial Research, a handsome building with marble columns, across the street from the Mellon-endowed Cathedral of Learning. I joined in watching men and women in stunning evening gowns and full dress suits leave the building and pass under a canopy into waiting limousines, which came to the entrance one by one. As a young couple emerged, a murmur went through the crowd. It was Richard King Mellon and his wife. A uniformed chauffeur made his way. "The car is right across the street, Mr. Mellon," he said. "It will take some time for me to get around here." "The car is across the street, Kate," Mellon repeated to his wife, waiting. The decision was hers. She was tall, slender, pale. "Oh, Dick, I don't want to, it's raining." The chauffeur bowed out. I went home, a block away. Yes, a few raindrops fell into my hair on the way, and I thought, "Those people have everything, but they miss a lot of living."

I moved to the South Side to be close to work. I lived with an elderly German woman who treated me well, serving pork chops for breakfast and packing an ample lunch. Another young fellow, whom the landlady called Alabama, roomed there as well, but one day Alabama vanished. Evidently he had caused a young girl of the neighborhood to become pregnant. She came around several times looking for him and asking for a forwarding address, but he was gone—to Alabama or parts unknown.

When I was on the three-to-eleven turn, I would try to stay awake until four or five in the morning and then sleep until noon. Milan Karlovich, or Karlo, sometimes helped me stay awake. He ran the newsstand across the street from the main gate to the mill. Eleven o'clock was his big hour because he sold hundreds of morning papers to the men coming off the job. I went home, cleaned up, and changed clothes, then went to Milan's stand where he and his two little brothers were getting ready to carry papers and magazines back to their little red brick house in a dark alley a block away. Everybody lived in an alley. I helped them carry the papers. The street was almost deserted; there was stillness in the dark and a gray mist in the air, with abundant dust particles from the mill. When we arrived, Milan and I drank coffee in the lighted kitchen. He liked to sit and talk in the light because he was deaf and had to read my lips. He was a product of life in a mill town, frail and delicate and deaf, unlike his sturdy father who had worked in the mill for twenty-five years.

Sam Bielich lived near me with his wife and two children and I often went there to learn about unionism and politics and to connect with the family. Their gray house hung out over the cliff and looked as though all it needed to fall off was a good push. They were the best and warmest of people. Martha lectured me gently about being away from home: "Suppose something happened to you? How would your mother feel? Suppose something happened to you and your mother didn't know about it?"

Martha was absolutely right, though I failed to realize it at the time. My parents were continually concerned about me, and with good reason. One day my father showed up, unannounced, at the old German woman's house where I lived. I hadn't written and hadn't answered my mother's letters, which were piled up unread in my box at the post office on Carson Street. He was relieved to find I was well.

I failed to grasp the meaning of Martha's questions to me until many years later, when my own two children went their separate ways, barely staying in touch with their parents. In 1991, Thelma, ten years after we had separated, sent me a copy of a letter she had written to our children:

> You'll never really understand unless, or until, you become parents yourselves. There are times when I honestly think the parental instinct is greater than the instinct for self-preservation—I know it is. Until the day we die we will miss you, we will love you and, yes, we will worry about you—especially when there is no communication to assure us that all is well. And yes, I still do love you.

And then she wrote to me of our son: "He can go for three or four weeks without a note or a call; then, bingo, he calls and you melt at the sound of his voice!" That was the way with my parents too, and probably with all parents. It took me a long time to realize it and then, alas, it was too late to make up for it.

The best I can say, for whatever it may be worth, is that I was busy learning history and living it. On a Sunday in May 1937, I was present when about 2,000 steelworkers crammed into Lithuanian Hall on the South Side. Many were probably frightened to be seen at a union meeting, but were part of the massive turnout. Sam Bielich was deeply involved (and in time left the mill to be a full-time union organizer).

The center front of the hall was taken by several hundred Serbians, some of whom barely spoke or understood English. They had the most to lose, for they were aging, had large families, and knew nothing but millwork. Still, they were the first to join the union.

The papers said negotiations with the company were under way. F. Patrick Hannaway, an aging veteran of the Mine Workers Union, neatly dressed with silver gray hair, explained carefully:

> Union brothers, negotiations for a contract are now being conducted by the representatives of *your* organization, the Steel Workers Organizing Committee, and the heads of Jones & Laughlin Steel Corporation. The Steel Workers Organizing Committee is asking for complete bargaining powers for all the workers in the Jones and Laughlin mills, both in Pittsburgh and Aliquippa.[7]

He declared that since the union began its drive, J&L workers had received three wage raises and reduction in hours to forty a week; that without the union they would be back to forty-eight hours a week; that the largest corporation in the steel industry, United States Steel, had signed with the union; and that Jones & Laughlin must do likewise.

> We of the United Mine Workers of America have the largest labor organization in the country. Our people work thirty-five hours a week under the best conditions. This has come about because we built a strong and fearless union, ready to strike whenever the employers refused to accede to our demands. And now I tell you, brothers, the United Mine Workers and the entire Committee for Industrial Organization stand behind you and will give you every possible financial and physical support.[8]

That was the essence of it. Everybody felt the meeting was a complete success, that the whole mill was behind the union. The saloons filled with steelworkers whose voices were high and happy. The strike could still be avoided. Next day my silent partner, Andy, wore a light blue CIO button in the center of his hatband. When I went to get chisels for the first time, the grinder looked through me and past me, then leaned toward me over his bench. "I seen you at the meeting last night," he whispered.

Pete was quiet all morning, in his own thoughts. Usually he was the chipper heard above the noise of the hammers, but now he was silent, with a gloomy, brooding expression. He walked away, didn't want to talk. Yet I knew he had something on his mind. When something went wrong, he either acted cross or sulked. When I went to eat my lunch, he came over and said, "I'll trade you a ham sandwich for an apple."

"I only have one apple, Pete."

"I'll give you a damn sandwich anyway. I got an extra one."

He brought the sandwich and walked away again. I realized the reason for Pete's perplexity was the issue of negotiations, bothering everybody in the mill. Was it work or fight? His chipping hammer was in his hand. He pressed the trigger, making it splutter air into the palm of his other hand. Pete was the only chipper whose hands were so tough he didn't need to use gloves.

"Hey, Mike, what do you think about the CIO?"

I told him if we could stick together—

"Yeah, it's all right for you...." he said, looking very distressed. "You can't strike against J&L. They're big, there's Andy Mellon's money behind this mill. You can't fight Andy Mellon. And I got too much to lose."

Then he lowered his voice. "I know the CIO is a good thing. I signed a card last month. But suppose I haven't even got a job."

That was the spirit of most of the men. They felt the need for unity, for sticking together, but they feared the invisible power of the corporation. They were uneducated and puny, while the mill was run by smart, rich men. They were uncertain about the CIO, about trusting something they did not understand.

The next couple of days, thousands of workers milled in and around union headquarters. The union leadership was still in conference with management. The strike deadline was postponed. The craneman came out of his cab, showing that he had been wearing a union button on high all along.

Finally, the strike was on, the first big strike in steel since 1919. Men picketed all along the wall, wherever they felt the need for a picket, in the rain, on the muddy earth. Nobody went in, everybody came out. The union let the company keep the blast furnaces lit. The union office, the street, the saloons overflowed. A union officer passed out chewing tobacco. Emil, the bartender, served sandwiches and coffee.

"A man don't have to be told to fight for his rights, " somebody said, then complained that a lot of guys went home and out hunting, because they knew others would fight. I ran into the chipping bed grinder, hurrying to the Eliza blast furnace, on the north side of the river, where his son worked and was picketing. "This time we got 'em," he shouted happily. "I work in mill twenty years. Boss always big shot, treat us like dirt, like rain that fall in river. When mill say work you work. Otherwise, you got nothing, you stay home. Wife and kids got nothing. Twenty years wait for today!" Somebody on the street asked whether the blacks in the mill were with the strike or were scabbing. Around the steel towns, they were commonly called "jigs" and "jigaboos." They were solidly with the strike and someone ventured to explain: "You know how blacks came into the steel industry? They were brought North to scab. They couldn't get work any other way. Besides, when there was a union years ago, the white leadership wouldn't take in the blacks and that made them scab. Mill bosses kept everybody apart by making the men curse each other's nationality: hunkies, dagoes, sheenies, and the rest, but blacks got it worst."

Now there was a new power on the South Side. The company could open the factory gates, but the CIO could close them. The strike lasted thirty-six hours, until a billion-dollar corporation conceded it had been humbled by 30,000 steelworkers. When it was declared over, thousands of workers jammed the hall on 17th Street, while thousands more flooded the streets outside. Within two weeks, the National Labor Relations Board would conduct an election to determine if the workers wanted the Steel Workers Organizing Committee to represent them. The three o'clock shift went to work that afternoon and soon smoke streamed out of relit stacks. I found a note from my landlady that the mill had called for me to report to work at seven the next morning.

Later that year, I teamed up with a fellow named Ralph Rudd, who worked at the Aliquippa plant of J&L to publish a newspaper called the *Union Press*. Ralph was a New Englander in his early twenties, whose father I believe was a college professor. The initiative was his so he was the editor and I was associate editor. The paper reflected the changes in steel country. Working people could hold their heads up, take charge of their lives and the way they were governed. The lead story of November 3, 1937, read:

> Democratic, CIO-endorsed candidates won most of the offices contested in the balloting yesterday throughout Beaver Valley, as the two organizations united to defeat conservative Republicans and replace them with liberal friends of labor.
>
> In Aliquippa the whole Democratic slate was elected, and the Republicans, some of whom had held office many years and had been unfriendly to the organization of labor, were defeated decisively.[9]

And a related editorial, titled "Victory," began:

> Next to our strike victory and the contract we won last May, yesterday's election is the greatest single victory the people of Aliquippa have won. We have defeated the political machine which tyrannized over us for so many years. We have defeated the powers which kept Aliquippa like a feudal preserve, notorious throughout the country for the completeness of the machine's control over the lives of our people.[10]

The *Pittsburgh Press* on page 4 reported, "The Democratic Party has been reelected in Pittsburgh. And the steelworkers of Jones & Laughlin helped to reelect Mayor Scully and the entire slate...." Moreover, on the job the contract was in force and working, as evidenced by this headline and the story that followed:

Union Scores Big Triumph on Seniority: Company Agrees to Rehire Men in Compliance With Contract

But perhaps the best feature in the newspaper was written by Abraham Lincoln—an excerpt from his message to Congress of December 3, 1861.

There is one point... to which I wish to ask a brief attention. It is the effort to place capital on an equal footing with, if not above, labor, in the structure of government. It is assumed labor is available only in connection with capital; that nobody labors unless somebody else, owning capital, somehow by the use of it, induces him to labor.... Now, there is no such relation between capital and labor as assumed.... Labor is prior to and independent of capital. Capital is only the fruit of labor, and could never have existed if labor had not first existed. Labor is the superior of capital and deserves much the higher consideration.

Starting from March 1, 1937, I lived and worked in Pittsburgh almost two years. I was laid off by J&L when work slackened. Then I was called back, but I had already returned to New York. I had that option, which Pete, my mentor and good buddy in chipping, pointedly made clear he did not have. Pete offered to trade me a ham sandwich for an apple and when I did not have an apple to trade, gave me the damn sandwich anyway. But then, the less people have, the more willing they are to share and care.

CHAPTER 4

Not a single one of our stories was worth publishing – Stavisky liked the camaraderie of the small, dedicated staff – I registered for the draft – Lots of hurrahs, but what was war really all about?

My parents and brother welcomed me home again in the Bronx, but I was still restless. At nineteen years old, I didn't know what to do with myself or how to make a living. I returned to evening sessions at CCNY to earn a few more academic credits and to write for *Main Events*. Working for the school paper was a tantalizing hint of the real thing, an exercise in inspiration and frustration.

Then, somehow, my close friend Howard Silverberg discovered in his family a contact with the editor of Street & Smith, which published pulp fiction magazines filled with stories of hair-raising adventure and mystery. We felt encouraged to collaborate and submit our work, so every morning for about two months we met at *Main Events* and wrote. The office was empty and quiet so we were able to concentrate undisturbed. We began each story by discussing and outlining the plot. Then one of us would write the opening, the other the ending, and we would meet somewhere in the middle. We wrote about ten stories; I saved three of them.

Murder—Made to Order
Five would get you ten anywhere on the Taunton campus that one fine day there'd be a murder in Professor Forrest's class in sociology. And another sure thing was that half the juries in the world would call it justifiable homicide. You couldn't expect a six-foot husky like Clint Forrest, once an all-American star on Taunton's championship eleven, to restrain himself forever when he was being heckled by a snip of a student like Thomas Peterson Jr.

Tommy Peterson was the chubby, pink-cheeked son of the county's district attorney. And the D.A. was Clint's favorite subject. So sooner or later it had to happen....

Band of Blood

Ray Torrance clambered up the gangplank of the giant Queen Anne. Crowds lined the deck, waving farewell to mobs on the pier.

The *Times-Star* ship newsman hastened to the far side of the deck, anxiously seeking a certain cabin number. Away from the jamming throngs he moved freely, rapidly. Shouts of exuberant voyagers mixed with the rhythmic lapping of the water to produce a dreamy melody in Torrance's ear.

"Good morning, amigo," a high-pitched voice greeted him from behind.

The reporter spun in his tracks.

"You!"

Dynamo of Doom

Headlines screamed at Chuck Regan as he emerged from a honky-tonk west of Broadway. The tall, lanky flier bought a paper and read the lead article with interest.

"Amy Hart Still Missing." Somewhere out in the Pacific America's greatest woman pilot had gone down. Although preparations for her flight had been shrouded in mystery, Chuck knew she was testing a new Army pursuit plane and that numerous "accidents" had delayed her takeoff.

Regan crossed Times Square, headed straight for his hotel. As he strode into the lobby he heard a familiar voice call out his name.

Wheeling around, he confronted Howard Fromm of Military Intelligence.

"I knew you'd show up," Regan greeted coolly. "Where do we go from here?"

"We're expecting you to take off from San Francisco the day after tomorrow."

We sent the batch of stories to our contact, who forwarded them to John Nanovic, the editor at Street & Smith, who soon agreed to meet us to review our work. We came to his office on 4th Avenue, north of Union Square. Nanovic's desk was piled high with manuscripts; his office was plain and cluttered. So this, I thought, is what it's like. He was cordial, frank, and forthright in reporting that not a single one of our stories was worthy of publishing, but we were welcome to try again if we wished.

Howard went back to work at a regular job that had nothing to do with writing or publishing and I went back to tracking my fantasy about breaking into the publishing world, somewhere and somehow. I answered advertisements in *Editor & Publisher*, a trade publication of the newspaper industry, and *Publishers' Auxiliary*, a trade publication for small dailies and weeklies. Pretty soon, I had nibbles and bites and accepted an invitation to come to work at the *Tribune-Telegraph* in Pomeroy, Ohio, a dreamy little town on the Ohio River.

It was a minimal daily, low in circulation, advertising, and coverage of news. It wasn't big enough for a teletype machine. In fact, every day at noon the city editor would put on a headset and take dictation of the fifteen-minute daily quota of news over the "pony wire" from the Associated Press in Columbus. After a week or so, the general manager told me that he had made a mistake, that he had really intended to hire "a thoroughly capable and experienced all-round advertising man and salesman," and paid my way back to New York.

But I had another job waiting in the wings and off I went to a weekly in Silver Spring, Maryland, a suburb of Washington DC. This one turned out to be a disaster, like the dry cleaning job in Pittsburgh. I mean, the publisher was slick and sleazy. For twenty dollars a week, my assignment was to solicit advertising, report and write the news, lay out the pages at the printer, and then turn newsboy to distribute copies. I stayed two weeks and considered myself lucky to get paid when I quit.

Thus, early in 1941, I came to Washington DC to seek my fortune. In those days it was an entirely different city than it later became, an amiable, genteel southern town, with abundant trees, monumental gardens, landscaped grounds, and century-old office buildings still in use—and segregation was in full force. I walked into the *Washington Post* on E Street, a little street at the edge of 14th Street and Pennsylvania Avenue, the main downtown intersection, climbed the narrow, creaky stairs to the second floor newsroom, and asked about employment. I was interviewed by an assistant managing editor, a bit of a victory in itself, miles ahead of being handed an application form by a clerk at a personnel office. I showed the editor the last issue of the Silver Spring weekly and said, "This is what I can do and I would like to be a reporter here." He scanned the paper with some interest and returned it to me. "We don't have an opening for a reporter—" and he paused. "However, we may have one soon for a copyboy. If you are interested, leave your name and check back in two or three weeks."

That was a welcome offer, my first real break in professional journalism, and I agreed. Meanwhile, I followed up on a newspaper ad and was hired as a Gray Line sightseeing guide. I knew nothing about the city, to be sure, but spring season was at hand and the Gray Line was desperate for guides. New hires were scheduled for a weeklong training program, but after three days the instructor said, "You are starting on the buses now. You have the manual. Use it." I made mistakes, but learned about the city and surroundings, and passengers were tolerant. Busloads of touring school groups and I learned together. I earned a decent wage, aided by the sale of sets of postcards on the way to Mount Vernon (dividing the profit with the driver). I found a place to stay with a family on Buchanan Street in northwest Washington, paying $6.25 per week for room and breakfast, plus 50 cents for every dinner or large meal I ate. I paid $1.25 for a streetcar pass. I earned more on the buses than at the *Post,* but in about three weeks, the call came from the newsroom and I jumped for it. For two or three days, I actually worked both jobs. Hugh Miller, the head photographer, got a kick out of seeing me run around the building in my Gray Line cap and sometimes reminded me of it much, much later.

The *Washington Post* of that time certainly was not dominant in its area, nor was it especially successful. It was a struggling newspaper, competing against the *Evening Star,* which had more circulation, more advertising, and more prestige, and the *Times-Herald,* a recent merger of papers belonging to Hearst and the *New York Daily News–Chicago Tribune,* which published both morning and afternoon editions. The Scripps-Howard *Washington Daily News,* a kind of noontime quick-read tabloid, was about the only paper less likely to succeed. Still, the *Post* was rich in personality and character. Sam Stavisky, who worked on the city desk and in time became a good friend, many years later wrote a book about his wartime experience in the Marine Corps, in which he recalled that he had joined the *Post* in 1938 at the age of twenty-seven because he "liked the camaraderie of the small, dedicated staff and could tolerate the low salary scale."

Sam worked under John Riseling, the night city editor, who was five foot six, maybe 120 or 130 pounds dripping wet, and was totally committed to his mission of getting the news, getting it right, and getting it out on time. He was a chain-smoker, like many in the newsroom, with one ear fixed on the police radio at the side of his desk. He could be caustic, barking to a copyboy, "While you're resting, take this to the composing room," or sentimental, when it was approaching three AM and we were waiting for the presses to roll on the final edition, telling me about his daughter who was preparing to enter a Catholic sisterhood.

A copyboy did whatever he was told to do by whoever told him. "Boy!" shouted Alfred Friendly, a chain-smoking top reporter sitting in the middle of the newsroom. He wanted a cup of coffee from the restaurant next door. "Copy!" shouted Walter Wood, the picture editor. He had something for the art department on the fifth floor. Or another editor or reporter wanted something from the library, called the morgue. "Copy," I thought, was a more respectful term, though all the copyboys were boys, or rather, young men. The newsroom was no place for women. If a woman ventured to enter, someone was likely to straighten her out, declaring, "The society department is on the third floor, one flight up." Working in the steel mill, I heard the *rat-a-tat-tat* of pneumatic hammers. Now I heard the *rat-a-tat-tat* of fifty typewriters and the lively talk of today's events and tomorrow's headlines. It looked chaotic, yet everybody had an oar to pull, from Edward "Eddie" T. Folliard, the number one reporter on politics and national affairs who had been at the *Post* for years, on down. At the deep end of the room, George James, the copy chief, or the "slot man," sat surrounded by his copyreaders, the men "on the rim." He was a heavy man who looked like an intimidating Buddha, with a loud voice that carried authority. Behind them in a glassed-in room were the teletype machines recording dispatches of the wire services and various syndicates. In the front of the newsroom on the left side was the glassed-in office of the managing editor, Alexander F. Jones, or "Casey," gray-haired, spectacled, and serious, but then he was in charge of it all. Around to the right, in another room, was the sports department, where the principal personality was Shirley Povich, who wore a broad-brimmed fedora and looked like the actor George Raft. He was like Folliard: both had been there for years, both were tops in what they did, yet both were modest and soft-spoken.

The role of copyboy was not exactly a thinking job, but it gave me plenty of exercise. Inside the building, I had occasion at one time or another to go to every department from top to bottom. The ancient elevator was notoriously slow, so I took the stairs two or three steps at a time. Outside the building, I was dispatched to the National Press Club around the corner to pick up news releases and down Pennsylvania Avenue to the Associated Press photo lab in the Star Building (from which I sometimes was late in returning since the fellows there had a peeping-Tom's view of bedrooms at the back of the Walter Raleigh Hotel).

In those years, Americans got their news from the newspapers. The first edition of the *Post*—the "bulldog" edition—was on the street about nine PM. The second was the mail edition, scheduled to catch the trains to downstate Virginia and rural Maryland; third and fourth were suburban editions, with makeups, changes, and corrections as needed until the fifth and final, the late city edition, rolled through the presses at three AM every morning no matter what. Newspapers still printed extras if the story was big enough. At that time—early 1941—the United States was not yet at war, but was getting closer to it by supporting Great Britain with massive lend-lease shipments. One evening, President Franklin D. Roosevelt was to make a major declaration and the *Post* scheduled a speech extra. I was sent to the White House along with George Bookman, a talented young reporter just a few years older than me, who covered the president. Bookman sat poised at a typewriter in the pressroom, while I, along with other newspeople, gathered around Steve Early, the president's press secretary, in his office. At 7:30, Early passed out the text. I took my copy and dashed over to Bookman in the pressroom. He wrote, paragraph by paragraph, then pulled each completed sheet out of his typewriter, handed it to me, and I read it over the telephone to a rewrite man at the *Post*. At 9:30, when the president began to speak, the *Post* had an extra on the street with the text and an article reporting it. Bookman told me I did a good job, for whatever that was worth, and I thanked him.

The truth was that I didn't want to be a copyboy. I wanted to be a reporter and writer and hoped for a chance to show that I was able. I made a deal with Robert Allan, the church editor, known as "the bishop," to come in Sundays on my own time and help him report the sermons of the day for the Monday morning paper. For several weeks in a row at "the bishop's" direction, I telephoned and interviewed various ministers and wrote up their activities, but that ended when the Newspaper Guild chapter at the *Post* complained.

I could understand and accept the Guild's position—if the job was worth doing, it ought to be done by a professional paid at scale. I supported the Guild and, even as a copyboy, paid my dues as a member. When Heywood Broun, the Scripps-Howard columnist, founded the Guild in 1935, he took a large step to making journalism a true profession. James Stahlman, publisher of the *Nashville Banner* (and president of the American Newspaper Publishers Association in June 1937), declared: "A closed editorial shop means a closed editorial mind." But then he was the most close-minded of them all, a reactionary's reactionary. Publishers claimed the Guild threatened freedom of the press. On September 22, 1935, the *Los Angeles Times* (reporting about Seattle radical organizations at work) stated in a news column that one purpose of the Guild was "to control news of radical activities by 'advising' editors." But at Christmas 1937, when department store clerks struck for higher wages and better conditions, Los Angeles papers, led by the *Times*, headlined: "Assassination of Santa Claus" and "Murder of the Spirit of Christmas." Publishers were basically businessmen, not journalists. William McLean, of the *Philadelphia Bulletin*, who was president of the Associated Press, the Kauffmanns and other families of the Washington *Evening Star*, Robert McCormick of the *Chicago Tribune*, the Chandlers of the *Los Angeles Times*, Frank Ernest Gannett—they all qualified for what William Allen White, the sage of Kansas, called the "unconscious arrogance of conscious wealth."

Another time, I picked up the first edition and read a front-page story by one of the top reporters. But the lead, I thought, was buried in the fourth paragraph rather than the first. Just for exercise, I sat down and rewrote it. At that moment, I heard Casey Jones complain to one of the editors, "But the lead here is buried in the fourth paragraph." I took my copy out of the typewriter, handed it to him, and said, "Yes, I just rewrote it." He looked at me as if to ask, "Who in the heck are you?"

My rewrite showed up in print, but it didn't do much good. Two reporters left for military service and the paper was shorthanded. Soon two journalism school graduates were hired. I concluded that if I stayed at the *Washington Post*, I was destined to remain a copyboy at $15 a week forever.

Now I had a little experience and knew a few people around town. My outlook on life had changed considerably. I would always keep my old sympathies for social justice, but I wanted to get on with my career in journalism, rather than with revolution. A friend sent me to the International News Service (or INS), which hired me as a dictation boy. This was definitely a step up, since I now made $18 a week, worked daylight hours, and nobody shouted "Boy!" or sent me for coffee. In fact, I actually had a chance to do a little writing. My fellow dictation boys were bright, able, and ambitious. They included Edwin Newman, later an NBC correspondent in London and Paris, Eugene Rachlis, later a magazine and book editor, and Bill Umstead, later managing editor of the *New York Daily News*.

The INS was a wire service, competing with the Associated Press, which was much larger, more prestigious, and plainly number one in the field (and owned by the newspapers it served), and with the United Press, which was owned by Scripps-Howard. The INS was owned by William Randolph Hearst, part of the communications empire of an earlier day when Hearst newspapers around the country screamed jingoism in banner headlines and featured top writers working for top pay. By now some of the papers had folded, but there were still the Hearst-syndicated comics like "Blondie" and "Barney Google" and popular Hearst features like Louella Parsons, the Hollywood gossip, and Bob Considine, the sports columnist (who was carried in the *Washington Post*).

What we dictation boys did was take dictation. When a reporter had a story, he would call in from his beat (whether covering Congress, or the White House, the State Department, or one of the executive departments), talk briefly to the desk, then switch to dictation. Wearing a headset freed both hands for the typewriter. I listened to and typed news stories in the process of composition, so I almost felt like I was there on the scene with the reporter. As soon as I finished, I gave the typed copy to the desk for editing and then out it went via teletype to INS clients. The process was taut and swift. The object was to get there first with something instantly usable, special, and respectable. I confess that Ed Newman, rather than I, took the stories from the White House. I was a pretty good typist but he was faster. The truth is that all these years I've never learned touch-typing. I don't hunt-and-peck but use about four or five fingers in my own unorthodox manner.

I saw the INS people as able professionals. They were all men and all white, like almost everybody in the news business in Washington at the time. Even after World War II, when the issue of admitting blacks came up before the National Press Club, George Durno, who covered the White House for the INS, fought against it. At the Cosmos Club, certainly elite and supposedly intellectual, President Kennedy withdrew his application for membership because blacks were still barred there as late as the 1960s.

The INS office was on the top floor of the *Times-Herald* Building, in one tremendous open room like a loft in a warehouse. The bureau chief, William K."Hutch" Hutchinson, had a little cubbyhole, but mostly he was somewhere else around town and would telephone now and then with the same salutation: "Hutch. Anything?" The men on the desk, Bob Humphreys and Harold Slater, who ran things, and all the others, were very decent to me. They allowed me to write a number of articles for the "mail sheet"— undated material the newspapers, mostly the smaller ones, would use as filler. The articles were based largely on news releases from government and private agencies and carried this byline:

By Michael Frome, International News Service Staff Correspondent

I almost felt I had arrived! Here are the leads of two of my stories:

Washington, Sept. 25 – While men in every section of the country leave their work benches in increasing numbers to take up Army life, American women are stepping into the breach to maintain a steady flow of defense materials from the factories to the armed forces.

Washington, Oct. 17 – The United States, as a result of the national defense effort, is today witnessing the greatest boom in its history.

Overall national production and income—factory turnout, farm yield, wages and business profit—are at an unparalleled level. After one full year of national defense economy, the cost of retail commodities is at an all-time high.

Yes, in the fall of 1941 the United States was nominally still at peace, but the war boom put virtually everybody to work, creating far more jobs and bigger profits than the earlier New Deal make-work projects ever did. Scant attention was given to the root cause of war, of any war, of one war that carries with it the seeds of the next war. America was distant from and free of the death and destruction that already engulfed civilians and foot soldiers around the world; many Americans were puzzled while world leaders connived with each other in strange ways. Winston Churchill, for example, hated communism, but England and the United States needed the Soviet Union. Joseph Stalin hated Hitler, or so we thought, until they signed a nonaggression pact in 1939—that didn't last anyway.

I registered for the draft but did not foresee my number coming up. The other dictation boys and I scrambled for better jobs opening in the news field (to be replaced once war began by dictation girls). I answered an ad for a position as managing editor of the *Main Line Times*, a weekly newspaper of substance in an upscale suburb of Philadelphia. We corresponded, and the publisher, A. E. Hickerson, telephoned, proposing to come down by train the next day, pick me up at the office, and take me to lunch. When I explained the prospect to Humphreys and Slater at the desk, they cheered. "Never mind the headset and dictation," they said. "Tomorrow you sit at that desk and look like a reporter." When Hickerson arrived, they summoned me with deference. We went to Child's, a popular chain restaurant, directly across the street. He impressed me as a sober, small town businessman. I showed him samples of my work and he offered me the job. I would start at $25 and go to $40 within six months. We got everything settled and he walked me back to the *Times-Herald* Building. A few minutes later, he came up again and said there was one point he forgot to make: Was I a member of the Newspaper Guild? When I acknowledged I was he said, "That sort of thing isn't good on a weekly, where people are trying to work things out for themselves and don't like somebody on the outside trying to tell them what to do." He said he wouldn't ask me to resign, but you understand how things are, don't you? No, I really did not. It didn't seem right for a publisher to tell employees what organizations they could belong to. But I let it go and moved to the *Main Line Times*.

The paper was located in a sizable one-story building where two sister suburban weeklies, the *Germantown Courier* and *Upper Darby News*, plus assorted commercial jobs, were also printed. As the managing editor, my staff consisted of a society editor and sports editor-photographer who took care of their own pages, plus correspondents in the towns, mostly housewives, who were paid (meagerly) for what they turned in and needed editing and rewriting. The paper usually ran in two sections of twelve and eight pages, abundant with advertisements from the Main Line branch of Strawbridge & Clothier, the Philadelphia department store, and others, with plenty of space for me to fill. I worked hard, late nights, covering and writing stories, editing the correspondents, writing headlines, laying out pages, and working with the printers to make it all fit. I learned a lot and learned the area, so that reporters from the Philadelphia dailies, *Inquirer, Bulletin,* and *Record*, assigned to cover the Main Line, stopped by periodically to see what I was working on. I doubt it meant much to the *Record*, a liberal Democratic paper with working-class appeal, but it certainly did to the *Bulletin*, whose publisher, Robert McLean, lived on the Main Line.

The area's name was derived from the main line of the Pennsylvania Railroad running through upscale towns, with old Welsh names like Bala Cynwyd, Narberth, and Bryn Mawr. It was very Republican country, with station wagons when they were high-priced and made of wood, chauffeured limousines, mansions, and estates; small elite colleges like Haverford, Rosemont, Bryn Mawr, and Villanova; and the ultra-elite Lower Merion Cricket Club, one of the championship golf courses of the country. Here was another side of Pennsylvania, and another side of life, for me to peek into and learn from. Here it was said that the New Deal people had a complex that made them go out and persecute classes. It was also said that Democrats were so scarce in Montgomery County that the Pew family, the conservative oil moguls, would nominate the Democratic candidates.

I lived in Ardmore with a landscape architect, Bill Mulford, and his wife for $5 a week. Bill was from an old established family in the Social Register; he was also a Harvard graduate (class of '28) and when Harvard whipped Yale, Bill had a good reason to tie one on. During that late fall football season, I was treated to a visit from George Bookman, my friend at the *Washington Post*, who had come with his betrothed, Janet, to watch his alma mater, Haverford, in its homecoming game. I gave them a tour of the *Main Line Times* and George was pleased to see me make good. Janet later said she disliked sharing George with me, but for me it was a treat. (In time, George worked at *Time, Fortune,* and the New York Stock Exchange.)

Then, on Sunday, December 7, I was visiting my parents in New York. My father had suffered the first of several heart attacks. My brother had graduated from CCNY with a degree in chemical engineering, married his sweetheart Mollie, and begun his career. We heard the radio report the Japanese attack on Pearl Harbor, so sudden and unbelievable that at first we barely discussed it. I think most Americans hoped to stay out of the war, but now "Remember Pearl Harbor" became a battle cry to curdle the blood, especially after President Roosevelt denounced the "day of infamy." The United States could now drop all pretense of neutrality and mobilize for war on a large scale.

My brother had been rejected for the draft because of his poor eyesight, but I was prime draft material. When I returned to the *Main Line Times,* I had plenty of news about our boys at war, people busy being air raid wardens, serving the naval auxiliary or the Red Cross, or growing victory gardens. I worked for a couple of months, and then returned to New York to enlist. That gave me the option of choosing my branch of service instead of having it chosen for me. There were lots of hurrahs, but scant attention to the question: what is war really all about?

CHAPTER 5

The Air Corps was my home – We learned to salute smartly and recognize authority – Studying astronomy, stars, trigonometry, and angles – She was a loner – "But I can't let you go without seeing you first"

In March 1942, two months before my twenty-second birthday, I volunteered for service in the U.S. Army Air Corps. I would have had to face the draft and go anyway. Volunteering gave me a choice. I went to Governors Island (reached via ferry from the Battery in downtown Manhattan) and passed various tests for skills and aptitude that qualified me for training as a pilot. I was willing and eager to go, to get the training behind me and fly into combat. That, however, wasn't the way it worked in a military system where you were apt to hurry up only to wait. I was accepted in the Air Corps but sent home on furlough without pay. I continually called and wrote letters until June, when at last I was ordered into uniform.

The delays were understandable in a way. When I entered the Air Corps (then still a branch of the Army) it was less than fifty years since the Wright Brothers pioneered the age of flight, almost yesterday when pilots flew the mail in open cockpits, when planes were flimsy, held together by wooden spars, struts, and wires. With the war, all that changed. The war modernized aviation and transformed air transport into an industry, with ocean flying, long runways, reversible pitch propellers, long-range navigation, and height and speed beyond the wonder of natural things. New planes—bombers, fighters, and transports—rolled out of factories, and new pilots and flight crews rose out of schools, all in a scramble, with enormous energy released to get up and go.

The Air Corps became my home for the next three and a half years. The first year I spent moving from one training base to another in the South and the Deep South, showing me that part of America largely unchanged for generations, impoverished and backward. It was rural and racist; everything was separate and unequal. Blacks rode in the back of the bus, they entered a movie house on the outside and climbed to "nigger heaven," toilets in public places were plainly marked "white" and "colored." Towns and cities were plain, old, worn, unpainted. I was looking at the South as it had long been. People were poor and powerless. Being in the South, I met southern boys, many of them racist, who found strange pleasure in telling nigger jokes over drinks, in card games, or in the shower. Racism was their chance to be better than somebody else.

My experience and observations were not unique nor limited to the South. Through much of the war, I corresponded with Sam Stavisky, my friend who had worked on the city desk at the *Washington Post*. At first he had been rejected for service because of poor eyesight. He was devastated, but in due course was admitted into a new Marine Corps cadre called "combat correspondents." They were assigned to write articles for hometown consumption about men with whom they served in frontline actions. Years later Stavisky wrote a book about it, *Marine Correspondent*, in which he recalled that after boot training he was "burning for combat." He was sent to San Francisco where he was stuck so long that he went to work as a copy editor at one of the daily newspapers. In his book, Stavisky recalled an old-line Marine sergeant he met in training. The sergeant hated Franklin D. Roosevelt as a dictator who would never give up the White House, and furthermore hated Secretary of the Navy Frank Knox and First Lady Eleanor Roosevelt as "nigger lovers," and hated the Army as well for accepting "rabble" under the draft.

My own first station was the preflight school at Maxwell Field, Alabama, where fellow raw recruits and I, now uniformed aviation cadets, learned to right-face, left-face, about-face, march, salute smartly, recognize and respect military authority, and chant "Off we go into the wild blue yonder" in unison; and to survive in an Alabama of summer heat and humidity, daily downpours, muddy raw red earth, and southern accents as thick as mush. I advanced from there to primary flight school at Douglas, in the piney woods of south Georgia. It was a pleasant setting, with 250 cadets housed four in a room in one-story buildings like little villas and served nourishing food in the mess hall by local civilian employees probably glad to have the work. We were issued goggles, helmets, and leather flight jackets to wear while flying in the primary trainers, PT-17s, the yellow two-seater open cockpit Stearman biplanes.

My roommate, Herb Goldstein of Buffalo, became a buddy. He was only nineteen, three years my junior, but had been flying privately for two or three years and was ready for acrobatics. He was way ahead of me, but we wanted to stay together. "I hope you don't wash out," he said. "If you do, I think I'll wash out too." Washing out in one of the periodic progress checks meant losing the good life and starting over in navigation or bombardier training, or going into something else as an enlisted man. It was a hard, ever-threatening fact of life. A friend, Stuart Schuyler, wrote me after washing out of basic training: "They say nobody washes out of basic, but I never could seem to be really sure I wanted to make it through. It became a lot of trouble and I became careless." I enjoyed flying and tried to be careful in my climbs, glides, rectangular course, stalls, and spins. I soloed at eight hours, then soloed again. I was up almost an hour, shooting landings and takeoffs, looking at shadows cast by trees, and trains that looked like toys. But I wasn't good enough and washed out. "All you do in the army," lamented Goldstein, "is make friends and lose them."

It was night, the first Sunday night in November 1942, when I arrived in Nashville, Tennessee, to start over at the reception center. Thirty washouts on the train, coming from different training fields, were all worn out and brooding, swapping stories and whiskey, shooting craps and playing cards. It did not help to find Nashville that night overrun by a huge host of soldiers, 300,000 of the "Red" and "Blue" armies, all in from training maneuvers for the weekend, and outnumbering civilians on the streets of the city. That was the South during World War II, and it was clearly good for business.

The cadet center was miserable, unsanitary, and unhealthy. So many were sick, it took a fever of 102 to get in the hospital. New cadets felt washouts were inferior for failing; officers disliked us for wanting additional liberties. We did kitchen police and guard duty with wooden sticks on wintry nights. Everybody wanted a furlough, but it took critical trouble at home to get one. Some talked about sending phony telegrams. One declared he would never do it: "I would rather not go on furlough than get such a telegram for fear that something bad might accidentally happen." When he became a father, they would not let him go home to his wife and baby.

Three nights a week, we were allowed off the post. One evening, I walked into the newsroom of the morning newspaper, the *Nashville Tennesseean*, where I felt the atmosphere familiar and warm and found the city editor accessible. "We have a reporter here who flies and covers aviation for us," he said, leading me across the room and introducing me to a young woman reporter. Her blond hair was uncombed, covering part of her face. She had a small body, small round face, with large, faraway sad eyes. We talked about flying. Her name was Gene.

I returned again and again to see Gene and look into those large, faraway, sad eyes. She appealed to me, with her sensitivity and appreciation of beauty in different forms. She spoke thoughtfully and knew how to listen. I went to the newspaper and walked her home where she lived with her mother. One afternoon, she took me flying from the little airport outside Nashville. After a while we kept circling and I wondered why. "Mike, I'm lost," she confessed. "Help me find the airport." We couldn't have gone far enough to be in trouble. Once on the ground, she laughed, "You must think I'm a terrible pilot." I didn't think she was a terrible pilot at all. Nor did it matter. She was five years older than I was, but that didn't matter either. She wasn't beautiful, she didn't cultivate the feminine, but there was depth and tenderness to her. She was a "ridge runner" from the hills of east Tennessee, a barefoot girl climbing a mountain alone with a dog. She showed me sketches of birds and dogs, poetry and short stories about "sliding over the edge of a cloud like a child sliding down a snow bank and dropping off to space below." When we embraced, she clung tightly to me, as though I mattered in her life, or she hungered for affection. When we went out she paid her way or we would eat at her house with her mother. That was sheer necessity, since we cadets didn't get paid at the base. The military camp was a miserable place and a disgrace, but nobody in authority cared.

I was based in Nashville from November 1, 1942, until mid-January 1943. At Christmas we exchanged modest gifts. She gave me a writing kit and told me to write a book while flying around the world. Then I went home on furlough to see my parents. Before I left Nashville for my next assignment Gene wrote a poem for me with a mystic message to us both.

> In bitterness you scorned the earth
> And nursed your scars,
> forgot the sky was wide with room
> for other stars.
>
> I, too, having felt the weight of chains
> held out my hand,
> saying there would be time for our feet
> to leave the land.

You asked what I saw within the dark.
I could not tell you that I saw my heart,
wild with passion as the twisting trees
sinking in chaos with the falling leaves.

You watched the shadows move across my face.
Neither your lips nor mine found answer for their ache.

I felt Gene was a loner, afraid to let me intrude in her space, but afraid, also, to let me go. I left Nashville for preflight navigation training in Monroe, Louisiana. Gene left too; she enrolled in the Women's Air Service Pilots, the WASPs, and went for training in Sweetwater, Texas, which apparently proved more than she bargained for. "I feel as if life is going on outside my little sphere and leaving me behind," she wrote me. "I feel I'm missing all the little sensing I used to have that made life beautiful. I'm missing music; and lazy days spent in the sun listening to the bright coins of Negro laughter spilling across the streets; nights with jangling telephones and death and love going by beneath my fingers; nights just looking at the sky and being alone." My face was in the locket the newspaper boys gave her when she left. When I sent her a record of my voice, she heard in it "the same little-boy wistfulness that I remember so well. And I remember the day we went up in a plane and got lost. You gave me some gum. I 'licked down' and found our way again."

Monroe, Louisiana, in 1943 was a small southern town with one main street, seven movie houses, hundreds of training planes flying over the rooftops, and assorted saloons and bars. It was a redneck's heaven. One of my friends told me how he had been riding on a bus when a pregnant black woman came on. He gave her his seat, but then a couple of stout southern boys warned him against violating local custom by doing it again. On the base, we kept on the go with calisthenics, drill, and classes. I studied logarithms, math, isobars, physics, maps, and charts. Still, some of us washouts making the second try were homesick and bored, tired of training. Gamblers in the ranks ran blackjack games (starting with dimes and working up to dollars) between classes, before and after formations, and all evening. I did not have money to lose and thought I could have gotten to the war faster as an enlisted man.

Rumor ran around that advanced training would not be through the program at Monroe, but at the University of Miami at Coral Gables, Florida, where the school was operated by Pan American Airways under contract to the government. A letter from Win Hird, a friend who had washed out of pilot training and was already at Coral Gables, previewed it for me.

> The first week here you are absolutely positive you'll never be a navigator—if you live. The second week you're scared stiff you'll live and *be* a navigator. The pressure keeps up right through the 40-day check. Washout rate is about 10 percent. Passing grade is 80 and it's easy as hell to drop 20 or 30 points in a test. The university has 600 co-eds, well developed, on the campus—swell for scenic effects, but you haven't time to do more than look (no shit!).
>
> You learn plenty of navigation here. Emphasis on celestial. Six weeks on Dead Reckoning. No Pilotage. All oversea trips over the Gulf and Cuba. Twelve flights total—a lot less than Monroe. The course is ten weeks long. Chicken shit at a minimum with Pan Am.
>
> Miami is a gorgeous place, weather 100 percent-plus. Am hot on the trail of Miami's most gorgeous brunette. I have a date for Sunday. Looks like a lulu.

His words proved true. Going to navigation training with Pan Am at Coral Gables was equivalent to winning a reprieve from the warden and leaving the dungeon to live in the sunlight as people do for a little while. Coral Gables, at the southern edge of Miami, was a synthetic upper-crust picture-book town, complete with coconut palm trees on manicured, landscaped streets with Hispanic names and lovely Mediterranean-style homes. We lived in the middle of it all, in the old San Sebastian Hotel, converted into a dormitory by the University of Miami. Under Pan Am, "chicken shit"—that is, military regulation, rigor, and formality—indeed was at the minimum. Pan American in those days was the U.S. flag carrier, whose vaunted, luxurious clippers pioneered routes overseas. Our instructors apparently were required to open every class session with a salute, but never took it seriously or made much of it. "If you haven't been lost," Captain Charlie Lunn, the director of the school, told us the first day, "you haven't navigated." That proved the gospel throughout my flying career (and I later adapted it to freelance writing: "If you haven't been rejected, you haven't submitted a manuscript to an editor").

We were housed five in a room, arranged alphabetically: Fournier,

Ford, Frome, Fuquay, and Freehafer. Ford, from southwest Minnesota, and Fuquay, from Piedmont, North Carolina, became friends, lasting throughout my military service and my life. The day began at six, when we were awakened by a popular show tune over the loud speaker: "Buckle down, Winsocki, buckle down. You can win, Winsocki, if you really buckle down." It struck home every day and made me vow to buckle down and not to wash out again. We poured out in front of the San Sebastian to do calisthenics and run for reveille; then back to clean the room, breakfast at 7:00; and meteorology at 7:30, studying the movement of air masses—high cirrus, stratus, cumulus, cumulonimbus altostratus, and nimbostratus cloud forms, all changing constantly and affecting the work of navigation. Then followed four hours studying astronomy, trigonometry, angles, stars, how to use the E6B computer (the navigator's best friend), plotting radio bearings, and plotting lines on a mercator projection.

We had to keep pressing, studying for tests to make it through the eighteen-day check, and then the forty-day check. Every day included time for physical exercise—handball, running through the streets, swimming in the classy Venetian pool and at the luxurious Biltmore Hotel, converted to serving as a military hospital. When I was given a sextant to use in practice, a whole new world (or, rather, a universe) opened for me. I was required to learn to identify fifty-five stars and, once we took to flying, to plot accurate positions derived from the stars. We trained in aging, dated Pan Am flying boats that took about twenty minutes to take off from the Dinner Key terminal and about as long to land. We never went very far—the planes averaged about ninety to one hundred knots—but always over water, at night over dark water through a blue sky, returning at three AM.

"If you don't think washing out is a serious problem, you're nuts," my old buddy Goldstein wrote from advanced training. "Spence Field [Moultrie, Georgia] is really a bitch of a school. The C.O. said he doesn't give a damn if he washes out the whole batch of us. Nineteen of our upper class have washed already. Plenty of chicken shit; no or little open post and other things too numerous to mention. A fellow in my room washed out the other day and, believe me, I'd rather go home in a wooden box than wash out." Navigation was nowhere near as severe, but in the very last week, even as the parents of my friend Tony arrived from Tampa to celebrate graduation with him, Tony was washed out.

Gene and I were both graduated on August 7, 1943. She thought I would go overseas as navigator in a bombing crew and had written me: "I feel as though I can't let you go without seeing you first. I've never thought, Mike, that I was in love with you, and yet for some reason to think of you going and not seeing you is hard to take. It is like dreaming a dream in which you look for something desperately. Then, just as you find it, it is no longer there." My two roommates, Ford and Fuquay, and I were not assigned to bombing, but to the Air Transport Command (or ATC), with ten days before reporting to our station at St. Joseph, Missouri. I telephoned Gene and we shared our happiness on graduating. She wanted me to come meet her in Nashville; it was a pleasure to agree. I found her tanned and happy. We went downtown to the newspaper office, then to the officers club in town. She wore a simple little blue dress and her eyes sparkled. We walked to the state capitol, sat a while, and I asked her to marry me. A tear rolled down her cheek. She said she wanted to marry me and yet the thought scared her. I felt I was in love with her, but neither of us was sure she was in love with me. If her feeling wasn't love, it bordered on it. "Let's both think it over and if, after a while, you still want to marry me, maybe we'll do it."

Gene went to the ferry command, a division of the ATC, at Long Beach, California, and I went to St. Joe. The letter writing began again. "I don't want to give you up. But I won't say I love you until I fight a few things out with myself and know better what the score is. Can we leave it at that for a while?" And then: "Mike, I want things to be always right for you. Every night I ask whatever faith I believe in to keep you and give you whatever you want out of life. I hope you get it. I think perhaps if I had known you better there could have been something for us. I am slow to love." And then again: "Before, I never had the courage to let you go completely. I am lonely and wanted to keep you as a sort of buffer. I wanted you there to turn to. In critical self-analysis, I can even admit you were a boost to my ego—not a pretty admission. I don't know, Mike, that I ever came or ever will come as close to marrying someone as I did you. Mike, I'm so confused, so discontented, so restless."

St. Joe, meanwhile, was little more than a way stop, a three-month holding tank, while I made practice flights to places like Dallas, Denver, and San Antonio. Ford and Fuquay did about the same. Finally our numbers came up. Fuquay went to the ferry command at Memphis and Ford went to Michigan, where he was not happy at all. His new base had more navigators than needed, but everybody had to report at nine AM and stick around all day, except for lunch break. He had landed "in the asshole of the world." The Bachelors Officers Quarters, or BOQ, was named Pneumonia Row, with flimsy barracks and outside latrines. When my turn came, I was assigned to Long Beach.

Unlike Ford's station, mine at Long Beach was anything but shabby. The air base was snug in a valley between oil wells and mountains, across the runways from the huge Douglas aircraft plant. It was first class, perhaps because of its proximity to Los Angeles and Hollywood. A few celebrities actually were on base in uniform (as they were at bases throughout Southern California). One was Sergeant Red Ruffing, New York Yankees pitching ace, with whom I played Ping-Pong and talked baseball. Ziggy Elman had played trumpet in Benny Goodman's orchestra, and now played in the dance band on base. Major Terry Hunt, formerly a fitness guru for the stars, presided over a fitness center for officers, with baseball players and other jocks as masseurs. It should have been a treat to be assigned there.

Then there was Gene. Maybe I realized all along it would never work, that it would be like trying to stop a star from its path in the heavens. When I arrived in Long Beach, she was friendly but not much more. We went to dinner and walked around the pier at the ocean front, my first glimpse of the Pacific. She told me she had flown copilot on a B-17. She was standing there with me, and yet I felt a gulf between us as wide as the ocean. She begged off to do computer study and catch up on her correspondence. After that, we would meet now and then along the flight line or in the mess hall and appear as two casual acquaintances. It hurt to greet her, then watch her move on.

Gene was a loner, that was true, and perhaps she thought I was immature or too needy to let me intrude into her space. I should have said, "Listen, Gene, what's going on here?" Or, "Gene, we need to talk." Instead, I kept it inside—perhaps, after all, I *was* immature and needy. I ate without appetite and was glad to be transferred a few months later. During the following summer (of 1944) a friend wrote from Nashville: "You will perhaps want to slit my throat for enclosing this clipping, but I thought you had probably heard of it anyway, and so I am sending it regardless. Don't go out and shoot yourself, for, remember, you are not the first to have gotten the gate." The clipping announced the recent marriage of Gene to a sailor from Seattle. While I appreciated the news, it was a crushing blow.

CHAPTER 6

Around the world, and around again – I loved the stars, brilliant, cobalt blue, glistening, red, flamboyant – The cockpit was a room, an office, living and working space – A Marshall Islander smiled with friendly eyes, free of guile

I welcomed my first overseas mission the last week in December 1943. It was a long, long time in coming, but once it began I traveled virtually around the world, and around again, over oceans and touching down on islands and continents, finding more adventure going places than most people could envision for a lifetime.

On that first trip my crewmates and I were assigned to deliver a C-47 twin-engine Douglas transport from California to Australia, turning it over there for use close to the fighting in New Guinea. Before takeoff I was terrified, empty, and hollow in the pit of my stomach. The youngest member of the crew, a twenty-year-old radio operator, was the only one who had made the crossing before, and the only one with enough sense not to be scared. Fourteen hours of flying lay ahead on the first leg to Hawaii, the longest overwater flight in the world without an alternate airport. Two small ships stationed midway in the Pacific sent radio signals for guidance, but they had to be careful, since the Japanese were still considered threatening, even in this area. The pilot worried, the copilot slept, the radioman told another radioman that we were still going. The engineer checked the gauges and transferred fuel from containers in the cabin. I had the most to do on the plane and never felt so much responsibility.

The flight dragged on, hour after hour, and it was still night. As black night faded into blue dawn the fatigue loosened. Stars dipped into the still dark horizon before us. To the east, where the sun cast its first shadows, the sky brightened; between east and west colors ranged from white through pink and white to pale blue and black. Soon waters below became visible and we realized the difficult part of the first leg was done. Clouds were billowy and bulging with sunlight streaming through when we descended over Molokai, then skirted Waikiki and Diamond Head, into Hickam Field, our destination, dead ahead.

That was only the first leg. We had a long way to go, to Christmas Island and Canton Island, mere atolls in the vastness of the Pacific; Viti Levu in the Fiji Islands; Nouméa in New Caledonia, and finally into Brisbane, Australia. I gained confidence and shortly made two more flights over the same route, both in twin-engine B-25s, medium-range bombers. The B-25 was a plane that everybody loved, but it couldn't carry much fuel or allow for navigational error. Then I was transferred to another ferry command base at New Castle, Delaware, outside of Wilmington. I flew missions from there for a while, then was transferred to the ferry base at Nashville, and from there to Presque Isle, Maine, and then back to California, at Hamilton Field, in Marin County.

Every time I felt satisfied, they moved me. I wasn't alone in this kind of treatment. During the war the commercial airlines operated as "contract carriers" for the government doing much the same work as we did in the ATC. Ernest K.Gann was a pilot for one of the airlines and later wrote popular books about his experience. In *Fate Is the Hunter,* he related how twenty TWA crews and their planes were dispatched to Presque Isle. Then they were ordered to load their planes with contents of a freight train, without direction of where to fly. Just as loading neared completion a new order came down to unload the planes. Then all the TWA crews were ordered back where they had come from. They flew south empty and bewildered.

I was bewildered too. But if I had not been moved as much, I would not have seen as much or learned as much about the world, its geography, and history; about the science of navigation and the mysteries of the universe; or about the relationships of people, men and men, men and women, and about myself. I was part of a generation that grew up in a hurry flying in wartime and was lucky to make the most of it and to survive.

In the navigator's compartment, my little office, usually located behind the pilot, I would contemplate my own small role. Planes were slower then, and navigation still a painstaking personal effort. I flew over distant watery wildernesses: the Amazonian equatorial trough where massive clouds rise to carry moisture outward to other portions of the world, and the high latitudes of Greenland where glaciers break into icebergs that sail majestically southward to their doom. I was exposed to weather in many moods. I saw it display violence while providing a balancing effect—regeneration—to the earth's atmosphere. A hurricane brings rain to the tropics, shifting heat to warm the temperate zone.

In my training I learned four different types of navigation: pilotage, radio navigation, dead reckoning (or DR), and celestial. Pilotage meant identifying railroads, highways, cities, physical features of the land, which every pilot ought to be able to do on his own without a navigator telling him "that looks like New York." Radio worked well to a degree, but the farther you traveled from the station sending out the signal, the weaker and less dependable the signal became; besides, pilots learned to follow beams and beacons in their own training. Dead reckoning was basic and essential. It came in handy when weather made it difficult to take celestial readings; DR involved using the best available data, primarily about wind direction and velocity, in order to calculate the aircraft's position and speed, and to determine the best heading to the destination. Celestial was the most accurate and best at night when stars were abundant and visible.

Whenever a flight crew boarded a plane, the navigator was easy to identify by what he carried. In one hand, in a square wooden box with a metal handle, was his octant, adapted for use in the air from the mariner's time-tested sextant. In the other hand, he carried a leather briefcase containing his maps, celestial almanac, E6B computer, Weems plotter, plus letters he meant to write, or a deck of cards. Once aloft, the navigator's job was to use his charts and tools (altimeter, compass, and chronometer) to track headwinds, tail winds, and cross winds, select alternate places to land, and figure ground speed (actual speed over the ground), the precise direction the plane was flying, and estimated time of arrival.

I had two lights to work with, one bright and one very small to illuminate only the desk itself whenever I was engaged in shooting the stars, while the rest of the cabin remained in darkness. The window glass was clear as air. During the long night, I stood on a stool in the Plexiglas astrodome to shoot celestial fixes, then plot them on my chart and calculate the wind vector, the ground speed, and the location of the aircraft. I looked through the chemical bubble floating in kerosene in the chamber of the octant—that was my artificial horizon. I selected my star, held the octant firm and began clicking at the trigger, which activated a pencil to make vertical marks on a small metal drum. I clicked for one minute, checked my watch, marked the time, and chose the average. Then I turned to the almanac, which provided celestial latitudes and longitudes relative to Aries, prime meridian of the sky, with Greenwich mean time (GMT) the prime meridian on the earth. That yielded data for plotting a line of position (or LOP) and the knowledge we were somewhere on that line. Directly I shot again for another LOP and then, granting favorable conditions, again, fully aware that a three-star fix was always best. I would move one line up and one back, based on estimated speed aloft and there it was: the smaller, or tighter, the triangle, the better the fix.

I loved the stars—brilliant, cobalt blue, glistening, red, flamboyant—Sirius (the brightest star in the heavens), Aldebaran, Arcturus, the North Star, and planets Mars and (my romantic morning star) Venus, and the moon. During daylight, I would shoot the sun, which normally gave only one LOP, except around noon, when angles changed rapidly and I could get the equivalent of a three-star fix between ten minutes before to ten minutes after. I also relied on the driftmeter, an instrument built like an inverted periscope, looking down instead of up, fixing grid lines on waves, showing drift to the right or left.

We were far from combat, but not from danger. I remember one terrifying night in late autumn 1944. We had come north beyond the St. Lawrence River to Goose Bay, at the edge of frozen Labrador wilderness, where the temperature was -40 degrees, to join a flotilla of C-47s, twenty-five twin-engine transports, all headed for delivery to embattled England. My crewmates and I walked to the plane through frigid, penetrating night air, examining the vapor of our breaths as a relief from the briefing we had just received from the meteorologists, the weather officers, warning that we faced a challenging night ahead.

Once in the cockpit, the pilot and copilot ran through the checklist: the control wheel, rudder, ailerons, and switches, buttons, and knobs in panels before them and curving above their heads. The cockpit was an office, living and working space that brought the crew together, and where the pilot must show us all he had trust in himself. "Gear up!" he shouted and away we went. Almost at once, we were enveloped in North Atlantic weather at its worst, a combination of ice, snow, sleet, and severe gusts. That night was not simply tough, but terrifying. We were floundering in the sky; the other C-47s were all around us, but we could not see a single one of them.

Soon ice accumulated on the wing. The pilot switched the landing lights on and off almost every minute, to see if the deicers worked. The leading edge of the wing looked like an unbroken bar of ice. The wing lost lift and the plane lost air speed; the altimeter showed us dropping two thousand feet to only five thousand feet above the water. The pilot pressed the throttles forward and back, chunks of ice the size of baseballs banging off the propeller blades against the fuselage.

Navigation was impossible. I relied as best I could on dead reckoning, based on the briefing before departure. I huddled in my chair, fearful we were going down, writing little notes to myself anticipating the end. The storm and night seemed interminable. Then both lifted; we were over the top of the massive Greenland ice cap, ten thousand feet thick, with hundreds of uncharted fjords and the sun rising to glare in our faces. From there, it was an easy, joyous ride to Iceland, with all planes safe.

Getting out of Iceland was another story. Prestwick, Scotland, was socked in and so was everything around it. So was Reykjavík, Iceland, where it seemed forever blustery with clouds, wind, and rain. One day on the ground led to another. The weather was too foul to see anything of Iceland, so each day we stayed up later, reading, writing, and playing cards until by the end of a week I was awake most of the night and sleeping most of the day. Finally on the eighth day, all crews were alerted for takeoff. The first fifteen got away, then the field was closed again, leaving my plane second in line. The following day, we made it to Prestwick, where we learned one plane from the preceding day had gone down, with the navigator who had beaten me in cards the night before.

Another time, another ocean. In May 1945, I was navigating a hospital plane across the Pacific. Okinawa at that time was bloody. Mangled Japanese dead lay to rot where they fell. American wounded were picked up, given emergency treatment, and evacuated by air. Sulfanilamide powder was poured over their wounds, thick, ugly plaster casts were molded around them, and they were moved to Hawaii or the mainland to rest and heal.

Litters occupied with wounded servicemen lined both sides of the cabin of the C-54 now converted to a hospital ship. Late at night, the plane landed at Kwajalein Island in the Marshalls to change crews and refuel. Once rich with palm trees, Kwajalein now was devoid of vegetation, flat as the Pacific around it. Patients able to walk stirred in their bulky casts and climbed down for dinner. Food was brought to the others in their litters. Red Cross workers came with magazines, books, and a smile.

A fresh flight crew and fresh flight nurse and medical technician boarded the plane. Walking through the cabin, through the heat and stench of rotting torn human flesh and bone, was like a malaria sufferer running through a jungle in search of quinine. We slammed the cabin door to close out the odor and looked forward to the cool, clean night.

We flew, oblivious to the pain and suffering of the human cargo. The nurse and her technician knew we had this barrier. They were locked in the rear with thirty sick boys. The nurse came forward to sterilize her needles: morphine to relieve agony, penicillin every three hours for eight patients.

Then she came again, worried and unhappy. "I have one in critical condition," she said. We never knew his name. He was a prisoner to his cast, which covered both legs, much of his body and one arm. He was feverish, poison spreading through his system. She had tried to make an intravenous injection but his vein was so tight she couldn't force the needle into it. He was already full of morphine.

Venus rose, my morning star, the sun rose soon after. Tiny Johnston Island, 715 nautical miles from Hawaii, lay ahead of us. The nurse asked the radio operator to call for a medical officer to meet the plane.

"I don't think there's any need to take him off here," the doctor said. "Pearl Harbor is only four hours away and they can give him proper attention there. While you're on the ground, we can give him an injection and refrigerate the bad leg. He'll have to lose it, of course, as soon as you get him up there."

Breakfast on the ground at Johnston tasted peculiar. That horrible stench permeated eggs and coffee. So did the image of a boy who had been walking and running having a leg hacked off. We departed again, all of us anxious to reach Hickam Field. Halfway out the nurse came forward. "My boy is better. His temperature is down."

We landed about noon, one night's flying and more than two thousand miles from our point of departure at Kwajalein. We were very tired, ready for a hot shower and clean sheets, but we all waited to see the patients loaded into the ambulances. The very sick boy was blond and slender, we could see that now, and he badly needed a shave. The odor came off the plane with him, foul and nauseating. The casts on his leg were green and black. His eyes were open in a blank stare. They took him away to cut off his leg to save his life. Hawaii's warmth, tempered by a lovely breeze, brought sleep to a weary crew, but I wondered if the surgeon sweat much as he operated. The smell of the sea was like an acid bath engraving on my mind the picture of a plaster cast and amputation.

Another time I was in Belém, Brazil, a city hacked out of the jungle a hundred miles up the Amazon River, strategically located in the bulge of South America where it reaches out toward the bulge of Africa. Belém was the jump-off to Ascension Island, "the Rock," thirty-four square miles of upthrust lava. Ascension was the lonesome home of seventy-five Britons, keepers of the South Atlantic cable, and thousands of terns until 1942 when U.S. Army engineers blasted and bulldozed lava rock and built a runway to handle transport planes. I made various trips through Ascension to Accra, capital of the Gold Coast (now Ghana), to Natal, and to Marrakech and Casablanca in Morocco. The war had been fought back and forth across North Africa; by the time I arrived there, the Germans under Field Marshal Rommel, the Desert Fox, had been chased out, while the Italians I saw at Tripoli seemed delighted to be prisoners of war, as though they never had it so good. Natives trudged along with bored-looking camels, their backs piled high with rugs, shawls, baskets, and jugs—everything their owners owned—crossing the windswept African dust bowl.

Most pilots I flew with were skilled and conscientious in their work. At first they would look over my shoulder, but once they learned to trust me we could enjoy things. I mean, we might have marathon gin rummy games, starting on the ground and continuing in the air once the automatic pilot took over. Or we would make a deal that I would show the pilot celestial navigation if he would allow me to fly the plane. Generally the pilot soon learned that the octant and tables were too complicated and we went back to gin rummy. I was fair at flying as long as the sky was clear and I was able to concentrate on the gyrocompass for direction and the altimeter for elevation. Once, heading into Marrakech in a C-46, a large-bodied, twin-engine transport, I was sitting on the left side, in the pilot's seat, and flying the plane, while the pilot sat on the right, the copilot's seat. He throttled back and ordered, "Bring her down." I lowered the nose, flying the pattern between the lower ridges of the Atlas Mountains into the final approach. Then he said, "Bring her in," giving me the chance to land the plane, but my legs were weak on the rudders and I needed him to take over.

We spent the day wandering through the ancient streets and markets of Marrakech, crowded with Berbers, Arabs, and French; on returning to base, I found a note directing me to report to the operations officer. I feared I was in trouble for trying to land an airplane. *Au contraire*, it happened that a squadron of B-24 heavy bombers was on the way to Bari on the Adriatic coast of Italy. One navigator in the squadron had broken his leg, so I was offered the option to substitute for him in "detached service" to Bari. Yes, of course, I could. Delivery of the C-46 was completed and I was only waiting to deadhead home. I welcomed the opportunity to go to Bari, joined my new crewmates, and scrambled into the nose of the B-24. I watched the imposing formation of twenty-plus heavy bombers strung out all around me, flying along the North African coast, over villages built into the cliffs of Sicily and into Bari. Those aircrews were unlike those of the ATC. They were *really* going to war, to drop bombs on targets, killing people in the process or being killed themselves. *That* was what war was about.

I thought of a letter from Goldstein, who was in the advance phase of training to be a fighter pilot: "We think of gunnery as the highlight of our training. For the last week all we've been doing is diving at targets with camera guns and then trying to better our scores through practice. Much to my disappointment, it seems that all this training is for one thing and that is to kill—to be able to shoot straight and true. Don't think I'm afraid of combat because I'm not. My goal is to learn to fly—at least that's why I joined—love of flying and not killing." And also one from Tony, who had washed out in the last week at Coral Gables and wrote to me from bombardier school at San Angelo, Texas. He was encouraged about soon earning his bars and wings, and hoped he would go into heavy bombardment, maybe even B-29s."I have been doing a lot of flying and bombing the last two weeks. Today I soloed, that is, I went up without my instructor and dropped a few bombs without help from anyone. If anyone drops two bombs off the range, and the range is a mile and a half long and a mile wide, he is up for elimination. Also, if he flunks two exams, he is up for elimination.... Out of fifteen bombs that I have dropped, I have two shacks [direct hits] and I am very proud of that record."

It was heroic to drop bombs and patriotic to support the bombing and killing that are the essence of war. In Bari, I saw the consequences of war and the legacy of *il fascismo* in poverty, filth, and stench: children shoeless, women with scabby sores on bare legs. I was glad to get on to Naples on the way home. Mussolini already was dead and gone, which gave Naples a sense of relief and a future. It was lively and spirited, a city built on hills, with a wide harbor, signs painted on the walls—"VV Roosevelt," "VV Stalin," "VV Churchill"— and slumbering Vesuvio overlooking all. Streets were filled with uniforms of French, English, Yugoslav partisans, Polish, New Zealanders, Canadians, and

Americans, soldiers and sailors at the gateway to the battlegrounds of northern Italy and the beachhead in southern France, which had been established that very week. In Naples, I was conscious of song. At the mess hall, the little waitress hummed opera; so did the salesgirl at the post exchange. I felt I was hearing it in the streets, leading me to the elegant, ornate San Carlo Opera House, where singers and musicians ignored the hardships of the day to perform with gusto Rossini's timeless *Il Barbiere di Siviglia* for an audience of assorted Allied servicemen and Neapolitans. War or no war, they would have their opera, and they were better at opera than at war.

At an airfield in Abadan, surrounded by the oil fields of southern Persia (later Iran), Captain Howard Hunt was about to give me a flight lesson in a single engine Piper Cub. No sooner did we take off, than our little plane was engulfed in a blinding sandstorm and we were lucky to reclaim terra firma; never mind the flight lesson. This happened again the following day when we took off for Karachi through layers of cloud, mist, and a tremendous dust storm with particles of sand banging against the fuselage of our four-engine C-54 transport. That sort of experience is enough to make one wonder: How much of earth is the human species meant to conquer? I might have wondered again when we reached the Assam Valley and transferred our cargo to other crews who would fly it over Japanese territory, across tortuous, windswept fourteen-thousand-foot passes in the Himalayan Mountains to Chinese forces in Kunming who were otherwise cut off from Allied supplies. I saw where those crews flew from a narrow strip on a converted tea plantation, an airfield without hangars, imposing modern machinery on an ancient oxen-powered world.

In August 1944, Paris was liberated, and in October I flew there twice within eight days from my new base at Presque Isle, Maine. I had little time in Paris, but plainly it was alive again. On my first trip, I joined a tour guided by an old professor who bummed cigarettes and knew the value of an unfinished butt on the sidewalk. When I went into the Métro, an old lady blocked my way at the turnstile. "Don't you pay!" she commanded. "The Bosch never paid!" In Paris, as I saw it, everything was built for art—boulevards, cafes, hotels, parks, elegant in bronze and marble, and now, after the misery of the Occupation, gay once more.

Presque Isle was a little Northeast New England country town, surrounded by hills of potato fields, and the restaurants served lobsters with all the potatoes you could eat. I spent an enriching fall and into the winter there in 1944/45 in the Second Foreign Transport Group. The base was as far north and east as one could get and still be in the United States, but strategically located for missions to Europe. My crewmates and I would be aloft for many hours, sometimes groping through heavy blizzards that characterize the wintry North Atlantic. But then there was the return to Presque Isle, touching down at the end of a fierce night, secure at the sight of the friendly clear morning sky and familiar white hillsides massed with snow. It was more than home base; it was home. "We never came home from an absence," wrote Mark Twain of the elegant steamboat house he built at Hartford, "that its face did not light up and speak out its eloquent welcome—and we could not enter it unmoved." So it was in returning to Maine, despite its cool climate and cool temperament.

I loved being in Presque Isle and took long walks dressed in parka, boots, and mittens. The air was clear and dry and I felt at times as though I was part of a Rockwell Kent painting come alive, touching golden sunlight on a snowbank in one of his thoroughly natural and undisturbed settings. I would share my encounters and observations, often on those long walks, with Harriett, a native of upper New York and a Cornell graduate, who was a Red Cross worker at the air base. She was quite different from many of the women to whom we were normally exposed. She was literate and loved to talk of books, but even when we walked in silence across the frozen plain, I felt as though we were sharing thoughts, and perhaps dreams.

It was a time when my peers and I lived as though there were no tomorrow. We transport pilots and navigators were mostly in our early twenties and yet suddenly worldly. On one continent we would hear this line: "No momma, no poppa, no per diem. Baksheesh, Sahib!" And on another: "You like to screw my sister? She's thirteen years old, plenty good!" On returning to the States, many headed for dim little bars and hotel rooms for sex before the next mission, which might prove to be our last.

We were making money, with flight pay (50 percent extra) and all. One fellow tried to see how fast he could run through it, how many different girls he could date and sleep with in a week. "What the hell, I won't be able to spend it in India." Moods ranged from abandon to melancholia. In every town, one bar was the place to meet women "on the make." Often they were married, with husbands in the armed forces at distant places.

I was no different from the rest, but Harriett was. While my colleagues were rooted in barracks card games or downtown beer parlors, I had the pleasure of her company. On evening walks, we often went to the compound of Siberian huskies, malamutes, and Saint Bernards used on search and rescue missions. Each had its own doghouse, yet all slept out on loose snow or on the rooftops of their houses. They were not unfriendly as we approached, one howling, then another and another, chanting some strange harmony that broke the stillness of a cold northern night. Something might have come of the relationship with Harriett, but then I was transferred again, this time to Hamilton Field at San Rafael, California. Although it was a choice, desirable assignment, I did not want to go. I discovered anew, "All you do in the army is make friends and lose them."

At least my old roommates, Ford and Fuquay, joined me at Hamilton Field. We took up residence in the BOQ and our navigation duties in missions across the Pacific, flying four-engine C-54s (Douglas DC-4s), the largest transport then in use, usually carrying supplies out and bringing personnel and wounded home. We no longer flew the South Pacific to Australia. That entire region was now secure, although the Japanese were far from beaten. My friend Stavisky recorded the reaction of men on the ground who were killing and being killed. He wrote about Japanese charges in gory nights of horror at Suicide Beach, Suicide Ridge, Suicide Point, Suicide Creek, with shouts, "Banzai! Banzai! To hell with Babe Ruth!"

From Hamilton, the usual pattern (if there was one) would be about sixteen to twenty days out, maybe including a turnaround out again from Hawaii, and then back to California. From Hickam Field, we would go to Johnston Island, a Navy-administered atoll, then to Kwajalein in the Marshall Islands, then to Saipan or Guam in the Marianas, or maybe to Manila in the Philippines. And then, later, to Okinawa, in the Ryukyus, three hundred miles from the home islands of Japan.

During the course of one mission, we landed at Kwajalein, a small place girdled by the sea, hardly known in the world beyond. At dusk, after a day's rest, the pilot and I strolled along the beach. The western ocean breeze cooled the air. Most of the palm trees were victims of the war. We walked past a deserted Japanese pillbox. Other Micronesian islands had been hit worse, suffering heavier bombing in World War II than any part of Europe or Asia. Those atolls were the home of a peaceful people highly adapted to an oceanic environment. Their most serious disasters had been thrust upon them by technologically advanced nations, including my own.

Before long, we encountered a Marshall Islander fishing with a net.

He was bronze-skinned, well built, wading in the surf. He smiled with friendly eyes, open and free of guile; as we watched, he cast gracefully several times until he caught a fish, then patiently brought it in. The net has been unchanged for three thousand years, since humans first tapped the wealth of rivers, lakes, and seas, and this fellow was proving that it still remains a valid tool. His people, their culture, and their environment were innocent victims of a brutal war conducted by twentieth-century civilized nations. In the lower ranks of our armed forces, they were denigrated as "Gooks" and "Wogs" and the Japanese were called only "Japs" and hated for being slanty-eyed, yellow-skinned unchristian heathens. But was it only in the lower ranks? Following the war, as a reporter in Washington, I was sent to interview a Navy lieutenant commander, Roger Revelle, who was preparing for the atomic bomb test at an atoll named Bikini in the Marshall Islands near Kwajalein. Revelle later became director of the Scripps Institution of Oceanography and president of the American Association for the Advancement of Science. He is considered "an articulate spokesman for science." When I interviewed him, he told me how valuable the bomb test would prove and about all the good things that would come to and through science because of it.

The war in Europe ended May 7, 1945, enabling the United States to concentrate all its power in the Pacific, and enabling the best and brightest of science to prepare for the imminent delivery of a frightening benefaction to history. In June, I was flying missions from Guam and Saipan to Okinawa. Americans controlled sea and air, but ground fighting was still heavy. At the Okinawa airport, we were greeted with a huge red sign: "Welcome to Atsugi—4th of July Every Night," referring to the kamikazis, skilled Japanese pilots now reduced to pesky, futile suicide missions. From the air, I watched U.S. warships off the south shore firing shells one after another. In the waters of the Marianas a thousand ships gathered—they were the invasion fleet readying for the advance on Japan. Crews at Hamilton Field were alerted to a possible shift to Guam. Then, the last week of August, the president authorized dropping the bomb on Hiroshima. I read about it in the newspaper while in Hawaii. Despite the big, bold headline and detailed account, I could not fully understand its meaning. It was justified as the sure way to shorten the war. It would save American lives likely to be lost in the invasion. Yes, Hiroshima was stricken with tragedy and death—but the Japanese *were* the enemy. Anyway, after the war, the energy in the bomb would be converted to peaceful purposes, America's gift to the world. Then followed the second bomb, dropped on Nagasaki, and the Japanese surrender, VJ Day in the Pacific, September 2, 1945, was wildly celebrated across the United States, while the Japanese counted their dead and disfigured, and the age of weapons of mass destruction began.

I was at an upscale watering hole in San Francisco, the lounge at the St. Francis Hotel in Union Square, with my copilot, Bailey. He was a tall, smiling, good-looking Southerner, barely twenty-one and full of life. It was a pleasure to be with him, on the ground and in the air. I had flown with Bailey before, with one pilot or another. Sometimes I flew with the same crew on four or five missions, and sometimes only once. Bailey really aspired to be a fighter pilot, what was called "a hot pilot," but instead the luck of the draw made him copilot on a slow-moving transport plane. Still, he yearned to become a first pilot, the captain of his own plane, meanwhile compensating by enjoying a carefree life and driving a flashy convertible automobile. While we were at the St. Francis an attractive, stylish woman in her thirties in a group at the next table apparently was taken with Bailey and gave him a come-hither look. He excused himself and left with her. Later, on the way west, he reported that she was lovely, a Navy wife, and that she took him home to bed with her. That sort of thing happened.

The war was over. We were crewmates flying Occupation troops from Okinawa to Tokyo, returning with liberated prisoners of war. At Guam, the only place to rest was a hastily erected tent at the base of a hill. While we slept in the afternoon, the rains came. The water ran downhill into the tent as though it had been a planned catch basin. Bailey in his shorts stood up on the cot and screamed. Half his clothing was drenched. Although the tent was crowded with baggage, cots, and rising water, he soon had his gear hanging from the canvas flaps. The rain stopped and the sun bore down. The new river soaked into the ground and sank away. Bailey took his clothes outside and hung them up to dry before taking off for Okinawa that night.

The pilot, Archie, was short in height, about five-foot-five, and long in talk. Repeatedly he told us all he should have been a major, the story of his life in Kentucky, and all the girls he had ever been to bed with. He talked about his wife and two children, how his little boy didn't eat when Archie wasn't home. My theory was that he didn't like to fly, that he was a pilot gone stale, that he talked so much for the skill he had lost. He was nervous and irritable.

Dawn had just broken as we neared Okinawa. The sky was overcast. Okinawa looked as grim as it did during the fighting. Bailey was at the controls, giving the engineer instructions for power reductions and application of flaps, while Archie sat in the copilot's seat, plainly agitated.

"You're too low. Too low!" Archie shouted. "Raise the nose!" Bailey raised the nose of the plane on the base leg over the airport before the final approach. Archie was overwrought. He thought Bailey would undershoot the runway, and shoved the throttles forward to increase power and go around again.

We landed at Kadena airfield, carved out of the hills by American bulldozers. It was a new field for us, for during the war we had used Yontan airfield, a former Japanese base several miles away. We loaded our gear on a truck and headed for tents near the other airfield. Bailey spotted several Navy bombers on the apron. "Mike! Mike, my buddies are over there."

"Over where?"

"Over where those B-24s are parked. No kidding, they are. My very best friend from home is flying one of those things. Let's go over there right away, okay?"

"Damn it, Bailey, when are we going to sleep?" We had been up all night and I had had a hard time of it.

"Let's go over there right away. You can see how bad the food is going to be around here. Their outfit has been set up a couple of months. They'll have good food and whiskey and maybe they'll even be able to put us up for the night."

I agreed, especially after we reached our tent. We were crowded, more than thirty in a large tent. Crews were coming in all the time for the operation to Japan. Cots were on bare ground and everybody was getting in the way. Since there was no chance that flight operations to Tokyo would start for several days, we told Archie where we were going and headed off.

"That guy is a blind panic," Bailey said, as we reached the dusty road and started hitchhiking to his Navy friends. I knew that he meant Archie.

"I don't like to talk about anyone like this, but, honestly, that guy doesn't have any right to be flying these planes. He really messed up my landing. A bloody blind panic, that's what he is."

We chased all over Yontan airfield, but finally found Bailey's buddies from Georgia. There were two of them, Arnold and J. R., both of whom had gone to school with Bailey and now flew in the same Navy bomber crew.

They lived in a neat, almost palatial, tent with their plane commander, Sam Pepe, a serious and studious fellow from Brooklyn.

They passed around their last three remaining bottles of warm coca-cola, mixed with healthy portions of whiskey. I curled up and fell asleep, but the last words I heard were, "This guy I'm flying with is a blind panic."

"Wake up, Mike. Damn it, wake up!"

It was late afternoon. Navy fliers came in from adjoining tents, each with his own whiskey bottle. We all staggered down to the Navy mess. After dinner the drinking started in earnest. We met Navy pilots by the score, each of whom seemed to come with his own bottle. We drank and talked, comparing notes on Army and Navy flying. The party grew higher and higher. We drifted from tent to tent. I was shown photos of girl friends, wives and children in Georgia, California, Toledo, and Brooklyn.

The drunken brawl was still going strong after midnight when Arnold said, "Listen, Bailey, we're going to take you and Mike home."

"I don't want to go home. I like it here," Bailey said. He was very drunk and sleepy.

"Well, we're going to take you home anyway. Let's go."

J. R. and Arnold owned a jeep they had bought from the Seabees for four quarts of whiskey and we all piled in. I fell asleep while Bailey leaned over the side and puked.

When we got back to our tent nearly all the crews were asleep Two of the men were sitting up, playing cards by flashlight. We staggered back and forth without finding our cots. Five cots were outside the tent, unoccupied. We crawled out, fell down and went to sleep.

I awoke in the middle of the night. The world was turning dizzily. I looked straight at the sky, but it would not stay still. In all the nights of my life, I had never seen so many stars. So many stars! But what are they? I should know, I am a celestial navigator. There were too many, I could not even recognize a constellation. But I would not need them much longer.

CHAPTER 7

At the end I wondered about wars – Whether any side ever wins – At least I learned to view the spangled heavens as a pattern for knowledge and beauty – They don't navigate that way anymore

When the war ended and I was discharged from military service, I felt it was a little like graduating from college. I was twenty-four years old, about the right age to graduate. I wondered what I had learned, and how much I had grown and changed.

I had been around the world and back, an education in itself. I had started as a raw recruit and become an officer, a first lieutenant by the time I was through. It wasn't very high in the ranks but high enough for me. "RHIP," the saying went: "Rank has its privileges." However, in an airplane crew, everybody had to work together and it didn't help to take yourself too seriously. The enlisted men in the crew were sergeants and corporals—a first lieutenant carried rank enough for them.

On leaving the service, I received a document called the Separation Qualification Record, which included this official Summary of Military Occupation:

NAVIGATOR
Navigated aircraft over land and sea by dead reckoning, pilotage, and celestial and radio navigation to reach objective at a predetermined time. Tested and inspected all navigation equipment prior to mission. Navigated aircraft by use of navigation instruments such as drift meter, pelorus, aircraft octant, radio compass, and periodic compass. Computed effects of various factors on course and plotted projected courses on chart. Checked data for errors after completion of flight and recalibrated navigation instruments.

That was, in a way, like an academic degree. There was little if anything I could do with it, and yet it testified as a measure of attainment in discipline and learning. Additionally, I was awarded an Air Medal for extensive flights over water in unarmed aircraft in active theaters of combat. The Air Medal could not compare with more lofty decorations like the Silver Star or Distinguished Flying Cross, yet I felt honored to receive it. I was proud to have served and glad my side won. But in due course I was troubled, and have been ever since, questioning whether any side ever wins, or whether war is a valid method of resolving conflict among presumably civilized nations, considering the evidence that one war leads only to another, with more death, destruction, and suffering to its victims.

I've already mentioned that on Sunday, December 7, 1941, I was visiting my parents in New York when we heard the radio report the Japanese attack on Pearl Harbor, the U.S. naval base in Hawaii. It was to Americans a sudden, shocking, unbelievable, and immoral act. The next day, President Roosevelt denounced the Japanese "day of infamy," and "Remember Pearl Harbor" became a battle cry to unify the nation. Japanese-Americans immediately became suspect of espionage and sabotage; they were rounded up and held in concentration camps for as long as the war lasted.

Pearl Harbor was not unlike the terrorist strike of September 11, 2001, when suicide squads of Middle East zealots hijacked commercial airliners and crashed them into the World Trade Center in New York and the Pentagon. Congress gave President George W. Bush authority and funding to invade and wage war in Iraq. Middle Easterners, Moslems, Arabs, and dark-skinned people in general became suspect, much the same as the Japanese had been during World War II. Wars are like that—they evoke fear and hate. I can say that now, but at the time, following Pearl Harbor, I was all for the U.S. entry into World War II, and was prepared to join the armed forces and do my part.

There was a lot I didn't know, about wars in general and that war in particular. I didn't know the critical issue between Japan and the United States was economic influence and economic power in the Far East and Southeast Asia. Or that the United States participated with Great Britain and France in the appeasement of Hitler, even while talking about saving Jews in Germany. But a war makes for good politics. Franklin D. Roosevelt felt himself essential to the war effort and was reelected to serve four terms as president. In the election of 2000, George W. Bush barely squeaked into the presidency, but then 9/11 and the subsequent war in Iraq helped his reelection in 2004. Or as Socrates said to Adeimantus in the *Dialogues of*

Plato: "When he has disposed of foreign enemies by conquest or treaty, and there is nothing to fear from them, then he is always stirring up some war or other, in order that the people may require a leader."[1] My war, World War II, was broadly accepted as a "good" war. Americans were encouraged to feel a stake in it, whether by buying war bonds, volunteering as air raid wardens, growing victory gardens, or sending V-mail to servicemen overseas. Everybody who wanted a job could find one—factories worked at full blast, with huge profits for their owners. Airlines became subsidized auxiliary contract carriers. In fact, the president of American Airlines, C. R. Smith, was appointed a general and made commanding officer of the Air Transport Command, a branch of the Army Air Corps. College campuses became training schools for one branch of the military or another, so they too were engaged and benefited with government funding.

The finest moviemakers in Hollywood produced a stream of star-studded films all designed as propaganda. *Mrs. Miniver* with Greer Garson won six Academy Awards and was meant to rally American support for British allies. In *Action in the North Atlantic,* Humphrey Bogart served stoically in the U.S. merchant marines. *The Commandos Strike at Dawn* starred Paul Muni as the lead commando; *Air Force* with John Garfield showed the heroics of a bomber crew, with the gunner exclaiming after scoring a hit, "Fried Japs going down!" and *Thirty Seconds Over Tokyo* starred Spencer Tracy as General Jimmy Doolittle. Movies made miracle workers out of infantrymen, the "dogfaces" in the trenches. But as a soldier explained to me, it wasn't the way the movies showed it. When a man in battle was hit, he would fall forward, on his face, his hands digging into the ground, clutching, trying to pick himself up, without glamour or glory to it.

As an institution, the military certainly was not democratic or open. Personnel were trained to take orders, not to question them. When you met an officer of higher rank, you were expected to salute; if you failed to, he could make an embarrassing or costly issue of it. If you walked in company with an officer of higher rank, you were expected to walk to his left, always to his left. There was little if any intellectual or cultural stimulation, and there was no recognition of the enemy as human beings, just as we were.

I mentioned the privileges of rank. My friend Stavisky in his book noted that officers were granted exclusive social contact with nurses and Red Cross ladies. They had access to jeeps, recons, station wagons, and liquor at the officers' mess or club. I witnessed that many times—it was a different war at different levels.

Men in the ranks comprised a cheap and easily expendable resource. In the Pacific, diarrhea, dengue, dysentery, malaria, fungus, and coral infection were widespread. The troops were afflicted with filariasis or elephantiasis spread by mosquitoes, with enormous swelling of testicles and scrotum. There was no way to keep dry in monsoonal downpours, which continued for days into weeks. On one flight into Hawaii, I met a lively, outgoing nurse, a major, returning from the Philippines. She was carrying a bottle of Philippine snails that were believed to host protozoan parasites, apparently infecting soldiers with a disease science knew nothing about.

On-the-ground frontline fighters were not the only ones thrust into harm's way. Once I was drinking in a bar with two or three navigator friends when we were joined by a young Navy pilot. He was determined to get drunk, repeatedly sobbing, "All that training for one flight...." He was a torpedo bomber pilot, which meant he expected to be assigned to strike a Japanese warship at water level, in much the same way the Japanese kamikaze suicide pilots attacked American ships. In Europe, fighter squadrons were led by twenty-five-year-old colonels who might never get to be twenty-six, while bomber crews called General Curtis LeMay "Low-Level LeMay" for sending them into combat at dangerously low elevations.

When the Japanese closed the Burma Road, the Himalayas fenced the route to the north. Flying "the Hump" became the only means of moving supplies into China. To cross the mountains, however, required flying through the worst weather and the tallest mountains in the world. Aircrews joked about following the trail of C-46 transport planes that had crashed in the mountains. They joked, but it wasn't funny. Now and then I would run into old classmates who had been on duty flying the Hump or in combat. They seemed changed, with ashen complexions and deep-set, piercing eyes, as though they had confronted death across the great divide.

The bounties of the "good" war were spread everywhere in the world. Far-flung Pacific atolls, little bits of land upthrust from the sea by reef-building corals, had been patiently developed by natural processes over thousands of years. They served as resting places for migrating oceanic birds until they were abruptly disrupted and obliterated by war. In August 1945, I was in Hawaii when the atomic bomb was dropped on Hiroshima, killing 100,000 innocent civilians. Then a few days later, the second bomb laid waste to Nagasaki, killing tens of thousands more. The bombings were difficult for me to understand or justify. The following spring, in 1946, already back in civilian life, I went to Berlin for the first time and was overwhelmed by the spectacle of that great city in ruins—from the aerial pounding it suffered.

"I hate war as only a soldier who has lived it can, only as one who has seen its brutality, its futility, its stupidity,"[2] said Dwight D. Eisenhower in 1946. But as Supreme Commander of all the Allied forces in Europe he had been party to it. At least he learned enough to voice regret.

When I refer to my own personal growth and change and learning, still another important side of my time in the service comes to mind. In 1954, a fellow named Guy Murchie published a wonderful book, *Song of the Sky*. He had been a writer for a Chicago newspaper who became a navigator, then an instructor in navigation, and now told about it in detail. Navigation for Murchie represented "a pursuit of truth"; it was something like that for me too. Certainly navigation proved a lasting influence, in pursuit of truth in the mystery beyond all mysteries of the universe and of my own small connection to it.

I appreciated the science of navigation, but I loved the mysticism. The night was my best time. Living in and out of flight bags, I might have felt rootless and lost, but surrounded by the night skies, listening to the invisible wind that transcended the humming of engines, I felt the nocturnal spell and the mystical quality of floating in space and being a part of it. Centuries ago in ancient Greece, Cephalus (in Plato's *Republic*) put it this way: "Astronomy compels the soul to look upwards and leads us to look from this world to another…. The spangled heavens should be used as a pattern and with a view to that higher knowledge; their beauty is like the beauty of figures excellently wrought by the hand of Daedalus, or some other great artist."[3]

One thing I can attest to: the stars never lie. Many times I watched and marveled as the thin pencil line representing our intended course became crossed with other lines that revealed our location on the face of the earth. I wondered at my perception of wilderness horizons of the universe and my ability to transpose the infinite of the universe into the practical finite of celestial distances on the plotting table. This was possible because of celestial mechanics, an achievement of the human intellect—the combined work of astronomers and mathematicians from the ancient Egyptians and Greeks on to Kepler, Galileo, Laplace, Newton, and Simon Newcomb. Here was a rendezvous of history, nature, and technology without conflict.

As any typical night wore on aboard our little plane and the canopy of the heavens changed, I felt navigation brought me closer to the harmonious pattern of the universe, of time beyond time, of space beyond space all joined as one. The celestial navigator can expand the dimensions of his experience, freeing himself of the containment of the moment—like a high without drugs—to become part of the continuum of history. This the ancients knew instinctively, being close to the source of existence, feeling rhythms and cycles that bind the brief hours of human life with centuries of time and with stars and seas and all living things.

I was an ancient mariner in a new ocean, an ocean of the sky, in which I could feel kinship with navigators before me, the Portuguese, and the Polynesians before them, who followed currents, wind, and wave, then stars, adapting shells as sextants. In midocean, the sky for them was compass, clock, and map. They knew the custom of stars, rising earlier each night, and the regular nightly and seasonal rotation of the Southern Cross. They learned to follow clouds hovering over atolls, and to follow boobies and gannets in late afternoon coming home from fishing grounds to feed their families, and the cries of seabirds that said to them, "Land is near."

I learned there is a logical connection between all things in the immense connected body of salty water that covers more than two-thirds of the earth's surface, a grand pattern embracing all the storms and calms, the deeps and shallows, the animals, plants, and birds, and the humankind traveling the surface and the skies above and living on the shores of all the oceans. I appreciated that volcanoes and undersea earthquakes disturb the water to the farthest drop on the other side of the world. Each small particle in the entire ocean, even in the deepest part, feels the pull created by the sun and moon. So does each little particle on the land, but the water responds by moving in ebb and flow, joyous, unfettered, and free in the cyclic movements of the universe. Always the waters are in motion, rolling and lifting the waves, beneath birds, ships, and planes.

I didn't think about the environment then, but my wartime experiences roused me later to work for a wholesome environment. I didn't think about religion either. I wasn't exactly an atheist, but perhaps my experiences led me to wonder about the possibility of a transcendent unifying spirit in the universe.

They don't navigate that way anymore. In my time, we traveled in the shallow layers of space, usually between 8,000 to 12,000 feet, finding guidance from stars and planets, aided by the almanacs and tables we carried along. Planes today travel three times higher and three times faster. They don't have time for a navigator to shoot and plot celestial fixes. They don't even include a navigator in the crew, instead using loran, radar, and computers that provide virtually instantaneous reports on the wind vector, actual speed in flight, and advice on the correct heading to follow. It impresses me as an extremely efficient system, geared to the accelerated speed of the age.

Still, whenever I talk with a young modern pilot, he is likely to ask, "You mean you really practiced celestial navigation, shooting the stars and all?" And he is thoroughly impressed when I reply, "Yes, I really did."

CHAPTER 8

"Okay, you're hired" – The entire building was perilous and problematic – Still, everybody on the paper pulled together – Becoming a bit of a celebrity around the newsroom – Then choosing, perhaps, the wrong turn

And then it was over, time to return to life or to start another one. I was fortunate that I had no scars, no physical wounds, and no battlefield nightmares. I had not been trained to kill. I had been issued a sidearm, but had never used it and barely knew how. I could look back on my work in navigation as an attainment of mind and spirit, even while meeting the obligation to serve. In the military, your basic physical needs were cared for. You knew that you had three meals a day, a bed for the night, access to goodies at the Post exchange and officers' club, and a paycheck at the end of the month. It was a highly structured system that repressed individualism. But now we were all directed to face the world on our own, mandated to choose a career without the support network tending to our needs.

The government professed to care for veterans by providing benefits through the GI Bill of Rights, including a free four-year college education. Richard Fuquay bade farewell with a toast and a final drink, returned to his home state, and entered the University of North Carolina. Harold Ford chose to pass up the GI Bill, instead returning to his hometown in western Minnesota to deliver the mail and marry his sweetheart.

I thought about accepting the opportunity offered by the GI Bill; perhaps I should have. I might have benefited from systematic, guided study in philosophy, language, and literature. I might have been influenced by a professor who wanted to bring out the best in me. I might have adapted to campus life, then qualified for a position with a future that required a college degree. I will never know. In my case, for better or worse, I wanted to get on with life, catch up on time lost, and never mind the GI Bill.

When I returned to civilian life late in 1945, I went first to see my parents. They had left New York early in the war and were living now in Westwood, New Jersey, which I recall as a pleasant community beyond the metropolis, north of New York on the west side of the Hudson River. My father had recovered to a degree from his cardiac problems and they were doing fairly well. He had grown a substantial victory garden of diverse vegetables and flowers during the war, but now was back in business with a fur shop on the main street and with WILLIAM FROMM, FURRIER bravely lettered in the window. Though he had never driven in the Bronx, now he owned a clean and modestly classic 1937 car, complete with running board.

I visited but did not stay. I wanted to find a job in journalism where I could emulate Lincoln Steffens, my hero. During the war my writing had consisted largely of diaries and letters to my mother, who saved them all, but I yearned to break in somewhere. The compass needle in my brain pointed dead ahead to Washington DC. I followed the arrow that led to the *Washington Post* and up the steps I had known before. I applied for a job as a reporter and was interviewed by Casey Jones, the managing editor. He was not much for smiling, but he looked me in the eye and seemed to smile around the edges when he said, "Okay, you're hired." Was it because I already had some connection with the *Post* and had served my country? Or had he detected, and remembered, some special aptitude for journalism in me? I was too elated to care and eager to begin.

Casey Jones seemed austere, preoccupied with important responsibilities, yet he had a way of adjusting his spectacles with his fingers while looking right at you to remind you he was listening. His prematurely grayish hair made it hard to tell his age—somewhere in the midfifties, I thought. I respected Casey as a thoughtful, able editor. Later he lost favor and was kicked upstairs as "assistant to the publisher" with little to do but look for another job, which he found in Syracuse, New York; he was executive editor there, but it wasn't the same as being in Washington.

One evening early in my employment, when the newsroom was quiet, Casey called me into his office, sat me down, and lectured to me on news writing. He said it takes a certain kind of writer, that not everybody can do it. He used the example of William L. White, son of William Allen White, the noted editor of the *Emporia Gazette* in Kansas. The younger White had come to the *Post* but didn't work out—he simply wasn't suited for writing news for a daily newspaper. Then he became an associate editor at *Reader's Digest*, where he did very well. The point being passed along to me was that news writing should be terse, without adornment or embellishment.

That was one way to look at it. I was reminded years later of this little lecture while reading a biography of Horace Greeley, the celebrated nineteenth-century editor of the *New York Tribune* (later the *New York Herald Tribune*). In a letter to a friend who wanted to start a country paper, Greeley counseled the new editor to cover all the news people cared about, and then: "If a farmer cuts a big tree, or grows a mammoth beet, or harvests a bounteous yield of wheat or corn, set forth the fact as concisely and unexceptionally as possible."[1]

That wasn't the way I looked at it. It has always seemed to me that a journalist's strength is his or her credibility and use of language, and that the best journalism has authority and a sense of purpose; but for now, the lesson was to set forth the facts concisely but no, I would never go for doing so unexceptionally.

I started to work in December 1945 (and here I go embellishing the story). That much I remember because on New Year's Eve, I was sent to cover a party at the Mayflower Hotel attended by Eugene Meyer, the paper's owner and publisher, his wife, and a group of their friends. When I arrived on the scene, I found all the men in tuxedos and the women in formal gowns. That was their idea of a New Year's party. I was not, however, about to be privy to it. Meyer and someone else politely sent me away. "Look," they said, "somebody made a mistake. This is a private party and really not meant to be covered in the press." Later I made many trips to the Mayflower and other hotels covering luncheons, dinners, receptions, and press parties hosted by all kinds of organizations, trade associations, and corporations wanting to dispense their version of the facts.

As a reporter on general assignment, I made it to my full share of those affairs, but not at first: I wrote obituaries. Editors were reluctant to send me on assignments of consequence. I worked from seven at night to three in the morning, sometimes waiting idly and hopefully for something to do. Eddie Folliard, the paper's star national affairs reporter, saw that I was idle but eager and spoke sympathetically, reminding me that we all served just by being ready and available. Sam Stavisky was also sympathetic. He reassured me, "Mike, first you will write the lead overset [a story that almost but doesn't quite make the morning paper], then the lead on the split page [the local news], and then the lead on the front page." He was not far off, as it turned out.

The *Post* building itself had not changed much since I had last seen it before the war. In her memoir, *Personal History*, Katherine Graham described it this way:

The *Post* was still operating from its plant on E Street [until its new building was completed in 1950], several doors away from the National Theater. The entire building was perilous and problematic. Everything in it was old, except some of the people. The small, dark lobby housed a cashier and a counter where back copies of the paper were sold and the public was dealt with. There was a small cagelike elevator run by a man who had to manage the old-fashioned gate, and a dangerous ride in it took you past the city room on the second floor to the editorial offices, women's department, and the editors' and publisher's offices in the front of the building on the third floor.

And elsewhere:

The front steps opened into a dark, shabby, small vestibule, large enough for the bottom of a long flight of wooden stairs and the creaky, rickety elevator that people wisely avoided. The city room, located on the second floor, was a small town of constant activity. Clouds of smoke hung low over men, still in their hats, hunched over typewriters at their desks.[2]

That is about how I knew it. In those days everybody on the paper pulled together. Katherine Graham later went to war with the printers, yet in her memoir mentioned a civil conversation with one printer who came to see her:

Hoot [Gibson] recalled the early days of the *Post*, when "We all enjoyed our work and each other.... We used to come in fifteen minutes early just to visit before we went to work," he recalled. And he emphasized how much easier it was to relate to each other when the paper was smaller.[3]

True enough. During World War II, the printers published a newspaper, the *Chapel Post*, for the benefit of *Post* employees and former employees in uniform (to which I sent two articles from the Pacific). The Allied Printing Trades Council granted special permission to use the union label. After the first issue, Eugene Meyer wrote, "Your enterprise has my hearty approval and enthusiastic support. Let me know at any time if there is anything I can do to be helpful."[4] In the October 1945 issue, the editor, Harry Deering, wrote, "The *Chapel Post* is more than so much paper and ink. It is a living spirit that has few parallels. It represents the cooperation of hundreds of people and each one of them feels as if they are part of it, and rightly so."

But I found changes, too, in the building and the way things were run. For one, women had come to work as reporters during the war and were still there, doing as well as the men alongside them. Women softened the edges of the newsroom; they made it look better, smell better, and feel better. It certainly did that for Dillard Stokes, a top reporter, activist in the Newspaper Guild and a friend of mine, who returned from military service and found a bride, Jane Smith, writing the local news.

Other changes were evident or under way. Stavisky was no longer on the desk, but carved a niche writing news and columns about veterans' affairs. John Riseling still presided over the night side. His work was his love and his life and nobody questioned his ability or his devotion to the paper. One night I was out covering a large fire at the Navy Yard in southwest Washington. I checked in by phone, reporting to Riseling that the opposition *Times-Herald* had three reporters on the scene, but he advised me to keep calm and keep working—that it took three of them to equal one of us.

The *Post* management, however, wanted change, a new, modern approach to the city side. As Katherine Graham wrote in her memoir, "Black citizens and black crime were not considered news. John Riseling, the night city editor, had a map of the District in his head, and when something happened in a black area, no one was sent to cover it."[5]

Thus Ben Gilbert was appointed as city editor with authority over both day and night sides. (The national desk was separate, the upper crust of the newsroom.) After graduation from the University of Missouri Journalism School and experience with the *St. Louis Star-Democrat*, Gilbert had come to the *Post* during World War II to cover national news (physical problems kept him out of the service). He brought a new approach to covering city news that did not make him universally popular, although I found him fair, encouraging, and helpful. Many years later, he sent me a copy of the forty-four-page monograph he wrote in 1993, titled "A Recollection: Lifting the Veil from the 'Secret City'—The *Washington Post* and the Racial Revolution," that may explain his lack of popularity. Gilbert's monograph sought to reconstruct the paper's institutional memory of its coverage of the racial revolution in the District of Columbia and the nation. He wrote:

> Newspapers mirrored pervasive segregation and entrenched racism. The *Washington Post* did not employ a single black reporter or editor nor could one of its reporters share a meal with a black

person at downtown restaurants. That was academic because few staff members knew any members of the Capital's black community well enough for lunch.[6]

I remember those days clearly. "Don't bother, it's black," Riseling would say, meaning we would not cover the event, although crimes by blacks against whites were generously reported. And to identify black persons in the news by race was a traditional practice, which the *Washington Post* ultimately defied and demolished. But Washington was a southern city, controlled by segregationist southern politics in Congress. The YWCA was virtually the only place where whites and blacks ate in the same dining room. When a bus or streetcar crossed the Potomac into Virginia, the driver stopped and blacks moved to the rear. Such are the facts of history.

"Daily newspapers," wrote Gilbert, "were chameleons—as white, black, or color-blind as their readership, management, editors, reporters, and prevailing social patterns suggested, which meant generally 'white.'" In his monograph, he quoted a recollection of Murrey Marder, who covered Washington racial issues in 1948 before transferring to national and international affairs:

> For true-blue or ersatz southerners, of whom we had our abundant share in editors as well as reporters, the notion that segregation was news was itself subversive. They were journalistically reared on the conviction that Negro news was not news except in mass-disaster figures or examples of the genetic stupidity or criminality of the race.[7]

Yes, indeed, even the *Post* had its share of editors as well as reporters who thought southern and thought white, and that was true in the period coming out of the war as well as going into it.

Another change at the paper, early in 1946, was the arrival of Philip Graham, who had married Katherine Meyer, daughter of the owner, Eugene Meyer. Graham was not trained as a journalist but as a lawyer, yet came in at the top, as associate publisher. Still, he was a nice guy who seemed to want everybody to think kindly of him. I would not call him good-looking but he came across as outgoing and earnest. He spent considerable time around the newsroom, talking and listening to everybody who would talk with him. Gilbert once passed along to me a memo from Graham about an unusual cabdriver who he thought would make a good story, but nothing came of it.

At that phase of my career, I was one of two reporters who stayed on duty until three AM, mostly to be there in case of something late breaking. Then opportunity knocked—and just about knocked me over. One afternoon in April, while walking through the lobby of the Willard Hotel, I ran into two pilots I had known in the military. Cooper Walker had been stationed at New Castle, Delaware, when I was there. Both now were civilians, preparing to fly to Prague, in Czechoslovakia, the very next week on a civilian mission for UNRRA, the United Nations relief agency. Their charter plane would be loaded with hatching eggs to help regenerate Czech agriculture. They said they needed an experienced navigator. Could I possibly join them?

It wasn't that easy, since I was struggling to make it in a new career, but I walked across the street to ask permission of my employer. The *Post*, as it happened, editorially supported UNRRA, so I was given leave from the obituary page for a little while and instructed to file a report by wireless from Prague if I found something worth writing about.

We flew north from New York to Newfoundland, refueled, and continued to Paris. My navigation was rusty, but I was looking for a whole continent and not some tiny atoll. From Paris, we flew on to Prague. The timing couldn't have been better: We arrived early on Easter Sunday, 1946. The Czechs loved the hatching eggs. I dashed to the telegraph office, typed and filed my dispatch in time to make the Sunday edition—on Easter Sunday. The editors featured it at the top of the front page with my photograph in the top center. This is how it began:

> PRAGUE, April 20. – "You have brought us the most wonderful and appropriate Easter present possible," Jan Masaryk, Czechoslovakian Foreign Minister, yesterday told the crew of an American transport plane which landed the first direct shipment of hatching eggs from the United States.
>
> The crew, this reporter included, landed here two and a half days after taking off from LaGuardia Field without a crack to even one of the 55,000 hatching eggs, flown by Veterans Air Line on a mission for UNRRA.
>
> We took every precaution to keep the unborn Rhode Island Reds and Leghorns in good condition. Before we left, the walls of the big four-engine Skymaster were insulated with padding and the 155 cases tied down tightly. In the air the ship's heaters were set to ensure a constant temperature of 55 degrees. The wings of

the plane were like the wings of a huge hen mothering an entire nation of baby chicks. On landing the eggs were immediately moved to a cooperative hatchery in Moravia, where they will help to redevelop Czechoslovakia's depleted poultry population.

Two weeks later, we returned to Prague with a second shipment of eggs. I wrote impressions of the Czech capital and of the country. A few weeks later, I rejoined the charter crew on a mission to Warsaw. I felt more confident. I was still a general assignment reporter but endeavored to conduct myself like a foreign correspondent. I determined to interview leaders of the government and the opposition. Those interviews became the basis of a five-part series that ran in the *Washington Post* from June 2 through June 6, 1946. The first article began:

> Out of the ruins of Warsaw, the most thoroughly destroyed city in all Europe, there is emerging the heart of a new Polish nation.
>
> This once great city, of 1,500,000 prewar population, has been reduced to one-third. Millions of rats roam the city's ruins, gnawing at its vitals and spreading disease. All through the night the sound of rifle shots pierce the dark. Thousands on thousands of corpses lie still and buried and mangled under the wreckage and rubble.
>
> This is Warsaw, securely screened behind the so-called iron curtain of the American press and State Department, which only recently suspended 90 million dollars worth of credits from the Polish government on the grounds that one American news correspondent's news account was suppressed.

I wrote of how various British and American correspondents welcomed me with Scotch and vodka, and stories of government suppression and inefficiency. "You might as well not even try," they said. "The government won't tell you a thing." Nevertheless, I went to the press section of the Polish foreign office, which arranged interviews during the next few days with five cabinet ministers from three different political parties, all of whom spoke freely with me.

In my second dispatch, I tried to give a picture of Warsaw, a city in ruins, almost leveled, a mass of wreckage and rubble, the most completely shattered city on the continent, where its only redeeming feature was the spirit of the people to clear away the debris, live on, and rebuild:

When I walked amid the ruins people would point to jagged, twisting steel and say, "That was our railroad station."

Or, "That was our theater; that was the best hotel; that was the monument to our unknown soldier; that was the city hall, the palace of the kings, the cathedral. That was. ..."

And all we saw were gaping holes in the ground and bricks and plaster.

Probably the worst sight of all was the ghetto, the walled city of Warsaw's large Jewish population. Here nothing was left, the walls were as crumbled and shattered as the buildings, still and lifeless as the hundreds of thousands of murdered Jews.

Here and there among the ghetto ruins we saw an old man or an old woman picking around, lifting up the stones. I asked the guide what they were looking for.

"They're looking, that's all," he said. "There still are many people buried under here and they're looking for their families, that's all."

Back in Washington, I became a bit of a celebrity around the newsroom. Phil Graham stopped to say he liked my work and ask about my goals and my views on various issues. Alfred Friendly, then a top reporter (later the managing editor), stopped by too. He said Phil was interested in me. "After your Polish stories, he asked if you were a commie and I assured him that you were not." I thanked Friendly. That was a fair statement since my adherence to the communist movement had long faded. For me, communism was like Judaism, doctrinaire and inflexible, without room for imagination or individuality. Communism was another religion, requiring acceptance of the Soviet Union as the mother church and Stalin as the father figure, with fitting homage to Lenin, Marx, and Engels. I chose to take the best I learned from communism about peace, equal rights, and social justice, and to move on.

At that time, I rented a room from an elderly couple in Georgetown, a thoroughly democratic corner where you never knew whom you would run into at the pub or the corner drugstore on Wisconsin Avenue or on the scenic towpath along the C&O Canal. People would come and go, waving as they passed or stopping to talk. I lived just back of Alfred Friendly's tennis court, which was behind his substantial and attractive Georgetown home, and so I was fortunate to be invited to the Sunday tennis sessions. On one Sunday,

Friendly's vivacious wife, Jean, cheerily served refreshments even while heavily pregnant. The following Sunday she was serving refreshments again and equally cheery, even after giving birth to twins. I played in a foursome with editorial writer Alan Barth, who may have been the best player on the court, as my partner, against Friendly, also an excellent player, and Phil Graham. Though not very skilled in tennis, my experience in Ping-Pong and handball helped me keep my eye on the ball and hit it hard, mostly against Phil Graham, who was not a great tennis player, at least not at that time.

In this same neighborhood I sometimes visited another *Post* personality, Mary Haworth. That was not her real name, but the one management gave her with the assignment to write her column, "Mary Haworth's Mail." It was pretty revolutionary in its day for discussing sexual and other real-life questions with thoughtful, lengthy replies. It made for a hard day's work; when I came around, we would walk in Georgetown and talk about other things. Herblock, the editorial cartoonist, was another *Post* personality I was privileged to know. His work was his life. He was a bachelor who hung around the paper all the time, soaking up ideas, then finally retreating to his studio to create another brilliant, biting cartoon. My best friends at the *Post*, however, were Jack Burness, the head of the library, and his wife, Ann, Casey Jones's secretary. I felt that Jack and his staff contributed as much to the paper as any editor, columnist, or reporter by clipping, filing, and storing fragments of news for year after year and then digging them out and making them available when they were needed. In the new age of computers, Internet, and dot-coms, that system has probably long been replaced, but it was essential in its day. Ann and Jack were dearest friends, proud of me for my reports from overseas. A day came when I accompanied them to Holy Cross Hospital in Silver Spring, a Maryland suburb, with Jack complaining of the unbearable pressure in his head. It was a brain tumor, and he did not survive. Later, Nate Haseltine, who covered science at the *Post* and was also close to Jack, said, "We lost a good friend." Yes, that was so, but what is friendship when friends are lost? What did I do to deserve the friends of my life, and whatever did I give back to them for all they gave to me?

At work I drew better assignments and bylines. Ben Gilbert assigned me to write front-page stories about inflation with the end of price control in Washington. One day I was working on a major story about the latest development. I was on deadline, completing my coverage on the telephone. John Riseling stood over me. When I finished typing the first paragraph, he pulled it out of the typewriter to edit quickly and send it to the copy desk and composing room. I wrote two more paragraphs and he pulled them out. Finally, I had the chance to finish the story undisturbed. But I did not have the time to read my work; I was too busy setting down one word after another, too busy to feel the excitement or thrill of writing what proved to be the lead article on the top right of page one.

That was on some days. On other days, John Singerhoff, the day city editor, sent me back to the obits and the local civic associations that generated little news of consequence. Singerhoff had been a police reporter for years until his recent move to the city desk. Based on what little conversation we had, I thought he had a policeman's (or a police reporter's) view of the world. I didn't see him as much of an intellectual. I might have been wrong, but then we hardly talked. In fairness, he had his job to do. I was still a cub reporter and somebody had to write obits.

I thought I had proven myself and didn't want to be treated as a cub reporter. I was paid thirty-five dollars a week, pretty meager even then, and thought I deserved more. Probably I should have talked with someone about it—probably Ben Gilbert or Casey Jones—but I was as impatient and eager as when I came out of the service, and now I was foolish too. I began scouting for a new job elsewhere and presently found one.

I was offered the position of managing editor of the *Herald-Journal*, the morning daily in Spartanburg, a modest city of about 30,000 in upland South Carolina, about midway between Atlanta, Georgia, and Charlotte, North Carolina, with two small respectable colleges, Converse and Wofford, and an economy based on textile mills and surrounding farmlands.

I resigned from the *Post* and prepared to leave. Gilbert invited me to lunch at a restaurant near the paper, but not to say good-bye. "The boss wants you to stay," he said. "If you stay, we'll give you a raise and better assignments." I wasn't sure if "the boss" in this case was Casey Jones or Phil Graham. I told Ben the arrangements with Spartanburg had gone too far for me to back out and reverse course.

Mary Haworth bade me farewell with a present of a book, the collected essays of Ralph Waldo Emerson, from which I learned, "The one thing of value in the world is the active soul,"[8] and that the active soul responds to the earth as alive, poetic, dramatic, and musical. Emerson has been my companion ever since, thanks to Mary Haworth. And Herblock sent me off with a gift I yearned to own: an original Herblock, which I treasure.

I went to say good-bye to Casey Jones. At first he was angry with me—as well he should have been—but when I said, "I want to leave with your blessing," he mellowed and smiled a little, shook my hand, and wished me well. Ben Gilbert provided a letter of reference, in which he wrote: "Michael Frome is an alert, aggressive reporter, determined to go places in the newspaper business. While working for the *Washington Post*, he gave us good service. He worked hard and produced many original and worthwhile stories. He left the paper under his own power to push his climb upward in the business."

Maybe I made a mistake and took the wrong turn, but life is full of crossroads to look back later on and think, "If only I had taken the other turn...." However, it never works that way. For better or worse, I was obliged to live with my choice and to get on with life.

CHAPTER 9

Racism was deep, virtually inbred – The South was a province in poverty, and in transition – On the road again – Leading to southern mountains and mountain people – Uplifting majesty of the moment

On my first day on the job in Spartanburg, someone on the staff whispered to me that I was the third managing editor of the year. That was a bad sign. I wondered briefly what I had gotten into, though I was too busy to spend much time on it. Besides, I felt encouraged on finding bright, progressive young people on the newspaper staff. One of them, John Lofton, was later an editorial writer for the *St. Louis Post-Dispatch*. Another, John Thomason, pursued social justice as an organizer for the textile workers union. The staff had mostly come from other parts of the country and were trying to make their way in journalism, just as I was. Alex McCullough, the city editor, was a diligent and experienced local fellow who brought practical knowledge the rest of us lacked. The *Herald-Journal* was owned by the International Paper Company. William A. Townes, the publisher, was a well-schooled journalist who allowed me latitude without looking over my shoulder.

I worked hard. I came in early and stayed late. This was not a weekly like the *Main Line Times*, but a daily that had to be produced every night and appear fresh every morning. I was expected to be a model for the staff, but they were all about my age and about as experienced.

The telegraph editor who handled all the wire copy was a serious, able young woman who had been raised in China by missionary parents. I was with her in the composing room one night when she pointed out to the printer a line of type that began with the word "Negro." He corrected her quickly and vehemently: "That word is nigger—n-i-g-g-e-r—it says it right here!"

Many people in Spartanburg and South Carolina felt that way. Racism was deep, virtually inbred. They usually called blacks "nigras" or "Coloreds" and cheered Governor Strom Thurmond, later a U.S. senator, hoping the South would rise again under its Dixiecratic hero.

I was living and working in the turbulent postwar South, a different and strange culture, a region in transition and in struggle with itself. During my military service, I had experienced portions of Alabama, Georgia, Louisiana, Florida, and Tennessee (and would see more of it in years to follow). Somehow, I never felt like an alien, never had difficulty communicating with people at various stations in life. I was helped to some degree by acquiring a taste for illicit moonshine whiskey. When a southerner dared me to drink it with him, I always said, "Sure," licked my lips when I was through, and was ready for the next one if he was.

I confess that I did not meet a black person who was not a waiter or server of some kind. But whites could be just as poor as blacks were and they suffered just like poor blacks, which explains why they were chosen as messengers of hate and why in this period, governors like Orval Faubus in Arkansas and George Wallace in Alabama stood in the schoolhouse door vowing to safeguard white purity. Birmingham was probably the most segregated, most racist city in the South, nicknamed "Bombingham," until it was shamed in 1963 by the Ku Klux Klan bomb that killed four black girls in the 16th Street Baptist Church during their Sunday school lessons.

I saw the South as a province in poverty. Tenant farming had replaced slavery. Hills never meant for farming were cleared, burned, and plowed. Tons of sand and soil washed down the hillsides, leaving gullies of gaping red earth. Farms overgrazed by livestock and overcut by loggers were burned, slashed, eroded, and decimated. Lumber companies that came to harvest virgin pine built the sorriest kind of towns. The industry was based on a short life that left land and people in desolation.

"It is red hills now, not high," said Jack Burden, "with blackberry bushes along the fence rows, and blackjack clumps in the bottoms and now and then a place where the second-growth pines stand close together if they haven't burned over for sheep grass, and if they have been burned over, there are the black stubs." Jack was the fictional ex-newspaperman created by Robert Penn Warren to narrate the life and times of a backwoods Louisiana political boss in *All the King's Men*. "There were pine forests here a long time ago but they are gone," Jack recorded. "The bastards got in here and set up the mills and laid the narrow-gauge tracks and knocked together the company commissaries and paid a dollar a day and folks swarmed out of the brush for the dollar and folks came from God knows where...."[1] Jack saw the land at its worst, between 1935 and 1940.

I failed to see it at its best, but in places where the hills had not been farmed nor the forests cut, where the South was still a natural wonderland. William Bartram, the "flower hunter" of the colonial period, called the Deep South "the very palace of Madame Flora." In the spirit of a pantheist, Bartram envisioned birds like people and people like birds. He saw the Seminole in their Florida habitat as blithe and free as winged creatures, active, tuneful, and vociferous. In my day, Marjorie Kinnan Rawlings likely felt much the same, as evidenced in her 1938 classic, *The Yearling*. Rawlings told the tender, feeling story of the backwoods settlers, the "crackers" of the piney woods, who knew little about life beyond their own small clearings and of a sensitive lad named Jody, who was struggling to mature with an understanding of wild creatures.

> Magic birds were dancing in a mystic marsh. The grass swayed with them, and the shallow waters, and the earth fluttered under them. The earth was dancing with the cranes, and the low sun, and the wind and sky.... The sun was sinking into the saw grass. The marsh was golden. The whooping cranes were washed with gold.[2]

Hodding Carter, who published the *Delta Democrat-Times* in Greenville, Mississippi, was one of the rare southern editors with courage to face the racial, economic, and religious problems of the region. Who can tell—in time I might have been another. I thought I was making progress and gaining respect of the staff and a grip on my job at the *Herald-Journal*. But perhaps I wasn't ready to run a daily—or at least not that one. After two months, the publisher, Bill Townes, called me in and said it just wasn't working. It was a Monday morning and the proof was that I had not played the Sunday stock car race on the front page when by all odds that was the biggest story in South Carolina. He was decent about it, offering to call the *Washington Post* and ask them to take me back, but I declined. Townes didn't last either. I met him several years later in Miami, where he was working as Sunday editor at the *Miami Daily News*.

My dismissal was a heavy blow, but I was not bitter. I might have even felt relieved the pressure was off. I was struggling to get ahead in my field and determined to continue. Once again, I checked the compass needle. It told me that since I was already in the South, I ought to go back to Nashville and try the *Tennessean*, regarded as a liberal southern newspaper published in an enlightened state capital and a university town.

Nashville was not yet the commerce-driven country music capital, although the Grand Old Opry packed the Ryman Auditorium, mostly with country people who couldn't care less if the music they enjoyed was called "hillbilly." I liked those folks and liked writing about them. I felt fortunate that the *Tennessean* took me on and that I was meant to come here. Both the city and newspaper were the right size for me.

From the outset, I wrote features and many front-page stories. The newsroom was congenial. My colleagues were mostly but not entirely local. I became friends with Les Barnard, about ten years older than me, an experienced hand who had worked in public relations in New York and for various newspapers. I could always go to him for guidance and answers. We both wrote front-page stories without any sense of competition.

In one piece, I recorded an interview with General Jonathan Wainright, the acclaimed hero of Bataan, while he was stopping in Nashville on December 7, 1946. It was exactly five years after the Japanese attack on the Philippines, simultaneous with Pearl Harbor; General Douglas MacArthur had left Wainright in charge to await certain capture in the Japanese advance. That interview led me to realize how far—and how much—I had traveled since the year before when I was hired by the *Washington Post*.

In another piece, I wrote about the opening concert of the new Nashville Symphony featuring Helen Jepson, the Metropolitan Opera star. That was very big news, the main story of the day, but something else about it sticks in my memory. My article was about the concert as an event. There was also a review, assessing the music itself. The paper had a reviewer, but his report did not appear; instead, it carried a review written by an editorial writer, a sophisticated fellow obviously in favor. Sometime in the morning, after the day's paper appeared, I saw the reviewer come into the newsroom. It was raining outside and he was drenched. He waited to see the managing editor, looking dispirited and gloomy. I assumed he wanted to know why his review had not been used—I could be wrong, but that was how I interpreted the episode. His review did appear in the next day's paper, after the fact, and I thought "This can be a heartless business."

I wrote a piece about the state penitentiary and prisoners being released on Christmas pardon, thinking I ought to come back to write about the daily lives of prisoners. One day I went to the state mental hospital, where I observed the medical director clearly frightened by the inmates and I thought I ought to come back to write about that. I was invited to contribute book reviews by the book editor, who was really a copy editor who wrote about books on the side and received at least five hundred review copies a week. I didn't have any love life, but I loved my work; every day I was learning something new and becoming a better reporter and writer.

I may have been ready to settle in Nashville, but Nashville, alas, was not ready for me. Two city editors were alternately in charge of things at the *Tennessean* and they were as different as, say, Strom Thurmond and Jesse Jackson. Ed Freeman (who later became managing editor) was friendly; he assigned me to top stories and often complimented me on my work. Jack Setters was, in a word, officious, as though he felt he had to prove he was a hard-boiled city editor; he never called me by my first name. He was, like John Singerhoff at the *Washington Post,* a city editor who had worked up from the police beat. One day, I was writing a story about a young woman who had jumped out of a window and committed suicide. He wanted me to get a photo from the aunt, with whom she had lived. "Tell her," he said, "we've got a picture of the girl splattered on the sidewalk and we'll run that if we must."

I came to work one day after two months on the job to find a sealed envelope addressed to me. It was from the managing editor, John P. Nye, thanking me for my services, which were no longer needed past the end of the week. I looked to his office for an explanation, but Nye absented himself all day. I shared the letter with Les Barnard, my fellow reporter and friend. "Yes, I know," he said. "I heard." He led me outside the building to a nearby coffee shop and explained Setters had seen a letter to me from the American Newspaper Guild. He carried the envelope to Nye for a serious conference. They speculated I had come on a mission to organize the *Tennessean* and decided to get rid of me before I was able to plant the seed of dissent among my fellows on the staff.

As far as I knew, my work had been satisfactory. That was not the issue in Nye's letter to me. Had he asked, I could have shown him that the Guild was merely confirming my change of address. But, then, America's publishers were frightened by the idea of their employees asserting rights, and those who were liberal in print, as I learned, could be as conservative as the rest in dealing with people working for them. As George Seldes told it, the owners "were in the habit of referring to their 'loyal' employees in much the same way medieval lords referred to their faithful serfs."[3]

I was hurt and confused. To lick my wounds and calculate the next move, I withdrew to Gatlinburg, a place I had heard of at the foot of the Great Smoky Mountains in eastern Tennessee. The town had a certain grace and charm; it was an attractive country crossroads, with four hotels, about a dozen motels, and a few craft shops producing mostly genuine old-time woodwork and woolens. I was lucky that a couple of good-looking mountain girls took a liking to me. They drove me here and there, voiced their amusement and amazement at the "derned tourists," and taught me square dancing in country places where we drank local moonshine.

That was my introduction to southern mountains and mountain people. I learned that, in earlier generations, the mountaineer and his family slept and dwelled in a one-room cabin he had built himself, alongside a stream, hugging the mountainside against the wind, maybe with ten children in a single room. Those people lived in poverty; homespun was the common wear and anybody under the age of nineteen in shoes was either moving to the city or getting married.

One day my mountain girlfriends and I went to the Great Smoky Mountains National Park to walk the trails. They explained that a "cove" was a small valley; a "run" was a brook; a grassy meadow summit, a "bald"; a peak was a "top" or "knob"; and a crown with a tangle of shrubs, a "slick." I saw flowers and shrubs abundant and thriving in the dense woods, open clearings through the branches of tall trees and mountain hollows. I looked up to giant virgin trees like the yellow poplar, or tulip tree, growing in sheltered coves to heights of 150 feet with diameter of eight to ten feet. I saw a stunted chestnut rising out of the roots of an old stump, but that tree would never reach maturity, for the blight that came from Asia had almost totally eliminated the once-abundant chestnut by the 1930s.

At Newfound Gap, I stood in the very place where President Franklin D. Roosevelt had dedicated the park only seven years before. I knew little about conservation or national parks. But with the majesty of the moment and amidst endless mountain splendor, I knew I was meant to come here, and that somehow life would work out.

CHAPTER 10

Every experience brings something positive – Working in public relations – I met and married my first wife – Introduced to conservation and conservationists – Learning there is no such thing as a fixture that lasts

After the interlude in Gatlinburg, I returned to my parents' home to think things through and chart my next move. Soon after I answered an advertisement in the *New York Times* for a writer with travel aptitude and experience. I went for interviews, first with an employment agency in mid-Manhattan, then for another with the potential employer, and was hired for a position that was not in New York but in Washington DC.

My new employer was the American Automobile Association. I started at $5,000 a year, a respectable salary in those days—more than many reporters made and certainly the most I ever received up to that time. I assured myself that since the AAA was a well-established civic organization, I would have the opportunity to do good works.

That proved true, to a degree. At the same time, I found myself removed from the mainstream of journalism. My work now was in public relations, or PR. Looking back, I often considered that move to the AAA the worst career mistake in my life. One evening, during the intermission of a concert at Constitution Hall, I met Katherine Graham and she asked what I was doing. When I told her, she snickered, as though it was a comedown from the *Post*. She may have been absolutely right. On the other hand, my work at the AAA ultimately led elsewhere: to a thoroughly challenging and fulfilling career as a writer and activist I would never have achieved otherwise. Besides, while at the AAA, I met and married my first wife. We had two bright, good-looking children, and stayed together thirty-two years. I had no way of foretelling all of this when I began. But, just as there is no rewriting one's life, every experience brings something positive to it.

The national headquarters of the AAA was in the Mills Building, an old landmark at 17th Street and Pennsylvania Avenue, directly across the street from the ornate, gingerbread State Department building (later a White House annex called the Executive Office Building), and one short block from the White House. When I came to work for the association, Harry Truman was president. In 1948, he moved across the street to the Blair House on the north side of Pennsylvania Avenue while the White House underwent reconstruction. The streetcar stop at the corner was eliminated, but anyone was free to walk past the president's front door—that is, until two Puerto Rican nationalists tried to assassinate the president, but succeeded only in killing a White House guard and getting themselves killed. I heard the shots from the fourth floor of the Mills Building and later saw the street spattered with blood and bullets.

Truman was an earthy Missourian who seemed surprised to find himself as president. He was noted for his early morning walks and for poking into little stores and shops, like Paul Pearlman's, the bookseller in the ground floor of the Mills Building, and the haberdasher across the street, who had been there long enough to have sold collars to Herbert Hoover. Pennsylvania Avenue between 17th and 18th streets was a street out of yesteryear. On the south side, adjacent to the Mills Building, was the Colonial Café, where I sometimes went to get coffee or lunch a table or two away from Secret Service men who had walked over from the White House, and next to it, Rinaldi, the dry cleaner. At the corner of 18th Street, an old office building housed the U.S. Information Agency (USIA), where Edward R. Murrow, the foremost radio news personality during World War II, became the USIA director after CBS decided he had outlived his usefulness. Across the street was the Roger Smith Hotel, a second-class hotel, but a convenient meeting place, and next to it Jack Hunt's, where the drinks were better than the food, and Jack was genial and his own best customer. All these places, including the old Mills Building, are gone, except perhaps the USIA, replaced by big and modern structures.

The Washington Redskins, the professional football team, was proudly and defiantly all white. So were the teams of the largest southern universities until they realized, one after another, that they could win more games with the best players, many of whom were black. The AAA was that way too. It did not have black employees or accept black members. My boss, the director of public relations, A. J. Montgomery, had been there for years. He was energetic and lively and played golf once a week, but he looked old, with thinning grayish-white hair, thick glasses, a cigarette cough, and spats on his shoes every single day. He was a Scotsman who still spoke with a brogue, who had come to America in his youth and worked in Washington as a reporter for the *Christian Science Monitor*. One day he showed me a newspaper clipping about the year he worked in public relations at the White House under Calvin Coolidge and humanized the unsmiling "Silent Cal." That was how far back A. J. Montgomery went.

The AAA began early in the twentieth century when horses and buggies outnumbered motor cars many times over. Motoring was a sport, mostly for people of means. They organized clubs and outings in the same way that bicyclists, hikers, and skiers do, and promoted roads suited to their vehicles. In 1902, the clubs established a federation to serve their common interests. They needed national coordination to ensure a uniform and systematic production, wide distribution of maps and guidebooks, and emergency service provided by automobile service stations under contract. But the clubs made certain to maintain their independence; the central headquarters in Washington (which they named the American Automobile Association) was meant to serve them, not to run them.

With the mass production of automobiles and the construction of new highways, the motor clubs grew and expanded their services. They sold automobile insurance and later other insurance as well. They expanded into the travel agency field, selling tours, cruises, and tickets for airlines and railroads, showing they recognized a business opportunity when they saw it and were not so old-fashioned after all.

On the surface, they appeared to be a federation of clubs, but they were never consumer groups daring to criticize the automobile manufacturers the way Ralph Nader did in the 1950s. When the rapidly increasing number of cars on the road brought about an increase in traffic and highway accidents, instead of pressing manufacturers to produce safer cars, AAA made the public conscious of *its* responsibility through school safety patrols and driver education in high schools. Some clubs operated as civic groups, motivated by public service as they saw it. Others were privately controlled and corporate driven. All had directors chosen from the communities, but the directors were mostly businessmen too.

The first person I met in the public relations department was Montgomery's secretary, Thelma Seymour, whom he called "Annie." It was "Annie, do this" and "Annie, do that." He probably would have discounted this as playful familiarity, but secretaries today would not stand for it. She was an attractive, prematurely graying brunette, extremely conscientious and efficient. These were the days, mind you, before computers and photocopiers, and even before electric typewriters. A secretary had to know how to take and transcribe dictation, type with carbon paper and five or six onionskin copies, and type on a blue stencil for reproduction on a mimeograph machine. Thelma did all of those things swiftly and skillfully.

She was unattached and took a liking to me—it may have been because I was the only unmarried man around the office. Or perhaps because she respected my writing skill, or intellect, or my life-experience. She made no pretense at intellectuality, but she was bright and able and honest to a fault; and she was motivated by a powerful sense of responsibility. She was still young—four years older than me—and had already worked there fifteen years, starting before World War II.

We went out a few times. Thelma, the eldest of five girls, still lived at home in Alexandria, Virginia, with her mother and stepfather. She was devoted to her family, job, and church. At one point she confided that she had once been in love with a prominent young Jewish fellow in Alexandria who had died prematurely. Then I came along. She wanted my company more than marriage or any commitment from me. For my part, I liked her and her family; they were blue-collar people, all close and loyal, who always welcomed me and made me feel comfortable. So did Thelma. We enjoyed simple pleasures and became devoted to each other and inseparable.

The trouble was that I became disenchanted with the AAA and was not keen on staying. During one particular meeting at headquarters, I saw the heads of the Automobile Club of New York and the Chicago Motor Club in action for the first time. Both were powerful personalities in the AAA councils. They came across as successful, self-assured, rough and tough entrepreneurs; they treated Montgomery, my boss, and the other headquarters executives like messenger boys. I did not want to work for them. I wanted to return to newspaper work and said to Thelma, "Let's get married and go somewhere else." With little hesitation, she agreed. But when she went to share this decision with Montgomery, he talked her out of it.

He called me in and closed the door. "I'm thinking of both Annie and you, and of your future together," he said. "You want to marry and I applaud you for that. But let me tell you about yourself. You are bright and able—or Annie wouldn't want you—but look at your employment record. You have changed jobs too often to do yourself much good or to support your wife and whatever family you two may have. You are well liked here and have a career with a future. You can travel, which you like to do. You can take on public issues you care about and write about them."

He talked me out of leaving the AAA, but not out of marrying. Thelma wanted a church wedding, but I was terrified at the idea of standing up before a crowd of people and suggested a small wedding at her home, to which she agreed. First, however, we went to counseling sessions with her pastor, Reverend Ernest Campbell, a gentle, graying southern gentleman of mature years. He was fond of Thelma and evidently of me too.

I returned to him alone one day and said, "I have a problem here. I'm not a Christian and I don't want to pledge marriage vows to Christ." He was understanding and sympathetic. "The important consideration is your love for Thelma. That will carry you through. When you hear something in the service to which you cannot in good conscience subscribe, make a mental reservation to yourself. I believe that God will accept that." Later Thelma repeated her conversation with Reverend Campbell to me. He said he had read some of my writing and felt that I could not be an atheist. That may have been true, but I can't imagine, even now, that I was writing anything in those days of spiritual value.

We were married in June 1949 at Thelma's home with family and a few friends present. It was a lovely ceremony filled with warmth and good spirit. My brother and his wife came, but my father disapproved and would not. He believed I should keep the faith and marry a nice Jewish girl. Later, following the birth of our first child, his grandson, he relented. We went to visit my parents and were well received. My father was still trying to make it in business, remodeling and repairing furs and buying skins from local part-time trappers. It was good that my father could meet his grandson, for he died in 1953 at age 67.

At the outset of our marriage, Thelma decided it was improper for her to continue working at the AAA and got a job as secretary to a lobbyist and a lawyer. She had a $5,000 war bond in the bank, which we set aside together with her earnings for the down payment on a home where we would raise a family. My earnings (I had little in the bank) would go for current expenses.

During my ten years with AAA, I was encouraged to do civic things because it enhanced the organization's public image. I was spared from promoting freeways or apologizing for them, although they certainly were high on the association's agenda. I developed expertise in travel and tourism and was designated travel editor. Editors and writers would call about trends and article ideas. I got to know many of them; I sent them news releases and special features about travel forecasts and reviews, and they would ask me to write articles for their special summer or winter travel sections.

There was still another dimension to it. In the postwar boom, people had jobs, earned money, bought cars, went places on paid vacations over new highways, stayed in new motels (with a private toilet in every room, which was first an innovation), and discovered Yellowstone, Yosemite, the Grand Canyon, and other national parks. I traveled to a lot of places and wrote articles about them. In due course, I became involved in civic programs that extended my horizons and introduced me to new people. For instance, the AAA was part of a national antibillboard campaign and participated in efforts to protect roadsides from commercial "ribbon development." Those were good causes that I wish had proven more successful. I became aware of conservation groups interested in this phase of landscape protection and began communicating with them.

I went to national parks and got to know National Park Service officials. National parks were new to me, but from the outset I saw them as sanctuaries of idealism, meant to stimulate the mind with new learning and to challenge the spirit. The Blue Ridge Parkway—the first park I got to know well—was a model for recreational motoring, extending 469 miles along the mountain spine of Virginia and North Carolina, free of truck traffic and billboards, with access to parks, forests, and mountain vistas along the way. In Wyoming I found the towering, jagged peaks parading across the sky in Grand Teton National Park inspirational, even more so with the network of waterfalls and wildflower gardens sheltered around ledges and at their base. In Florida, I visited the newly established Everglades National Park and read *River of Grass*, in which Marjory Stoneman Douglas reshaped the public image of this watery wilderness from an obstacle to progress to a world treasure of untamed nature.

The national parks were clearly significant touring destinations, and of long interest to AAA clubs and their members; however, the parks had been virtually closed during the war and their new popularity was soaring beyond adequate staffing and protection. Bernard DeVoto wrote a classic piece on the subject called "Let's Close the National Parks," in *Harper's Magazine* of October 1953. I met DeVoto and others in and out of government who played particular roles in park policy, including publisher

Alfred Knopf, chairman of the National Parks Advisory Board, and Wallace Stegner and Sigurd Olson, authors who concerned themselves with the preservation of nature. I became acquainted with the conservation column by John Oakes in the *New York Times*. His column appeared in the Sunday travel section, which I read regularly as part of my work; it was buried in the back pages, but it was alive with news of goings-on in America that I found in no other paper. Friends who were travel editors increasingly asked me to contribute articles about parks and preservation. My early articles were published in the *Christian Science Monitor* and the *New York Herald Tribune*, and so I began to make my own contribution.

Thelma and I saved our money and bought a modest new home (for about $20,000) and soon after, welcomed our first child. I enjoyed writing—it's never been a chore. After we moved into our home, I submitted a piece for the personal essays section of the *Christian Science Monitor*, which appeared in print May 19, 1951, under the heading "My Journey to Washington." The opening portion of it follows:

> The birds were awake first and I heard them before the alarm clock; sweeter music, too! Otherwise, it was a quiet, tranquil morning in northern Virginia. Beyond the window blinds the great oaks reached skyward—they've been around this place a long time and I looked out, wondering which was the oldest and which the tallest.
>
> And were they here in General Washington's time? Had he ever seen them on a trip through the woods? He might have, for this land, five miles from the mansion at Mount Vernon, once was his; and, in fact, the original settlement of his father's Hunting Creek estate was only a mile or two away.
>
> But I had to be getting on: with shaving, dressing, breakfast and an early departure. Even so, driving to Washington, I was to follow the dreamy trail of nature and history. The broad Mount Vernon Memorial Boulevard was lined on both sides with green lawns and Virginia's loveliest trees and shrubs, red and white, pink and green, all of them as alive as spring and as cool as the morning....

All in all, we were doing well. Soon we had two children and Thelma was happy being a mother and homemaker—that was what she wanted. I was reasonably happy too. I settled in at the AAA, earning raises doing what

I wanted. Around Washington, however, I learned there is no such thing as a fixture. Only friends last—for those lucky enough to find them and savvy enough to keep them. All the rest may think of permanence, but they, like the rest of us, are merely passing through their current addresses.

Paul Pearlman, the bookseller, was a fixture, doing business at the same stand on the F Street side of the Mills Building for thirty years. In his bookstore, I could never find what I wanted, except by mistake. But Paul or his helper, Bill, could find it. Bill was a little old man, who I think was with Pearlman since the beginning. He was a bachelor, small and frail with a thin face, pointed nose, and humped back, like a gnome, and he walked slowly. Bill complained that Paul went off for hours, leaving him alone in the bookstore. Paul in turn complained about Bill, saying, "I pay him, don't I?"

In the mornings, Pearlman visited auctions, hunting for bargains in old books to add to his collection. Three afternoons a week, he played handball at the YMCA on F Street. He was considered one of the best players in the city, even though he was over fifty. He played throughout the year, including summer when younger men would wilt in Washington's humidity. He was healthy, with a round red face, spry, quick, and alert. The ceiling in his store was at least fifteen or twenty feet high, with books piled to the top in the back, old prints and paintings on the high walls in the front. "There is no price on them," he said of the prints and paintings. "They're mine and not for sale." He was not much of a reader; he collected books because he liked the smell of them, and because he liked having readers come in and browse and ask for volumes only he could find. He did a considerable business in secondhand books, which he also sold from shelves on the sidewalk. There was usually a crowd during lunch hour, but Pearlman didn't care whether people bought or not.

When Thelma and I were married Pearlman gave her a cookbook. Occasionally I brought in old books to sell to him. Sometimes I would try to trade, but he wouldn't hear of it: "Absolutely not! I'll give you money but no books. I didn't ask for yours and I'm not giving up mine. I love my books."

Then one day, the building manager brought him the news. Another bookstore would open soon, three doors from Pearlman. "But don't worry, Paul," the manager said to soften the blow. "It's an art bookstore. No competition to you." Pearlman told me about it in the street in front of his store; he was distraught and grieving to the world. A short while later, Franz Bader came along and opened his store. I'm not sure how long Pearlman lasted, but he closed his doors, after all those years. Bader, in due course, turned his store into a gallery and moved to Dupont Circle when the old building came down and was replaced with a new upscale Mills Building.

Sometimes I would meet a friend for lunch or a drink at the National Press Club, across from the Willard Hotel on 14th Street. The AAA paid my dues and I might even charge the meal to my expense account. The Press Club was a rendezvous for ambitious young journalists and PR people on the way up and also for those who had been there, done it, and were on the way down. Former senator Robert La Follette Jr., son of the famous "Fighting Bob" La Follette, was a regular without much to do. We would exchange smiles and greetings, though he didn't know me at all. Then one day he jumped out of the Press Club window and killed himself, probably in despair of losing his Senate seat to the infamous Joe McCarthy, an accident in history who was riding roughshod over constitutional civil liberties and manipulating the media in the process.

At the Press Club, I would run into Scot Hart, whom I had known as an able, popular feature writer at the *Post*, which he left to become the Washington editor of *Esquire* and its sister publication, *Coronet*. The trouble was that *Coronet* folded and so did *Esquire*, for a while, pending resuscitation. Scot was trying to make it as a freelance writer. He certainly had the talent for it, but the best he could say, with a smile and shrug, was "I go to the mailbox every day looking for checks and assignments. All I find are bills, news releases, and rejection slips."

I used to meet Edwin Newman, my old sidekick at the International News Service, for lunch at the Old Ebbitt Grill, on F Street near the Willard Hotel. It was convenient and we could afford it. He was bright, critical, and acerbic. He worked for a while for Esther Van Wagoner Tufty (known as the Dutchess), doing what he considered menial chores covering Washington for several Michigan newspapers, and for which Tufty got the credit. Then he was a leg man and writer for Eric Sevareid, the thinking person's radio commentator. Ed would tell me, "Every evening they like to say, 'This program is under the supervision and control of the Columbia Broadcasting System.' What they don't say is the sponsor's option is up every thirteen weeks." We were in this period good friends. He was away at the time of my wedding, but his wife came. I drove him to Union Station when he went off to Europe to try his luck as a network correspondent, uncertain if he would ever make it. A few years later, I ran into him at a party, when he, as a prominent correspondent for the National Broadcasting Company, came back for a visit; I hoped we could get together, but he said, "Why bother?" and turned away.

That sort of episode was not uncommon in Washington. In time Ed Newman became past history too. Decline in fortune and influence can happen to the best, as it did to Scot Hart and to Frank D. Morris. Frank walked into the AAA in Washington one day, introduced himself as a staff writer for *Collier's* magazine, and it somehow fell to me to be of service to him. *Collier's* evidently was working on a story, or a series that might take a year or more to develop, on the impact of new highways on cities around the country, or something like that. *Collier's* was a highly respected weekly, top of the line along with its principal competitor, the (seemingly) invincible *Saturday Evening Post*. *Collier's* had lately been through upheavals, with old editors fired and new editors hired. Frank had weathered the storm and survived. He had graduated from the Naval Academy in the 1920s and looked as though he could have played an admiral in the movies, tall, well dressed, with graying, sad eyes staring far off, half smiling. He had been at *Collier's* for years, the executive editor or articles editor for a long period before serving as war correspondent covering the Pacific.

I tried to help him, then later he tried to help me. One day I stopped to see him at *Collier's*. He was in a large room with fifteen desks and a few glassed-in cubbyhole offices along the windows. He was at one of the desks in the middle of the room. "Come into my private office," he said with an exaggerated gesture. After I left the AAA, Frank counseled me on magazine writing, that to make a living as a freelance required having five articles in the works, at various stages of research and writing. He showed me how to write a narrative or anecdotal lead: start with a story to catch the reader's interest; don't tell it all, let it grow (Casey Jones would certainly not approve). He told me to get an agent in New York and sent me to Kenneth Littauer, who had been fiction editor of *Collier's* for twenty-five years, dealing with the finest writers in America. I went to see Littauer, who wore suspenders and a belt, and I thought would soon be an old man. He was on the phone, presumably talking with his wife. "Yes dear, we made exactly as much as we did yesterday—nothing." We talked for an hour. I showed him newspaper articles I had written. He suggested I send him outlines, and that I try fiction. "How about a novel?" He was willing to represent me. I was elated at having an agent. I did nothing, became embarrassed at not having sent him anything, thought about the big pile of manuscripts he had to read through and how badly mine would compare with the rest of them.

Presently *Collier's* folded. Frank was out of work, but not for long; he landed on his feet as executive editor of *True*, a handsome, well-written, well-respected men's magazine, but for whatever reason that did not work out. He was unemployed for the longest time, until his old Naval Academy classmate, a vice president at Pan American Airways, helped him get a job as a bookkeeper at the ticket counter at the midtown airline terminal on 42nd Street. That was a comedown, one of life's little reminders that whatever works today might not last through tomorrow. When I was in New York, I would stop by and we would have lunch. He was glad to see me.

Many people smoked in those days. My father smoked, and suffered from emphysema, which contributed to his death. Frank Morris smoked, leading to his death. The two doctors giving prenatal lectures that I attended with Thelma paced up and down puffing on cigarettes while telling parents-to-be how to have healthy babies. I smoked from the age of fourteen until I was forty. I wised up and finally decided to quit. It wasn't easy. I appealed to Thelma to quit with me, and so did our children, but she didn't, not then. Smoking is a miserable, dirty, and deadly addiction. Her old boss and mine at the AAA, A. J. Montgomery, smoked and died from it.

Following Montgomery's death, the AAA hired a consultant who decided to make changes. Alas, I was chosen as the subject of one of the changes. The consultant called me in and said management wanted to try something different with somebody else. Though it hurt at the moment, I did not argue or try to make a case of any kind. Maybe deep down I recognized that it was time to move on and raise my sights. I had felt secure—too secure—or maybe trapped, not recognizing that regular employment can be as addictive (and seductive) as smoking: going to work every morning and saluting the paymaster before going home every night. I was frightened at losing the security, yet I felt, I believed, that change would prove a blessing.

CHAPTER 11

Breaking in as a freelance writer — It wasn't easy but it worked — Stories on conservation were not being covered — My friend in New England "reaping the sweet fragrance of an apple orchard in full flower"

After leaving the AAA, I faced the challenge of providing for my wife and two children and making the monthly payment on the house. I couldn't find a job I wanted, but maybe I didn't want a job, believing that now I could do something more in my life than publicize and promote automobile clubs or some other commercial venture, or even work for a daily newspaper reporting facts without interpreting what they meant.

Although I thought of myself as a travel writer, I recognized deeper issues and opportunities. In making the rounds, I found that former contacts were now friends more than willing to help. One of the first, Jack Hazard, at *Changing Times* (later renamed *The Kiplinger Magazine*), urged his editor, Herbert L. Brown, to assign me to write travel articles since I knew the field well. At *Changing Times*, everything was staff-written and Brown had a serious misgiving about giving work to anybody with a PR background. He relented, however, and gave me a chance. After I wrote two articles, he offered me a position on the staff. It was tempting, and hard to turn down, considering benefits and security, but we finally agreed that I would be a contributing editor, getting paid for what I wrote.

My first regular connection, in late 1958 or early 1959, was to write a monthly Washington report for *American Motel* magazine for $75. Soon after, I started writing another Washington column for the *Interline Reporter*, an airline publication (published by the same outfit that owned *Travel Agent* magazine) for $50 per month. A year or so later, when I was ready to give these up, Thelma asked in her cautious, conservative way: "But they're regular, aren't they?" I laughed and assured her we would make it somehow without them.

It took time to get my feet firmly on the ground and to feel that I was making it. At first I wrote travel articles for the *New York Herald Tribune* and *Christian Science Monitor*. They were respectable, but didn't pay much. Magazines paid considerably more, but required more effort and a better (or at least different) kind of writing. Once I connected, I wrote regularly for *Holiday, Woman's Day, Parade,* and *Changing Times,* plus assorted others, some of which no longer exist.

But something big and important was going on around me in those years of the late 1950s and through the 1960s. As a journalist, I saw many stories on national parks, national forests, and conservation in general that were not being covered but needed to be. One evening early in 1963, I listened to an intensely impressive speech in Washington by Gaylord Nelson, then a new senator from Wisconsin. Nobody sent me, but I thought I should go, listen, and learn. Nelson warned the audience that conservation of woods, lakes, streams, and other natural resources constituted the most urgent and crucial domestic issue facing the nation. But to find a report of his remarks in the *Washington Post*, I had to look to the bottom of the obituary page, where it lay buried below the deceased, like a very dead issue.

That wasn't right. Although I was lucky to get assignments from respectable magazines for articles on travel with some reference to conservation, I wanted to do more, to report on exciting changes in public policy then under way. I wanted to be part of what was going on in the 1960s, a period rich in landmark decisions aimed at protecting wilderness, rivers, trails, air, water, and endangered species of plants and animals—all components of a healthy environment. Americans in that time generally learned to accept the new word "ecology," reflected in 1970, with the first Earth Day, passage of the National Environmental Policy Act, and the emergence of environmental organizations as important players in shaping public attitudes and government policies.

My own transformation, or emergency in a new role, had begun while I was still with the AAA. Then, in 1958, a friend, Doug Larsen, telephoned me out of the blue. "Call so-and-so at Doubleday in New York right now," he said. "They want to publish a family travel guide and I have recommended you. Here is the number—call now!" Minutes later, I talked with the editor, who wanted me to get an outline of the guide in the mail that very night. This led to my first book, *Better Vacations for Your Money*, published in 1959. The book was simply a guide to family touring in the United States, but it made me a published author. *Better Vacations* was a Doubleday Book Club selection, and was featured in one of those full-page advertisements in the Sunday supplements.

The director of the National Park Service, Conrad L. Wirth, was kind enough to contribute the foreword to the book. He wrote that I was a good friend to the national parks and that personnel in the field knew and respected me. But then I loved the national parks: they gave meaning to America and meaning to my writing.   Then I wrote a guidebook to Washington, also for Doubleday (published in 1960). I enjoyed the research and writing about the city, and the book actually sold well.

Much of my work and income over the previous decade had come from writing for magazines, mostly about travel. Editors knew of my interest in conservation and to varying degrees tolerated and encouraged it in their pages. As a freelance contributing writer, I was vulnerable to the whims of the editors, but they were vulnerable too, in their own way, to their publishers, although they had to act secure and in command. But I felt they cared about me and wanted me to succeed. We would often go over stories and story ideas together, leading to something better than I could have come up with on my own.

When I first came to *Changing Times*, "a monthly service on personal and family business … no advertising," Herb Brown, the editor, was initially reluctant to take me on. After my first piece in March 1959 and my second in June 1960, I wrote a stream of articles for him about travel in Mexico, Europe, Africa, and China—about big cities, tipping, train travel, hassles in air travel, bicycle travel, overage and unsafe cruise ships, and "silly souvenirs and how they sell." While working on these articles, I discovered that Brown was just as concerned about the environment as I was. Our conversations led me to write "America the Beautiful: Heritage or Honkytonk?" (November 1962), "America the Beautiful: Let's Not Lose it" (September 1963), and "America the Beautiful Needs More Friends: Your Town's Open Spaces and How To Save Them" (October 1976).

Brown, unfortunately, was fired as editor and left the magazine. Luckily, his successor, Bob Harvey, shared the same concerns so that (in addition to the travel articles) I was allowed and encouraged to write pieces like "The Battle Over Wilderness," "Why Are We Ruining Our National Parks?" "The Controversy Over Snowmobiles," and "Conservationists: A Field Guide to the Many Organizations That Are Defending Our Natural Heritage."

At *Parade*, the Sunday supplement, while I began by writing travel stories, one day I came to Ed Kiester, my editor there, to discuss my experience at the Gettysburg battlefield in Pennsylvania, which I had just visited in connection with another project. This conversation led to a cover story published December 14, 1958, with a huge spread inside headlined:

> Neon signs, junk yards and dollar-grubbing are invading many great shrines. And the most hallowed of all is being desecrated in ... *The New Battle of Gettysburg*.

Kiester encouraged me to write another cover story titled "What's Happening to Our Shoreline?" in the February 15, 1959, issue. Two days later, Senator Richard L. Neuberger of Oregon introduced the article into the *Congressional Record* and sent it to me with a letter of appreciation. There was nothing unusual about that—congressmen load the appendix to the *Congressional Record* with all kinds of relevancies and irrelevancies—but I admired Richard Neuberger as a writer with a cause who made his mark in public life. Subsequently Kiester went to *True*, where he assigned me to write "Our Campgrounds Are Turning into Slums," which was picked up and reprinted in *Reader's Digest*. That was all his idea.

At *Holiday*, I had started by writing a how-to motor tour of Georgia as the prototype of a series. I did two more motor tours as models for other writers, then wrote about twenty-five articles for *Holiday* over the next ten years. *Holiday* was an absolutely superlative magazine of the postwar period, edited by a genius named Ted Patrick who engaged the best writers and photographers to do their best work. These included John Steinbeck, whose *Travels with Charley* began in the pages of *Holiday*. Once when I was traveling, I received an urgent message to call Harry Sions, the magazine's editorial director. "Ted is mad at you," he said. "You wrote an article for us and here Ted found an article by you on the same subject in another magazine. Promise you won't do it again." I promised. The rule was that you could rewrite the same story for another periodical as long as it wasn't competitive, which I thought was the case here. Harry wasn't angry but Ted was; I took it as a compliment that he would notice and care.

My editor, John Roberson, was in charge of a section in the back of the book called the Holiday Handbook. He continually designed handbooks for me to research and write about Indian crafts, national parks, national forests, historic places, neglected American treasures, summer studies, the Rocky Mountains, and more. In one 1963 issue, the table of contents listed as contributors Paul Engle, John Steinbeck, Jerome Weidman, John McNulty, Bruce Catton, Ogden Nash, Arthur C. Clarke, and Clifton Fadiman, all in the same issue. I was listed too, for my latest handbook on America's public gardens, prefaced by a little note John Roberson had written: "Michael Frome has written many articles for *Holiday* on the fight to preserve America's beauty. His latest book is on our national forests, *Whose Woods These Are*." My handbook to gardens began:

> There it was, as large as life, the elegant *Franklinia*, as legendary a plant as grows in any garden in America. It was the ancestral *Franklinia* itself, grown from seeds that William Bartram carried from the Southern wilderness to his father's renowned garden by the Schuylkill River two centuries ago. "A beautiful flowering tree," the younger Bartram described it, and so it struck me, with its fragrant blossoms—golden-yellow stamen encircled by silky white petals—and its glossy dark evergreen leaves. Yet we might have lost this plant forever. A few years after Bartram collected its seeds, the *Franklinia* was observed in the wild for the last time— though it has since been searched for carefully and repeatedly. The plant has been propagated here and has spread to other gardens, but for some reason it has vanished from its natural setting.

That sort of lead might not have worked elsewhere, but it worked for *Holiday*. I could have written handbooks ad infinitum, but Ted Patrick died. The parent firm, the Curtis Publishing Company, became a money loser after being profitable forever. Somewhere in this time period, *Holiday*'s older sister, the *Saturday Evening Post*, collapsed and died. Harry Sions left to be a book editor and a new team took over *Holiday*, headed by Don Schanche as editor and Don Gold as managing editor, and at some point the magazine moved from Philadelphia to New York.

To my surprise, I received more and bigger assignments. The editors noted the natural beauty movement and asked me to analyze it, both in Washington and across the country. I observed President Lyndon B. Johnson in a bill-signing at the White House, interviewed cabinet members, senators, congressmen, and industry and conservation leaders, and I visited the Grand Canyon and the redwoods. It was a great writing exercise: twice the editors returned what I considered the finished manuscript, raising pointed questions, forcing me to learn more about my subject. The feature that emerged, "The Politics of Conservation" (published in *Holiday* in February 1967) dealt with public desire to meet the onrushing environmental crisis and the inadequate response of politicians and public officials. Perhaps the essence of it is in this paragraph:

> Lyndon Johnson pursues in practice a course of halfway measures and "consensus conservation" designed to gain support from everyone and to please all. Secretary of the Interior Stewart L. Udall, during a recent interview, was asked about his mistakes or regrets. "All of us," he conceded, "overcompromise and therefore fall short of our ideals." Such compromise results from mixing conservation so deeply with political considerations that principle becomes a matter of secondary concern.

I've been writing on the same theme, with variations, ever since. It went over well at the time, but times were changing. Schanche gave me more assignments. He wanted to devote a whole issue to the national parks illustrated by Dennis Stock, a top photographer, with me as guest editor. But he got fired and Gold went with him. All my assignments were canceled, but in due time *Holiday* folded, so it didn't matter.

At *Woman's Day*, I wrote my first piece about vacation planning for a front-of-the-book section called What Goes on Here in July 1957 and became good friends with Evelyn Grant, the managing editor. The magazine had been started by the A&P grocery chain and for years had sold for five cents. When I came along, it was owned by Fawcett Publishing, sold for a dime in the supermarkets, and had a circulation in the millions. In July 1960, after I wrote my second piece, "A Guide to Our National Parks," I approached my friend Evelyn and said, "Miss Grant, I would like to write a regular travel column for *Woman's Day*." She smiled and responded politely: "Michael, Miss Tighe [Eileen Tighe, the editor at that time] likes to assign articles to people who have written for her before."

Magazine editors were that way. They wanted new talent, but preferred to work with professionals who understood their needs without taking a lot of time for questions, explanations, or rewrites. That is why they paid well. Or as one writer explained the secret of his success: "I get my copy in on time and it's neatly typed." Happily, Miss Tighe did like my work and assigned me to write for the series on "treasure towns," usually illustrated with beautiful paintings. Besides the treasure towns, I wrote

"The Wonderful World of Covered Bridges" and "Ten Lovely Train Rides." *Woman's Day* sent me to Banff, Alberta, Canada, to do a piece on the Banff School of Fine Arts. I felt good about doing something worthwhile.

Miss Tighe in due course was replaced by Geraldine Rhoads, who continued to keep me busy. When I came to New York, she and Evelyn would take me to lunch next door at the Alqonquin; after the magazine was sold to CBS and the office moved to Times Square, they would take me to Sardi's or some other swish place. One day Evelyn called me: "Gerry wants you to come up for dinner." They were both over six feet tall and towered over me. They were good to me and I adored them both. "Now, Michael," Gerry began, "we're not going to call it a column, but we are going to make you a contributing editor with a regular monthly feature...." But it *was* a column, called On the Go, that I wrote for every issue for the next eleven years, until Geraldine Rhoads retired in 1982. Years later, the three of us met for an evening in New York. Both were living well in retirement, Gerry a volunteer with the Literacy Council. "Remember when you called me up to dinner and assigned me to write a column?" I asked. "That was a big night in my life." Neither remembered it at all and we laughed.

Like almost every editor I've known, Gerry Rhoads read everything in the magazine—every page, every line, every word—fulfilling her responsibility for it all. No one at *Woman's Day* ever suggested what I should write about. Once I told her I wanted to be critical in print, but she said, "We don't have the space. We criticize by leaving it out." I was also called on for additional travel copy for regional editions. It was like writing two or three columns per issue. I had to keep files and keep up with my travels. I followed the seasons and covered the country. I felt my column should be good reading even for people who would not visit a particular place. I wrote about gardens, hotels, historic sites, cities, saving money, airline bargains, national parks, state parks, nature reserves, and lodgings of all kinds. I had an expense account but, yes, I accepted invitations to free trips. But I always had to anticipate questions from the reader and the editor: Are you working for me or for the people giving you the free trip? Is the plan you suggest for me worth my spending the money? Is your advice useful and helpful? The reader and editor would know if I was playing games.

In the February 20, 1979, issue, the magazine carried a profile of me:

"On the face of it a travel writer's job sounds like a constant round of fun and games," says Michael Frome, "and it's true that you have to enjoy travel in order to write about it effectively. But it also takes a lot of work and involves considerable responsibility. Personally, I would not recommend a vacation trip to readers that I would not recommend to a member of my own family." The effectiveness of Mike's popular "On the Go" feature (p. 56) can be judged by the fact that when he mentioned the offering of a free brochure on the Kutztown, Pennsylvania, Folk Festival in our June 14, 1978, issue, requests from 5,000 readers were received by June 15. Mike, who has been writing "On the Go" since 1970, dates the start of his travel career from World War II, when he flew over all six continents as an airplane navigator. "My first overseas flight, from California to Hawaii, took almost fifteen hours in a twin-engine transport," he recalls. "Now it takes about four and a half. There have been some tremendous changes in the travel scene during the past thirty years. People are now ready to travel anywhere on earth, but they are growing steadily more selective in their tastes. My goal is to stay ahead, so that I'm able to supply the kind of advice readers want." Home for Mike and his wife is in Alexandria, Virginia, where Mike does his writing. He is the author of ten books, including the *Rand McNally National Park Guide*, now in its thirteenth annual edition. Last spring he served as a visiting professor at the University of Vermont. "It was about the longest time I'd been able to spend in one place in years," he says. "Most of the time I'm on the go—just as the column title says!"

I could not have done all of this, or done it at all, without Thelma. She organized a cozy office for me at home by closing in the breezeway between the house and garage, and by doing my typing, filing, and bookkeeping. Once, in the late 1960s or early 1970s, she came to me with our income tax statement, which she had just completed. "Last year you made $74,000 and will earn about the same this year." That was more than I could imagine, but one editor or another would call on the phone asking me to send a story tomorrow that I had written for somebody else yesterday, so I would rewrite it and send it off and the editor would send a check for $1500 or whatever. One year, the *National Geographic* assigned me to write a section in a book to be called *Wilderness USA*. Sigurd Olson was to write the lead essay, while I was to describe wilderness in the East. I was told to go wherever I wanted, but to keep a record of expenses in a little booklet, which included a provision for "tips to native bearers." I went all around the East (without native bearers), turned in my assignment, which the *National Geographic* editors massaged a little, since they had to keep busy too, and they paid me $2500 or $3000. Several years later, *National Geographic* asked for an update for a new edition of the book, which took me about forty-five minutes or an hour to complete. After I turned it in, the editor telephoned. "We don't want you to feel put upon," he said. "Will $700 do for the update?"

As a child of the Depression, Thelma was frugal, while I was ever fearful the big paydays would end. Besides, my mother, who lived in Alexandria until she died in 1963, would be critical of any wasteful ostentation on my part. With Thelma, everything was for her children and home. We underwrote music lessons and sent our son and daughter to the National Music Camp at Interlochen, Michigan, for three summers, and later to expensive private colleges, Williams in Massachusetts and Bethany in West Virginia. Both were spared hardship, but they were also denied the learning experience that comes with it.

During this period of my career, I was able to write about conservation even in the travel pages. Advertising paid the way for travel sections in Sunday papers and many of the pages were filled with saccharine servings and how-to writing, but some of the travel editors wanted to do their share to protect the land and landscape. Travel editors and writers had every reason to care. In 1967, I wrote a series of five articles on national parks for Leavitt Morris, travel editor of the *Christian Science Monitor*. Then Kermit Holt, the travel editor of the *Chicago Tribune*, published a two-part series of mine also on the parks. It appeared on August 3, 1975.

How long will the quality last?
As millions of persons around the world seek out beauty, peace, and solitude on their vacations, the throngs of tourists as well as 20th century progress exact their tolls.

The main story I wrote for the front page of the *New York Times* travel section of June 2, 1974, followed under the headline, "After 50 Years, the American Wilderness Still Stands—in Peril." One of the best of my newspaper stories appeared in the *Washington Post* of April 12, 1981.

Parks in Peril: Critical Problems Facing America's Wilderness
Our national park system is now engulfed by the gravest threats in its entire history of more than a century.

Pollution of air and water, commercial encroachment, improper assignment, and lack of field personnel to protect the resources, are some of the critical problems that must be faced and solved in the 1980s—that is, if our parks are to remain unspoiled, peaceful havens for travelers in search of inspiration and wholesome recreation.

Another favorite story appeared in the *Miami Herald*, February 25, 1979.

Add Tropical Islands to the "Endangered Species" List

Tropical islands across the planet face the same serious plight of intense overdevelopment in the name of progress. The Seychelles of the Indian Ocean, the Canary Islands of the South Atlantic, the Hawaii chain in the mid-Pacific—all the enchanting green sanctuaries in the sun are being stripped of the very qualities that make them popular and loved.

Of islands under attack, I daresay that none are more endangered than those of the Caribbean. Over the past 30 years, one West Indies island after another has been "discovered" and despoiled, in the same pattern that earlier swept the coasts of continental United States.

Today there is little left of sparkling beaches, tropical forests and untouched coral reefs. Caribbean islands have been deprived of their special identities and reduced to carbon copies of continental cultures, complete with industrial blight, crowds, noise and pollution.....

That piece had been published first in the *Los Angeles Times*, where the travel editor, Jerry Hulse, gave me a weekly column, starting June 19, 1977, called Environmental Trails, which allowed considerable latitude, though in the end I may have been *too* environmental and too critical of tourism for the travel pages. My first column was about the Clean Air Act. I wrote about clear-cutting, coral reefs, commercial blight of tourism, bottle bills aimed at recycling, billboards, rail travel, off-road vehicles, the California desert (which I thought the *Los Angeles Times* might have covered on the front page), the Sagebrush Rebellion, convention centers, caution with cameras in game areas, the Serengeti at age fifty, the United Nations World Heritage List, and a range of environmental issues in various countries around the world.

I knew most of the travel editors and travel writers of the time. While at the AAA, it had been my job to know them and tell them all the good things we were doing. They came in a variety of different sizes and flavors. A state tourist official once said to me, "All you need do is give a travel writer a drink and a press release." Yes, there was that type. Some freelancers would sell their work for little or nothing just for the free trips. On the other hand, Ann Wyman, of the *Boston Globe*, would take the freebies, go birdwatching almost every time, and after two or three years as travel editor quit to become an editorial writer. Kermit Holt had been a foreign correspondent for the *Chicago Tribune* who enjoyed going places and won almost every prize open to travel writers. Jerry Hulse, of the *Los Angeles Times*, was a serious fellow who wrote a best-selling book about the search for his wife's parents and could have written more. I think most of my colleagues were serious and responsible journalists. So were many of the PR people in the travel field. A few became friends and helped me on my way.

Leavitt Morris of the *Christian Science Monitor* and I went through various issues together and were close friends for years. He would often refer to the personal essay I had written for the *Monitor*, and considered it a literary achievement of some kind. He held my hand when I was fired by the AAA and was struggling to make it on my own. Then I held his hand when he confided to suffering from neurosis and depression. He was a faithful Christian Scientist, yet confessed he had seen a medical doctor for help, and he cried. He edited a travel page or section twice weekly for thirty-eight years, and then retired in New Hampshire. He and his wife lived very well, but he despaired the decline of the *Christian Science Monitor*, now reduced to a shadow of itself after the glorious years when he had worked there under the noted editor, Erwin Canham.

When I visited, Leavitt and his wife were living atop Sugar Hill, where they communed with the high peaks of the White Mountains. With vistas of snowy Mount Washington and the Presidential Range from their front lawn, they had no need to pack and scramble. I pored over columns he wrote for the *Monitor* from all over the world and was struck by the idea he was writing ecologically without even knowing it. He wrote in 1947 that New England was accessible but not to be seen in haste:

> Tourists streaking across New England highways, darting through
> its villages and towns, take away with them a few mementos of
> dust and a blurred view of the countryside.
>
> New England wasn't made overnight. Neither can it be seen
> overnight. One travels too fast to reap the sweet fragrance of an

apple orchard in full flower or to thoroughly enjoy the flavor given off by an old weather-beaten house sheltered by a sweeping elm.

Most of what we wrote in the travel pages and magazines *has* been filed and forgotten, but I'm glad to slow myself down to reap the harvest once again, including "the sweet fragrance of an apple orchard in full flower" and the pleasure of the company of colleagues with whom I shared it.

CHAPTER 12

Following the path of Devoto and Neuberger – To 11,000 feet in a Rocky Mountain wilderness – Forestry friends and teachers – Finding "the woods are lovely, dark and deep"

After my first two books, I was ready to advance from guidebooks to something of more substance. I was fortunate at Doubleday to work with an able and encouraging editor, Sam Vaughan, but I had no theme to propose to him, at least not yet. Around Washington, I was on a growing and learning curve, knocking on doors and asking questions of government bureaus and conservation organizations, meeting people with experience and ideas to share with me. I read assorted periodicals and books. My favorite role models were Bernard DeVoto and Richard Neuberger. They were like latter-day Lincoln Steffenses, writers I admired and aspired to emulate.

DeVoto was an essayist and historian, who won the Pulitzer Prize in 1948 for *Across the Wide Missouri*. He was born in the West (Utah) but lived in the East (Cambridge, Massachusetts). He wrote a provocative column, The Easy Chair, every month in *Harper's*. That column was almost as old as *Harper's* itself, dating back to October 1851. DeVoto described it as "a column of personal opinion" and made the most of it with his own view of topics of the day, including activities of the FBI and book censors in Maine. He contributed to other magazines as well (including *True,* for which he wrote a celebrated article on how to mix a dry martini). I met DeVoto several times, finding him as vigorous in person as he was in print. He had a broad nose that looked to me as though it might have been flattened by a punch. A friend of mine, William K. Wyant, a Washington correspondent for the *St. Louis Post-Dispatch*, described DeVoto as "a magnificent freestyle barroom brawler in debate," which was exactly as I observed him.

In one of his pieces in *Harper's*, DeVoto explained the call to advocacy. Some judgments, he said, are quite simple: express yourself and you have nothing else to do. "But there are also judgments that require you to commit yourself, to stick your neck out. Expressing them in print obliges you to go on to advocacy. They get home to people's beliefs and feelings about important things, and that makes them inflammable." In the 1950s, he tackled a major issue of the time: the proposal by the powerful Bureau of Reclamation to build dams across the Green and Yampa Rivers in Dinosaur National Monument, a remote, haunting, little-known wilderness in eastern Utah, his own native state. If Congress approved those dams, it might well set a precedent for intruding in other national parks as well.

In columns and articles with titles like "The Anxious West" and "The West Against Itself," he championed public lands and their importance, excoriating industries that sought to exploit those lands. Stockmen grazing (often overgrazing) livestock on national forest rangelands were a favorite target. Wyant wrote that DeVoto "applied his scourge with a remarkably effective mixture of humor, sarcasm, and gentlemanly abuse." The "Cattle Kingdom," as DeVoto called it, roared in anguish and charged that the Forest Service was feeding him material to generate public support for its own position.

Following DeVoto's death in 1955, Senator Richard Neuberger of Oregon called him "the most effective conservationist of the twentieth century," which may well have been true. Neuberger was a significant figure in his own right. He was a Jewish boy born in Portland with a taste for journalism and politics. As a student journalist at the University of Oregon, he became editor of the student newspaper, through which he campaigned for abolition of mandatory military training and compulsory student fees. His grades were low and he left without graduating, but that did not stop him from a career writing for a wide range of periodicals, including *Esquire, Harper's, The Nation, Holiday,* and the *New York Times.*

Neuberger grew from an observer into a participant, first as a member of the Oregon legislature and then the state senate. After his wife, Maurine, took his old seat, they constituted a formidable team, championing progressive legislation in both houses. Then in 1954, he ran for the United States Senate. With little funding and without staff or PR people, they covered the cities, towns, and crossroads of Oregon and won. Once elected and until his untimely death in 1960, he was associated with every piece of environmental legislation and was considered "Mr. Conservation." He supported efforts of citizen groups to block devastating dam projects, like Dworshak in Idaho, despite the pressure for these projects by the power brokers of the Senate. Sometimes he dispatched Maurine to attend social functions while he stayed home to meet a magazine deadline, since he thought of himself foremost as a writer.

The Neubergers worked diligently in the legislature to eliminate billboards from Oregon highways. I first learned of them while working on the same issue at the AAA. It was a phase of my environmental awakening. As part of my job, I would read and track Sunday travel sections in various newspapers. Thus, the first time I read about the Wilderness Act (called the Wilderness Bill at that time) was in the *New York Times* of May 15, 1956. In the column headed Conservation (on the back page of the travel section), John B. Oakes reported that Senator Hubert Humphrey of Minnesota was sponsoring legislation to establish a national wilderness preservation system. "The idea is certainly worth exploring," Oakes wrote, "if what is left of our country in a natural state is worth saving, as many of us believe it is." That stirred my conscience and my curiosity to learn more.

So it was probably no accident that in 1960 a fellow named Clint Davis came into my life and added a new dimension to it. He was the director of information and education (another way of saying public relations) of the U.S. Forest Service; I had met him at various functions around Washington and had called at his office. At that point I understood little about the Forest Service or the national forests. I did know they were much larger and covered more of the country than the national parks, and that many scenic areas were available for recreation; unlike the parks, however, the national forests were also open for commercial uses such as logging and grazing. Perhaps it was incongruent, but the concept of preserving wilderness had originated in the Forest Service years before and the agency actually was administering large areas of the West as wilderness.

That much I knew, in a vague way. Davis had seen some of my published writing on the national parks and wanted to interest me in writing about the national forests as well. We talked a few times and then he invited me to join him on a pack trip into the Bridger Wilderness of Wyoming, south of Yellowstone and the Grand Tetons, with a group sponsored by the American Forestry Association called Trail Riders of the Wilderness. We would visit other national forests in the area and be gone for three weeks.

That invitation was easy to accept and the trip turned out to be a magic time for me. The fifteen or so trail riders were city people, mostly professionals wanting a different kind of vacation. Few were expert riders.

Neither was I—in fact, I was glad my horse, Midnight, did the heavy work, enabling me to explore a side of America I had known only from picture books and history books. We rode uphill, downhill, alongside sheer rocky crests, and across streams and green meadows in the Wind River Mountains, one of the most rugged sections of the entire Rocky chain. Woods and valleys were abloom with wildflowers. At one point, we came to the confluence of plunging streams forming the headwaters of the Green River. The color really was green, caused by milky glacial particles suspended in the water. At 11,000 feet, we were in the country explored by General John C. Fremont in 1842. Overcome by the power of natural stillness, he described it as "a concourse of lakes and rushing waters, mountains of rock, dells and ravines of the most exquisite beauty, all kept green and fresh by the great moisture in the air and sown with brilliant flowers."

For myself, now above timberline, beyond civilization, and free of its artificial noises, close enough to touch stars, I felt connected with the universe as I had while flying over the wild oceans years before. Later, after the trip was done, Jim Harrower, hardware dealer in the town of Pinedale and local historian, drove me to a summit above town where he had taken Bernard DeVoto while helping in research for *Across the Wide Missouri*. So I felt a kinship with DeVoto as well.

While on the trip, Clint and I talked at length about the national forests, the Forest Service, and the issue of preserving wilderness, which Congress was then considering. He didn't try to convince me of anything as far as I could tell, but wanted me to see things for myself. He was a likeable, outgoing southerner, a very big fellow, at least six-feet-three with a large body on his frame, which made me sorry for the horse he rode. He carried and used a movie camera for a film he said might be made about the trail ride. This was before cell phones, but he had a phone with him and somehow kept daily contact with various Forest Service installations (which to me did not seem appropriate in the wilderness), and he also dispatched local forest rangers to ride out on one mission or another.

It struck me while we talked and while we rode in the Bridger Wilderness that I was privy to something important here. National forests were spread across the country; they had been established around the turn of the twentieth century to protect the public interest from exploitation by commercial logging, ranching, and mining. I thought I was fairly informed about such things but I was wrong. Actually I knew little about them, so how much could the public know? Besides, I was experiencing in the Bridger Wilderness a marvelous fragment of America that I hadn't realized existed, and there were more of them—I didn't know where or how many, but I believed them to be rich in history and adventure as well as scenery.

This was the book idea I was looking for. When I returned home I wrote to Sam Vaughan at Doubleday, outlining my idea. It took a little time but he responded with approval, a modest advance and helpful advice: "Remember that you are not writing for *Parade*, where you have to write tight. Let yourself go, and write up...."

When I shared the news of my book contract with Clint, he was pleased. That was to be expected. Then I said something like, "I would like to get your help when I go around to visit the forests." I meant in terms of research data and contacts with Forest Service field personnel, but he saw something else in it. For a moment he was thoughtful; then he cited a provision in law directing the Forest Service to encourage public understanding of forestry. That became the basis of the help—the support, I should say—he was able to provide to me. In due course, the Forest Service paid me a consultant's fee to research and write my book, plus transportation expenses and per diem. I like to think I was not co-opted, and that my viewpoint would have been the same without the fee, but it was far more than I could have hoped for. I do not believe that I was co-opted, though in retrospect I should have acknowledged this arrangement in the book.

Subsequently I made a series of trips around the country exploring forests and interviewing forest people. In those days I respected and admired foresters as professionals serving the public interest. They were my friends and teachers, who introduced me, through lessons in the field, to taxonomy, dendrology, silviculture, hydrology, and wildlife science; they conducted their business as individuals with social conscience, sound science, and vision, while the Forest Service was still proudly pursuing the conservation crusade that Gifford Pinchot had started. That was my view.

I learned about forest policy and administration, and forest history. I went to the national forests of southern Appalachia, beginning at the Pisgah National Forest in North Carolina, the "cradle of forestry" where Pinchot began his career in 1891 (when it was still part of the Biltmore estate of George Washington Vanderbilt). I called at byroads and backcountry because that was where the forests were. Everywhere I saw wonderful wild gardens scarcely known beyond the local communities. I became acquainted with rain forests of the Pacific Northwest and desert gardens in the Southwest.

In Georgia, I visited the Chattahoochee National Forest (whose name comes from the Cherokee word for "flowering rock," a reference to the many waterfalls tumbling in the highlands), with the beauty of the mountains accented in spring by dogwood, redbud, mountain laurel, azalea, and rhododendron.

I was impressed by the Forest Service management system without seriously questioning it. I felt there was drama, personality, and even romance in forestry and forest history, yet the national forests were run by technical people. They were trained in commodity production, like agronomists, with scant attention to philosophy or the values of scenery in its own right.

Fortunately nobody told me what to write. I recognized that timber had a place, but when I looked at a forest I saw trees and the message that comes with them. So, in choosing the title, I turned to the opening of Robert Frost's poem, "Stopping by Woods on a Snowy Evening": "Whose woods these are I think I know, / His house is in the village though; / He will not see me stopping here / To watch his woods fill up with snow."

I dedicated the book to "the inspiring memory of Bernard DeVoto and Richard Neuberger, who loved and championed the national forests." The book was well received when it appeared in 1962, doubtless in some degree because of the rising tide of environmental awareness. The public had a fair notion of national parks, but national forests were something else—larger but more amorphous and less understood. This was my first serious work in conservation. It was a selection of the Literary Guild and the Outdoor Life Book Club; it was reviewed by Senator Clinton P. Anderson of New Mexico in the *Washington Post,* and by Alfred A. Knopf in the *New York Herald Tribune.* All the conservation and natural resource publications paid some attention to it. Monroe Bush began his review in *American Forests* by calling it "the most mature survey that I have seen of the vast Forest Service lands which comprise one-tenth of the United States." He concluded: "Frome loves these rich and magnificent forests. As a practical reporter he understands the forces which maintain and utilize them. He obviously respects the skill and dedication of the U.S. Forest Service itself. Other than that, he is entirely his own man."

I received a stream of mail from Forest Service foresters, their wives, mothers, and widows. The book made them feel good about themselves, their work, and their organization. They wrote to me about earlier times, when life in this country was less complicated by technology, and when public agencies were run by people who functioned as individuals rather than as cogs in bureaucratic machinery. Though often untrained by professional institutions, foresters could still be called professionals, considering that they learned by doing—through direct observation and experience in the forest and through direct communication with some of the most rural communities in America. Those forestry pioneers were called "custodians," though "guardians" might have been a more fitting term, for they protected vast areas of this country.

"We should look at forests as a source of 'good' as well as 'wood,'" Arthur Woody, a celebrated ranger in north Georgia, would tell young foresters training under him. Woody, in 1925, negotiated the purchase of Sosebee Cove from a farmer who had held it all his life and then was over seventy-five. Believing it to be the finest stand of unlogged tulip poplar in the state, Woody convinced his superiors to purchase it for ten dollars an acre, the highest price the Forest Service paid in those days. When he died in 1946, funeral services for Woody at a backcountry church cemetery were attended by 1,500 persons from all parts of the state.

That was really something. Through my research and writing, I had absorbed a great deal about forests and forestry, including science, history, civics, politics, and culture, but those were external matters. The story of Woody taught something about inner truth, just as I had learned from Robert Frost directing me to listen to "the sweep / Of easy wind and downy flake," to the many voices of the forest that I somehow had been chosen to hear.

CHAPTER 13

I became a magazine columnist – Sticking to the truth, really bad enough without stretching it – Writing about politics and bureaucracy, naming the wrongdoers – "Please help us save this park"

In 1966 I became a columnist for *American Forests* magazine. No, I can't say that it was one of the country's leading journals, but it gave me a platform, a monthly space from which to express my views on conservation and natural resource politics, without fear or favor, as I liked to say. Moreover, a little over one year later I began writing a second column for a much larger periodical, this time as conservation editor of *Field & Stream*. I did not solicit or apply for either of these assignments. I was open to them, but both came after me. The editors may have thought I was producing particularly outstanding work, but not necessarily. At that time, few if any in the media were tracking issues in conservation and the environment as I was. Most newspapers and magazines didn't think it was worth covering.

John Oakes told me how it worked at the *New York Times*. We had become friends at some point following Oakes's appointment in 1961 as editor of the editorial page of the *Times*; we would meet now and then, based on his personal, longtime interest in the environment. He told me of a conversation he had had with Turner Catledge, the managing editor of the *Times*. Oakes said, "Turner, the environment is getting to be big news. Why don't you assign somebody to cover it regularly?" But Catledge brushed him off. "When there's a story there, we'll cover it." In short, it wasn't important enough and a good reporter could handle it easily as the need arose.

This may explain why the *Times* ridiculed *Silent Spring*, the landmark book by Rachel Carson, soon after it appeared in 1962. The *Times* called it "wholly inaccurate" and said it would "unnecessarily frighten the readers." But that newspaper was not alone. *Time* asserted that accidental poisonings from pesticides were "very rare," though Carson and history have shown otherwise. That was the media at work: deriding Carson as a bird lover, fish lover, cat lover, and devotee of a mystical cult, reacting without serious research or investigative reporting, and more willing to heed the public relations material furnished by the pesticide industry than the substantive scholarly work of a diligent crusader.

For my own part, through contacts with the Forest Service, I met and came to know the secretary of agriculture, Orville L. Freeman. He was a former governor of Minnesota, young and progressive. He liked having me around. Once he included me along with eight or ten news reporters at lunch to discuss conservation perspectives. I was appalled at the shallowness of the questions, the lack of knowledge or perception, the inability to penetrate the superficial and come to grips with basic issues. "Yes, I think I've answered that question a hundred times, " as Freeman said at one point, referring to recurring media queries that were often off the mark. "I don't expect to be fired, to quit, or to be appointed an ambassador."

I began writing for *American Forests* in January 1960 with an article about the pack trip of the summer before in the Wind River Mountains of Wyoming. After I had contributed several more articles, Jim Craig, the editor, made me a columnist. My first column, in March 1966, was about the Lueneburger Heide, a German nature reserve on sandy heathland that I thought might serve as a model for consideration in America.

American Forests was not a first-class magazine, maybe not even a second-class, but a likeable, readable third-class. It published articles and essays by Jesse Stuart, the Kentucky poet and novelist, and Leonard Hall, St. Louis columnist, conservationist, and author (known as "the squire of Possum Trot"), plus a literate column of book reviews by Monroe Bush. The magazine had a bit of a split personality. On one side, most of its readers were everyday people who grew trees in their backyards or who liked trees and parks. On the other side were professionals trained in forestry or employed in the forest products industry; forestry deans and professors contributed technical (sometimes polemical and pontifical) essays, and abundant letters to the editor extolled the virtues of industrial forest production. *American Forests* had a substantial circulation for a conservation publication—about 80,000 at its high point—and the longtime editor, Jim Craig, tried to keep a balance to it. He told me that he wanted to edit the magazine as a forum open to diverse ideas; that was why he hired me—to "ward off blandness."

It was the official publication of the American Forestry Association, an old-line organization headquartered in a small, attractive old building near the White House. The AFA called itself the country's oldest conservation organization with some justification. It was established in 1875 under the auspices of the American Association for the Advancement of Science at a time of rising concern over privatization and fires threatening America's forests. By the time I came along, the AFA was at the conservative end of the conservation movement. It endeavored to appeal to a broad public, but was controlled by a timber-first cadre. I mean that most of its directors came from the timber industry, Forest Service, and forestry schools.

Field & Stream was a much larger magazine with a circulation of almost two million. Before joining the staff, I assumed it was read mostly in barbershops in rural communities and was aimed at that level of readership. But I also knew that Corey Ford and Robert Ruark, two formidable writers of the 1940s and '50s, had been columnists, and that in years gone by Aldo Leopold and Zane Grey had contributed articles or essays to it.

I was not a hunter and not much of a fisherman. I enjoyed and loved the out-of-doors, true enough—more as an activist and advocate for nature than as a writer. I thought Field & Stream's appeal was to users rather than conservers of the outdoors, and that I was hardly meant to write for it. At the time, I was reading Willa Cather's Death Comes for the Archbishop. I had been on a travel writing project in New Mexico and when I came to Santa Fe someone showed me the church that figured in the novel. I thought I should read that book and learn something about the author. I found Cather had been a newspaper journalist and an editor at McClure's during the muckraking days in the early twentieth century. She felt a love of the land and advocated what today would be called the counterculture of antimaterialism. This was clear in her description of Father Latour, the young pioneer priest (later the archbishop), traveling on horseback through Navajo country with his Indian friend, Eusabio. It took them almost two weeks between blinding sandstorms and brilliant sunlight to cover the 400 miles to Santa Fe.

Riding with Eusabio was like riding with the landscape made human; he accepted chance and the weather as the country did. When they left the tree or rock or sand dune that had sheltered them overnight, Eusabio was careful to obliterate every trace of their presence. He buried the embers of the fire and the remnants of food, unpiled the stones he had piled together, and filled the holes he had scooped in the sand. It was the Indian's way to pass through a country without disturbing anything, like fish through water, or birds in the air.

> It was as if the great country were asleep, and they wished to carry on their lives without awakening it; or as if the spirits of earth and

air and water were things not to antagonize and arouse. When they hunted, it was with the same discretion; an Indian hunt was never a slaughter. They ravaged neither the rivers nor the forest, and if they irrigated, they took as little water as would serve their needs. The land and all that it bore they treated with consideration; not attempting to improve it, they never desecrated it.

Clare Conley, the editor of *Field & Stream*, never asked me what I read or questioned my views on wilderness, or hunting, or politics. He had read my articles elsewhere and wanted to give his readers something more than stories about the old fishing guide and the gore connected with killing a bear. After assigning me to write two articles for publication, he expressed confidence that I could bring something of value to the magazine. He proposed to engage me as conservation editor and brought me to New York for an interview with the publisher, Franklin Forsberg. In this period *Field & Stream* was owned by CBS and shared a floor in the Madison Avenue building with Holt, Rinehart (or perhaps it was still Holt, Rinehart & Winston), an old respected book publishing firm that had lost its independence and was now another CBS subsidiary.

We were well into the age of conglomeration, in which publishers were swallowed whole, only to be devoured again by larger fish and spat out to be gobbled up by another profit-seeking predator. At this time, Forsberg appeared to run *Field & Stream* without interference from CBS. He was courtly and genial; he asked how much money I wanted. "Go for it," I told myself and when I gave a figure, he agreed without blinking. I don't remember the amount, but Conley was impressed and, after we left the publisher's office, said that I had just become the magazine's highest paid columnist.

From then on, I spent considerable time with Conley. He was a native of Idaho, a state with wildlife and wild country still abundant, who had studied at Stanford and then came east to work in New York, first as managing editor and then as editor of *Field & Stream*. I was fortunate with both magazines, *Field & Stream* and *American Forests*, that nobody told me what to write or how to write it. I was fortunate also that they were essentially noncompetitive, although I tried to assess the difference in the readerships and provide accordingly. From the outset, readers responded with many letters either to me or to the editor, mostly but not always supportive. At *American Forests*, the foresters were checking me out, and at *Field & Stream*, the hunters were. One wrote to complain that my first feature was "the year's best propaganda piece in support of the game management bureaucracy who defend mammalian predators...." With some hunters, it was all about game birds and animals and never mind the rest.

In reviewing my early columns at *American Forests,* I find that at first I wrote rather gentle reports and commentaries: about coastal islands off the Carolinas and Georgia, my visit to the forestry school Gifford Pinchot attended at Nancy in France, and citizen efforts to save Sunfish Pond in the Kittatinny Mountains of New Jersey from a dreadful water storage project. Then I grew bolder. I wrote critically but spread the criticism around. All sorts of people sent me tips, confidential government and industry reports, and appeals for help regarding one eco-calamity or another. They were hard to resist: for example, when a reader sent me the Neiman Marcus Christmas catalogue offering an exotic selection of jaguar coats, vicuna paw pillows, natural cloud leopard coats, belts made from sea turtles, alligator belts, and natural kit fox skins.

I let the chips fall where they might, while always trying to stick to the truth, which was really bad enough without stretching it. This led people with special interests to complain:

> "I wish to take this opportunity to categorically deny the allegation in Mike Frome's column in the May issue of *American Forests* that any of our California State Fish and Game biologists have buckled under political pressure...."

> "We see little to be gained in sweeping emotional statements to rally public opinion against 'spotted cat' coats and 'alligator' shoes...."

> "Mr. Frome's 'facts' concerning the predator control program as it is carried on in Arizona today are completely out of date and wholly untrue...."

> "Using misinformation, insinuation and innuendo to generate controversy may buy shoes for a clever writer's children, but it serves no other useful purpose...."[1]

I didn't mean to write mean things and upset people, but the facts were waiting to be written and they had not been. I did my homework, often following expressions of concern from private citizens. Once I turned to the tule elk of California, a rare and endangered species, because of an appeal from a California woman, Beulah Edmiston, who headed the Friends of the Tule Elk and had already knocked on many doors. She sent me data showing that great herds of untold thousands of tule elk had once roamed the central and coastal valleys of California before they were slaughtered by ranchers and market hunters. A few animals hid in the bulrushes, or tules. From that slender group, the elk made their miraculous comeback and in 1933 were transplanted to become a famous herd in Owens Valley, east of the Sierra crest. The area served primarily to ensure metropolitan Los Angeles water supply but also was used, under lease, for livestock grazing. In recent years, cattlemen complained about having to share their range. Consequently deliberate efforts were made to restrict the numbers of elk.

Whenever the tule elk increased to more than 300, a legal hunt on October weekends was held to reduce the total to 250, a figure set arbitrarily by the California Fish and Game Commission as "the carrying capacity." All the evidence strongly indicated the exercise was far more of a slaughter than a sport, and that it bore scant relationship to scientific game management. I was glad to publicize Ms. Edmiston's cause and to cheer when she ultimately succeeded in stopping the slaughter mistakenly called a "hunt" and in gaining protection in various California preserves for the tule elk at a minimum of two thousand in number.

In another instance, I wrote a column in tribute to Edward Meeman, a noted newspaper editor and conservationist who had died in Memphis at age seventy-seven. This led to several letters from members of the Friends of Overton Park in Memphis. They were touched to read the tribute to their friend Meeman and missed him in the fight to save Overton Park from construction of an interstate highway through the heart of the park. They felt that even though he was editor emeritus of the *Press-Scimitar*, Meeman's hands were tied, and that Scripps-Howard in Memphis was in league with downtown commercial interests in support of the freeway. They wrote:

> Please help us save this midtown park. The park's 300 acres have trees 350 years old and it is sorely needed as high-rises go up in this area and an old people's home is on one side. Why take federal funds to build an unneeded freeway through a park, then take 50 percent to buy open space (having destroyed a natural, existing one), then use 75 percent to fight air pollution which the freeway has helped bring to the city. How wasteful can we get?

I investigated and found that Scripps-Howard (which controlled both Memphis newspapers) had ridiculed the park defenders and tried to create a public impression that the issue had been settled irrevocably and that nothing further could be done by public interest. It belittled any politician who dared to challenge the proposed park invasion. In March 1968, I devoted a column to Overton Park, writing that "an established park is an integral and sacred part of the American city—when the choice must be made between open space and a highway it makes more sense to locate the highway elsewhere than to invade the park."

Overton Park ultimately was saved, thanks to the persistence of a group of citizens who pursued their concerns to the United States Supreme Court. Ironically, the *Memphis Press-Scimitar* bet on the wrong horse and folded, while Scripps-Howard blithely continued to present an annual award for conservation writing in memorial tribute to Ed Meeman.

Inevitably I turned to forestry in my column, although I did not make up or choose the issues. They were already evident and debated in the pages of *American Forests* and elsewhere. In a letter to the editor pubished in the August 1970 issue, Leon Minckler, a forestry professor at Virginia Polytechnic Institute, wrote:

> Clear-cutting is not necessary for successful hardwood regeneration and it is not the only way that hardwood forests can be managed. If foresters say it is the only way, they are misleading the public. As professionals, foresters must know the alternatives which will meet the needs and desires of woodland owners and the general public.

In the West, the Sierra Club engaged its own staff forester, Gordon Robinson, a professional with many years' experience managing large blocks of commercial timberland. He confirmed suspicions that serious mistakes were being made in the public forests and gave thoughtful arguments in contesting them. In the Northwest, Brock Evans for the Sierra Club, and the North Cascades Conservation Council made a national issue of Forest Service plans to clear-cut the last stands of scenic old growth.

Dale Burk, the outdoors editor of the *Missoulian* in western Montana, wrote a series of nine articles about clear-cutting and "terracing"—a harsh means of adapting crop farming to forests—in the Bitterroot National Forest. Burk interviewed loggers, ranchers, and old Bitterrooters; he showed clear-cutting on a large scale as a victory of technology over nature, with new types of machinery upending 1,500 to 1,800 trees in the course of a day.

I found that I shared these concerns. My friends in the agency had taught me to ask questions, but now I asked questions they could not answer. Thus, in February 1970, I wrote:

> The difficulty is that Forest Service people, or any other group of land management officials, deals largely with men experienced in their own fields. Competence is judged to a great extent within the bounds of their professions. They are not at home in the thought world of our environment....
>
> The day when "the forester knows best" is over. The sooner this is recognized the better off we all shall be. Foresters, with all credit to them, rarely have the depth and breadth of vision to make ecological and environmental judgments.

Foresters didn't like that, but other readers did. Jim Craig, the editor, had no objection and ran my columns as I wrote them.

In *Field & Stream* I sometimes covered the same ground but focused on showing the effects of logging on wildlife and its habitat. I traveled around the country, investigating and writing about politics, bureaucracy, and corporate power, naming the wrongdoers, trying to involve and activate readers so they would not feel helpless against the odds. That for me was good journalism, as Lincoln Steffens had inspired me to pursue it. I found hunters and fishermen receptive and responsive to the conservation message. Rednecks who wrote in penciled scrawl and university professors alike told me of their concern over degradation of particular places they cared about. In looking back, I believe that I struck a chord among outdoors men and women who wanted to rise above themselves, and above exploitation. They needed to be told who was responsible and what they could do to save what was left, and Conley encouraged me every step of the way.

Besides, I learned that I was not the only one who cared, that *Field & Stream* published a variety of memorable pieces by gifted writers. Ted Trueblood, an Idaho-based columnist, was at the top of the list. My wife, Thelma, read him religiously, and I'm sure other women did too. He was a hunter, but Ted described the walking, the stillness, the physical exercise, life around the campfire, the pride in roughing it, and working for game—all the components showing the human place in the natural scene without being intruder or stranger. "You must respect your fish or game, " he wrote.

"Otherwise, it has no value. And nobody respects fish and game so much as anglers and hunters, nor loves them so well." That was true of him and of sportsmen who followed his ways.

As a contributing editor, I worked at home but also had a base at the magazine's office in New York, plus income and an expense account, and latitude to pursue other activities. On the masthead I was listed as department editor. *Field & Stream* and its competitors, *Outdoor Life* and *Sports Afield*—"the big three"—concentrated on how-to articles: how to catch fish and kill game based on secrets from an old guide named Joe. The advertising was about fishing tackle, rods and reels, high-powered rifles, telescopic lenses, outboard motors, trail bikes, snowmobiles, and game preserves mostly preserving game for the kill. They made me feel that I was in the wrong place, but at least in the wrong place at the right time.

I think part of what my bosses at *Field & Stream* wanted was a presence in Washington. Forsberg came down a few times and I would arrange lunch with a senator or congressman or the secretary of the interior. I don't mean to be a namedropper, but with the *Field & Stream* connection, I could reach these people. Conley and I would go see bureau chiefs, politicians, and environmental leaders, even hosting a few affairs. He wanted to know what I was doing, who I was talking to, what I asked, and what I was told. I never felt he was looking over my shoulder, only that he wanted to be part of the action. He was a sportsman's sportsman who felt the urgency of protecting the environment and of blowing the whistle on despoilers and destroyers.

We talked on the phone almost every day. Early in 1970, he asked for my input on a seventy-fifth anniversary issue in June. I thought about it and proposed "A Symposium on the Shape of Tomorrow," with a contribution by President Richard Nixon, followed by essays by five leading scientists and educators. Nixon didn't know or care anything about the environment, but somebody in the White House certainly did and wrote a progressive and formidable statement for him that included this call to action:

> What we need today is not only *conservation*, but *restoration* as well. We must continue to conserve our remaining natural resources and wild places—but we must also restore to our nation and our people much that has been taken away from them. Our task is not so much to bring Americans "back to nature," but to bring nature back to Americans.

We could not have hoped for more and I was pleased to play my part. For the Symposium on the Shape of Tomorrow, I chose (with Conley's approval) five leading scientists: Barry Commoner, then at Washington University in St. Louis, who told about the effects of technology on modern society; Paul Ehrlich of Stanford, who had electrified the nation two years before with his book *The Population Bomb*; Hugh Iltis, noted botanist and preservationist at the University of Wisconsin; Eugene Odum of the University of Georgia, pioneer in ecology; Douglas H. Pimlott, of the University of Toronto, much honored for work on the ecology of wolves; and Charles Wurster of the State University of New York at Stony Brook, a scientific leader in the campaign against DDT. I called each one, explained what it was about, and offered a modest fee. All were willing—they too felt the sense of mission—and did great work addressed to outdoors people. There was still time, they warned, but we needed to be concerned, involved, and active. Odum summed it up, warning that human ecology, rather than wildlife ecology, must become the chief concern.

> If we don't intelligently "manage" our own population, there not only will be no outdoor recreation as we now enjoy it, but the quality of human existence in general will deteriorate just as surely as the quality of the individual deer and elk deteriorates on an overcrowded range. Fortunately, attitudes toward the natural environment are slowly changing so that people (and especially the youth) realize the optimum density is something less than the maximum that could be supported, and, therefore, that control of both population growth and economic development is necessary.

Conley wanted to make the most of that particular issue and so we distributed copies to all the members of Congress. They receive that kind of material all the time; still, a number acknowledged and thanked us. Over the years I interviewed and came to know various members of both parties in both houses. I found that generally they were not ecologists, historians, or scientists, either by education or experience, and only occasionally by inclination. Politics they knew better, intuitively responding to local interests and pressures, but a few along the way actually understood and cared about land and landscape in a personal way.

Conley and I came up with another idea: in September 1968, we published a feature showing readers how to "Rate Your Candidate" for Congress on thirteen key conservation issues including public land management, water pollution, and endangered species. We told readers to clip out the questions and mail them to congressional candidates, then rated fifty of them (incumbents and aspirants) in the following categories:

Out In Front: Deserve cheers and support
Good Men: Usually can be counted on
Faced In the Right Direction: Need occasional reminders
Too Late to Be Great
The Expendables: Won't be missed by conservationists

Some of those who were rated low ignored us; others wrote letters of protest, insisting we did not appreciate how they really were working for conservation. But the point we were trying to get across was that promises printed in party platforms bore little relationship to actual performance. In 1970, we expanded the feature, rating all one hundred members of the Senate and more than one hundred members of the House, this time using a point system (from excellent, 85 to 100 points, to poor, below 40 points). Along with their voting records I used interviews with national and grassroots conservation organizations to help in making assessments.

Early in 1972, I proposed to rate every member of Congress. Conley approved and authorized hiring a special assistant for the project. We recognized that congressmen tend to cover their tracks by amending and emasculating legislation until it looks good but has lost its meaning. As we explained to readers:

Congress itself has devised and compounded an intricate, tricky legislative system that utterly overawes and befuddles the American public. It is difficult to dig behind the surface into the cogs and wheels that make things go. Many key decisions are not reached in open view, but rather by a handful of power brokers behind closed doors. Our mission is to open the doors.

We sent a questionnaire to every member of Congress and almost three hundred replies were received from both houses. We endeavored in our questionnaire to look past the consensus votes. Representative David Obey, a Wisconsin Democrat, acknowledged that we had a point in doing so:

Politicians are, I think, the least able to judge their own contributions to enhancing environmental quality. In fact, after reading 100 or so letters from congressmen and senators in response to your letter of March 7th, you may be wondering why we are not living in an environmental paradise.

In the September 1972 issue, we published the ratings of all 100 members of the Senate and 435 members of the House. We showed their voting records on eight important environmental bills in the Senate and twelve in the House. Percent figures were calculated by dividing the number of correct pro-environment votes by the number of total votes cast. We weighed other factors as well: degree of understanding, degree of commitment, extent of involvement, and effectiveness in getting things done. Replies were received from 220 members of the House and 58 members of the Senate, surprising in the case of the latter since many were not up for election in 1972.

Some readers responded gratefully. One southerner wrote: "Put a little heat on Dixie; we've got sportsmen down here as well as moonshiners. Prod us up a little, we could use it." The Idaho Wildlife Federation sent a bulletin urging its members to read the September issue: "With the tool provided we may be able to curtail some of the farces being foisted on us and be more effective."

I felt that we were on the right track, breaking new ground and showing the way for our readers. In both magazines, *American Forests* and *Field & Stream*, I believed I was writing truth to power, as I was meant to do.

Chapter 14

A new and different experience at Yale – Students rocked the boat, demanding answers – Meeting mountain people, all helpful – Joining the defense of Smoky Mountains wilderness

My work in conservation and natural resources attracted some attention in the 1960s and '70s. I received invitations to write, and to speak at workshops, seminars, grassroots rallies, the 1967 Sierra Club Biennial Wilderness Conference in San Francisco, and at various colleges and universities. Maybe it was because the time was right in the light of rising environmental concern, or maybe I had something to say worth heeding, or a way of saying it. Over the years, I heard many exceptional speakers and never considered myself one of them. I just did the best I could to "tell it like it is."

One of the first universities to invite me was Yale, specifically the School of Forestry. This was a new and different experience for me, meeting with refined young ladies and gentlemen, and with their prestigious professors. When I arrived at New Haven, the dean, at that time François Mergen, and two or three professors took me to lunch. The fare was more than ample, well served and leisurely, as though we had the afternoon to eat and talk. I won't say they took themselves seriously, but they certainly were self assured. Although I felt like a stranger in another world, they treated me as if *I* was the expert and worth taking seriously.

I spent that evening alone. I remember the date clearly. It was April 4, 1968, the very day that Martin Luther King was assassinated in Memphis. I felt depressed by radio and television accounts of outbursts of violence and fires in the inner cities of the country. I kept waking up during the night, thinking again and again that in modern America the educated and affluent escape crowds, concrete, and crime, breathing cleaner air in a cleaner environment, while the poor, especially the nonwhite, are trapped, disenfranchised from the bounties of our time. The lower the income, the lower the quality of life.

But how could I tell that? The next day I spoke in two or three classes and then to an assembly of students and faculty at Sage Hall, the headquarters of the graduate forestry school Gifford Pinchot established in 1900. He was a Yale man who studied forestry abroad because there were no schools for it in America. Now, as though forestry had run its course, the institution was called the School of Forestry and Environmental Studies, with the emphasis clearly on "environmental studies." It seemed appropriate to start by quoting the prominent Yale ecologist, Paul Sears: "Conservation is a point of view involved with the concept of freedom, human dignity, and the American spirit." I suppose that could mean anything, but nevertheless the white, middle-class students in the audience showed they were enthusiastic and eager to make a difference in their lives and in society.

It was much that way at one campus I visited after another. In the late 1960s, students started to rock the boat and demand answers. They lambasted the "misuse of science and technology" that led to pollution and a mode of production based on waste; they charged that the federal government and large corporations controlled science. They weren't sure how to proceed, but they wanted a change. On the first Earth Day, April 22, 1970, students all across the country showed their dissatisfaction with the status quo. I went around to speak at different schools, four in one week, to large and responsive audiences. They cheered when I urged them to challenge their professors and their textbooks, and to tackle tough environmental issues on their campus and community.

I could get away with speaking and thinking like that since I was a journalist, who came to hit and then to run, and not a professor meant to stay. Bernard DeVoto lived at Cambridge, Massachusetts, and lectured for a time at Harvard, though he was never hired to the full-time faculty. Nevertheless, he taught conservationists a key lesson: that while they themselves may exercise limited influence on social attitudes and values, through the media they can increase that influence many times.

DeVoto died in late 1955 (at age fifty-eight). Soon after he departed the scene, I entered it. Possibly people in the Forest Service thought I had the makings of a new DeVoto. Several years before Clint Davis, the Information and Education chief of the agency, had made it possible for me to receive a fee while traveling across the country and writing *Whose Woods These Are*. We never discussed it, but perhaps he expected that I would defend the Forest Service against its critics in logging and grazing, as DeVoto had done. Or maybe he hoped I would write kind words about recreation in the national forests as I had about the national parks. Whatever the reason, he befriended me, gave me writing assignments, and took me with him as a consultant on trips to various national forests and conferences.

One assignment was to write the script for a short film, *Wilderness Trail*, based on our pack trip in the Bridger Wilderness. The Information and Education office of the Forest Service, which Davis headed, produced credible films about fire prevention, courtesy in the woods, and other themes, but *Wilderness Trail* was a slapdash piece based on his camera work plus stock footage. One of his colleagues cautioned me while I was working on the script to be sure to provide adequate treatment of "multiple use"— that is, of legitimate sanctioned commercial use of forest resources outside of designated wilderness. Multiple use was the alpha and omega that sustained support for the agency from diverse and sometimes contradictory public quarters.

The same proviso arose anew when I was commissioned to write the text of a booklet, "Trees of the Forest—Their Beauty and Use." I confess that I loved looking at trees in the forest and learning that each of them was composed of root, stem, bark, branch, bud, leaf, flower and fruit, and also that I looked for the spirit of the tree. Considering it breathed, drank water, nourished itself, and transmitted qualities of heredity through reproduction, it seemed logical to believe there would be a spirit too. But my forester friends endeavored to set me straight, explaining that the tree had no nervous system; it couldn't move to water or shelter, and that, unlike humans and other animal species, it reacted unconsciously to stimulus. They were certain the tree couldn't have a spirit. To most foresters that tree was meant for use—and for them that was the beauty in it.

Another time, Davis asked me to come to the Forest Service office to see a film that might serve as a model for a project he had in mind. It was *Wilderness Alps of Stehekin* written, directed and filmed by David Brower, executive director of the Sierra Club. Though I had not yet seen the film, I had heard of it as part of a campaign by the Sierra Club and other conservation groups to promote the transfer of nearly one million acres in the North Cascades of Washington State from jurisdiction of the Forest Service to the National Park Service as a new national park.

Brower in this period of the 1960s was a singular and influential personality in the conservation movement. He was tall, erect, and athletic from his days in mountain climbing, and prematurely white-haired. He had attended the University of California for four years without graduating, and worked as an editor for the University of California Press and as a PR person for the concessionaire in Yosemite National Park. When he became the Sierra Club's first full-time paid executive, he transformed the club from a mostly California group of polite outdoors enthusiasts into a militant national organization committed to advocacy. He was a genius in communication, as is obvious in the *Wilderness Alps of Stehekin.* It was a marvelous film, beautifully photographed, and striking a spiritual chord, and thoroughly convincing that the heart of the North Cascades deserved protection and preservation (which Congress in 1968 voted to secure).

After viewing the film, Davis said, "I have in mind something with the same feeling, but about multiple use." I was glad and relieved that we both got busy with other things and nothing came of it, so the project did not interfere with our relationship. I valued our friendship and learned much from Clint; the best thing he gave me was a lesson in how to live. He would eat long breakfasts and insist on cooking Georgia-style redeye gravy if he had a chance to cook. He charcoaled steaks with moist hickory chips when he was at home, and ate a long, late supper wherever he was. He was kind and generous to people who had nothing to do with his work. He certainly was generous to me—and he probably never thought I owed him a thing.

It was probably wise to keep a little distance from the Forest Service, especially as I perceived flaws in forestry, and to refine connections elsewhere. And then, fortuitously, I received in the mail one day a cordial letter from Sam Vaughan, my editor at Doubleday in New York, asking if I would be interested in writing a book about the Great Smoky Mountains of western North Carolina and Tennessee. Apparently a Doubleday salesman in the field had determined there was a market for such a book and after *Whose Woods These Are,* I seemed the logical author for it.

Maybe so, but I questioned whether I was qualified, how long it would take, and whether it was something I really wanted to do. I had first seen the Smokies in 1947, when I found Gatlinburg to be still off the beaten path, a country crossroads, certainly with little resemblance to the traumatic, frenetic, and tawdry Gatlinburg of later years. I knew little about conservation or national parks or southern mountains or mountain people, but when I went to Newfound Gap and saw the bronze plaque marking establishment of the park amidst endless mountain splendor, I felt elevated and enriched in spirit.

Then I returned two or three years later as a travel writer on a tour for writers hosted by various regional promoters. I was introduced to mountain crafts people—woodcarvers, weavers, and makers of pots, dolls, and dulcimers—and to Cherokee Indians, park rangers, and forest rangers. Tourism was different then, more civic and cultural instead of overblown with commerciality and crowds as it later became. Tourism for the most part was compatible with the natural setting, rather than contradictory to it.

I kept coming back, traveling down the crest of the Blue Ridge, the eastern rampart of the Appalachian Mountains, first on the Skyline Drive in Shenandoah National Park and then the Blue Ridge Parkway, which links Shenandoah and the Smokies. I thought there was nothing like it—there were no billboards or high speeds as on the freeways; I could stop at mountaintop wildflower gardens, restored mills, weathered cabins, and overlooks facing farms and national forests. While researching *Whose Woods These Are* I was fortunate to visit byroads and backcountry of Appalachia. I saw the region had a unity to it, comprising a cultural and ecological province, yet each and every creek, creek valley, and ridgetop was distinctly its own.

I talked on the phone with Sam Vaughan and, once we agreed I would write the Smokies book, he challenged me again to raise my sights and foresaw the end result as "a small classic," to use his words. My initial thought was to make it something of a history and travel guide, but once I got into the research, I set the guide part aside for somebody else or some other time. I collected and read old and new books, booklets, and periodicals; I visited the Library of Congress, university libraries, and assorted bookstores and libraries in North Carolina and Tennessee. These excursions opened the door to new ideas and new personalities. I discovered *The Travels of William Bartram*, the record of a thrilling adventure into the natural domain still covering much of the South in colonial days. Bartram had failed in a variety of business undertakings in his native Philadelphia, then found his true calling when he set out to hunt plants and to paint and draw the natural world. Like a precursor of the modern ecologist, Bartram described the interdependence of creatures: the spider preying on a bumblebee that had lit to feed on the leaf of a plant, a coachwhip snake wreathing itself around the body of a grounded hawk, the battle between crayfish and goldfish, the swarming assembly of alligators feeding upon a vast solid bank of fish. To Bartram, every little thing had purpose, personality, and beauty. He taught friendship even with the rattlesnake, who is "never known to strike until he is first assaulted or fears himself in danger, and then always gives the earliest warning by the rattles at the extremity of his tail."

At Lowdermilk's, a venerable Washington bookstore that featured old and out-of-date government publications, I made two prize acquisitions: the *Fifth Annual Report of the Bureau of American Ethnology* (1883–84) and the *Nineteenth Annual Report of the Bureau of American Ethnology* (1897–98), oversized books of more than five hundred pages each, with maps, photographs, and illustrations. Those works were inspired by the director of the bureau, John Wesley Powell, a Civil War veteran and one of the great adventurers in American history. Powell was the first white man to lead a party in boats down the Colorado River through the Grand Canyon. Later, at the Bureau of Ethnology, he endeavored to record and interpret everything possible about America's native peoples before they were lost to civilization.

Powell dispatched one of his most able associates, James D. Mooney, to the Great Smoky Mountains to unlock the Cherokee storehouse of prayers, sacred songs, and formulas relating to all of human existence. Mooney collected and labeled more than five hundred plants used by the Indians for their food, medicines, and rituals, and which I was privy to examine in their repository, the herbarium of the Smithsonian Institution. Exactly what each plant revealed was beyond me, and yet I felt pleased that it had been saved and I should have the chance to see it.

I conducted considerable research on the ground. I hiked all over the park, often with rangers and naturalists, but found myself not nearly as interested in writing about trails and the plants as about the story of the mountains and their people and the story of the park itself. I met all kinds of people and virtually all were helpful to me—the old banker, bear hunter, fiddler, weaver, innkeeper, older people who told of times past. One summer, my family stayed for several weeks in a cottage above Maggie Valley on the North Carolina side. When my wife decided to take the children to Sunday school, she chose the Macedonia Baptist Church in Cherokee, where lessons were given in English and Cherokee. My son and daughter met Indian children, while I called on Jarrett Blythe, the chief of the Cherokee, who shared recollections of his childhood days and his grandfather's talks with him.

And then Harvey Broome came into my life. On my first hike with him, we ventured to the Chimney Tops, a steep climb, almost vertical for several hundred feet, hand over hand from one rocky perch to the next. It was raining and I dared to complain. Harvey was a gentle spirit, always with tolerance and good humor, and he set me straight with a laugh. "You don't complain about weather in the Smokies. You learn to accept it!" That story became part of the opening paragraph of *Strangers in High Places*.

Harvey was my friend and mentor. He was a Knoxville native who first came to the mountains as a boy and knew the Smokies intimately. He was graduated from the University of Tennessee in 1923 and three years later from Harvard Law School, but his love for the mountains transcended his professional career. Harvey took me on hikes and to his home in Knoxville. I observed that he walked sure-footed but lightly on the land. That was consistent with his commitment to a cause that went beyond sheer enjoyment of the out-of-doors to the preservation of wilderness as a natural resource in its own right.

I learned lessons from Harvey and lessons about him. For example, in 1936 he met with a handful of others—appropriately in the Great Smoky Mountains—to conceive a new organization to be called the Wilderness Society. Those present included Robert Marshall, a young man in his thirties who was pioneering federal programs in wilderness protection. Marshall as a boy in New York had tramped all across the Adirondacks (in the same way that Broome had tramped the Smokies) and gone on to adventurous hikes across the continent and to a creative career in government. Another was Benton MacKaye, a regional planner, philosopher, and social reformer who in the 1920s had originated the idea of the Appalachian Trail as "a footpath in the wilderness" extending from Maine to Georgia, or, as MacKaye saw it, "a sanctuary from the scramble of everyday worldly commercial life."

From the very beginning until the end of his life, Harvey Broome was a central figure in development of the Wilderness Society's ideology and advocacy. I came to him when he lived through his absolutely finest hours. I saw him in 1966 as tough and tenacious, never once countenancing the possibility of defeat on the issues of principle. In that year, the National Park Service announced its first wilderness proposal under terms of the Wilderness Act of 1964. That law directed federal land management agencies—the Fish and Wildlife Service, Forest Service, and National Park Service—to review potential wilderness under their jurisdiction, conduct public hearings, and submit recommendations to Congress for additions to the National Wilderness Preservation System. The Park Service chose for its precedent the Great Smokies, of all places, but its proposal could not have been worse. It was, in fact, an *anti*wilderness proposal. As the *New York Times* editorialized June 14, 1966, on the eve of public hearings:

The Park Service has come up with a meager, unsatisfactory and essentially bureaucratic proposal that six different areas covering less than half the park be held inviolate as wilderness. It is the Park Service, supposedly the prime protector, that has plans to destroy major parts of the Smokies wilderness by constructing several highways.

Instead of a plan for wilderness, the Park Service offered a design for roads to solve seasonal traffic jams, including a new transmountain road that would cross the Appalachian Trail, plus corridors for additional inner loops. What was left—less than half the park—was offered for inclusion in the National Wilderness Preservation System in six broken blocks, ranging from 110,000 down to 5,000 acres. The wilderness proposal was part of a master plan to accommodate ever-increasing numbers with massive campgrounds of two hundred, three hundred, and six hundred units.

Harvey Broome may have been a gentle soul, but he was determined to protect the wilderness and to block the transmountain road. Responding to the challenge of providing for more and more visitors, Harvey wrote:

It must be clear that the demand which now looms over us can never be satisfied. Slow attrition follows development. Almost without exception, wherever there is a road or dug trail or shelter facility in the virgin forest, there is slowly spreading damage. The areas contiguous to developments become littered, eroded or threadbare from heavy use and abuse.

No further development of any character should take place. No more trails; no more shelters; no more roads; no expansions, extensions, or additions to existing facilities. To protect what is left we must learn to live with facilities we now have. The hardest thing will be the decision itself.

The antiwilderness design was the personal concoction of George B. Hartzog Jr., director of the National Park Service, who had made a commitment to local North Carolina politicians for commercial-boosting highways across the Smokies and had resisted wilderness designation everywhere. But then, as I observed him, Hartzog was at his best as a political wheeler-dealer and at his weakest as a preservationist of principle. Hartzog evidently thought the Smokies would make an easy beginning, but he could not possibly have anticipated the public's reaction. More than two hundred witnesses presented oral statements at hearings in Gatlinburg and across the mountains in Bryson City, North Carolina; 5,400 letters were later received for the hearing record. A handful of local politicians and business people supported the Park Service plan, but a parade of preachers and schoolteachers, scholars and scientists, scouts and scout leaders, hikers, trout fishermen, botanists, and birdwatchers spoke for wilderness. They spoke of the joys of wild places, the spiritual exhilaration, the threats of a political road-building boondoggle. They identified with love of land, idealism, a qualitative experience as the essence of our national parks.

Editorials in newspapers across the country were part of a mobilization of public opinion; it was an education to observe and an enrichment to feel as a part of it. Harvey and his closest comrade-in-arms and old hiking buddy, Ernie Dickerman, gave the spark that fueled the fight. On Sunday, October 23, 1966, a total of 576 people joined the "Save Our Smokies" hike, walking some portion of the route from Clingmans Dome parking area out along the Appalachian Trail to Buckeye Gap, where the proposed road was intended to cross the crest of the Smokies, and then down to the Elkmont Campground. A total of 234 persons walked the entire seventeen miles, the last completing the trip by moonlight.

"It is amazing how many persons from all over the country supported wilderness designation in the Great Smoky Mountains," Dickerman wrote years later, "and opposed any new roads in the course of the campaign which lasted six years until George Hartzog finally threw in the towel." A new report, issued in January 1971, declared the Smokies "a natural treasure of plant and animal life living in an ecological balance that once destroyed can never be restored" and the transmountain road plan was withdrawn.

That made sense to me. I was glad to join in defense of wilderness and to assert that national park policy must transcend local politics and be determined in full public view. I wanted my book to speak for preserving and protecting wilderness, for I believed the Great Smoky Mountains were one of God's special places, even while much of the world was going downhill, and that the national park would become more of a treasure with passing years, deserving the same love and care society bestows on works of art. So, after my book was published, I was shocked when a friend on the park staff told me it was banned from sale in the park. That struck me as a mean-spirited act of state censorship—fortunately, the publisher and I protested and the ban was removed.

People count. Were it not for everyday people who cared, the Smoky Mountains likely would be another parcel of real estate, developed and probably overdeveloped. My interest was in the relationship between mountains and people, how they influenced and cared for each other, and how they cared for the earth. Through the research for my book and participating in these activities, I became involved with a new set of mentors who dealt in sheer idealism.

I saw Harvey for the last time early in 1968, a matter of weeks before he died. A few months earlier he had climbed Mount Katahdin in Maine. Then, near Thanksgiving, he learned that he had a heart ailment. Still, he came to Washington on Wilderness Society business and had dinner with a small group of friends. While walking with him back to his hotel, I saw that he looked pale and weak. The once tireless hiker felt he must stop to rest every few steps. On March 8, 1968, Harvey collapsed and died in his yard while sawing a segment of a little hollow log to make into a wren's house.

In this same period, Clint Davis became critically ill. He was a big, strapping fellow, but cancer reduced him to a mere shadow of himself. When I visited him in the hospital, however, he was cheery, or made a good act of it. I knew that he was disappointed when I had started writing critically of the Forest Service, but we were able to set that aside and enjoy a good visit. He died soon after. I remember the pastor at the funeral sermonizing how there comes a time when your friends have departed the earthly province and are calling you to join them. At this stage, I was not through talking in college classrooms; as it turned out, I was just at the beginning and yet my own education had plainly come not from the classroom, but from friends in the process of living.

CHAPTER 15

Foresters and loggers did not approve – Congressmen complained – Time said I was "tough and tendentious" – But what, after all, is a writer really worth without freedom to bring hope into the realm of grace?

"The Lord giveth," as the saying goes, "and the Lord taketh away." And maybe the taking away was bound to happen to me, first at *American Forests*, but it didn't stop there. Early in March of 1970, James B. Craig, the editor of *American Forests*, invited me to dinner. Nothing was wrong, he explained—well, not exactly wrong, but perhaps it was time to review things. Yes, he had encouraged me to express myself frankly, forthrightly, and critically when need be. So had William E. Towell, executive vice president of the association. Towell was trained as a forester and had come to the AFA after a career with the state conservation department in Missouri. He was always cordial to me, supportive, and seemingly appreciative. Now, over dinner, Craig suggested it would be a good idea to lay off forestry for a while. I could see his point and agreed, maybe for his sake as well as my own, and, besides, I had other subjects on tap.

A week or so later, I received a call from Ernest H. Linford, professor and head of the journalism department at the University of Wyoming and a former editorial writer at the *Salt Lake Tribune*. He was calling as a member of the board of directors of the AFA. He told me he had been advised in a memo to the board that I had agreed to be censored and not to write critically of the Forest Service, the forest industry, or the forestry profession, and wanted to know if it was true. I assured him that it was all news to me.

I was angry Craig hadn't mentioned anything about this to me. I immediately wrote him a letter stating that "at no time, and no manner, have I agreed to having my column censored." He responded that he was shocked when Towell showed him the memo to the board with "that ugly word used not once but two times." Craig explained that he didn't want to show me the memo, he wanted to ride it out; restating that "the whole idea of starting the column was to present an outside opinion in an effort to ward off blandness in the magazine."

On April 8, Towell replied to an inquiry from Linford saying the board had instructed him to "control" Mike Frome and that his March 4 memo had been written at the explicit request of Charles A. Connaughton, the AFA president (a high-ranking Forest Service official who immediately on retirement became a timber industry lobbyist). On April 13, Towell sought to clarify things, changing the word "censorship" to "editing." This stirred Linford in a way that really had little to do with me. He wrote Towell:

> Do you honestly believe anyone could write conservation under such a stricture? Mr. Towell, I cannot find the words to express my amazement and distress that a spokesman for the AFA would impose such an outrageous and crippling rule on a columnist for *American Forests*. In 30-odd years of writing and editing I have encountered some weird obstacles, but this breaks all records for sheer audacity.

I did let up in my column, but in June 1970 could hardly resist writing:

> The tide of disaffection with the management of our national forests, which I have touched upon in recent columns, flows increasingly stronger and deeper, both within the Forest Service and among the broad ranks of thoughtful people in everyday life. I see visible evidence everywhere I go. I receive mounting pleas for help from concerned citizens distressed over abuse and misuse of the public forests.
>
> A memorandum dispatched from the Regional Forester in Missoula, Montana, to the Washington Office at the Department of Agriculture confirms the wave of "unrest" (to use his very word) inside the agency. "Some of our own people are feeling and expressing doubts," according to Regional Forester Neal M. Rahm. "The doubts are whether we can perform as well as we tell people we can."

Foresters and loggers did not approve of this kind of writing in what they considered *their* magazine. A letter to the editor in the July issue declared:

> I for one trust the professional judgment of our Forest Service men far more than the prejudiced judgment of Mr. Frome. I am sick of the cynical condemnation of lumbermen as rapists of our natural resources. In my humble opinion they are the true conservationists,

the builders of this wonderful nation of ours.

And one in the August issue:

> Of late I have become concerned that *American Forests* is leaning
> much more heavily toward preservation, particularly in Mike
> Frome's unwarranted attack on the timber industry in the April
> 1970 issue.... When are we going to get on with responsible
> journalism and work toward something constructive for the good
> of all our people and the nation?

Starting with October 1970, a note appeared above my column: "In
response to inquiries from readers, this is a column of opinion. Mr. Frome's
views are his own and do not reflect the policy of the American Forestry
Association. Editor." I didn't mind, but some readers did. As one expressed
it in the June 1971 issue: "From the preface to Mike Frome's column, I get
the impression that you get a lot of letters criticizing Frome and criticizing
you for publishing the column. As one A.F. reader I have only this to say:
'Give 'em hell, Mike!'"

By then it was too late. Towell ordered Craig to cancel the column and
I was gone. Old-line foresters cheered at the elimination of a pesky critic.
Kenneth Davis, a professor at the Yale School of Forestry, then president
of the Society of American Foresters, stated that I should never have been
allowed to write the column since I was not a professional forester—as if
public policy dealing with vital natural resources should be left to narrowly
oriented technicians like himself. Various people wrote asking why and
say-it-isn't-so. Interior Secretary Walter J. Hickel on August 3, 1971, wrote:
"I have gathered that Mike's column was one of the magazine's most
popular features because Mike tells it 'like it is,' not necessarily like we'd
like to think it is. This independent viewpoint and this willingness to face
the naked truth of issues before us has been one of the strong appeals of
American Forests." But it was too late.

Various news media wrote about my dismissal. *The Living Wilderness*,
the quarterly of the Wilderness Society, in its Autumn 1971 issue went into
great length, headlining its report "The Strange Case of Michael Frome,
lover of trees and bête noire of the lumber industry," with this preface:

> In his *American Forests* column Mike used to probe into anything
> and everything related to our nation's forests and rangelands. His

approach was direct, his style incisive. He gave quarter to no one he thought deserving of criticism. Oftentimes he was critical of the U.S. Forest Service and/or the timber industry.

We always thought it was to the credit of the American Forestry Association that it published Mike's column, which began in 1966 and was preceded by occasional articles going back to 1959. Here was convincing proof that the association could look objectively at itself and its many close friends in government and industry and fight for change where change was needed. With at least seven industry representatives and several former officials of the U.S. Forest Service among its officers and directors, the association needs to show this kind of independence.

and then fully reprinting the pertinent exchanges.

Stewart Udall and Jeff Stansbury wrote a syndicated column for the Los Angeles Times Syndicate: "With no great pleasure we write this obituary for the American Forestry Association. It is not dead in a literal sense, but its leadership has sold out its birthright and therefore its future claims to our attention."[1]

I was upset but far from crushed. I'd had a good run at *American Forests*. Neither timbermen nor foresters could take away my words already in print. Besides, I still had my column in *Field & Stream*, a much larger and more influential magazine, and plenty of other things to do.

At *Field & Stream*, I received a steady stream of letters from our readers. Most were positive, suggesting issues to discuss, asking me to come visit and go see one area or another with them. Many cheered our pre-election Rate Your Candidate features. Others, however, were painfully upset, especially when they found pro-gun control congressmen and senators—their absolutely mortal foes—with the highest ratings. One sporting goods dealer in Kansas issued an irate bulletin calling on advertisers who did not want to promote an anti-gun position not to advertise in *Field & Stream* and urging dealers not to sell products of those who did advertise in the magazine.

Congressmen complained too, belittling and attacking *Field & Stream*, beating their breasts in righteous wrath about all the good they had done that this scurrilous magazine refused to acknowledge. Conley held firm against the challenges; he wrote an editorial explaining that we were dealing here with the environment, and that gun control was a separate issue we would take up another time. I was proud of him.

The trouble was that Forsberg retired and was replaced by a new publisher, Michael O'Neill, with ideas of his own. Conley felt his editorial judgment was threatened and that slickness was creeping into the magazine. It grieved me to see him go. We were not pals, I'm not sure that he had any, but I was indebted and grateful for the platform he gave me. When he was cleaning out his desk Conley mailed me a letter that had come to him from George Hess, a Weyerhaeuser public relations man in Tacoma, Washington, spelling out a bill of particulars against me. And at the bottom of the page, Conley wrote in red ink: "WATCH OUT!" Conley subsequently worked for a time in public relations, then became editor of *Outdoor Life*, the principal competitor of *Field & Stream*. Curiously both later were acquired and owned simultaneously by the Los Angeles Times Company, but that did not last after that firm was taken over by the Chicago Tribune Company.

I had good rapport, I thought, with the new editor, Jack Samson, who had been on the *Field & Stream* staff about two years. Following the 1972 election, he wrote me: "You are an excellent conservation editor and we sure as hell will continue to back you, as we have done during the past few months of heated controversy over politics." That sounded pretty good to me, but the first sign of trouble emerged in 1973 when I went to New Mexico to investigate questionable land transactions conducted by the state director of the Bureau of Land Management. Staff personnel of the BLM were deeply disturbed, fearful of speaking openly; yet they risked their jobs to alert me. Once in New Mexico to check it out, I learned that a prominent real estate company had completed a sequence of major land exchanges with BLM, obtaining title to more than half a million acres of federal land, including key areas close to El Paso and Santa Fe.

I wrote a report on my findings for publication as my regular column in the June 1973 issue. It never appeared, nor did I receive an explanation. That was my first taste of censorship. I attributed it to the fact that Samson had lived in New Mexico; perhaps I had touched some hidden nerve. On a trip to Montana, I met my colleague, Ted Trueblood, who shared my concern. He had written to Samson about the absence of my column and had received this reply: "I agree that Mike Frome is one of the best conservation editors around. Nothing was amiss about his July column not running. It was just a priority matter and I think we have our priorities ironed out."

That was not exactly so. In the next issue I found key expressions deleted and the article cut abruptly. The space for my column was cut, my secretarial allowance was eliminated, I was instructed to write in generalities without naming names, and plans for a new Rate Your Candidate feature were scrapped. "The energy crisis has caused a backlash which I don't want to subject *Field & Stream* readers to at this time," Samson wrote to me. In late September, I submitted my column for the December issue dealing with the Forest Service's new Environmental Program for the Future, which struck me as a scheme for accelerating exploitation of the forests. Within a week of sending it to New York, I received an envelope marked "Personal and Confidential." Thelma opened the mail. She said, "You better have a drink first," and it was only eleven in the morning. The word from Samson was: "We contemplate handling our conservation department in a slightly different manner. This will not only require a modification in the editorial approach, but will mean a change in editorial personnel."

That letter came in October 1974. Maybe Samson was right. Maybe he understood his audience and his market better than I did. Maybe I should have gone quietly, grateful for the opportunity that Conley had given me. I felt deeply wounded, but I had been there before, with *American Forests*, the *Nashville Tennessean*, and AAA, as though I had been bred to be wounded. It wasn't the money; it was more like closing prematurely on Broadway, and then waking the next day to realize the footlights were out to stay. In a way, I felt stripped down, naked to the bone. But I had been bred, or was moved by some inner force, to pick up the pieces, keep going, and keep fighting.

I determined not to feel lonely, nor to go quietly. After I shared the bad news with friends, Marian Edey, founder and director of the League for Conservation Voters, proposed to organize a mass picketing of the Washington headquarters of CBS; and in a few days fifty citizens turned out toting posters proclaiming "Fairfax Loves Mike Frome," "Friends of the Earth Love Mike," and "CBS—Censored Broadcasting System."

I was flooded with messages, warm and supportive, from former readers, primarily hunters and fishermen. They enriched my life and deepened my commitment. For Samson's part, he wrote inquiring readers, "Mr. Frome's removal concerns only him and *Field & Stream*." Presently, however, he disclosed "the real reason" for my dismissal: that I was antihunting. In a widely circulated letter he wrote,

> when someone writes antihunting material in another publication
> and also submits a monthly conservation column to this eighty-

year-old hunting and fishing magazine, it is more than sufficient grounds for dropping that column. No one who is antihunting will remain on the masthead of *Field & Stream* as long as I am the editor.

As evidence of my presumed antihunting bias, he disseminated a photocopy of a page from Cleveland Amory's new book, *Man Kind?* Amory was a highly successful author and also the eloquent, intellectual founder and president of the antihunting organization called The Fund for Animals. He was the man the gun crowd loved to hate, and in his book, Amory had quoted from my own latest, *Battle for the Wilderness,* in which I wrote that although hunting is a valid outdoors experience,

> the need to hunt for food is gone. Much of sport hunting has scant relevance to primitive instincts or old traditions. It does little to instill a conservation conscience. Blasting polar bears from airplanes, hunting the Arabian oryx—or deer—from automobiles, trail bikes, or snowmobiles, tracking a quarry with walkie-talkie radios, killing for the sake of killing annihilates the hunt's essential character. There can't be much thrill to "the chase" when there is little chase. At one end of the spectrum, "slob hunters" shoot farmers' livestock, road signs and each other. At the opposite end are the superpredators: jet-set gunners whose greatest goal is to mount on their walls one of everything that walked Noah's plank.

I was simply telling the gun crowd to clean up its act and to eliminate from its ranks those who violate the basic rules of outdoor sportsmanship. Samson's argument, I felt, would convince only fools. *Time* in its issue of November 4, 1974, devoted almost a full page headed "A Voice in the Wilderness" with my photograph. The magazine said I was "tough and tendentious," that I had been fired because I made enemies in big business, the gun lobby, and on Capitol Hill, and it quoted Representative Henry Reuss of Wisconsin: "If *Field & Stream* has no place for Frome, then we have come to a time when the voice of conservation is, quite literally, a voice crying in the wilderness."

Many friends and organizations protested my dismissal, leading Samson to strike back with angry letters and statements. Yes, he might discount Brock Evans's article in my behalf in the *Sierra Club Bulletin* as

pure preservationism, but others expressing outrage in print included Ray
Scott of the Bass Angler Sportsman Society, Jack Lorenz of the Izaak Walton
League, and fish and wildlife agencies in Massachusetts and Montana. After
Outdoor Life did an interview and accompanying profile of me, Samson sent
a hot missile to the editor, Chet Fish, challenging him to hire me.

More than a half dozen senators and congressmen discussed my dismissal
in the *Congressional Record*. Representative Silvio Conte, a Massachusetts
Republican, declared: "With the dismissal of Mike Frome, the media barons
have tarnished the CBS halo. It appears that when the chips were down, the
public interest was sacrificed to the corporation's self-interest. If so, then the
firing of Mike Frome must be interpreted as a selfish and hypocritical act."

Representative Ken Hechler, a West Virginia Democrat, introduced
into the *Record* of January 10, 1975, the article from *Time*, plus others from
the *Roanoke* (VA) *Times*, *Vancouver* (WA) *Columbian*, *High Country News*,
and *Missoula* (MT) *Missoulian*, declaring: "The firing of Michael Frome,
the noted environmental writer for *Field & Stream* magazine, by CBS is a
sad chapter in recent history, reflecting hysteria against those who fight to
protect planet Earth. Mike Frome is a straight shooter." I was deeply moved
that Conte and Hechler, men of integrity and attainment, would speak of
me in those words.

It would have been too much to expect reinstatement at *Field &
Stream.* Yet I felt an obligation to cite my experience as a case of censorship
by conglomerate media that boded ill for journalists cherishing free
expression, and so I turned to writers organizations for help. The Society
of Magazine Writers (later American Society of Journalists and Authors, or
ASJA) was responsive. Patrick McGrady, the chairman of its Professional
Rights Committee, declared: "Where a man is chastised for expressing,
not an antihunting opinion, but an antislaughterhouse opinion, in *another*
publication, I think they've got a lot to answer for."

McGrady talked with Samson, who told him I wasn't doing the job he
wanted, and then noted:

> I said, "What wasn't he doing the way you wanted him to?" He said,
> "Well, when he was doing those exposés...I mean he was going so
> heavy on the exposés.... Above all, the thing I really objected to was
> when he was doing those exposés—I mean filling the whole article
> with names of people. He didn't have to do that! I don't mind an
> exposé every now and then, but when you start putting the names

in, embarrassing people, you're going too far."[2]

The ASJA conducted a study and issued an exhaustive white paper, concluding: "The circumstances surrounding the dismissal of Mike Frome as a columnist for *Field & Stream* pose a threat to the intellectual freedom—the freedom of expression—of every independent writer in this country."

And what, after all, is a writer really worth, to herself, himself, or society, without independence and intellectual freedom? This sort of question was asked to me early in 1975 by Donald McDonald, editor of *Center Magazine*, published by the Center for the Study of Democratic Institutions. "People have to know what other avenues, if any, are open to outspoken environmental writers such as you," he wrote. "What other recriminatory actions have been taken against other writers who 'name names'; the degree to which writers self-censor their own work, anticipate trouble and sanitize their writing to the point of banality; the connections between congressmen and special business interests (mining, lumbering, etc.) and the mass media with its cross-ownership of interests?" I tried to answer his questions in an article published in his magazine (July–August 1975) under the title, "Freedom of the Press—For Those Who Own One." That was an old saying, but the meaning was ever new, ever challenging.

I could find some further salve, for whatever it was worth, in a column written by Ernest Linford, whom I mentioned earlier as the head of the journalism department at the University of Wyoming, appearing in the *Salt Lake Tribune* of September 22, 1975. It was all about me and my editorial battles for conservation, including this assessment: "No critic has been able to pinpoint factual errors in his articles, but he is controversial. He angers the businessmen and politicians he lists as enemies of conservation."

I put the controversy behind me, but this was not the end of the Jack Samson/*Field & Stream* story. After I left the magazine, Samson set a new tone for it. An editorial he wrote in the January 1975 issue asked the question "Oil and Water: Can They Mix?" with an answer about cooperating with the great oil companies, keeping their employees working, and avoiding the pitfalls of preservation. It sounded as if it came from an Exxon annual report.

Soon after publication of the article in *Time*, I received a call from Frank Sartwell, the editor of *Defenders*, the bimonthly (six times a year) magazine of Defenders of Wildlife. "I am authorized to offer you a column," he said, adding with a laugh, "as long as you don't get us sued for libel." Defenders of Wildlife had carved a place for itself by picking up issues that other groups like the National Audubon Society overlooked. Defenders of Wildlife had come into money from a sizable bequest, enabling Sartwell to edit a presentable magazine with a circulation of about 50,000. My column was titled Michael Frome's Crusade for Wildlife, with the first one, in December 1974, titled "Clear-cutting: A Frightening Pattern." It began:

> The recent reintroduction of DDT into the forests of the Pacific Northwest was a shocker in itself. It also reveals basic and scary lessons about the long-range prospects for forests everywhere in America, and especially for the native wildlife—mammals, fish, birds, insects, and plants—which they embrace. The worst, I fear, is yet to come.

With *Defenders* I was writing for a gentler, more intellectual audience. Maybe a writer must find his or her own level and this was mine. I think of Colman McCarthy, whom I have never met, but whose work I admired for years. From the 1960s his columns graced the pages of the *Washington Post* until 1997, when the editors decided his work had "run its course," and he signed off by asking, "What should be the moral purpose of writing if not to embrace ideals that can help fulfill the one possibility we all yearn for, the peaceable society?" I asked the same question about the moral purpose of writing. At *Defenders* I could answer it as I wished. I wrote my column through the tenure of three different presidents at *Defenders*, John Grandy, Joyce Kelly, and Rupert Cutler, all good people who never bothered me. I kept writin,g the column through three different editors until 1992.

As long as I kept wildlife in mind, I could wander off into other issues. In November/December 1989 I wrote about imagination that opens the heart to feeling and opens the mind to articulate compassion. I cited a report by a paleobotanist, J. E. Potzger of Butler University (Indiana), written after probing for fossil pollen grains in the mud of lakes and peat of bogs covered by foot-deep sphagnum moss. He found himself viewing an ever-changing scene of throbbing life. The imaginative analyst, he wrote,

> reads into tiny pollen grains great forests. He hears the purring west wind in furry boughs. He pictures snow and ice, cloudy and sunny days, rushing streams of spring freshets, death crashes of great tree giants weakened by centuries of combat, germination of seeds and new forests. As he counts he wonders how many deer, wolves, bears, spruce hens and varying types of scurrying animal

life were associated with these changing forests.[3]

In the same column, I mentioned a compelling article in the pacifist publication *Fellowship*, titled "Seeing Through Peaceful Eyes," by Mary Evelyn Jegen, a nun, teacher, and poet, who wrote:

> Many of us learned to despise or at least to undervalue our imagination as unreliable, deluding, sometimes dangerous, or at best something to be left behind as quickly as possible in the pursuit of truth. We were wrong, of course....
>
> Today it is the imagination that is crying for the grace of redemption. Our world is mortally ill and for the most part does not even know it. Those of us who do know can bring the illness of our time into the realm of grace. One of the effects will be on our own imaginations, on our energy and our hope.[4]

I know now that I was crying for redemption by seeking a moral purpose. That must be what made me feisty, as they said of me, why I wrote as I did, and why I insisted on viewing defeat as opportunity. Maybe it began in the Depression years when I wore my brother's hand-me-downs, and the communist period when I learned of the need for social justice, and the time I spent with steelworkers and immigrant furriers, and my search for infinity over the oceans of the world during World War II. Whatever it may have been, throughout my life, without truly knowing it, I was searching for redemption by trying to find some way, through my imagination, energy, and hope, to "bring the illness of our time into the realm of grace."

CHAPTER 16

Doors closed, others opened – A woman rose to ask my advice – The English teacher frowned on Allen Ginsberg – Schoolchildren saw something special in the varmints

Doors closed to me. I was too outspoken and independent. But other doors opened. Soon after my dismissal from *Field & Stream*, I went to speak to the Montana Wilderness Association in Missoula, feeling rather downcast. The hall was packed. My friend Dale Burk, the outdoors editor of the daily newspaper, the *Missoulian*, introduced me. Everybody stood up and cheered, and I hadn't yet said a word.

I went to New Hampshire to speak to the annual meeting of the Society for the Protection of New Hampshire Forests, where I was introduced by Sherman Adams, former governor and former chief of staff to president Dwight D. Eisenhower. Adams was trained as a forester, so he knew the field. He recited my record and then warned foresters in the audience to buckle up their armor because "here comes Mike Frome." I went to Portland, Oregon, to speak for the Friends of the Columbia River Gorge, where I was introduced by former senator Maurine Neuberger. She said thoughtful, kind words that touched me to the core and kindled a sense of unity with her and her heroic late husband, Dick. I went to Madison, Wisconsin, to speak to the Madison Women's Club, which had made a particular point of inviting Nina Leopold Bradley, the oldest daughter of Aldo Leopold, to come hear me. She invited me to visit the farm that was the subject of her father's classic work, *Sand County Almanac*.

During a question period that followed my presentation at Madison, a woman rose to ask my advice. It was about her son. He was a college graduate who had gone to New York, where he lived close to poverty while aspiring to write plays. She was concerned but did not want to discourage him. What could I tell her that would help him? How could he make a living? Those were not simple questions to answer. I turned inward to

my own circumstances and struggles, but they only complicated things.
I thought of Ralph Waldo Emerson, who wrote in his *Essays*, "To the poet,
to the philosopher, to the saint, all things are friendly and sacred." But
poets, philosophers, and saints don't think of making a living, they think
of poetry, philosophy, and saintly, sacred giving. I thought of writers who
loved land and landscape and whose work had helped me on my path.
Mary Austin, early in the twentieth century, defied the norm, proclaiming
the rights of women, Indians, and wild nature. She went west to discover
mesquite-covered ranges and sky-reaching mesas, lands beyond human
occupancy. Her book, *The Land of Little Rain*, published in 1903, shows a
stylish, ecological approach:

> Go as far as you dare in the heart of a lonely land, you cannot
> go so far that life and death are not before you. Painted lizards
> slip in and out of rock crevices, and paint on the white-hot sands.
> Birds, hummingbirds even, rest in the cactus shrub; woodpeckers
> defend the demoniac yuccas; out of the stark, treeless waste rings
> the music of the night-singing mockingbird. If it be summer and
> the sun well down, there will be a burrowing owl to call. Strange,
> furry, tricksy things dart across the open places, or sit motionless in
> the conning towers of the creosote. The poet may have "named all
> birds without a gun," but not the fairy-footed, ground-inhabiting,
> furtive, small folk of the rainless regions.[1]

Thus, the best answer I could give the lady in Madison went like this:
"Yes, I understand your concern. I hope that you can understand your
son's creative need and allow him the flexibility to work out his own life."
Creativity is a tough row to hoe, but where would society be without those
who dare to follow their hearts into lonely, unexplored territory?

There is another aspect of the same question. One day around this
time, I spoke in two high school classes near where I lived in northern
Virginia. Between classes several students clustered around me. One said he
enjoyed writing and reading poetry. He especially liked Allen Ginsberg, but
his English teacher had scolded him for it, criticizing Ginsberg's poetry as
crude and rubbish. Maybe she was right. Ginsberg indeed was the "Hippy
Poet." Still, his major work, "Howl," has become one of the most popular
poems in U.S. history. A little later, when I spoke in the class, students asked
for my reading suggestions. The teacher—the very one who had scolded

the student poet—stood in the back of the room, as though on guard. I advised the students to read widely, to find their own favorites from works that institutions and elders might frown upon. I especially recommended Allen Ginsberg, whose "Howl" I said might be the best American poem since "Leaves of Grass" by Walt Whitman. I said, "Start with Ginsberg's classic opening line, 'I saw the best minds of my generation destroyed by madness,' and go on from there. Make up your own minds, make your own choices."

Although in boyhood I had not been much of a student, and despite my chronic irreverence now, somehow I became involved in educational affairs and found one thing leading to another. At one point, I was invited by the publishing house of Coward-McCann to write a book for schoolchildren about Virginia, where I was living then, as part of a series called States of the Nation. I found that I enjoyed writing for young readers; I learned to write to their strength, not their weaknesses, and definitely not to write down to them. The book went through three printings in several years.

However, I did encounter a very serious problem. Before the book went to press, the editors sent me a proof of the edited manuscript. They wanted me to check it carefully but to approve and send it back in a week. I was aghast to find monstrous changes that distorted and destroyed everything I was trying to achieve. When I protested vehemently, the editors explained they had shared my manuscript with an elementary school supervisor in Richmond, Virginia. They believed that her review and approval would help in merchandising the book. Maybe so, but virtually everything that mattered was either distorted or destroyed. The following passages, for example, were completely eliminated:

> A reference to George Mason, author of the Fairfax Resolves of 1774 and Virginia Declaration of Rights of 1776, which proclaimed that: "All men are by Nature equally free and independent, and have certain inherent rights, which, when they enter into a State of Society, they cannot, by any Compact, deprive or divest their Posterity; namely, the Enjoyment of Life and Liberty, with the means of acquiring and possessing Property, and pursuing Happiness and Safety."…

> The fundamental rights of man, of *all* men under the sight of their Creator, were Mason's concern. As a member of the Virginia House

of Delegates from 1776 to 1788, he joined with Jefferson in the hard fight for religious freedom, and for separation of church and state. He was a delegate to the Constitutional Convention of 1787 in Philadelphia. But he refused to sign the Constitution because it failed to provide for the abolition of slavery or sufficiently safeguard individual rights....

Hard battles were fought in the legislature to secure freedom for all religious faiths—or, more correctly, for freedom of conscience—and to separate church and state. [Jefferson as governor] had devoted support from his friend James Madison, who later followed him as President of the United States. Together they rejoiced at the passage of the mighty Virginia Statute of Religious Liberty in 1786.

One of Jefferson's most important bills called for a public school system in which the most able students would be sent to a state university. But the wealthy objected to paying taxes to educate the poor and the bill was defeated. Education remained a luxury. A new generation was not trained. Virginia, as well as Jefferson, was the loser....

Jefferson fought issues, rather than individuals. Following his democratic principles, he sought again and again to abolish slavery and to keep it from spreading into the western territories. But he was blocked by the Deep South cotton planters and Northern slave traders. Finally he succeeded in obtaining a law prohibiting the importation of slaves, and he regarded this as one of his major achievements....

Whether factories are really better than farms I cannot say. They seem to be more necessary for prosperity in a modern age, although industry presents new problems. There is no better way of charting a healthy future than by helping young people to start thinking new about the changing shape of things.

The Virginia "money crop," for example, is tobacco. Danville, Petersburg, Lynchburg, South Hill, and South Boston rank among the greatest tobacco markets in the United States. Danville alone can store 250 million pounds of tobacco in its warehouses. Farmers grow most of the tobacco south of the James River, in the "Southside" of the Piedmont. When you drive through southwestern counties you see fields covered with the golden-colored, thin-leaved burley. At Abingdon, the principal burley market, you can hear the chant of the tobacco auctioneer during winter sales. In Richmond, you cannot avoid the aroma of tobacco from warehouses and factories which produce over one hundred billion cigarettes a year, in addition to snuff, pipe tobacco, chewing tobacco, and cigars.

Yet tobacco may be doomed. Cigarettes are harmful to the human body. This fact is established and accepted. Doctors all over America are now stressing this. In due course the popularity of tobacco will decline. What then of Virginia?

Happily, the editors heeded my protest and restored the manuscript as I had written it. Moreover, they asked, "What do you want to write next for us?" And the next became *The Varmints: Our Unwanted Wildlife*. It did well, and not only among children ages eight to twelve, for whom it was intended. In retrospect, however, I wonder about my presumption in claiming expertise. I knew little about wildlife, compared with the biologists or those who grew up with animals in the backyard, or with someone like Sterling North, a popular author of the 1950s and '60s who wrote memorable books like *Rascal* and *Raccoons Are the Brightest People*.

North grew up in rural Wisconsin in company with Wowser the Saint Bernard, Poe the crow, Rascal the raccoon, pet skunks, and woodchucks. In the haylofts there were always sounds of pigeons cooing, sparrows bickering, and mice rustling, music to fall asleep to in the hay, safe from wind and cold. He remembered the first signs of spring: when woodchucks came up from their holes under the barn to take a cautious look at the world and decided it would be wiser to sleep a few more weeks, when meadow mice broke through the snow crust to view the sky, and their big cousins, the muskrats, made similar forays from their ponds and streams to graze on any vegetation that showed a tint of green.

I had no such experiences in my own childhood. I had become concerned in my travel writing days with the sight of animals caged and confined at roadside tourist attractions advertising themselves with misleading and deceptive titles, such as Reptile Gardens, Kiddies' Barnyard, Prairie Zoo. Then, one day while researching *Whose Woods These Are*, I came to the entrance to the Pisgah National Forest, the historic gateway associated with Gifford Pinchot, Frederick Law Olmsted, and George Washington Vanderbilt, and was shocked to find a caged bear pathetically begging for a Coke and money. It wasn't right, not there and not anywhere. Zoos, I thought, were bad enough, but roadside zoos were worse.

This led me to Defenders of Wildlife, which not only shared my concern but introduced me to the widespread war against predators, conducted by "government trappers," or "gopher chokers"—a cadre of men paid by the federal government to spread toxic poisons with scant knowledge of ecology or wildlife science. They had been working at it for years, mostly for the benefit of the sheep industry, with little attention from the media. Through Defenders, I met able and educated people, including Victor Cahalane, the Defenders president, who had been chief biologist of the National Park Service, and the author and editor of monumental reference works like *The Mammals of North America* and *The Imperial Collection of Audubon Animals*. In due course, I was elected to the board, serving with Roger Tory Peterson and Rachel Carson. They were people of principle, who cared about the rights of wild animals in a supercivilized age. In *The Varmints*, I wrote about the mountain lion, coyote, badger, fisher, wolverine, wolf, wildcat, bear, owl, alligator, fox, and eagle in a way that young readers would understand and appreciate. At least, so I hoped.

Actually, Sterling North and I were not far off, despite the differing backgrounds. On the very last page of *Raccoons Are the Brightest People*, he wrote:

> As Thoreau suggested, all living things are better off alive than dead, be they man, moose or pine tree. And as John Muir believed, man cannot even survive without the wilderness to freshen his mind and revive his perception. We are but the ephemera of the moment, the brief custodians of redwoods, which were ancient when Christ was born, and of the birds of the air and animals of the forest which have been evolving for countless millenniums. We do not own the land we abuse, or the lakes and streams we pollute or the raccoons and otters we persecute. Those who play God in destroying any form of life are tampering with a master plan too intricate for any of us to understand. All that we can do is to aid that great plan and to keep part of our planet habitable....

In *The Varmints,* I put it this way:

> Almost every animal on earth is capable of accomplishing some-
> thing clever and beautiful. Almost every animal can show affec-
> tion and do very unselfish things for its young.
>   Wild animals observe their own code of justice and fair play.
> Cooperation among them is common in the wilderness. It is very
> possible they do not know hatred as humans do. Many give fair
> warning before they attack. The grizzly bear will often cough
> deeply, or tear at the turf. The rattlesnake will bare his tongue and
> shake his rattles....

At an elementary school somewhere in the Midwest—I think it was in
Iowa—one teacher assigned her pupils to read the book through and select
their one particular favorite animal. But it didn't stop there. Members of
the class were directed to write to me explaining their choices and asking
a question to which I had to reply. For the most part, they saw something
special in the varmints I had overlooked. So I benefited more from the
exchange than they did.

CHAPTER 17

Sigurd Olson's challenge was meant for me – Examining diverse aspects of wilderness – George Wallace gave his support – Brandborg's door and heart were open – A new experience in Vermont

In 1972, the Wilderness Society asked me to write a book. Two members of the Society's council came down from Washington to my home in Virginia to discuss the project. One was on the staff of the Smithsonian Institution, the other of the National Geographic Society. They were that kind of people: professional, literate, and involved. They said they wanted me to interpret wilderness and the Wilderness Act of 1964 and to explain how private citizens could safeguard particular areas as components of the National Wilderness Preservation System.

To research and write such a book was what I wanted to do with my life. Ever since I had worked on *Whose Woods These Are* in the early 1960s, I felt that wilderness preserved and protected forms the core of a healthy society, that wilderness, above all its definitions, purposes, and uses, is sacred space, with sacred power—the heart of a moral world. At the 1967 Sierra Club Biennial Wilderness Conference, I heard Sigurd Olson declare:

> My only suggestion to this conference is to consider, as wilderness battlers, ways and means not for reaching each other—we are converted—but [for] reaching the other 98 percent of the people. Make the wilderness so important, so understandable, so clearly seen as vital to human happiness that it cannot be relegated to an insubstantial minority. If it affects everyone—and I believe that it does—then we must find how to tell the world why it affects everyone. Only when we put wilderness on that broad base, will we have a chance of saving it.[1]

I believed he was looking right at me, or at least that his challenge was meant for me. As an author I could examine diverse aspects of wilderness, of science, art and literature, history, politics, and ethics. When *Battle for the Wilderness* appeared in 1974, it was well reviewed and received; the blurb on the dust jacket called it "a clarion call to people power,… a thoroughly optimistic work, offering an alternative to the waste and dissent that characterizes modern society."

The more I learned about wilderness, the more I came to recognize the Wilderness Act as reinforcement of what I considered right and hopeful about America and the American system, and about Americans too. Saving wilderness through law showed that individuals can and do work miracles. Over the years of the sixties and seventies, I visited many wilderness areas and shared experiences with committed wilderness advocates. I went to California to visit the first national forest area subject to review following passage of the Wilderness Act. My partner and guide on the trail was Dick Smith, an energetic reporter/photographer for the *Santa Barbara News-Press*, who knew the area intimately. Smith and the California Citizens Committee for the San Rafael Wilderness worked with the Wilderness Society to develop a wilderness concept far bolder than the official proposal from the Forest Service. Smith saw something special that others had missed in the chaparral slopes highlighted by grassy balds and dotted with rocky outcrops and ancient Indian cave paintings. His efforts led to designation of the first wilderness under the 1964 act—the San Rafael—but he wanted a large adjacent area added to it. After he died suddenly in 1977, that area was named the Dick Smith Wilderness with support of the entire community.

Shortly after publication of *Battle for the Wilderness*, I went to Alabama to help celebrate the dedication of the Sipsey Wilderness, a chain of deep gorges threaded with streams and waterfalls, that was part of the Bankhead National Forest. I had been there before, out on the ground with members of the Alabama Conservancy, who felt strongly that the Sipsey should be protected under terms of the Wilderness Act. The Forest Service insisted the area did not qualify, that there was no valid wilderness in the East. The Conservancy then undertook to prove otherwise, surveying wildlife, plants, geology, speleology, and history, the foremost authorities in these fields contributing their time and talent. They found many fish species driven out of major rivers elsewhere still at home in the Sipsey and its tributaries, and many species of birds depending on the Sipsey's specific kinds of food and cover. The conservancy convinced powerful Alabamans, including Governor George C. Wallace. And they convinced Congress too.

Now this was the citizens' day, and the Sipsey's. The local congressman, Tom Bevill, spoke cheerfully before the two hundred-plus celebrants. He was a conservative, but plainly proud of his people, and pleased they had prevailed over a powerful federal agency. The Alabama Conservancy and other citizen groups opened the way to a new grassroots movement in which local people could be heard in behalf of wildernesses they knew best.

The years following passage of the Wilderness Act were exciting, a marvelous period in conservation history. I traveled widely exploring wilderness areas. Around Washington, I knocked on many doors in Congress, government bureaus, and various interest groups. I went frequently to the environmental organizations, large and small, militant and mild, and knew, to some degree, all the environmental leaders of that time.

My best connection was Stewart Brandborg, executive director of the Wilderness Society. He answered many, many questions and was patient, with good humor, in contrast to some who seemed self-important, snobbish, and jealous of their peers. I could never fathom mean-spiritedness among people presumably working toward common goals. With Brandborg I observed that both his door and heart were open. I liked the way he would not quit and eschewed compromise. In the mid-1960s, when I became interested in citizen efforts to save the Little Tennessee River from being obliterated by the Tellico Dam project of the Tennessee Valley Authority, I went to see the conservation director of the National Wildlife Federation. "Oh sure," he said, "we wrote a letter." That was the total effort—the whole campaign. With Brandborg, it was all-out action, whether the cause had a chance or not—after all, who can predict the ultimate consequence of hearty determined effort?

Brandborg grew up in western Montana, where he studied forestry and wildlife at the university and activism from his father, Guy M. Brandborg, from whom I too learned a lesson or two. The older Brandborg was a two-fisted populist. In 1914, at the age of twenty-one he joined the Forest Service when the outfit was loaded with Gifford Pinchot's disciples who foresaw conservation as the foundation of a national destiny of freedom and brotherhood, and saw forestry as a leading edge in the fight against what Pinchot and Theodore Roosevelt called "the control of government by Big Money." After a long career, he retired but kept up the fight to protect the forests, only now he was forgetting to protect them from his old outfit. Like Pinchot, he believed that exhaustion of resources leads to war. I saw him as an evangelist, preaching that society too must be born again, out of an economy of exploitation into an economy of conservation.

The son, meanwhile, joined the staff of the Wilderness Society in Washington, where he served under Howard Zahniser, who had drafted the Wilderness Act and crusaded for it from the time it was first introduced in Congress in 1956. When "Zahnie" died in May 1964, a few months before the Wilderness Bill became law, Brandborg succeeded him, facing the new challenge of making the National Wilderness Preservation System a reality. Dave Foreman, a stalwart of those days, called Brandborg "a great man in American conservation, full of vision, courage, and a solid environmental ethic."

That is how I see him too, though I've known him in a personal way over many years and plead guilty to bias. But he had his weaknesses too. Verbal overkill was one of them—where one word would suffice, he was likely to use two or three. Sigurd Olson was a friend and supporter, but he once rebelled at the long, wordy letters he received: "Brandy, if you can't say it in one page, don't say it!"

I lectured at colleges and universities here and there. Eugene Odum had me for a seminar with his graduate students in ecology at the University of Georgia. At more than one school, students would take me out for beer and say something like "We never hear your viewpoint." I never expected to qualify as a teacher and was astonished to receive an invitation to join the University of Vermont in 1978 as a visiting professor. The invitation came from the head of the environmental studies program, Carl Reidel, whom I had known in his earlier life in the Forest Service. Carl grew up in Chicago, the son of a bookie. He surprised his family by taking to the outdoors, studying forestry, and working as a ranger in Nevada and in the regional office of the Forest Service in Utah, where he got in trouble for challenging old shibboleths. He was concerned with ethical issues rarely discussed in forestry classes or circles. Before they could get rid of him, he fooled his bosses by returning to school for a doctorate and a new career in education. He was at Williams College for a while, then went to the University of Vermont to initiate the environmental program.

I looked forward to a new experience in Vermont, the rocky little state that from a distance, seemed to cling to its pastoral past, out of step with the rapid beat and tempo of the rest of the country. Thelma encouraged me to go and came up to spend a weekend or two with me. When I arrived on campus, Carl was away on leave. During my first week, I approached one

of my new colleagues for guidance and asked if we could have lunch. "No,"
he replied brusquely, "I live sixty miles away. I don't spend a lot of time on
campus, no more than I have to, and when I'm here, I'm very busy." That
was my introduction. The professors weren't all like that, but many were,
there and elsewhere. I often heard the word "collegiality," but did not see
or experience much of it in practice.

I started with the theory that students learn best by doing, through
involvement in issues beyond the classroom. I probably overrated the students and my own ability to turn them on. Most were comfortable learning to
research in libraries, writing planning documents, and fulfilling their assignments to conduct interviews by interviewing their roommates. I doubt that I
ever became a great teacher. Some responded to my unorthodox system, but I
intimidated others. I was impatient, sometimes cutting them off, yet I myself
did not always follow a structured schedule as professors should.

But I felt I had nothing to lose by stirring the pot. I told my politics class
about Martin Luther King's campaign to desegregate Birmingham. Maybe it
didn't relate directly to the environment and maybe it did—it had *everything*
to do with political decision making in modern democracy. I told how
friends and allies pressured Dr. King to give up the Birmingham campaign.
President John F. Kennedy and Attorney General Robert Kennedy warned,
"Not now, later; we need legislation first." Birmingham black ministers and
a sympathetic rabbi insisted Dr. King's action would be illegal and endanger
lives. It was the chronic syndrome of seeing the challenge as "too big for
us, we can't beat it," the sure way to defeat. Martin Luther King, however,
wrote a bolder script: "We need to make people look at themselves. If we
desegregate Birmingham, we desegregate the South."

Whether I succeeded or not, I stimulated students to look at themselves;
I looked at myself as well, learning about assumptions and how wrong
they can be. Some students sat quietly in class, never speaking. I wondered
whether they were too timid to talk or disinterested and tuned out, and how
in the world I could tune them in. In an essay near the end of the semester,
one student explained that she had yearned and struggled to speak, but
her precollege background in Catholic girls' schools, where silence was
mandatory, prevented her from opening up. Another student wrote:

> I have come from a "traditional" schooling background of theory
> and rhetoric regurgitated. It is difficult for me to go beyond this.
> Many of the comments made about people who don't speak out

on their ideas can be directed toward me. It is refreshing (but hard) to be able to think without "losing out" for going against what the professor thinks. It remains for me to get myself out of the shell I've built for many years.

I learned how tough it is to be a college student. In my journalism class, students could spell well enough, but more than a few didn't know how to structure sentences or paragraphs (let alone to properly identify sources, or even to get the names of their sources). Nevertheless, we talked about issues on the campus and in the community, researched them, and wrote about them. I learned from the students. I went around Vermont, sometimes with them, other times on my own, traveling on quiet roads and an occasional modern highway through mountain notches, valleys, and villages. I joined a class in cross-country skiing and enjoyed it so much that I went to a different area every weekend. I found cross-country skiing uplifting, based on self-reliance and solitude, independent of machines. One moonlit starry night, I skied across the frozen surface of Lake Champlain; it was the kind of experience that develops not only the body but also the soul. In the end, I bought a pair of used wooden Norwegian skis that I diligently waxed and enjoyed for years.

The students made me aware that change was coming on fast: that the pastoral and natural qualities that made Vermont attractive were under attack. They felt the state was passive, living on its laurels, and that environmental groups were ducking hard issues. The governor of the period, Richard A. Snelling, was a businessman's businessman, busily engaged in promoting highways, industry, and development, clearly without environmental concern or restraint. Burlington, the largest and really the only city in the state, was afflicted with the urban condition and its growth problems. Yet voters had approved a costly bond issue for three new power plants, all environmentally hazardous, without assessment of future needs or consideration of energy conservation alternatives.

We researched what that meant for the future. One plant would derive power from a dam across the Winooski River, interfering with salmon, preventing canoeing and rafting, and turning the river into a stagnant pool. Another could burn trash, directly counter to the rising tide of collecting and recycling solid waste. The third was to be a 50-megawatt, wood-fire-powered generator, likely to mean intensive logging of state forests, the Green Mountain National Forest, and private lands, with inevitable adverse effects on natural beauty, water flow, and wildlife. Then we made our findings known; that was not considered a polite thing to do—not by public officials or by people on campus. One faculty member who taught environmental education complained that by encouraging student involvement in local issues, I was causing trouble for the entire environmental studies program, which made me wonder what environmental education was all about.

Much of what my students undertook originated in class discussion. One of them summed it up in her final paper:

> Especially after dealing with the various government administra-
> tions and public officials involved with my projects, I see that laws
> are not going to change the way people feel about a hydro facility
> on the Winooski River, a highway in Burlington's south end, or a
> dam on the Richelieu River [all issues the class considered]. The
> only way that the public will begin to examine its values more
> closely and perhaps reshape them is if individuals like myself
> bring forth (either through writing or some other active means)
> the important aspects of leading issues.
>
> By becoming an active part of the BED [Burlington Electric
> Department] issue I discovered how beneficial collective participa-
> tion can be. Working with others who were concerned with the same
> problems of the BED proposal [to use wood fuel for power] gave me
> enthusiasm to push forward and also gave more strength to the argu-
> ments we brought forth. My sense of environmental responsibility
> was encouraged because I was an active and necessary part of our
> group, working toward goals that were important and challenging
> to me. I think others in the group felt this same way.

Carl Reidel later invited me back two or three times. I lectured to students and met with the faculty. I invited Carl to contribute the foreword to the second edition of my book *The Forest Service.* He wrote: "On the several occasions that Mike Frome has been a guest lecturer at the University of Vermont, he has always challenged me and my students to recommit ourselves as advocates for conservation. He has not asked us to abandon our scholarship or professionalism. To the contrary, he called on us to work harder as scholars, teachers, practitioners, and citizens."

He was exactly right. Teachers of conservation ought to be advocates for conservation. They ought to feel empowered by humility, passion, and energy. They should work harder in the public process of decision making. Academics *should* stick their necks out to express themselves freely, to be actively involved in social issues, including the environment and human demographics, without fear of repression or reprisal. After leaving Vermont, I returned home and to writing, but I kept lecturing and learning more about the academic world.

Maybe I was better off writing for a living. The truth is, I never made a great deal of money writing books. In a practical sense, royalties helped and so did authorship in gaining credibility. For me, the real pleasure in books came from digging deeper and spreading out in print; in learning through research, and in working with editors, who almost always wanted only that I improve my writing and that it come through as mine.

CHAPTER 18

Piles of files spilled over – In Yellowstone, a wilderness romance – Walking old logging roads – The hot water was on for tea – While winds of change cleaned out the stale air

In 1980, I was sixty years of age old. Thelma and I had been married for thirty-one years; our children were through college and out of the nest. Son Will went west and daughter Michele remained in New England, leaving us alone in our comfortable home located about one mile west of Mount Vernon, George Washington's estate on the Potomac River. Thelma endeavored to revive our stale marriage by consulting a family counselor, to whom she had been referred by her church. I cheered her initiative, but declined when she asked me to join her for a counseling session, likely because I did not want to open my inner self either to the counselor or to my own wife.

She rarely complained or made demands of me. At the beginning of our marriage, we had few material possessions. I remember returning from our honeymoon to the apartment we had rented (and where I was already living). Outside of her bedroom set and a little borrowed table, we had hardly any furniture. We laughed and made the most of it. We saved our money, rarely splurged, and bought our first home for about $21,000. In the twelve or so years we lived there, Thelma underwent one miscarriage and two difficult pregnancies. Before each Christmas, we had a family photo taken and used it as a Christmas card. Years later, long after we parted, she made albums of the cards, one for each of the children and one for me.

We spent about $45,000 for our second home, the one near Mount Vernon. I thought it was a desirable location and a bargain, while she saw it as unnecessary luxury. Later she sold it for $185,000, which we divided, and she bought a smaller house nearby. She was continually frugal until she died in 2003. And she was devout in her faith: I believe she read a passage from the Bible every day of her life and was singing hymns with her caregiver an hour before her death.

But in 1980, Thelma decided she no longer wanted to do my office work. That was her right and was reasonable, yet I declined again when she brought up the counselor's recommendation that I relocate my office away from home. For me, working at home was the essence of convenience and economy. I made a small concession by finding someone to type the manuscript of *The Varmints: Our Unwanted Wildlife*, a children's book I had just completed. The lady did a credible job for a fair fee, but I missed the critical review Thelma had given while typing my manuscripts through the years.

I had piles of files in various locations in my office. Sometimes they spilled over into the living room, which Thelma resented and which led her to protest that I was invading her space. Her home was her pride; everything was neatly kept in its proper place. She traveled with me now and then, but never felt the need to get up and go. When the children were small, we spent a week or two during the summer at a family resort in the Shenandoah Valley, which seemed about right for her. She didn't care for crowds, being hard of hearing in one ear, and avoided prominence or recognition for herself. On cruises she enjoyed playing bridge, but did not care much for going ashore to observe the slums and poverty characteristic of ports in the West Indies.

My work was my primary love. I spent the morning in my office, came to lunch when called, then returned to work for a while before going swimming (at the pool two blocks away) or bicycling, then quitting for a couple of drinks before dinner. The routine certainly had its pluses, but I functioned with lack of feeling for myself or for the feelings of others. Basically, I was not proud of myself and needed always to keep proving my worth. Even later, at an academic seminar, when the instructor said, "Every time you complete a task along the way, no matter how small, allow yourself a break and celebrate," I piped up impulsively, "I don't know how to celebrate. I always feel the pressure. There is always so much to be done." Plainly, I must not have been easy to live with.

But perhaps I was struggling to come up with a better, or at least a different and more challenging way to live. I did not realize that I was entering what you may call a male midlife crisis; to me it was a life-altering period of discovery. It began in the summer of that year, 1980, when I accepted an invitation from a commercial outfitter to join a weeklong horse pack trip in Yellowstone National Park. I had made various visits to Yellowstone, a national park almost as large as the entire state of Massachusetts, but this would be the first time to start from the Lamar Valley, in the northeast corner of the park, relatively tranquil in contrast to the crowds and commerce that dominated the standard tourist loop. From there, we would climb almost 3,000 feet from grassland and sagebrush through fields of wildflowers and pine forests to the Mirror Plateau, a wilderness portion of the park— Yellowstone as it was meant to be.

We were a small group, as these groups really ought to be, led by the outfitter, Ralph Miller, and his girlfriend and cook, Candy, plus the riders: a sociable middle-aged couple, two unattached women (who came separately), and me. On the first night in camp one of the women, Jill, declined the offer of coffee, but wanted hot water to go with her herbal tea, a brand called Red Zinger, which she had brought along. She shared a teabag with me, and that was the hesitant beginning of our wilderness romance, an interlude in a fragment of time that neither of us could foresee at that moment. Jill was bright, lithe, and at first reserved, a little withdrawn. But the second night, she moved into the tent with me and all that changed.

She was forty-four, a graying blond sixteen years younger than me and recently divorced, with three children, though it didn't show in her body. She lived in Bucks County, Pennsylvania, and taught advanced nursing at a medical university in Philadelphia. She believed in healthful living, including vegetarianism and herbal tea. We talked about it at length and it seemed consistent with my own goals. Our little affair started as a game, a fling for me, and perhaps for her as well. I made it clear that I was married and intended staying so. Jill understood and accepted that

But being with her made things different. I felt for once able to give and receive affection and love. Everything was upbeat, filled with anticipation and joy. We shared the days on the trail with the others, though they could tell that each day brought the two of us closer together. We observed herds of elk and buffalo in their summer range and signs of grizzly bears. We saw varying species of birds—bald eagle, rosy finch, sandhill crane, and trumpeter swan—varying with elevation and terrain. From the top of the Mirror Plateau, views unfolded of the great ranges surrounding Yellowstone—the Bearthtooth, Snowy, Gallatin, Absarokas, and the snowy Tetons far to the south. Then there were nights in the tent, tender and loving. Jill was warm and responsive, scarcely out of my arms, her body fitting snugly and weightlessly against mine. One night near the end of the trip, she cried in my arms at what we thought would be a final parting.

But it did not end there. After returning home, I phoned her and we met in New York. Then we met in San Francisco, where she was attending a conference. And in other places. Whether in jeans or a dress or slacks and sport jacket, she always seemed sleek and stylish. One night at dinner, she reached across the table, touched my hand, and whispered, "I love you more than loving."

Maybe I should have dealt differently with Thelma before becoming involved with Jill. Maybe I should have joined her in counseling and saved my marriage. But maybe I did not really want to; but in that case, I should have confronted my wife and told her so. Now I recognize the misdeeds and wrongs, but maybe I would not have committed them, and would have gone on with my marriage as before, had I not met Jill or asked to share her Red Zinger.

The relationship at home deteriorated and disintegrated. One day early in 1981, after a sequence of misunderstandings, Thelma and I quarreled, leading her to declare the time had come for us to separate. With my thoughts focused on Jill, I agreed at once. The readiness seemed to take her by surprise, but now there was no room for either of us to give ground and turn back. When I shared the news with my children, my daughter said, "I'm not surprised." She knew, she could tell; children of any age recognize disharmony in their parents and are influenced by it. I remember talking with my close friend and confidant, Stewart Brandborg, the executive director of the Wilderness Society. He was a very moral fellow, married to the same wife for years, but who had been privy to all kinds of marital digressions among friends and associates. Since he already knew of my affair with Jill, he wasn't surprised either. Yet he told me, "Remember that Thelma will always be the mother of your children and the help she gave you in your work and career through the years." I tried to do that, through the process of settlement and later. The breakup was much more difficult for Thelma than for me. In due course, we at least established cordial relations, unlike some other couples who absolutely hate each other after splitting.

But now that I was leaving my home, where to go? The answer came forthwith. In this same time period, I was trying to complete the manuscript of an updated edition of a book I had already written and published about the Forest Service—its history, organization, policies, and problems, part of a series on federal agencies—but making little progress. One day I was lunching with the chief of the Forest Service, Max Peterson, whom I had known for years. Peterson was not a forester but an engineer, who had worked his way up through the ranks. I thought he wanted to be progressive in his leadership but was restrained by the industry-oriented culture prevalent in his agency. He recounted to me a letter he had received from a retiree. It went like this: "Dear Max: With reference to that speech you gave on multiple use [balancing wildlife, recreation, and wilderness with commodity production], why don't you cut out that horseshit?"

Peterson understood that my book was critical of his agency, but he saw room for criticism and suggested that I go to complete my work at the Pinchot Institute for Conservation Studies at Milford, Pennsylvania. This was the converted forty-room family mansion, called Grey Towers, which Gifford Pinchot, the first chief of the Forest Service and twice governor of Pennsylvania, had willed to his old outfit.

Peterson's invitation came out of the blue, but I accepted immediately. Soon after, I left my home and moved with few personal belongings to start anew at Milford. Grey Towers was a showpiece of the Poconos, built of stone in the style of a French country château with three circular towers, on a landscaped hill overlooking the Delaware River. At this center of research, however, little of consequence was going on, but then foresters are out of their element in actually studying conservation that might challenge dogma. I was given a large, comfortable office on the third floor of one of the towers, an ideal workshop. For a place to stay, I advertised in the local newspaper and received a phone call from a fellow named Tom Smith asking, "Are you the same Michael Frome who wrote—?" He was the resident director of the Millford Reservation, a large old estate being developed as a nature study center. He offered me accommodations without charge. As it turned out, they weren't worth much, but the setting was gorgeous, with 1600 acres of roadless forest around a peaceful lake without a motor or a boat on it, but only Canada geese or ducks stopping to rest during their seasonal migrations. Five old wooden cottages bordered the lake, but only one, which Tom occupied, was winterized; I was in one of the others. At the far end of the lake a modern, solar-powered brick building with dormitory accommodations for one hundred school children had lately been completed and stood waiting for the program to come to life and get going.

Jill came on weekends or I would make the three-hour trip by car to her house at Doylestown. After her divorce, she had pulled herself and three children together and moved into this house on an average street in downtown Doylestown, definitely not on the right side of upscale Bucks County, where she had grown up. The Yellowstone trip had been an expensive holiday treat to herself, paid for in part by her large, gentle golden retriever that she bred regularly for nine or ten puppies that easily sold for $300 each. Mother golden and pups began now to help underwrite the doctoral program in which Jill enrolled at Temple University.

With her responsibility of studies, teaching, and family, our regular weekends together grew irregular. The thrill of illicit pleasures in glamorous locations plainly was gone. I went through a period of guilt and remorse over leaving Thelma and home in Virginia. Once that passed, I yearned to be with Jill, but wondered whether we both were too strong-willed, busy, and competitive to make a go of it. Luckily, Tom Smith was good company at the Milford Reservation even while coping with endless delays in opening the nature study center. Some weekends, his fiancée, Gail (soon to be his wife), came to visit. He was Irish and she was Jewish and we talked about religious differences and dealing with them. Other weekends, Tom left to join Gail at Hightstown, New Jersey, near Princeton, where she was a science teacher, leaving me alone on the reservation. When fall came and the wind blew through my cottage I moved into the solar-powered brick dormitory, where I was the sole occupant. Almost every day, I walked old logging roads, now trails, through the reservation, never meeting another person, watching nature change with the seasons, with signs of beaver and signs of bear; I saw otter swimming and diving, different kinds of turtles, lots of deer, groundhogs, raccoons, porcupines, skunks, and butterflies, and Canada geese resting on the lake while heading south in autumn, north in spring.

After nearly a year at the Pinchot Institute, the work on my book was done. I had in mind moving to Doylestown, but Jill made it clear that she did not want me so close at hand. I was hurt once again but probably brought it on myself. Still, I remembered the consolation a friend had given me when I was dismissed from *American Forests*. "There is nothing like the winds of change," he wrote me, "to clean out the stale air." It was time to go and I chose to go west. I phoned a friend in the Forest Service in Denver. "Is there any place out there like the Pinchot Institute that would have me?" I asked. "Have you thought of teaching?" he asked. "No," I said, "but I would."

I would and I did. That phone call opened an entire career for me. It led soon to an invitation to come to the University of Idaho as a visiting associate professor. Saddened on one hand at parting from Jill, I was glad on the other at the prospect of relocating in Idaho. It was a state I had known and enjoyed since my travel writing days and my research on national forests for *Whose Woods These Are* twenty years before. Idaho was abundant with wildlife, wilderness, free-running rivers, and political issues involving public lands, maybe more than any other state. In the very heart of it, the Idaho Primitive Area (later designated the Frank Church–River of No Return Wilderness) comprised the largest wilderness in the lower forty-eight states—larger and wilder than Yellowstone.

I shared the news with Jill. I think she was a little relieved, a little dismayed, a little unsure of what to say or do. She came to Milford to bid me farewell. We spent the day canoeing the Upper Delaware River, watching hawks and vultures glide and swoop in graceful spirals, and then spent the night making love one last time. Then I drove west, but this wasn't the end, for late in the summer she flew out to spend a week with me and it was almost as precious as our first week together in Yellowstone. We corresponded during the fall, the warmth in the exchange suggesting that our long-distance romance could work. I planned to fly back for Christmas, but then early in December she changed her mind and wrote that she did not want me to come, but that she did not want to lose me either. We should have faced the truth that long-distance romances never work.

I was desolate, alone, and lonely, rejected by someone I held dear. In Idaho, daylight yielded to darkness early. Skies were chronically overcast, wind chilled the bones. Everyone around me had the holiday spirit, with somewhere to go, something to do, somebody to meet. I felt the need to get away. Not to flee, but to connect with a kindred spirit. I telephoned my friend Sam West at the Grand Canyon. "Sam," I said, "my plans for Christmas blew up. Can I come down?" "Perfect—we'll have a great time!"

Sam was a national park ranger, with whom I had earlier floated the Colorado River through the Grand Canyon. He wore a full red beard and had been boating all of his life, including rowing on the crew at the University of Washington. It was his religion, Buddhism, his way of looking at the world that appealed to me about Sam. Being a park ranger was the means to continue his adventure with rivers and mountains, which already had taken him to Alaska, Mexico, and Nepal, searching for spirit. He told of how he had been discontented with the values of life to which he had been exposed. He found the Tao, which relies on nature as teacher, and said, "Once you're on the path you become friends with yourself. You decide that material wealth isn't important. You become available to other people;

you can cut them a little slack, understand why they're pissed off when they are pissed off. In Christianity, there is too much separation between the spirit, or God, and human needs. 'Subdue and conquer the earth.' If you take it literally, that gives you carte blanche to run over anything; whereas, if you look at a Native American religion, or an Eastern religion, it says the earth is my mother. It's a sacred place."

I felt blessed to come to Sam. Where Jill had stirred my soul with depth and passion I did not know I possessed, Sam was a brother and teacher to me. At the Grand Canyon, it was chilly and snow covered the ground, but skies and air were clear. We passed our time on the rim of the canyon and hiking the trails down into it, looking at mountains visible one hundred miles away, the sacred sanctuaries of the Navajo and Hopi peoples. I stayed with Sam in his government quarters, a small old house clustered with those of other government employees. We meditated each morning and found peace. A few weeks after my return to Idaho, I received another letter from Jill. She had met somebody else. I should not have been surprised; at least now I was able to handle it.

During my time in Idaho, a small, upstart local publishing house called Solstice Press invited me to contribute a story to a book to be titled *Field Guide to Outdoor Erotica*. I didn't have anything to say about erotica, but did write and submit a piece, which the editors accepted and published. I called it "Red Zinger." I changed the relationship between the principals. I could do that in this little work of fiction. I think it brought some small measure of redemption in a troubled time. The story begins:

> Jane asked about the explosion of sounds they heard at twilight in the wild, but Mark didn't know much more about it than she did. It takes a lot of time and a lot of listening to fathom music, whether performed by professional musicians on human-made instruments or by water, wind, or wild animals. But if Jane wanted an answer, she should have one.
>
> "I think we hear the critters up here crooning in love, or calling for mates, or maybe challenging one another in conflict. Or singing and shouting about another day of life on earth." Mark wasn't sure that made sense, though he felt there must be some inherent rhythm, beyond human understanding and that he and Jane were part of it.
>
> He was a professor of journalism, nearing sixty, a widower.

Jane was a nursing educator, cool and reserved, who at first meeting had brought her own herbal tea and had shared, rather reluctantly, her Red Zinger.

Jane spent the entire night with Mark in his tent. It was her coming-out party, as she later explained. Her husband had been the first man she'd been to bed with (before they were married) and the only one she'd been to bed with before Mark. They nestled in his sleeping bag, their arms and torsos and cheeks and lips hardly ever out of contact.

And then the conclusion:

At the last kiss and embrace as the trip ended, her eyes filled with love and longing. Mark felt they would be going separate ways into separate worlds, that in no way could he be as appealing in Evanston as in Yellowstone. She was bright, youthful, with the best of a professional career ahead of her. He'd come into her life when she yearned for endearment. But to pursue it further—no, in due course she'd identify his abundant weaknesses, leading only to discontent and sadness for them both. It would be better to treasure the interlude as complete in itself.

Jane telephoned his office at the college, but he didn't return the call. When she wrote him his first instinct was not to open the letter, but he did, "I love you more than loving," it began. He decided to read no further. For him it ended when it ended. The hot water was on for tea. He crossed his office, reached for the pot on the counter, poured a cupful, and dropped in a bag of Red Zinger.

CHAPTER 19

The town had a scale about it, a human dimension – Peter would play Bach and Mozart by the hour – They read their work, sharing revelations and wonder – Why I was never neutral

The year after my marriage dissolved, I joined the faculty at the University of Idaho as a visiting associate professor. I was not on the tenure track and certainly not pursuing a life's career in teaching, but I was thrilled with this new opportunity. Politically Idaho was a conservative state, maybe the most conservative in the country, but still lightly populated and richly endowed with public lands and wilderness. It was the home country of Ted Trueblood, my old colleague at *Field & Stream*, whose essays I admired. I had looked forward to seeing and working with him, but he died shortly before I arrived. Ted recorded that early in his career he had been merely eager to hunt, but in time, as he said, he developed "a philosophy toward the outdoors and nature and all things connected to them." He was not basically an activist, but toward the end he became involved and spoke strongly in efforts to protect the public lands. He warned that Idaho had already lost some of its choicest wild country and said we were not looking at how much more wilderness we were going to have, but how much less of it there would be. I quoted that line many times in hopes of gaining public support for saving remaining wild country.

I owed the invitation to come to Idaho to James R. Fazio, the chairman of the Department of Wildland Recreation Management at the College of Forestry. Like Carl Reidel, he was an Easterner who studied forestry and worked for the Forest Service until he became disillusioned and turned to education. When I drove out from the East in the summer of 1982, Fazio and his wife, Dawn, were away, but they insisted that I stay at their home, even in their absence, until I found a place of my own. From then on, the Fazios became part of the network that sustained me through the four years I spent in Idaho. Such people somehow always showed up when I needed them.

I enjoyed Thanksgiving dinners and birthdays with the Fazios and their children. They weren't the only ones to embrace me, but they were the first. I was grateful and sought to give as well as to receive.

Fazio asked my advice about a book project he had under way with a local publisher, Solstice Press, which had asked him to write a book with practical stewardship ideas for owners of small woodlots. The trouble was that whatever copy he submitted, the editors rejected with criticism that bordered on scorn. I reviewed his work as he requested. It may not have been inspired deathless prose, but it looked okay to me. If anything, I questioned the quality of editing. "These people don't like your style," I told him. "I don't think you're going to satisfy them no matter what you do." I suggested that he publish the book himself and try to sell copies through the American Forestry Association. He did that and it worked to everybody's advantage. When *The Woodland Steward* appeared in 1985, he gave me a copy autographed "To Michael, Copy Number One to my number one advisor and supporter. You helped give life to this book." That was easy. It took little effort on my part, yet Fazio appreciated it and remembered.

Soon after my arrival, I moved into a basement apartment in a large home located in town. My landlord was a retired professor in the school of agriculture (which comprised a large part of the university). He explained that he and his wife were Mormons, and they spent their winters at their second home in Arizona. Then he questioned me closely about drinking and drugs. He wanted to be sure I was not about to host drug parties for students, as a former tenant, a professor, had done with abandon. The house was on a ridge, named Ridge Road, a choice address where homes of college deans and faculty overlooked the university and the town. It took fifteen minutes to walk to the forestry building. I bought a used bike and it took less, to say nothing of the exercise derived from biking uphill to home. Actually, I did more biking and walking than driving around town.

I could do that in Moscow, a minicity of about 20,000 people, including students. The town had a scale about it, a human dimension. It was off the interstate freeways. Spokane, the nearest *real* city, was 90 miles away. Washington State University was nine miles away, across the state line at Pullman (although Moscow had better bars and a lower age limit, attracting WSU students for their weekend drinking). Moscow was remote but not isolated. I heard Linus Pauling speak at WSU about war, peace, and vitamins, and Gunther Schuller about modern music at the University of

Idaho. The Washington Idaho Symphony played the same programs as major orchestras, maybe not as well, but well enough, and when Lionel Hampton adopted Idaho, he brought with him jazz greats for the annual jazz festival.

I did not miss the pace of the cities, where people are apt to commute an hour each way or ride on crowded subways or buses, and where office buildings are little fortresses with TV cameras in the elevators and access to locked offices is gained only after pressing a doorbell and passing inspection by the person behind the peephole. I had occasion to go back to Washington DC and found Georgetown, where I once lived, like a psychedelic tourist ghetto. I spent part of a day at the Senate Office Building. It seemed to be crawling with people, most working in cubbyholes and scurrying down corridors, highly compartmentalized in their functions, yet each convinced that he or she must be doing something absolutely critical to the fate and future of the Republic.

Washington struck me as the kind of place where people forget who they are. New York was that way too, or almost any large city. But Moscow provided a reverse stage set, where people can discover who they are. It wasn't Western-upscale like Boulder, Colorado, or Jackson, Wyoming. It was plain and earthy. My tennis partner, Jim Tangen-Foster, and I could find a court anytime, for free; in New York the going rate was $25 an hour, with advance reservation. I first met Jim in the noncredit physical fitness course he taught at the university. We became partners in racquetball, running, hiking, and backpacking. He was a doctoral student in recreation who took a course with me, then another and another, entering each with enthusiasm that spurred the undergraduates around him. One day in the middle of winter I returned from a trip away to find the snow piled high, but Jim had come by to dig out my car and clear the driveway. I spent a lot of loving time with Jim, his wife Laurel, who worked at the university as a counselor to students while studying for her doctoral degree, and their two children.

Peter Steinhagen was a German-born professor in wood products, whom I met in the physical fitness course with Jim. Peter told me, "The priority in my life is not my work, but my music." He had long ago set aside his aspiration to be a concert pianist, but would play Bach and Mozart for me by the hour, apologizing for mistakes that I didn't even hear. His colleagues chided him for hanging out with a critical nonconformist outsider like me, but Peter brushed them off. They were technical people, whose world revolved around wood as a product; few had ever read Aldo Leopold, John Muir, or even Gifford Pinchot, let alone listened to Bach or Mozart. Peter's wife, Elizabeth, was a pal, too. She was a librarian at the university, Hungarian-born, who loved to cook, and every meal at their house was a feast.

I exercised almost every day, one way or another, in every season. In the morning I did pushups, up to seventy-five or eighty. I went hiking in summer, cross-country skiing in winter. I started running, first around the indoor track at the university, then around the outdoor track. I was never much of a speedster and one day while the track team was practicing, I asked the coach to give me a tip or two. He watched me in stride and then said, "If I were you, I'd run faster." That was his advice. One summer I ran in the Moscow Mile, striving to keep up with an eight-year-old coming down to the finish line before a cheering crowd on Main Street. Then I trained for the Moscow-Pullman race. Fazio would help by taking me out a country road and dropping me off to run back six or seven miles. Finally, on a hot August day I ran the 9.25 miles to Pullman in a shade under two hours. I was the last one to finish, but others dropped out. I received medals for being the oldest to finish and the fastest in my age class (as well as the only one).

For a while I had a girlfriend (twenty years younger than me) who was addicted to bicycling. We would head out of town beyond traffic into the Palouse, the once diverse rolling upland prairie, practically none of which survived the plow. Now the Palouse was almost completely cultivated in wheat, peas, and lentils, but still we enjoyed refreshing smells and colors of gold and green. That country appeared beautiful but suffered from high erosion; looking closely, one could see soils blowing away, and that lovely landscape was heavily poisoned with pesticides. That too was Idaho, below the surface. Local people were not pushy, mean, or vindictive; they were generally courteous and helpful and enjoyed their steelhead fishing and elk hunting. But they didn't think much of government at any level and dumped Frank Church, a progressive United States senator, for Steve Symms, a hard and fast right-winger. They didn't think much of higher education either, nor of the university at Moscow, which sheltered liberals and leftists who dared, now and then, to challenge loggers and ranchers, the traditional powers in the state.

Perhaps this explains why the Department of Wildland Recreation Management, or Rec Management, was in the basement of the three-story forestry building, buried below departments of forest resources, forest products, range management, and fish and wildlife management. Yes, the emphasis clearly was on "management," the forestry schools of the country having emerged out of agronomy, a system based on taming the earth and producing commodities of commercial worth to human society. Thus, everything that grows was labeled "resource." A tree acquired value as board feet of timber. Fish and wildlife designated as game species were meant to be "harvested," like corn or cabbage. Nongame species, including predators such as coyotes and wolves, were considered vermin, beyond the pale and open to killing without restraint.

Despite the traditional agrarian worldview of resource management institutions and professions, I found progressive colleagues. Maurice Hornocker was the foremost authority on large wildcats in America and probably in the world. I had first known Hornocker when he worked with John and Frank Craighead in the study of grizzly bears in Yellowstone. Then he went on his own to concentrate on mountain lions and wildcats in America, and on lions and tigers elsewhere in the world. Through his initiative, energy, and indisputable ecological research, he reversed public attitude and public policy concerning the mountain lion, so the big cat finally was recognized and protected as a game animal instead of persecuted as a varmint. It wasn't easy for Hornocker. It never is; hurt is a hazard, risk is always there.

In 1986, when I received the Marjory Stoneman Douglas Award from the National Parks and Conservation Association, Hornocker sent me a note: "Congratulations—the system works!" That was the way I felt. I tried to work in the system, to make the system work. Wilderness management, after all, was part of recreation management and Idaho was a wilderness state. I lectured on wilderness in classes and wrote articles for various magazines in 1984 on the twentieth anniversary of the Wilderness Act.

As a teacher, however, I probably was regarded as quirky for allowing and encouraging students to think differently than they had been trained to. I would quote Einstein, who said, "Imagination is more important than knowledge," and then I would add that facts and figures and analytical thinking do not always furnish the right answers to the simplest inquiry. In a graduate seminar on current issues, most students did projects on practical matters, such as "Soils as a Resource System" and "Acid Rain: A Threat to Western United States," but one enterprising fellow came up with "The New Interior," a view of grizzly management in Yellowstone National Park. It was well researched but written as a fictional thriller, in which the park superintendent favors Alternative D, "to eliminate grizzly bears from the Yellowstone ecosystem." So does Interior Secretary James G. Watt, but he feels the grizzly kill should wait until after the next presidential election in 1984, so he opts for Alternative A, the continuance of present policy. When Watt is forced out, his successor, William Clark, decides to make Alternative D operational without public notice. This is accomplished by Interior's newest division, the clandestine Office of Covert Operations, staffed by ex-CIA agents posing as park rangers. After cleaning out the bears, they find they must turn to human protesters. "The maneuvers in Yellowstone were not winding down," the author concluded. "The war had only just begun." That paper was well written, creative, and all too prophetic. It showed what students could do when their imagination was freed.

A young forestry professor once invited me to lecture in a class he was teaching on conservation, for nonmajors in forestry. He wanted me to talk about wilderness, but at the top of the course outline he had written that the class would deal only in objective values. That stirred me to begin by saying, "For just this session let us set objectivity aside. Close your eyes and breathe deeply." I did a little visualization exercise, asking the students to picture the most beautiful natural place they had ever known and to examine it closely to determine what made it so. Then I asked them to write down what they had found and felt, and all of them in turn around the room read their work, sharing revelations and wonder.

I suppose logic dictated that I would get away with my disregard for orthodoxy for only so long. In time, Fazio moved upstairs as associate dean and was replaced as department head by Bill McLaughlin, an energetic go-getter who had always been friendly and helpful. But now McLaughlin and the other faculty members decided to change the name and focus of the department from wildland recreation management to tourism and recreation. They probably figured they could attract more students and bigger and better financial grants, but to me the change signaled downgrading wilderness research and studies, which were my interest. McLaughlin made me uncomfortable and out of place.

He disapproved of my teaching methods, warning me: "Michael, you're not training students to think. You're teaching them to be just like you. You're opinionated. You should provide the data and allow students to reach their own conclusions." He wanted to remove me from graduate committees because I was not a member of the graduate faculty and therefore

was not qualified, but my colleague Sam Ham interceded in my behalf.
One day I mentioned to McLaughlin that I was invited to deliver a speech
somewhere on the subject of recreation, but he dismissed me: "You're not
qualified to talk about recreation. You don't have the training."

Maybe I didn't have it, after all. I decided to go. And I went, after
four years at the university. My colleagues tossed a little farewell party and
made it sound important. The invitation ended:

> This reception will celebrate the donation of the Frome Archive
> of personal papers and manuscripts to the University and the
> establishment of the Michael Frome Scholarship for Excellence in
> Conservation Writing.

Jim and Laurel Tangen-Foster composed and sang a song for the occasion,
dropping in titles of books of mine:

> We'd like to thank our friend
> For seeing round the bend
> To a lesser traveled path
> And views we might have missed.
>
> He wanders near and far
> To ask whose woods these are,
> Invites us to come in
> To see the wilderness within.
>
> And step by step
> And hand in hand
> We're climbing up
> To the Promised Land.
>
> His classroom is afire,
> His students to inspire
> On contemplative walks
> To see the message in a rock.
>
> In struggles to preserve,
> We draw on his reserve
> When trails we walk are steep
> With promises to keep.

And step by step....

His warm and gentle smile
A gift to all that's wild;
Mountains, streams, and lakes,
And the forest's saving grace.

His vision won't be stilled,
His destiny fulfilled
When we take our rightful stand,
And the victory's at hand.

And step by step....

Stewart Brandborg had given me reassurance. "You've done a lot for a lot of people," he told me, "and have a lot to be proud of." Then he taught me an old Montana aphorism: "I'm one of the best. I'm better than most, and far above average." With that little verbal keepsake to guide me, in 1986 I went off to a one-year gig in another ecosystem, at Northland College at the edge of Lake Superior in Wisconsin. I had spoken at a conference there, and the people in charge had liked what I said and invited me to come with the fancy title of "environmental scholar-in-residence" and a comfortable office at the Sigurd Olson Environmental Institute, a community outreach branch of the college. Apparently I could do as much or as little as I chose.

I read and reviewed the life and writing of Sigurd Olson. He was a fine writer and activist, whom I had known before he died in 1981. He lived for years in Ely, Minnesota, where he worked fearlessly to protect the Boundary Waters Wilderness from commercial intrusion, mostly by local entrepreneurs. He started writing for publication at age fifty and completed nine books, all of which are still in print. He spent some boyhood years in Ashland, where Northland was located—that was the connection.

I explored the surrounding country of lakeshore, woods, and fields, mostly depleted and run down after years of logging and other commercial exploitation. I met summer people who came from Chicago and the Twin Cities to enjoy cool breezes on the Bayfield Peninsula, Madeline Island, and the Apostle Islands in Lake Superior and went home after Labor Day, while the locals endured harsh winters and hardscrabble. It saddened me that some of them vented frustration by demonstrating hatred for Indians living on reservations in the region. Those Native Americans were treated as strangers, or intruders, in their own land.

But they were not the only ones. I learned about wolves and loons, which also were regarded as strangers in *their* own land. Fortunately while adult wolves were being killed with few pups surviving to replace them, wolves were safeguarded on Isle Royale National Park, the largest island in Lake Superior, and on public lands in Wisconsin and neighboring Minnesota. They were making a comeback, slowly but surely. The Olson Institute through a variety of materials sought to encourage public understanding, acceptance, and protection of loons and wolves and their habitat. I felt pleased and proud to be part of this work. My colleagues and I organized and conducted the Wilderness Lecture Series, featuring leaders of national environmental groups, most of whom came at their own expense and did good works on campus.

I taught a couple of classes and advised students on writing, editing, and producing their little magazine. When the fall 1986 issue of *The Mosaic* appeared, it was devoted to the environment. The editor, Chris Strom, wrote:

> I have hope in the world we live in. I have faith in those with whom I share it. I think if we are to build a successful future we must all face the realities of our time, and be strong in our resolve to improve the world. Sharing our thoughts and pictures is a good start to a continued or renewed open line of communication.

I've always found students with such thoughts and striving to express them effectively. The contributors to *The Mosaic* were not journalists or literary majors, but they were trying to voice their care and concern. One fellow wrote about the marvel of clouds, proposing that "if each one of us sets some sort of personal goal for protecting the skies from unnatural clouds, society [will] benefit from our efforts." In the same issue, a young woman wrote about an internship she had completed, starting:

> The mysterious spirit of "the wild" has always been important to me. Why do I feel so restlessly responsive to the haunting cry of a loon? Why am I powerfully humbled by a quiet pond at dusk? What is so mystic about nature and her children that lead me into her enveloping branches? Though I may not have all the answers, I have discovered within me an overwhelming desire to help care for and protect the wilds.

On rereading those lines, it strikes me the roots of the "mysterious spirit" may lie in our own evolution, our own genetic history. Sigurd Olson expressed this idea of ancient feeling and ancient yearning many times in writing of his wilderness experiences. We are who we have been, bred in nature long before cities and machines. I wish that natural resource professors, or even I alone, had done more to expose students to principles of evolution in shaping the human spirit; I wish that I might have consciously responded to theories of creationism as taught at fundamentalist schools and colleges and extolled as gospel by right-wing religionists.

Following my year at Northland College, I had one last stop to make on my journey in academia. Somewhere along the line, I had met John Miles, dean of the Huxley College of Environmental Studies at Western Washington University. We discussed and corresponded about common interests and goals, and he invited me to join the faculty. The university was located in Bellingham, about ninety miles north of Seattle, with the San Juan Islands in Puget Sound on one side and rugged, snowy North Cascades less than an hour away. It was an outdoors person's paradise.

This time I became "environmental journalist-in-residence." That was fine with me, though it caused a little problem of jurisdiction with the journalism department. Students got confused when their journalism professors stressed objectivity and I told them there is no such thing. Nevertheless, we managed to establish a joint degree and turn out competent graduates who could hold their own. I stayed eight years, during which time I wrote *Green Ink: An Introduction to Environmental Journalism*. I didn't intend it to be a textbook, though it has been used as such. I quit because I was seventy-five, probably past the age of relevancy in dealing with young people, and newly remarried with other goals in mind. A graduate student of mine, Scott Brennan, was hired to teach my courses and probably did a better job. I mean, I may know a lot about yesterday, but he is more the expert on today and tomorrow.

When I first arrived, I decided it was time to settle down and stay. Bellingham was an attractive small city with a lot going for it. It rained more than I liked, but never got too hot or cold. I bought a home about four miles from the campus, at the end of a street bordered by undeveloped hilly woodland. The house, for which I paid $72,000, was more than I needed, but I had students coming for potlucks and they seemed to enjoy being in a regular house for a while. I could afford to buy it because Thelma had sold our home near Mount Vernon and moved to a smaller space. Under the terms of our settlement agreement, she was entitled to stay in the house as long as she wished, but if she moved we would share the income of the sale. The house sold for nearly four times what we had paid for it, so we each came out with a nest egg.

In 1990, three years after I arrived at Western Washington, I began thinking seriously of how and where to study for a doctorate. I was nearing seventy, but didn't feel at all like it. The idea of a PhD first came to me at the University of Idaho, where my department head wanted to remove me from graduate committees and told me I was not qualified to talk about recreation because I did not have the training. So, I thought, perhaps sometime I should acquire "the training." Then I was surprised to receive an invitation out of the blue to attend an introductory reception and seminar to be given by The Union Institute in Seattle. I actually had heard of The Union Institute, or TUI, from John Miles, my dean at Western Washington, who was a graduate of this nontraditional, experimental school. I was impressed with the presentation at the reception and by the discussion, especially by one visiting Union graduate recounting her experience. "I was accepted for graduate studies at Stanford but rejected by TUI," she said, "so I thought I should find out what the place was about, and I have never regretted it."

While at the reception I picked up a newsletter in which I noted an article by the associate dean, John Tallmadge, about John Muir, the pioneering conservationist and a particular hero of mine. I wrote Dr. Tallmadge, enclosing an essay I had written on the occasion of John Muir's 150th birthday, plus another piece critical of academics and their narrow world. Again I was surprised when he responded warmly:

> I agree with your observation that academia selects for people who prefer security and conventional thinking to creativity and risk-taking; thus universities generally cannot be expected to foster social change. One great thing about the Union is that we bring ideas and wisdom into the academy from outside, thus enriching disciplines and scholarly discourse. That's because here the learner, rather than department or the discipline, is the center of the educational process.

We corresponded and he encouraged me to apply. "Our community is full of seekers, visionaries, and real people of all kinds," he wrote. I responded:

"It's not leadership so much that concerns me as personal responsibility and self-fulfillment, living on hope, and spreading light by example in a sick and tired old world." He also sent me an essay he had written, "Meeting the Tree of Life," published in the Winter 1989 issue of a journal called *Witness* on his "tenure ordeal" at Carleton College, a well-esteemed small liberal arts college in Minnesota (later expanded into a book, *Meeting the Tree of Life: A Teacher's Path*). He wrote that four days before Christmas the dean and president told him he had not demonstrated "qualities of mind necessary to sustain a permanent teaching position." His first reaction was shock. Students petitioned for reversal, and supportive professors protested, but they did not succeed.

Tallmadge ultimately found his place at TUI, where he became highly regarded by peers and students. He was encouraging and helpful to me. In fact, everything I did for my PhD fit with my work of teaching, writing, and wilderness advocacy and helped me do those better. I received my degree in 1993. Six years later, I was chosen as the outstanding alumnus of the year. When I entered the program, I believed emotion is the most powerful force in human life, while my experience showed that the training of professionals generally represses emotion. I wanted to prove it doesn't have to be that way; I wanted to legitimize subjectivity, the expression of a heartfelt personal viewpoint. As I saw it, courage, honesty, and a sense of purpose are essential for the individual who wants to face the world with hope and heart to make it whole again. Conservation, as I knew it, responds to social needs. It treats ecology as the economics of nature, in a manner directly related to the economics of humankind. Keeping biotic diversity alive is the surest means of keeping humanity alive. But conservation transcends economics—it illuminates the human condition by refusing to put a price tag on the priceless. I wanted to help define the human condition in subjective values essential to personal transformation as the starting point to transformation of global society.

I wish I could say that I found higher education to be progressive, flexible, warm, and enriching, a community of caring, but I can't, notwithstanding the many wonderful individuals I met. In the course of my studies, I came across a great little book of dialogue between two nonconforming activist educators, Myles Horton and Paulo Freire, titled *We Make the Road by Walking: Conversations on Education and Social Change*. Horton was asked: "Is it possible just to teach biology?" He replied as follows:

Academicians, politicians, all the people that are supposed to be guiding the country say you've got to be neutral. As soon as I started looking at that word neutral and what it meant, it became very obvious to me there can be no such thing as neutrality. It's a code word for the existing system. It has nothing to do with anything but agreeing to what is and will always be—that's what neutrality is. Neutrality is just following the crowd. Neutrality is just being what the system asks us to be. Neutrality, in other words, was an immoral act. I was thinking in religious terms then. It was to me a refusal to oppose injustice or to take sides that are unpopular. It's an excuse, in other words. So I discarded the word neutrality before I even started thinking much about educational ideas. Of course, when I got into thinking more about educational ideas and about changing society, it became more and more obvious that you've got to take sides. You need to know why you take sides; you should be able to justify it.[1]

I appreciate that many scientists have worked hard to try to understand how the world's ecology works; their contributions are critical to positive action. Nevertheless, education, as I observed it, is largely about careers, jobs, success in a materialistic world, and elitism, rather than caring and sharing; it's about facts and figures, cognitive values, rather than feeling and art derived from the heart and soul; it's about conformity and being safe in a structured society, rather than individualism, the ability to question society and to constructively influence change in direction. A change in direction is critical and imperative. And that is why I was never neutral.

PART 2

When Ortonville Meets the Bronx

CHAPTER 20

Life was busy, but not complete – She drew a picture of three tulips – Meepul perched on the edge of things – Jack Nicholson explained why he pursued his sweetheart – "We only go around once"

In the spring of 1994, although well past midlife, I was still going strong, writing and teaching and hiking and skiing and living in the illusion that I looked younger than I was, and without much thought to how long it would last. Living alone in my cozy home at the edge of the woods in Bellingham had its strong points. I could withdraw when I chose to, fixing my own schedule to go when and where I wanted. I was with Percy Shelley, who wrote, "I love tranquil solitude / And such society / As is quiet, wise, and good."

I hardly knew anyone in the seventies, my own vintage. Students in their twenties kept me alert and lively. I would see them every day in class, where I likely learned more than they did, and not only about the subject at hand. One day we were all relaxed. I proposed to the class that we go around the room, each person sharing a self-evaluation of personal strong points and weak points. The students talked and assessed themselves in turn, with humored, healthy introspection. Finally it was Anna's turn. She was an attractive, bright student who struggled with a mild speech impediment that occasionally caused her to stammer and blush. Anna at the time was editor of the *Huxley Hotline*, the weekly student newsletter, for which she had volunteered without background or training hoping to explore and acquire new skills. "I feel that I get along well with people," she began. "I know how to motivate them...." She went on like that, exuding confidence, then abruptly halted, paused, and blurted out, "Then, I confess, there are times when I feel all fucked up." Everybody cheered and clapped. Anna had dared to introduce an earthy dimension to the discussion and was a hero for it.

Students came around to my house at various hours of the day and night. They wanted me to go over their writing with them, or they had questions about classwork or their personal relationships or issues at home, or they just wanted to get away from their ratty little rooms for a while. We enjoyed potlucks, when everybody brought goodies to share. We drank beer, but I can't remember anyone overdoing it. Porter, who had been a tennis instructor, took me out and helped me to improve my game.

Though my life was busy, it was not complete. For all the doings and all the people I knew, I was alone at those special hours meant for the magic that comes only from intimate emotional companionship. I had had lady friends, attractive and intelligent, but had failed to build a continuing or lasting relationship with any of them. In one way I was safe and warm, but in another way was essentially isolated and lonely, like a bird in a cage, yearning to share laughter, tears, hugs, and dreams with another bird somewhere outside and beyond the cage.

I was not religious, and so found no support in belief or prayer to a given god, but I was willing to take from religion whatever worked for me. My daughter, Michele, had sent me a gift subscription to a monthly bulletin, *Daily Word*, a series of short spiritual essays she suggested I turn to when I felt the need and desire. I began these daily readings as a means of reaching out in communion with my daughter, but in due course read from the *Daily Word* at breakfast each morning and felt I could better face the day. Some verses I underscored, others I copied; for example, from Luke 4:18:

> The spirit of the Lord is upon me, for he has anointed me to preach good news to the poor. He has sent me to proclaim release to the captives, and recovering of sight to the blind, to set at liberty those who are oppressed, to proclaim the acceptable year of the Lord.

Setting aside "the spirit of the Lord"—likely it wasn't relevant to me, but maybe it was in ways I did not realize—inside myself I wanted to be anointed to preach good news to the poor, bring release to the captives, restore sight to the blind, and set the oppressed at liberty. That was what I wanted my life to be about. But whoever could I share it with? I did not realize at that time that a woman pastor in Ohio named June Eastvold Nillsen had chosen this same text for her ordination service. I had no idea she existed, let alone that we were meant to meet and share our goals and lives.

"Frankly, I am more interested in what makes a person. A whole person—not just the form of a person. I enjoy ideas, humor, connecting with a living, thinking, creative feeling human being who grows through a mutual desire to share and give." Thus wrote Ms. Nilssen in the first letter I received from her. She described herself, mentioned that she had just been to see the tulips in Skagit Valley, a few miles south of Bellingham, and drew a picture of three tulips, colored red, orange, and blue, rising from green stems.

That was in April 1994, written in response to the advertisement I had placed in the pages of personals in the *Seattle Weekly*, a well-written, well-edited publication popular with Northwest upscale young professionals. Considering that I received more than forty replies, I've been asked many times by friends exactly what I said. Once June and I became serious, I discarded the advertisement and all the other replies to it. I do recall describing myself as a professor/writer who enjoyed the out-of-doors and was looking to meet a professional woman over fifty-five who was loving and lovable. I heard from, and then met, attractive and interesting women who worked as teachers, nurses, psychologists, a bookstore owner, a public relations writer, and a singer. They were many and varied, obviously feeling the incompleteness in their lives that I felt in mine, and searching for someone as yet unknown to talk to, touch and, hopefully, at some point to embrace and snuggle up to. It was more difficult for them than for me. Since I had placed the advertisement, I was identified only by a box number, to which they could respond with either letter or phone call—but in doing so they must tell who they were, and where and how to reach them.

One evening soon after receiving June's neatly typed letter with the drawing of three tulips, I called her. We talked for a while. She sounded cheerful. I asked, "What do you do for a living, if you don't mind my asking?" She replied, "Would you believe I'm a Lutheran pastor?" I thought (and may have said), "Well, I've never known or been out with one of them."

We arranged to meet at breakfast. I didn't tell her at the time, but my interview with her was the first of five I conducted with respondents that day (including coffee at ten AM, lunch at noon, another coffee at three PM, and then dinner at six before driving home to Bellingham). June chose as the venue Paul's Place in the university district, about four blocks from her church. I arrived first. The restaurant was comfortable and inviting, a converted private two-story home of yesteryear. The intimate dining room on the first floor had only seven or eight tables. I sat down at a round little table for two at the window and waited. June came promptly at eight, the appointed hour. She arrived with what I recall as a swish and a breezy warm smile that lit up the place, conveying self-assurance and peace with herself. She was middling in height and weight, with curled auburn hair and lively blue eyes. She looked in her mid-fifties, although she told me she was sixty-three. She was the oldest of the women I met through my ad, and probably the most youthful, energetic, and purposeful.

Her first reaction to me was cool. She told me later that I had spread various books of mine across the table, but she was not impressed. ("I didn't care about your books. I wanted to know about you.") Near the end of breakfast she looked at her watch and said she must get to her next appointment. I picked up the books, put on my beret, and walked with her to her car, parked a block away on University Avenue, and asked about getting together again. "You have my number," she replied and drove off, leaving me standing wordless at the curb.

Nevertheless, I soon called again. She said she was too busy to meet, since she was scheduled to go to South Africa on a study tour on the following Monday and had a wedding ceremony to perform on the Saturday two days before leaving. But an hour later she called back: We could indeed get together for lunch on Saturday if I understood that she was on the go. We met at Ray's Boathouse, an upscale restaurant in a choice setting above the marina at Shilshole Bay, on one of those patented brilliant Northwest spring days. Unlike the breakfast, this time it went well. Then she wrote me a note before leaving for South Africa: "The luncheon was delicious, the water and boats a delight, and the conversation provocative. I appreciate your candor and enjoy your caring responses.... Your warmth, hospitality and attention deserve my response. You are a charming fellow...."

She sent me a postcard from South Africa. I wrote her, sending a copy of the new edition of my book, *Strangers in High Places*. I was looking for some special chapter to commend to her and found the one titled "Mountain Missionary." I had no idea where I found the quotation at the end (which I later determined to be Psalm 126)—"He that goeth forth and weepeth, bearing precious seed, shall doubtless come home again with rejoicing, bringing his sheaves with him"—but it made sense and seemed fitting to quote to her. When she returned we talked on the phone, corresponded, and met again. Late in May, curiously, I received a birthday greeting from Thelma, my former wife. She, too, was reading the *Daily Word* and cited the verse appropriate to my birthday, May 25. It was from Isaiah: "And the Lord will guide you continually, and satisfy your desire with good things, and make your bones strong, And you shall be like a watered garden, like a spring water, whose waters fail not." Thelma reminded me that her Bible was a gift from me in 1955, and that it had since been rebound and handled with care and respect. She wished me well and blessed me in all that I would undertake. Her forgiveness and good wishes were typical of her, and doubtless of her faith as well.

That summer June attended a Lutheran conference on the Western Washington University campus in Bellingham. I was away but left a key so she could see where and how I lived. When I returned I found a note from her:

> Meepul [that, for some reason, became her name for me]—
> A deer was here to welcome me.
> Every house needs a guardian angel. This one [a brightly painted wood carving] flew in from El Salvador. Put it in a special place.
> It is strange being in this place without you here—lonely.

In a letter I received soon after she explained why she called me Meepul. When she lived in Ohio, a little girl, five or six, said to her, "I need counseling. Can I make an appointment?" The little girl came regularly twice weekly for months. Her father finally got his long-awaited kidney transplant, but his body rejected it. During those months, it was hard for Patty to deal with all the confusion, anxiety, and loss. Shortly after her father died, her mother decided to move close to her parents. Patty brought a gift so June would not forget her. It was a curious masculine creature made of wax. He wore a beret on his head—somewhat like my own.

"He perched on the edge of things," wrote June. "Popping from the center of his hat was a wick. Around his neck was a tag which read:

> 'I'm a mini-meepul.
> I bring warmth and love into your life.
> When you have me, it means someone cares.'

> The meepul has been with me for twenty years. His nose is banged and his big wide feet look like they have walked a thousand miles. I have never set him aflame for fear that he would melt away. He is solid. I seldom notice him.

> Then, one night you called. We visited briefly and I went back to my word processor to finish what I was writing. Meepul was perched in his usual place. His beret was cocked at the same angle. His hands rested on his knees. His eyes looked straight ahead. Of course, he was formed that way. Because of my fear of having him change, I never lit the match to free him to do what

the tag declared he could. That is Meepul.

Soon our acquaintance deepened into courtship. June's secretary, Hope (who answered the phone, "University Lutheran, this is Hope."), demanded to know, "Who is this Dr. Frome who keeps calling here?" I came to visit every weekend. We walked in parks, went to concerts and plays, enjoyed dining out and dining in. But she always imposed a curfew on Saturday night and I would stay with friends. They kept probing, to find out how far we were going. I told them June was a pastor but also a woman and let it go at that. On Sunday I went to hear her preach. Everybody listened and stayed awake. I thought she was awesome.

Following the service one Sunday after another, she introduced me to various friends, who clearly were curious and gave me the once-over. These friends included Randi and Steve, a young upscale professional couple. She had met them two years earlier at a seminar series on spirituality when all three, they and she, were single. In due course they had turned up at her church, individually and independently of each other, to hear her preach, and a few months later June officiated at their wedding. So they were well and firmly connected. I learned she had been visiting at their house when she found my advertisement in the *Seattle Weekly*, read it aloud, and Steve commanded, "Answer it!" I also had my own friends in Bellingham to deal with. Peter, my neighbor, a professor at the university, and Dean, my financial advisor and confidant, got a vicarious high from reviewing my progress and giving me encouragement and counsel.

The week arrived when June had a Monday off. With sheer seduction in mind, I suggested driving out of Seattle for a hike and staying overnight at some attractive resort. I consulted Hilda Anderson, a travel writer friend who wrote a weekly where-to-go newspaper column; she recommended Snoqualmie Falls, a classy place, but warned it would cost about $150. June at first was coy and reluctant. Early in the day we hiked around Tiger Mountain near Issaquah, reviewed the options, and June finally agreed to our overnight affair. It cost more like $250, but was worth it. We enjoyed room service and a hot tub and a night of intimacy. But there was much more to it: My clever little scheme turned upside down and backfired. First, when I signed the register on arrival at the hotel, I noted that June walked away from the desk to another part of the lobby—she did not want to be visible as party to the plan. Next morning, while we went sightseeing at the overlook high above Snoqualmie Falls, she met a woman she knew. Now it was my turn to walk away so she would not be embarrassed. I didn't like myself or the little game I was playing. It flashed through me that June was thoroughly lovable and loving. I admired her social consciousness and courage and her commitment to her belief. I liked her tenderness and affection for me. From the very first with June, I felt the body was a way for one soul to reach another. Peel it all back and call it love. In one of his films, Jack Nicholson explained to his sweetheart that he pursued her because "you make me want to be a better person." With June, I could have said the same, plus, "You help me to get inside myself; you lift up my spirit." Shortly thereafter I proposed, and she accepted.

On August 21, June announced our engagement in her sermon to the congregation: "Mostly out of curiosity and partly on a dare, I answered a personal ad in the *Weekly*. Ann Morawski, the young woman pastor at St. John's Lutheran, had been answering personals for months and kept saying how it got her out of the church box and in touch with the real issues of single life. So, thinking it was just a twenty-nine cent stamp and a bit of a game, I wrote back to this writer-professor who wanted to meet a woman over fifty-five who was lovely and loving. This led to breakfast, lunch, and dinner, many trips to Seattle from Bellingham, and finally a trip to the jewelry store for an engagement ring."

The following week, my friend John Lampl called from New York with congratulations and to say he was enjoying life after splitting with his wife (no. 2) after sixteen years. I knew her and felt they were both better off. He said he was enjoying life for the first time since he had always been married, from the age of twenty-two. Then he said, "We only go around once so let's make the most of it." Since John was the public relations manager in America for British Airways, we talked about the recent crash of a US Air plane, which led him to say, "You never know when the curtain will fall, so enjoy each day all the way."

In her church newsletter, June wrote that the announcement of our engagement from the pulpit marked a sacred passage: "Where love is, God is. The divine intersects with the human. Then surprise and joy. Spontaneous applause exploded from your hearts, lifting back a response of affirmation. It was a point of unplanned ritual. The wedding is New Year's Eve. You are all invited to share the blessings. We are all being enlarged and deepened. I am so grateful for Michael and for you, the wondrous people of God."

June told me she had a conference with her bishop about our plans to marry. He counseled that marriage would begin a new chapter in life that deserved full attention. Until then she had not mentioned giving up her work as pastor and I wasn't thinking much of practical issues. She also told me about consulting an old colleague. When she mentioned marrying a Jew, he laughed. "Oh, Jews make the best husbands!" I had never heard that before, but it was cheering.

The night of the wedding, New Year's Eve, the church was packed. A dozen or so friends of June came from Milwaukee. Her three children and two grandchildren and my two children came. At least twenty students and former students came. Paul Pritchard flew out from Washington DC. His wife, Susan, sent a message: "Love is like a butterfly in its beauty, fragility, strength and heights. As you begin your life together, we give you our warm support and wishes for many, many soaring experiences together." Several years before I had attended their wedding, Paul's second, in Washington DC. He had confided in me following his divorce and was gloomy about his future, but I had assured him romance would come his way, as indeed it did. Shirley Ford, now widowed, sent best wishes from Luverne, Minnesota, noting that she too was Norwegian, so we all had that in common.

I was nervous and thoroughly confused by the wedding procedure. Waiting in the vestibule outside the sanctuary, I heard the music, chatter, and laughter on the inside. "What do I do now?" I asked my son, Will. "Never mind," he responded, treating me like a child. "Just follow me." We entered the sanctuary and I saw all those people looking at me. June was waiting for me in the center, dressed like a bride, and full of smiles. She held my hand and I felt protected. Several years later she recorded her feelings at that moment: "There was a deep quiet assurance and joy. Although the church was full, I felt alone with you."

Her colleague Jon Magnuson, whom she had known for years, officiated at the wedding. We had been to him for premarriage counseling so he was fairly well acquainted with me. He blessed our union:

> Michael and June, windwalkers, pilgrims to the earth's far places,
> you each bring a world of wisdom to this journey. Michael, you a
> hiker of national parks, a friend and colleague of editors, foresters,
> writers, and politicians; June, you a priestess and church leader,
> a ringmaster of the circus, a lover of films and plays. Both of you
> bring for each other your own journey of the heart. Each of you
> knows, in special, still unfinished ways, what it is to stumble, to

wound, to be forgiven, to be born again....

May you soar high like eagles over valleys in hot air balloons; may you ride together upon giant turtles in Galápagos Islands beachlands; may you read poetry that you write for each other but will never be published; may you walk in the rain sharing a single umbrella; may you watch sunrises and sunsets holding each other's hand on park benches far from busy crowds; may you watch reruns of John Wayne movies together, bundled in blankets in the earliest hours of morning; may you whisper the words of German theologians and feminist philosophers; and finally, do not ask from each other that which God can only give.

Hold fast to that which is lasting; be bold with your honesty, fierce in your loyalty to stand alongside one another respecting your differences, while building something new and good. Also know that this night the carpenter from Nazareth, the one that speaks about treasures and hearts, the one that danced long ago in the shadows of Jewish country inns, remember that scripture tells us that he loved the wedding feast. Tonight, brother, sister, he dances with you. Amen.

Michele LaFontaine, one of my students, described the "joyful and loving event" in the next issue of the *Huxley Hotline:*

Here Comes the Groom: Michael Frome
Ties the Knot on New Year's Eve

Environmental journalism's beloved advisor started the new year with a lifestyle change and a big commitment. Michael Frome and June Eastvold Nilssen were married on New Year's Eve; it was a joyful and loving event. June is a pastor at University Lutheran Church in Seattle, where the wedding took place.

Frome's children, Michele and William, participated in the ceremony, as did the bride's daughter Fjaere Nilssen, an award-winning folk singer/songwriter. Fjaere composed a song especially for the wedding. As she sang, the pure, clear tones of her voice echoed throughout the chapel. Other music was provided throughout the evening by a saxophonist and a pianist.

Following his usual pattern, Michael broke with tradition and had two women ushers seating the guests, along with two men. Evergreen boughs, white flowers, and lighted candles gave a festive air to the ceremony.

A number of Huxley friends (both faculty and students) made the trip south to attend the wedding.

After the wedding ceremony, which was refreshingly brief and down to earth, guests passed through a receiving line wishing joy to the couple before passing on to the feast. There was good food, good drink and good company. A unique and enticing display was the community wedding cake. Twenty of Ms. Nilssen's parishioners baked twenty separate cakes of many shapes and flavors which were then arranged on a tiered stand. One cake, a luscious chocolate delight, was obviously too tempting—someone cut a slice before the bride and groom arrived and disappeared to indulge herself in solitude. (It was utterly delicious.)

As a token of their love and respect, church members presented a gift of $1,500 to the couple. After all the excitement and hurly-burly of the wedding, the Fromes left for a honeymoon in Hawaii. Can't you just imagine them lolling on the tropical sands in the moonlight? Congratulations and welcome back, Michael!

We enjoyed Hawaii, then returned to reality. We lived ninety miles apart, with different careers and different lifestyles. I drove to Seattle every weekend, knocking on June's door with flowers. She came north in midweek when she could. But during our short courtship, key questions had been left unresolved. We both had patterns that worked for us. Now June felt compromised, as though marriage must take full priority and her other commitments were to be dismissed. Still, she intended to share her life with me. She led us in open dialogue, which convinced me that if we could lead own lives and stay true to our own ideals, and did not try to change the other person, then, both of us would have far more together than we had alone, and the very place we met would be bathed in joy and beauty.

In June 1995, six months following our marriage, I retired from my position at the university. One month later, she retired from her position at the church, heeding her bishop's advice to begin a new chapter in life that deserved full attention. It was a much greater sacrifice for her. She was at her peak in a congregation that loved her. Nevertheless, on a bright Sunday morning in July, we drove away from the church, heading east on holiday to see her hometown in western Minnesota.

CHAPTER 21

Finding the Galápagos in a new era – Sharing a purpose – And sacred connections – June followed sisterhood in Beijing and Kodiak Island – The rain forest was a misty jewel out of the pages of Green Mansions

Initially June hesitated, wondering aloud, "What would the congregation say?" It was early in December 1994, three weeks before our wedding. But she did not hesitate for long, adding, "They all know we'll soon be married." Besides, she was thrilled at the idea of going with me to the Galápagos Islands, one of the world's treasured places, where I was invited, with tickets for two, to an international symposium on the occasion of the twenty-fifth anniversary of organized nature tourism of the Galápagos.

In going places, then and thereafter, especially to places where nature still prevailed, I believe we shared a purpose, or a goal. We looked at the world and the universe from different perspectives, that is true, and yet from a mutual base. June's view was not drawn from ecology or conservation, as mine was, but from theology and religion. Even so, her compassion led to recognize the sacred connection of all of life, or as she would say, "Humankind has forgotten that every tiny insect, small strand of algae, grain of sand, drop of water, lizard, fish, and fowl deserves its place in the chain of existence. God's design is transcendent."

In the Galápagos, we had come to a living shrine, a source of knowledge for scientists and of wonder for the rest of us. So it has been since Charles Darwin visited these islands in the Pacific and described his observations and deductions, Now, the symposium at hand was convened by the United Nations Development Programme (UNDP) in cooperation with Metropolitan Touring, a major operator in the islands, with participants representing institutions like the Center for Marine Conservation, Charles Darwin Foundation, National Audubon Society, Smithsonian Institution, World Wildlife Fund, and bureaus of the Ecuadorian government. If you ask what I was doing in such company, perhaps I was considered an authority on "nature tourism." Besides, I had been to the Galápagos before, not once but twice, and had raised questions about protecting the quality in tourism that needed answering. I felt the commercial tourist entrepreneurs wanted to protect the Galápagos so they could profit from them, but now they saw this was not easily done, as in the beginning, and they needed help.

I first visited the Galápagos in 1977, at the dawn of a new era. Before then, tourists were few in number; they traveled the six hundred miles from the Ecuadorian port of Guayaquil via slow boat, taking six days en route. When airplanes entered service, it took a little more than two hours. On that visit, I was part of a group invited by Metropolitan Touring to sample a new way of getting around, aboard an 80-foot trimaran. Early on, I learned that more tourists came to the Galápagos in the 1970s than in all preceding history. I learned that and more from Tui de Roy, our guide, who grew up and lived in the Galápagos. She was then in her early twenties, robust, bronzed by the sun, knowledgeable about natural history, and concerned about the islands' future. Later she became a renowned photographer who made her case for the Galápagos through her bold and brilliant photographs.

Charles Darwin arrived as a 26-year-old naturalist aboard the British survey ship HMS *Beagle* in 1835. Before and after Darwin's day, British and American whalers and sealers removed thousands of tortoises, weighing up to 550 pounds, stacking them alive one atop the other in ships' holds, to be brought out and slaughtered as wanted for meat and oil. Reportedly, the tortoises survived and stayed fresh more than a year, living on water and fat stored in their bodies. Few people lived in the islands until after World War II. A handful of Europeans, including Tui de Roy's parents from Belgium, came to get away from it all. But they were joined in a few years by immigrants from the mainland, mostly from the impoverished Andes, who brought with them goats, cattle, burros, and pigs, and who introduced fruits and vegetables to intrude on native species.

When June and I came late in 1994 to attend the symposium, we were told that official efforts to protect the environment at first appeared to work. Establishment of a national park, a marine resources reserve (second in size only to Great Barrier Reef Marine Park in Australia), and an international whale sanctuary enhanced Ecuador's showpiece and encouraged a thriving tourism. Programs were successfully conducted to protect and repopulate giant tortoises, land iguanas, and plants. Other projects eliminated, or at least controlled, feral dogs, cats, and rats. Limits on tourism were suggested and implemented to some degree.

But we found Puerto Aroyo, the main settlement on Santa Cruz Island, a city in the making, and Santa Cruz was only one of four populated islands—out of thirteen major islands—with a total population of nearly 15,000. And that was just humans, not counting many thousands of domestic animals and plants. Moreover, when I first visited in 1970, fewer than 5,000 visitors per year came to the Galápagos. They traveled through the islands on one large ship and four or five smaller ships. Now nearly 50,000 visitors were accommodated on ninety ships, large and small. Besides the tourist fleet, dozens of boats, with at least a thousand fishermen, were reported taking high numbers of sharks, sea cucumbers, lobsters, and groupers, and polluting waters with trash and bilge.

While I was in meetings listening to the horror stories, June was out seeing the Galápagos as they were meant to be. She told me of watching a seal birthing a pup on the rocks. We had time to explore together, too. We watched fur seals plunging in and out of rocky grottoes. Along another rocky cove, we encountered Galápagos penguins, northernmost and smallest of the penguin family—a peewee compared to the emperor and king penguin of the Antarctic. Many marine iguanas, dark bodies tinged with red and orange, rested like statues along the volcanic rocky coast. "Imps of darkness," Darwin called them. Birds were everywhere: in the mangroves and steep, pitted hills and swimming alongside our boat with the dolphins when we traveled island to island.

In sessions of the symposium, officials of the national park and the government of Ecuador complained continually of mounting public hostility to preservation of the islands. Imagine my surprise, therefore, when we were met at Puerto Ayoro, the main settlement, by a delegation of thirty-plus, children included, with an altogether different message. Their mimeographed appeal included the following passages:

> The Galápagos Islands have come of age. By this we mean that they have, like every other place on earth, including Antarctica, come, in the due course of time, under the hammer of man's restlessness and greed.... The observation of Chief Seattle that by destroying nature we will die of a great loneliness of spirit haunts us, for we sense that by the destruction of nature we wound and disfigure our own minds.

> We ask for the victory of moral responsibility in the case

of the Galápagos, a moral responsibility not compromised by motivation for personal gain and power. We ask that this unique archipelago, with its complexities of natural communities almost complete, be left in peace for all time, that we don't demand so much from the islands that we destroy their charm, magic, and deep breathing of their inner souls....

We ask you to join forces with us to save our islands, as a last chance for mankind to show an ability to live in peace with nature.... The islands require the concerned involvement of people everywhere to find solutions that will never harm the natural function of the Galápagos ecosystems.

Jacqueline de Roy, Tui's mother, was in the group. She said Tui had left the Galápagos in despair over the degradation of the islands and was living and working in New Zealand. I tried to say something encouraging. Then I went over it all with June that evening. I said that although the Galápagos are part of a single nation, they belong to the whole world—as the scene of evolutionary changes that led to a new understanding of life. Maybe we'll never have all the answers, but we ought to preserve the prime source of questions. Darwin challenges the mind in contemplation of life: "Seeing every height crowned with its crater, and the boundaries of most of the lava-streams still distinct, we are led to believe that within a period, geologically recent, the unbroken ocean was here spread out. Hence both in time and space, we seem to be brought somewhat near to that great fact, that mystery of mysteries—the first appearance of new beings on earth."[1]

I appreciate that it isn't a simple issue. One month later, early in January 1995, a band of armed fishermen stormed the headquarters of Galápagos National Park and the Charles Darwin Research Station. For several days, the fishermen held personnel, their wives, and children as hostages. They threatened to kill all the giant tortoises in captivity and to set fires on important islands of the chain. The uprising finally was suppressed by a military detachment from the mainland. There must be another way, a better way, of identifying and understanding the sacred connection of all of life, of people, plants, animals, water, sunlight, and clouds, and of establishing a way of life with a spiritual ecological dimension.

But, then, we have a hard enough time understanding each other. To illustrate: Several months after Galápagos, still early in our marriage, June flew to Beijing to attend the 1995 international women's congress. It was something she had planned to do long before we met; that didn't matter, she would have gone anyway. She was proud to be a woman and refused to be put down or mistreated for being one. She returned with accounts of women asserting themselves and claiming their rights, but also with accounts of women in many countries abused and exploited.

But that is only part of the story. In a subsequent summer, after we both had retired, she was invited to serve for one month as a substitute pastor at a Lutheran church on Kodiak Island, Alaska. I flew up to join her for the last two weeks and found her as enthusiastic as ever. Kodiak was like a little Galápagos of the north: mostly natural, green, wild, and fresh, isolated from mainland Alaska and accessible only by plane or private boat. She told me of her success in establishing rapport with the congregation, especially with the women. She had invited them to church for an all-day Saturday retreat to discuss women's issues and women's needs, and to bond in sisterhood. She expected six or eight, and forty came. They shared stories of loneliness, fear, and frustration. Husbands who worked as fishermen left them for long and hazardous journeys in rough seas, or for the Coast Guard at the largest Coast Guard station in the country, because of pressing demands for search-and-rescue. Kodiak was a machismo world, where men lived on the edge and women were expected to support them as needed. I was glad June shared her experiences with me and felt how much better things would be by recognizing the sacred connection of all of life.

That was during a summer. In a subsequent winter, she was invited to substitute for a month as pastor in San Juan, Puerto Rico, and she took me along. Grace Lutheran was not a wealthy congregation. Most parishioners were blue-collar Puerto Ricans or blacks from impoverished English-speaking islands like St. Vincent who had come to Puerto Rico to work. They welcomed us warmly. I was already acquainted with Puerto Rico. I first came there during World War II, when Borinquen Field, in the northeast part of the island, served as a stopover on flights to South America and from there to Africa. I recall observing massive slums that clearly reflected poorly on North American colonialism. I returned later as a travel writer to witness high-rise chain hotels and condominiums emerging along the Caribbean beaches. Now, as I saw it with June, much of this little tropical island—one of the most densely populated places on earth—was taken up by high-speed highways, high-rise hotels, factories, and fast food parlors. All those, too, reflected on North American colonialism.

Here and there were shreds of ageless tropical beauty. I remembered that many years before I had interviewed (and worked with, to some degree) a fellow who had contributed significantly to saving those shreds of nature. He was Dr. Frank Wadsworth, who had long been director of the Institute of Tropical Forestry and the administrator of the Caribbean National Forest, which covers about 27,000 acres in the Luquillo Mountains twenty-five miles southeast of San Juan. I telephoned him and, though now retired, he offered to go there with us and show us around and tell his story about it.

The rain forest was a misty jewel out of the pages of *Green Mansions*.[2] Wadsworth told us the forest included 240 species of trees, only six of them native to the continental United States. He led us past waterfalls into a grove of 120-foot-high giants—tremendous specimens of tabunuco, ausubo, laurel sabino—sheltering fifty varieties of ferns, plus orchids and lichens covering rocks and decaying logs. Another trail led through woodland filled with musical sounds of cascading waters and the chirping of the *coqui* tree frog and the shrill Puerto Rican parrot, in its last refuge.

Wadsworth recounted the history of the parrot and his connection with it. Once these birds flew in huge flocks, screeching and squawking over forests that were widespread a century ago—like the passenger pigeon on the U.S. mainland. They were emerald green over most of their twelve-inch-long bodies, with blue wing tips and reddish beaks. Then they were shot for food and taken for pets. In the 1960s, Wadsworth initiated efforts to breed the parrots in captivity and return them to the wild. Those efforts brought them back from the brink.

I remembered 1967, when a major military maneuver involving thousands of men was aimed at passing through the habitat of the parrot. Wadsworth succeeded in stopping it by refusing to grant a permit. He declared:

> Defense projects, road building, and recreational development (even some types of research), all may threaten the residual parrot population. One of the most important Forest Service responsibilities is to see that they do not. One result has been our refusal to grant permits to "develop" parts of the Forest, though it is inexplicable to many in the face of heavy recreational demands and pride in the development of Puerto Rico in other ways.

That sort of stand on principle doesn't happen much any more, but then there aren't many public officials like Frank Wadsworth either. To illustrate further: we took a couple of days off to visit the nearby Virgin Islands, easily accessible by a thirty-minute flight. I knew that place since the establishment of Virgin Islands National Park, on the relatively unspoiled island of St. John, in 1956. Certain improvements had been made, largely to the credit of people who worked in the parks and believed in them. On the whole, however, it was downhill, with new illusions substituting for the old reality. When the national park was new, coral reefs were its particular pride, equated with Yellowstone's geysers and Yosemite's waterfalls. Now we saw them as mostly shadows of themselves, deteriorated and dying from various forms of human disturbances and abuses. There wasn't much coral along the Trunk Bay underwater nature trail, once a showpiece. But snorkelers could still read the labels etched on submerged glass plates describing reef life and imagine they were seeing it. We saw where beautiful palm trees had been uprooted for pavement, parking, and a new high-speed highway to accommodate tour buses carrying cruise passengers for a quick sightseeing trip.

For me it was sheer sacrilege. June saw it all from a pastoral perspective, more lofty than my own, and yet derived from a mutual base. On the following Sunday, she began her sermon by declaring that day by day, we humans were being forced into exile, driven from the country of paradise into a faraway place called progress. She told that we had gone to St. John and at night had seen stars spread without number, intimate and distinct though lightyears away; but those stars were not visible in the city where their light was overwhelmed by electric power and pollution that obscure their brilliance. She talked of how one afternoon, a charming yellow-breasted bird honored us with a visit, landing on the bush next to where we were sitting. The bird lingered, sang a sweet tune, and took leave. It was just a flit of sound and color, but the image caused her to lift her eyes and follow the bird in flight up to the heavens stretching like a curtain and forming a tent for all of us to live under. She told the congregation that that enchanted part of the world hinted of long forgotten Eden. She said,

> The rulers of this day who would cover God's garden with concrete highways, turn the crystal pristine waters of the sea into a sickly sewer yellow, bleach the coral, and silence the parrot do not understand that they will be blown away like stubble by a Creator who does not grow faint or weary. We walk in a strange land. There is danger that our collective senses, forgetting that once the air smelled sweet with flowers and fruit, will accommodate to

gaseous exhaust from too many automobiles and trucks....

While God suffers with us in our exile from his kingdom, he does not abandon what he has made; nor will his word come back to him unfulfilled. We who wait upon him will be given strength to do whatever is required of us. Instead of accepting an abuser's mentality, we will be empowered to restore what is degraded and destroyed. In God's good time, just as we become weary and exhausted, we will see trees grow anew on the mountains and plants produce food again in fertile farmlands. When we feel powerless, he renews our strength and lifts us with wings like an eagle's....

In summary, we have a responsibility to protect and sustain the wonders and resources God has provided. There is nothing of material consequence that we can leave our children to approximate the legacy of his creation. Thank you for your hospitality and friendship during our time with you. Amen.

We traveled extensively, with more adventures ahead. We enjoyed living in the Northwest as well, making excursions nearby to the North Cascades, San Juan Islands, Olympic Peninsula, Seattle, Vancouver, and Victoria, all wonderful places that other people cross the continent to visit and for us were virtually at hand. We returned to Ortonville, Minnesota, for June's all-high-school reunion and to Milwaukee to greet her grandchildren. We celebrated life together in simple ways, too, like taking our doggie for her morning walk, sharing the *Daily Word,* mixing soups and salads to go with breads, playing Scrabble and card games, and forgetting who won and lost. We were engaged with neighbors in challenging the city's approval of a massive, ill-conceived housing development in the hilly woods above us. It's tough to fight city hall, and yet we felt encouraged to believe we could save our woods—as though hope might yet prevail, in our backyard, and across our benighted world as well.

CHAPTER 22

Ortonville meets the Bronx – How little we know of life beyond our place – Children should not fight over candy in Easter baskets – Rolvaag produced his own epic of prairie life – The governor refused to use troops as strikebreakers – Myles Horton set the tone

I liked June's hometown, Ortonville, a prairie town in western Minnesota, in the valley of the Minnesota River just across Big Stone Lake from South Dakota. I liked the stories June told me about growing up there in the 1930s and '40s, and I also liked reading in literary history about earlier times of Scandinavian settlement on the frontier. Now this is part of *my* story too, or perhaps I should note simply that I enjoy learning, living, and telling it.

We arrived on our first visit together in time for the Corn Festival in September, which included the parade down Main Street and all the corn we could eat served from a huge steaming vat on the lakefront. Another time we came to Ortonville for June's fiftieth high school reunion, bringing together people who had long migrated to cities and looked at each other thinking, "I hope I don't look *that* old." We stayed overnight with June's old classmate, who lived comfortably on the lakeshore with her husband, read good books, fished all year round, and felt she had everything she wanted without leaving town.

June told me that when she and her sister were growing up, Ortonville had a population of about two thousand and everybody knew everybody. It was not uncommon for the telephone operator to respond, "Oh, you're calling Hazel? She's having coffee at Marie's." In fall, men would go pheasant hunting in South Dakota, and in winter they would drive out on the frozen lake and fish through the ice. The town had one movie theater, the railroad station, two pharmacies, a grocery, meat market, and two hotels. There were two law firms, five Lutheran churches, one Catholic, one Congregational. Beyond the pale were two or three Jews, but no blacks.

As a child, June wanted to write plays and poetry. When she was about ten, she started publishing *The Neighborhood News*, first on onionskin paper, later in mimeograph form, and ultimately in print. She reported on shows at the movies, the dance at the ballroom, and the start of kindergarten. One editorial boosted establishment of a city youth center, while another urged children not to fight over candy in Easter baskets.

In June 1932, when I was twelve years old growing up in the Jewish neighborhood of the west Bronx, June was born in what Sinclair Lewis called "that most Scandinavian part of America, Minnesota." I knew nothing at that stage of my life about Minnesota, or about the great ocean of grass called prairie that clothed the earth there, or about Scandinavians and their Lutheran religion, and certainly nothing about June, who years later would be my wife. It strikes me now on reflection how little we know of life beyond our place, or even beyond our time in our own place.

In *Main Street*, published in 1920, Sinclair Lewis tells of Bea, the Swedish girl, who came from the farm to find work and a home in Gopher Prairie. She was overawed to see four whole blocks of stores. The Bon Ton alone had seven or eight clerks, while the drug store had a long marble soda fountain with silver soda spouts and bottles of new kinds of soft drinks nobody ever heard of. Bea walked in wonder past a hotel that was three stories high, and a regular theater just for movies. The roar of the city frightened Bea; there were five automobiles on the street, all at the same time. It might have been Ortonville in the same period.

Lewis noted that prairie towns did not serve the farmers, but the business people of the towns. Shrewd townsmen made money out of mortgages and wheat, and a whole culture—the culture of small town mid-America—grew up around them. Lewis's home town, Sauk Centre, a prairie village in the heart of Minnesota, became Gopher Prairie, a prototype of a thousand towns, where, as he wrote, "orgies of commercial righteousness" were common.

Carol, the librarian who came to Gopher Prairie as the doctor's wife, learned that to be "intellectual" or "artistic" was highbrow and of dubious virtue. Carol suffered but endured, finally concluding: "Not individuals but institutions are the enemies, and they most affect the disciples who most generously serve them. They insinuate their tyranny under a hundred guises and pompous names, such as Polite Society, the Family, the Church, Sound Business, the Party, the Country, the Superior White Race," and the only defense against them, Carol believed, is unembittered laughter.

During this period, leading to and through World War I, life changed in many ways for Sauk Centre, Ortonville, and across the prairie. The auto, the telephone, and rural free delivery brought farmers in closer touch with town and the world. They could hop into the car to get to the movies on Saturday. Scandinavian women at first made spiced pudding and wore red jackets; then changed to fried pork chops and white blouses. In a generation, they absorbed American ways.

Lewis drew a harsh picture, but then, as he wrote of himself, he "possessed the gift of writing books which acutely annoyed American smugness." He became important to me as a chronicler of a time in history in a region that produced my wife. Over the years, I learned more about where June came from and how she grew up, and who her people were and where they came from. Like the Jews, they were emigrants, leaving the old world to search for a better life in the new world; unlike the Jews, however, Norwegians shunned the cities for the frontiers of agrarian America. The immigration movement began in 1825, when the *Restauration* sailed from Stavenger. By 1840, only about 400 Norwegians had immigrated to America, but by 1850, the number had climbed to about 15,000. A 1925 estimate of the number of Norwegians in America placed the total at 2.5 million, about 2 percent of the population. In fact, Norway may have sent a larger percent of its population to America than any other country except Ireland. And most were farmers.[1]

One of those emigrants, Ole Edvart Rolvaag, came from a gloomy, perilous, and desolate cove on the fringe of the Arctic night, where he went to school nine weeks a year for seven years to the age of fourteen, walking seven miles each way, across rocks and moors. After he came to America in 1896, Rolvaag worked as a farmer, but put himself through school and college, taking up teaching Norwegian literature at St. Olaf College. In 1927, Rolvaag produced his own epic of prairie life, *Giants in the Earth*, but of an earlier pioneer period. It was written in Norwegian and ran through many editions in Norway, engrossing readers there, as he did later in America with his account of the hardships and human cost of planting root in new soil, reflecting the fatalism of the Norse mind.

His fictional pioneers in *Giants in the Earth* did not understand English. Like the Jews on the lower east side of New York, these settlers were clannish, wanting to be with Norwegians, especially those from their own region. The central figure in the book, bearded Per Hansa, and his family were moving west to the Dakota Territory in a small caravan of prairie schooners with canvas tops. They were little ships of the Great Plains, pushing their way through the tall grass. The prairie stretched in grass, sky, and space westward to the Rocky Mountains. Per Hansa worked sixteen hours every day, plowing and breaking up the land. He had to journey four days for supplies. With October, skies became bleak, gray, godforsaken, empty desolation on every hand. Cold wind howled about the huts. Winter was on the border of utter darkness, a gray waste, empty silence, boundless cold, blizzards lasting for days, stirring up an impenetrable grayish-white fury, the whole prairie a foaming, storm-beaten sea. Drifting snow flew wildly under a low sky, sweeping the plain like the giant broom of a witch.

Beret, Per Hansa's wife, felt that "here on the trackless plains, the thousand-year-old hunger of the poor after human happiness had been unloosed," but she saw an evil power among them. In her mind, the desolation called forth all that was evil in human nature. "No evil is quite so bad as that which man fosters," as she said. Then the Evil One struck with darkness, unleashing clouds of locusts to descend on their wheat and destroy it, followed by the grasshopper plague in 1877, when only the wild grass was left untouched because it had grown here ere time was and without the aid of human hand. The Power of Evil in High Places was felt again in the winter of 1880/81, when people and cattle smothered in snow and died. Only the roofs and chimneys of farmhouses could be seen. And after the great snow, famine came. But settlers somehow endured the worst; they survived and conquered the prairie.

Another young man, Carl Johan Eastvold, June's grandfather, came from the Stavanger area to work on a farm in Iowa. He studied English, taught parochial school, then heard the call and entered the seminary. He married a Norwegian girl and began serving his flock in both English and the old tongue. With his buggy and black horses, Reverend Eastvold traveled miry country roads, tending to funerals, illnesses, confirmations, and communions, and preaching to four scattered congregations on repentance, faith, everlasting bliss, the eternity of despair, and the doom and danger of the impenitent. In due course, he became bishop, in what was then called the Norwegian Lutheran Church of America.

They changed their names, both Rolvaag and Eastvold, choosing the names of the areas from which they came. It was a common practice among Norwegians to Americanize, or at least to simplify their names. When the bishop died in July 1929, the funeral service, at the request of the deceased, was delivered in Norwegian. Rolvaag, in the very same community, had two more years to live before going to his reward and likely was bade farewell in the language of his forefathers. But one generation is apt to change in ways the generation before it regards as mysterious and unacceptable. The bishop and his wife, Ellen Sophia, had ten children. Of the four girls, all were teetotalers. Of the boys, two were pastors. The other four were lawyers, and all four of them alcoholics, including June's father, Carl.

Carl was born at the family farm in Iowa, worked his way through college and the University of Minnesota law school, and then came to Ortonville as a young lawyer and partner in the firm founded by Aaron B. (A. B.) Kaercher, June's grandfather Kaercher. A. B. had been a leading light in the business life of the community, as well as county attorney and founder and owner of the local weekly, the *Ortonville Independent*. He had built a large, imposing home; it had to be to accommodate his eleven children.

Carl's wife, Marge, had enjoyed a privileged life until her junior year at Carleton College, when she was stricken with encephalitis, which leads to personality changes, mood swings, frustration, seizures, and confusion. In a period when treatment was primitive, Marge was subject to a variety of antiviral drugs. She recovered to a degree, but was plagued with problems for the rest of her life. Marge and Carl were married on the porch of the Kaercher family home, Carl's father performing the ceremony. Both were ambitious, but ambition was hardly enough to constitute a complete or fulfilling marriage. Carl was busy in progressive politics, helping to organize the Farmer-Labor Party in 1922, when it emerged from the former Nonpartisan League, a grassroots movement of the upper Midwest. The new party quickly became a force powerful enough to elect two U.S. senators, a very popular and populist governor, Floyd B. Olson, and many members of the state legislature, including Carl Eastvold (who became speaker of the house in 1937 and ran for Congress, unsuccessfully, in 1958, after the Farmer-Laborites merged with the Minnesota Democratic Party).

A century ago, progressivism swept across the upper Midwest and influenced the rest of the country as well. In 1912, Minnesota voted for Theodore Roosevelt, the third party Bull Moose candidate for president. In 1915, the Nonpartisan League had 40,000 members in North Dakota alone, while the La Follettes dominated the political scene in Wisconsin. Eugene V. Debs, leader of the Socialist Party, was a popular national figure; the Socialists actually elected mayors in Bridgeport, Connecticut, and Milwaukee, Wisconsin. In the 1920s and '30s, labor unions backed farm legislation, while farmer cooperatives supported the eight-hour day and old age pensions. Many farmers faced foreclosure and eviction, the victims of drought, plague, drop in farm prices, and their own poor farming practices, but once Floyd B. Olson was elected governor of Minnesota in 1930, he came to the farmers' aid, suspending mortgage payments and foreclosures.

Olson and Carl Eastvold were friends and allies. The governor was the son of peasant immigrants, but an orator and politician out of the pages of Sinclair Lewis, captivating audiences like a Viking. After one unproductive college year, he had wandered around the Pacific Northwest, observing lives of squalor and misery. In Seattle, he had joined the protest by enlisting in the International Workers of the World, the IWW, or Wobblies. As governor he dominated Minnesota politics, refusing to use troops as strikebreakers, combating accusations of corruption, communism, and demagoguery. He was barely forty-five when he died of cancer in 1936; he was preparing to campaign for the United States Senate, though some wanted him to run for president on a third party ticket.

The Eastvolds, meanwhile, lived well. Carl drank well, and often. Marge had one or two hired farm girls to do the housework, while she enjoyed the social life of upper-class matrons and of travel. She was stout, strong-willed, and belonged to the right women's clubs and often entertained lady friends at coffee parties and at the golf club. Marge strongly supported Carl's political campaigns. Once when he shared a venue with his opponent, she got into an argument with that fellow. To escape her, he fled into the men's room, but she followed him in and kept arguing. She did that kind of thing. Another time, when Carl and Marge were returning home from a trip, they had a disagreement and argued for a while. When Carl stopped at a cornfield to relieve himself, Marge took revenge by driving off and leaving him at the side of the road to get home as best he could.

Following graduation in her class of forty from Ortonville High School, June entered St. Olaf College at Northfield, Minnesota, the strongly Lutheran Norwegian college her father had attended. She had convinced her father that if she spent the first two years at St. Olaf, he would allow her to spend the second two years wherever she chose. He may have been surprised, or shocked, when she chose the University of California at Berkeley, but it made sense to her to spread her wings and explore the world beyond devout, agrarian Minnesota.

She entered Berkeley in 1953 without the foggiest notion of what to study for a career. She elected to major in rhetoric, after a professor counseled her that if she learned to express herself clearly and to motivate people into action, she would find abundant opportunity to make something of herself.

In due time that proved fortuitous, but not right away, for soon after she married a bright, attractive fellow she had known at St. Olaf.

I know little about my wife's first husband, Jerome. I know he and June raised three healthy and intelligent children. Apparently he was talented, tall, athletic, and intellectual. Moreover, he held what I consider positive and progressive values. He would not let the children join a segregated pool. He went to Washington DC to hear and cheer Martin Luther King deliver his famous "I have a dream" speech from the steps of the Lincoln Memorial in 1963. He wanted to write and teach, but was also interested in the ministry. In the early years, Jerome led and June followed: first to Duke University, where he studied for an advanced degree in English, then to Davidson College in North Carolina where he taught, to Chicago for his seminary studies, to Tyler in southwest Minnesota, for his first pastoral position, to Philadelphia where he was an editor on the staff of the Lutheran Church, and to Springfield, Ohio, where he joined a seminary faculty. The moves were not easy for June. Their three children were all born in different locations. In Philadelphia, June was close to completing a degree in filmmaking when Jerome announced it was time to move again.

June was driven by ideas, dreams, and goals of her own. When they came to Springfield in the early 1970s, she petitioned her way into the seminary. Her ordination, at the age of forty-two, was a major church event in 1974, considering June was the first ordained Lutheran woman pastor in Ohio and one of the first anywhere, opening the way for many other women to follow. As the text for the service, June chose from the book of Luke: "The spirit of the Lord is upon me, for he has anointed me to preach good news to the poor. He has sent me to proclaim release to the captives, and recovering of sight to the blind, to set at liberty those who are oppressed, to proclaim the acceptable year of the Lord."

She succeeded in her first pastorate in Springfield, but after four years Jerome's seminary position ended and it was time to move again. Now it was Milwaukee, where he would became a church pastor. As for June, she found the best was yet to come—as campus pastor at the University of Wisconsin–Milwaukee, where she ministered to students, their parents, and faculty. In the spring of 1982, she had a vision: the establishment of the Gamaliel Chair in Peace and Justice, named for a biblical teacher of law, Gamaliel, who called for reason and faith as alternatives to violence, thus moving people to reconciliation. She designed it so each year the invited Gamaliel would spend one month in Milwaukee and be accessible to schools, churches, and other institutions for lectures and seminars. And for the first Gamaliel, she defied convention by inviting Myles Horton, founder of the Highlander Folk Center in Tennessee, educator, civil rights activist, and advocate of economic reform. Horton was exactly the type of innovative nonconformist June respected and admired. He and his associates at the school were harassed, jailed, beaten, investigated, torched, and denounced.

Myles Horton set the tone for Gamaliels to follow. Thus, in 2002, when I accompanied June to a celebration of the twentieth anniversary of the Gamaliel program, I met recipients of the chair who came from Hong Kong, Tanzania, Chile, Haiti, Appalachia, New York, Nigeria, Palestine, Estonia, and Canada. They embraced and praised June; all were powerful grassroots organizers who worked in communities to realize shifts from violence to peace. It was a profound experience to sit in their company.

After eight years, June left the campus, accepting the call at Ascension Lutheran Church on Milwaukee's south side. Caught in the sweep of urban change, the composition of the congregation was far different from what the Scandinavian settlers had known in the upper Midwest. The church had a core of white middle-class commuter members, but also Hispanics and Hmong. June felt exhilarated and inspired by her work, but her vision of the multicultural witness and ecclesiastical progress was not altogether shared. "I think there's a certain grieving within the congregation about a lost period when they were extremely prestigious and large," she later reflected. Something else went awry, more serious, in her personal life. Her marriage of thirty-plus years foundered and collapsed. Jerome left his church, finding his way to social work in California. June resigned her position, applied for another in Seattle, then she went abroad on her own, learning while in Europe that she had been hired.

Before her departure, the religious editor of the *Milwaukee Sentinel*, Mary Beth Murphy, wrote a piece (published May 12, 1990), describing June as "one of the city's leading religious figures for the past fourteen years" who had made history in Lutheran ministry when she became the first female senior pastor to serve a large urban congregation. The article continued:

> After some reflection, Nilssen, who admitted to being in her late
> 50s, said she decided this was the season to chart a new direction
> in her ministry and life. The only thing for certain is she expects
> her new course will continue to be in the ministry. Nilssen said

she could think of no other profession with the human dimension of the ministry.

"It is a profession that gives you the privilege of being with people at their most intimate times," she said. "You're there as an extension of the Spirit, as a comforter and listener. You have the privilege every Sunday of having a place to stand to proclaim the Word. That is really quite an astonishing opportunity."

That was June, bruised but unshaken. She went abroad not knowing what she would do on her return, but certain she would continue in the ministry. She loved Milwaukee, which had a coast of its own, plus diversity, culture, and the nearness of family and friends at many different levels in society, but she was ready to start afresh. The Pacific Coast was a long way away, but when she returned late in 1990 she went to her new church in Seattle. It was in the University district, about five blocks from the main entrance to the University of Washington campus, uptown from downtown Seattle, but still had the smells and feel of the Northwest coast, maritime moist and misty, never hot, never cold, a rendezvous of seafarers, strangers, and down-and-outers competing to survive in the new world of yuppies and computer jocks and whiz kids. The "U district" had a feel of its own, centered on University Avenue, "the Ave," two blocks downhill from the church. The once classy shops along the Ave were now replaced by others selling T-shirts, trinkets, and souvenirs, interspersed with Vietnamese, Thai, Lebanese, and Greek restaurants, while traffic was enlivened with comings and goings of students, shoppers, and the street people who had no place to go but still seemed busy and added color and off-color to the Ave.

June loved it and fell in step. She may have grown up in a small prairie town, but she reveled in the cities. She found a cozy apartment overlooking the scenic ship canal connecting Lake Union and Lake Washington, naming the apartment "Hobbit Hole." She attended concerts, plays, films, opera, frequented upper-class and lower-class restaurants, and walked with parishioners and pastoral colleagues through the University arboretum and the landscaped park around Green Lake in the heart of the city. She found half a dozen women pastors at other churches in the U district and communed regularly with them. Several of her Seattle colleagues, she discovered, were social activists, speaking out for peace and for the poor, at times accepting arrest and jail as the price to pay for their principles.

Her congregation was composed mostly of university professors, architects, physicians, and other professionals. A few at first had difficulty heeding a woman in the pulpit, but they came to appreciate her vigorous, articulate sermons and her commitment to serving them. When the weather was fair, June walked from the Hobbit Hole to the church, over the University Bridge, watching small craft on the water purr and sputter on their way to the locks and the open water of Puget Sound; she felt the mountains, trees, and waters were lifting their praises to exalt a God who never quits creating, as evident in flowery fragrances potent enough to overwhelm the fumes of the growling, wheezing morning traffic. She had plenty of friends, but lacked a mate. She would go to dinner with one or two couples but always she was the one who went home alone. She yearned for companionship, affection, shared passion, and commitment. Then she answered the advertisement in the *Seattle Weekly* and we found each other.

In the December 1946 issue of *The Neighborhood News*, which June published when she was fourteen, the editor's column headed "Minor Details," included the following little aphorism: "Have you ever stopped to think that nothing on earth has the ability to smile but man? A face that never smiles is like a blade of grass that forgets to turn green and withers and dies before its time." And then, early in 2003, she wrote to my son on the death of his mother:

> My dear Will—My parents died alone without warning. I had always supposed I would be standing by their bed, sharing closure, making amends, praying them into eternity with the sense that angels hovered in the room. As it happened, my father dropped dead in the garage and laid there over the weekend in 95-degree heat (decomposing) before his law partner missed him and went to the house to see if he was okay. We had a closed casket so I never saw him again. My mother was in a nursing home, complained to the nurse that she didn't feel well, and when the nurse came back to help her to the dining room for dinner found her in a heap, dead on the floor. It was Easter Sunday.
>
> In this way, you are more fortunate than I. You have had time to be with Thelma and time to come to terms with her condition, age and your relationship to her. Grace. You will never regret giving your mother and sister care, time, and love. It puts us squarely in front of the realization that this earth is not our permanent address. Strength, comfort, and faith, my dear.

CHAPTER 23

All one world, all one life, indivisible – Students made a great day of Earth Day
– Lessons from Greek gods and poor Mexicans – We are all in turn victims of what
we are told and taught – Brock and Linda showed us the desert

Following retirement in mid-1995, I thought my teaching days were done. But not quite, not yet. In the spring of 1997, the director of the foreign studies program at Western Washington University invited me to spend an academic quarter of four months in Mexico, with June welcome to accompany me.

We were singularly blessed in those endeavors, enabled to combine career experiences, whether in teaching or preaching, with viewing at close range parts of the world in the throes of change and upheaval. Along the way, I sometimes thought that it's not hard to see the worst side of things—the worst is inescapable. On the other hand, wherever we went, we met people, a few (and sometimes more than a few) trying to make things better. I was moved by the very idea that those we met in the Galápagos would cite the words of Chief Seattle, a native North American. In pleading with us to join in assuring that their islands be left in peace, they spoke for the endangered great turtles, as others did elsewhere for butterflies, bison, whales, wolves, forests, and monuments left by ancient human cultures, causes larger than, yet including, themselves. In Puerto Rico, June made the point that every tiny insect, small strand of algae, grain of sand, drop of water, lizard, fish, and fowl deserves its place in the chain of existence. Thus each species at issue came across to me as a symbol of unity of people and places—all one continent, all one world, all one life, indivisible, manifest in differing forms yet all of the same source and spirit. In Morelia, the city where we were located in Mexico, we visited local headquarters of the Partido Verde Ecologista de Mexico (PVEM), the Green Party. Though I have no idea of how influential that party might have been or how many voted for its candidates, plainly it gave voice for the environment, for *Amor, Justicia y Libertad,* even in the midst of poverty, pollution, and political corruption. I loved especially the Partido Verde's coloring book designed for schoolchildren, *Nuestra Madre Tierra y sus Semillas* (Our Mother Earth and Her Seeds), a reminder that seeds properly planted and nurtured ultimately will bear fruit.

I've tried many times to define the differences as I saw them between the Mexicans and us *norteamericanos*. Simply stated, I think that possessions, property, and tangible reality dominate our worldview while Mexicans are more conscious of *espíritu* and *alma*—spirit and soul—in their lives. I think this influence is evident in the closeness of the Mexican family, in Mexican art, dance, and music, in the dignity of the poor without impoverishment, in contrast to our wealthy without riches.

During my first stint in the spring of 1997, the seventeen students in the program were from Western Washington University and other schools of the Northwest. Their main focus was to study *español* and Mexican culture. A few were excellent students, already fluent, socially conscious, and aspiring to serve in a serious, constructive way. Three of them came to me, quite on their own, to ask for guidance and help in organizing an Earth Day on April 22. They were Annika, Dana, and Erin, who we called "the Three Musketeers" and became good friends of ours. They organized a great day, conducting an open forum for high school students, a joint seminar with Mexican university students, and a program of cleanup around the school. They also distributed in the neighborhood a little flier in Spanish on how each person could do a little bit to make the earth a better place.

That was a positive happening. One student, however, wrote a report that included the following:

> The garbage, air pollution, health problems and hazards are all big enough, but the most insistent problem is the lack of environmental education. I found that a 22-year-old friend did not know the word "pollution" (or *polución*). This is no exception; I've noticed that most Mexicans have very little if any knowledge about the consequences of their actions regarding the environment.
>
> Garbage trucks ride through town daily picking up various bags of garbage (often recyclable) for as little as ten cents a bag to dump them in one deserted area just outside of town. Recycling is inconvenient and practically unheard of except for beer and glass pop bottle exchanges. The streets are already so dirty that many find it pointless to even use a garbage can anymore. The rivers

are filthy, everywhere something is stinking, and the air hurts to breathe. There are deadly floods due to excessive logging of surrounding lands. Mexico is a clear example of what would have happened to the U.S. if there weren't environmental protection laws—what can still happen if we aren't careful.

I taught one class, in environmental writing, while June and I were free to join classes in grammar, conversation, and culture and the excursions, or field trips. In my class, we discussed various aspects of Mexican life and the comparisons with life at home. I was pleased to have students examining the environment around them. Morelia was a lovely city of a million-plus population, one of the lesser-known treasures of Mexico. The heart of the city was still intact, with endless blocks of colonial streets and houses, probably even more extensive than any section in Mexico City. June and I appreciated and enjoyed the people, for the most part lively, friendly, and patient with us. But their city was not very clean or healthy.

Each student saw the surroundings and the experience of being away from home in a foreign country through a different set of glasses. They were all about twenty or twenty-one years of age, in the process of breaking the bonds with home, searching for self with a fair amount of knowledge acquired, but not yet much maturity. Being with and observing them led me to recognize how little parents understand their children. As one of the students wrote: "I only wish my Dad was in touch with my reality so he could lift the two blocks off his shoulders labeled Vietnam and sonless father." And another: "My real challenge remains in the United States, where I will have to confront my schooling and maintain a social life without substances."

One wrote that she "had difficulty feeling part of a community" and another found it "difficult to develop relationships with people in Morelia." One student considered herself a "lesbian feminist" and continued:

> I do not fit in easily. At first I felt isolated. I found the women standoffish and the men only interested in me to date. I felt helpless and depressed. Then I made a decision to carry myself wherever I go. Feeling disturbed by the condition of the street kids, I began working at the local orphanage a few hours a week. I also enrolled in Tae Kwon Doe. I have learned that I would never move back to this country unless I was surrounded by and working with other feminists.

And the other student wrote:

> The [Mexican] men usually want you for one thing and it is nearly
> impossible to get to know women your own age. I confronted
> this same problem when I lived on a kibbutz in Israel for a
> year. The residents were so accustomed to students coming and
> going that they kept their distance from us. For the most part I
> have encountered the same situation here. Not only have I felt
> myself an oddity as an American student but as a Jew. Yet, by
> the same token, I have a firmer, though not complete, hold of
> who I am: someone tied to tradition as well as independence,
> deeply emotional and committed, at the same time detached and
> indecisive. By understanding these basic elements about myself, I
> have become more secure in facing the future.

Some students spent a lot of time at fun and games, but maybe they
were learning and growing in the process and becoming "more secure in
facing the future." One student gave her own response, noting that during
her first month in Mexico she wondered how she could communicate so
well in Spanish and not always in English—where she had so much more
vocabulary to choose from. Then she concluded:

> The truth is that we keep it simple and direct when there is a
> linguistic challenge. There is more forgiveness, too. When I speak
> Spanish, my second language, people listen to my ideas instead
> of the exact significance of each of my words because they know
> I'm not a native speaker. We English speakers can't communicate
> in our native tongue because we are searching for and using the
> hidden meanings in everything instead of focusing on simply
> communicating.

That makes sense to me. Never mind the hidden meanings. Focus on simply
communicating. And the whole world likely will be better off.

A year later, in the spring of 1998, we spent another quarter with
students in the same kind of program, this time in Athens, Greece. Here
again I learned a great deal. I learned how little I knew—about Greek gods
and goddesses, about Socrates, Plato, the rise and fall of civilizations, art
and archaeology, religions and righteousness, hatreds and wars that seem
to have gone on forever.

People wherever we went were kind and helpful. I think people universally are meant to be that way, not to hate. One day, I was souvenir shopping in the Plaka, the ancient section of Athens at the foot of the Acropolis crowded with *tavernas*, cafes, and souvenir shops. The young woman clerk asked where I bought the bright, embroidered fez I wore on my head. When I told her I had gotten it during a long weekend in Turkey, she frowned disapprovingly. "They are not good people there," she said. "We are taught they are bad people." But I could not agree, remembering the pleasant encounters in Istanbul, particularly Turkish schoolchildren who thronged around us playfully, eager to practice English. I suppose they are taught in their schools that Greeks are bad people. So we are all in turn victims of what we are told and taught about Albanians, Bosnians, Palestinians, Iraquis, Gypsies, Jews, Muslims, and Americans, in ways that cultivate hostility and keep wars in style.

We were headquartered at the Athens Centre, which conducts courses for various American colleges and universities, and lived in an apartment nearby. The apartment was aging, adequate, and nondescript, except for access to a small, family-run store across the street, where I could pick up a bottle of *retsina*, the Greek national drink that tastes like varnish, for about fifty cents or a dollar. The curriculum in archaeology and art history included field trips in and around historic Athens to Sounion, Delphi, and Peloponnesus, and through the Greek Islands to Crete, home of the ancient Minoan civilization.

I taught environmental writing and journalism. I enjoyed these opportunities and challenges, although in Athens I taught U.S. students the difference between colons and dashes instead of environmental criticism. One young man said he had never seen a dash (—) in anything he had ever read. He also did not know the difference between the state legislature and national congress, and did not believe there was one. This came up when I asked the students to name their own representatives in Congress. Only one was able to do so. Their writing skills—vocabulary, grammar, punctuation, spelling, sentence structure, and composition—were limited. Like many university and college students, graduate as well as undergraduate, they confused "its" and "it's," "effect" and "affect," "there" and "their," "role" and "roll."

One day, I arranged a seminar with Lily Venizelos, one of Europe's leading conservationists, known as the Turtle Lady of Greece for her courageous campaign to save the sea turtle and its habitats in the Mediterranean. She recounted with eloquence the magic that drew her to the sea and sparked her desire "to put the turtles on the map as something of value." She told of founding Medasset, the Mediterranean Association to Save the Sea Turtles, and of its work in protecting nesting beaches threatened by tourist development.

The following week, we held another seminar with my friend Brock Evans, director of the Endangered Species Coalition in Washington DC, who stopped in Athens with his wife en route home from Israel. The students listened to these speakers passively, with scant questions or interaction. They were passive in class, more knowing and enthusiastic about pop and rock charts and their own extracurricular nocturnal social activities. But that is how they were trained—to take notes and regurgitate for their professors, not to write, not to speak, nor to analyze or to think.

Nevertheless, half a dozen students, June, and I celebrated Earth Day 1998 by joining a group of fifteen schoolchildren and members of a local neighborhood council in a cleanup of trash of the Arditos Hill above the Olympic Stadium. But even while we were cleaning the park, garbage bins on every street corner were piled higher and smellier because they had not been unloaded for days. The archaeology instructor (an American expatriate living in Greece) led a field trip to the Acropolis but members of the class couldn't see the mountains circling Athens because of the heavy haze of pollution. One group of workers after another was on strike or protesting against the government. Returning from field trips, we could always tell we were "home" in Athens by the chronic roar of motorcars and motorbikes, exhaust fumes from oversized tour buses, graffiti, and billboards (celebrating Joe Camel and other nicotine icons). Athens, the first great city of the western world, struggled in its stress. A newspaper poll of Athenians published while we were there showed that over 60 percent considered it unlivable.

The gods and early Greeks knew how to pick their special places. We saw the evidence on our field trips to the Temple of Poseidon at Sounion, facing the open sea at the tip of the Attica Peninsula, and to the ruins of Crete, and at Olympia and Mycenae, Corinth and Delphi. We enjoyed lovely mountain landscapes and seascapes combined with treasures of antiquity. The only trouble was that the people who chose those sites lived a long time ago, while the modern Greeks apparently have taken them all for granted. They figure that tourists will come from all over the world with money to spend, and we do. Crowds dominated without boundaries or limits; there were no safeguards for beauty and antiquity.

True, we were tourists, too. We took advantage of a long weekend break to fly to Istanbul, going around the mosques, markets, and fragments of ancient civilization that complement the Greek. We enjoyed the energies and warmth of the Turkish people and the surface sights of the weekend. But reading the *Turkish Daily News* (in English) showed me that Turkey was not really a happy, prosperous, or open country. The newspaper reported the arrest of opposition members of the assembly suspected of supporting Kurdistan separatists and a raid on their party's office by government antiterrorist teams. The same paper reported a study on censorship of media around the world, with particular reference to Turkey as the country with the most journalists in jail—fifty-eight. I also read an interview with the new ambassador from the United States, who didn't say anything about issues of free expression, but urged Turkey to achieve its "potential in global economy" by attracting investment by American corporations.

The ten-day spring break, we spent in Israel. The first few days, we were with friends Brock Evans and his wife Linda Garcia at the Arava Institute for Environmental Studies at a kibbutz in the Negev desert where Brock was teaching. It was impressive to observe Brock with all his enthusiasm and years of experience with the Sierra Club and National Audubon Society sharing lessons of politics and activism with students from half a dozen countries, including Israel, its Arab neighbors, and the United States, and breaking down barriers of misunderstanding. The students were impressive too. I spent one evening with them and found them highly motivated, eager learners, willing to discourse and debate until past midnight.

Brock and Linda showed us the desert in the region where the borders of Israel, Jordan, and Egypt meet. Portions reminded me of the red rock country in southern Utah and of Death Valley in California-Nevada with golden white dunes, canyons, and mountain walls. One day we crossed the border into Jordan, from Eliat into Aqaba to explore the incredible ruins at ancient Petra. On leaving the site, the cabdriver who had driven us from Aqaba took us to his father's house for tea and I remember that as much as I do the spectacle of Petra. The everyday people of Jordan were not different from those of Israel or Turkey or Greece. Take away the hate and there is no need for guns, warplanes, and tanks. Or maybe take away all the guns, planes, and tanks, and there is no need for hate.

We arrived in Israel on May 31, 1998, the fiftieth anniversary of the founding of the Jewish state, a day of celebration everywhere. I remarked to June that we were in the one country in the world where it's all right to be a Jew. She reminded me that not everyone was celebrating. We met Palestinians who wanted to get on with their lives, but felt victimized by the Israelis and by their own politicians. Plainly they lived in discomfort in shabby settlements in a police state. They deserved a better break; they deserved the compassion that had been denied to Jews during the dark days in Europe. I shared this later in correspondence with my niece Annette, a scholar versed in the Middle East, who was raised in the Greek Sephardic tradition of her mother's family. She responded there was another issue among Jews themselves: "Although Sephardics are the majority, the country is modeled after Eastern European paradigms and I don't think other Jews will ever be fully accepted."

That doesn't ring right to me. It reinforces doubts and questions about structured religions, all of them. Suffice for now to say that it grieves me to find so much of the world degraded and debased by that glorious global economic potential of which the U.S. ambassador had spoken glowingly in Turkey. Nevertheless, I felt uplifted by the three days we spent at the Sea of Galilee, still a beautiful, relatively unspoiled landscape, where Jesus did his preaching, teaching, and healing—he and his unshaven, hippy, hobo, and maybe even smelly, apostles. At the Church of the Beatitudes, the presumed site of the Sermon on the Mount, I picked up a copy of Pope John Paul's Prayer in Preparation for the Great Jubilee of the Year 2000. The refrain to the prayer was printed in boldface: "Come, Spirit of love and peace!" And two brief passages I found appealing:

> Spirit of holiness, divine breath which moves the universe,
> come and renew the face of the earth....
>
> Inspire solidarity with the poor,
> grant the sick the strength they need,
> pour out trust and hope upon those experiencing trials,
> awaken in all hearts a commitment to a better future.

Yes, I came away wanting to renew the face of the earth, and to exalt the spirit of love and peace. That experience and others like it made me appreciate the calling of peace. At Delphi, I learned how the god Apollo claimed the sanctuary from Ge (or Gaea), the earth goddess, by slaying the

My father, William Fromm, with my brother, Marvin, and me on May 30, 1922, a week after my second birthday. Shrubbery and private house indicate we were still living in the Flatbush section of Brooklyn, where I was born. Within a year or two, we moved to the Bronx.

My mother, Henrietta, with brother Marvin (already in glasses) and me on Labor Day 1927 at Rockaway Beach.

The flight crew on my first overseas mission, January 1944. We were in the air fourteen-plus hours from California to Hawaii, then island-hopped another five days to Brisbane, Australia.

Thelma and I in conversation
with Senator Theodore
Green, of Rhode Island,
at a black-tie function in
Washington.

Life was promising for the
growing family, wife Thelma,
children Will and Michele,
and Christmas at our first
home was abundant.

I went around with foresters and loggers, listening and learning from them. And then I made up my own mind.

I never felt I was a stranger in the Great Smoky Mountains or in Appalachia. The year 1966 was another landmark for me with publication of *Strangers in High Places* and the fight to "save the Smokies."

In the 1970s, I collaborated with North Carolina bear hunters in trying to block construction of a road into prime bear country. Sorry to say, we failed.

D

My first book, *Better Vacations for Your Money*, was published in 1959 and my second, *Washington: A Modern Guide to the Nation's Capital*, two years later. I enjoyed autographing books, but found I was meant for something more than travel writing.

Orville Freeman, secretary of agriculture, was easy to work with when we coauthored *The National Forests of America* in 1968.

I did my writing on a secondhand Royal typewriter, in an office with a view of trees and water and classical music playing on the radio. As I wrote in *Tools of the Writer's Trade*, "Precious little gadgetry is really needed. Much wonderful work has been

produced without it. I can't imagine Henry David Thoreau or John Muir writing their inspirational and challenging pleas for nature with anything but the simplest tools, to match the simple styles of their lives."

At Bellingham we had a lot of beauty nearby. This ranger, John Madden, invited us to scout for eagles on the Skagit River on Christmas Day.

With Lynn Kinter, a former student, on the bank of Torrey Lake, Dubois, Wyoming, in 1993, on her way to earning her doctoral degree in botany and university teaching.

With Tom Bell, who in the 1960s founded the Wyoming Outdoor Council and then *High Country News,* August 1993.

I came a long, long way to achieve my PhD in 1993 when I was seventy-three.

At my parents' grave at the cemetery in New Jersey. I placed a stone on the headstone, the traditional sign of respect.

And then came Brandy the terrier, so there were three of us going places, here on the Pacific beach of Vancouver Island.

In autumn 1995, June went to the international women's conference in Beijing. I met her when she returned and we went to Yosemite, where I spoke. We went on to the Great Smokies, where I spoke again at the Tremont Learning Center.

At Zihuatanejo almost every morning we walked down to swim in the bay, then returned to our apartment for breakfast and I began work on this book.

H

I was at the Federal Building in Bellingham every Friday with fellow protesters of the Bush administration and its war in Iraq.

The rebel on the road keeps going, one foot following the other.

guard python. To cleanse himself after shedding blood, Apollo went into self-imposed exile as a shepherd for eight years. Only after atonement and purification did he return to Delphi and by this example taught a great moral lesson: that expiation for bloodshed could be achieved by means other than new bloodshed, as had been the practice until then. The past is to learn from, not to repeat.

Early September of that same year, 1998, we returned to Morelia. It was a little like coming home: identifying with familiar streets, shops, restaurants, little sidewalk places, and colleagues at the school. The chronically gray, pollution-laden skies and poor air quality that hampered breathing recalled our stay in Athens. But at least now, we could speak and understand a few more words *en español*, definitely simpler to understand than Greek. Soon after we arrived, we joined in celebrating Mexico's Independence Day, another cause to *fiesta* with fireworks, parades, and *mucha música mariachi*. And on All Saints' Day at the beginning of November, we went to historic Patzcuaro and nearby cemeteries for la Noche de Muertos (the Night of the Dead) when many Mexicans follow the ancient custom of congregating at family graves with flowers and food and elaborate altars in anticipation of the return of their loved ones—in celebration rather than in mourning.

I found that two of my new students actually had heard of Rachel Carson, and one knew she was the author of a book called *Silent Spring*. She knew the title, not the book. But I suppose that everyone comes in somewhere, and that was the place to begin. I felt that while they would not all follow Rachel's path, some of them might if I encouraged them to believe in themselves. This was not easy to do. One young man was well motivated, but could barely express himself either orally or in writing; as he explained to me one day, he'd been intimidated and terrified for years by his father, a law enforcement officer. One young woman who had been in and out of drugs wrote to me: "My life had become one big rut. I returned to my parents' house, but it was still the home from which I had always needed to escape." Then she added: "I had exhausted two years of general studies and still had no idea of what I wanted to do...." That was a common theme among students, revealing the wide gap between them and their parents. As another wrote: "My parents were nagging me to declare a major. As my dad put it, 'Stop wasting my time and money.'"

Nevertheless, we held positive discussions in class. One key subject was the North America Free Trade Agreement (NAFTA). We reviewed the pluses and found there weren't any, and the minuses and found them abundant for U.S. and Mexican labor and for the environment, especially in Mexico. We considered the status of the *mariposa monarca*, the Monarch butterfly, endangered to the verge of desperation by tree-cutting, but with some measure of hope in the establishment of government reserves and the activities of butterfly advocates in both Mexico and the United States.

We read and clipped environmental news in English and Spanish journals. I read to the class an interview with a San Francisco hotelman representing a luxury hotel group about the coming boom he foresaw in tourism to Mexico. "It is one of the largest emerging markets, easy to get to, affordable, and the product is very good. I think what people fear most is just the internal situation, economically and that kind of stuff. Take away that and it's one of the most enjoyable places to visit." The students reacted. One said, "Well, it isn't easy to take away 'the internal situation and that kind of stuff.'" Another cited drug-related corruption rampant in the administration of *el presidente* Carlos Salinas. And another held up a report on the official number of children living on the streets of Mexico. It was 500,000, though the actual figure was thought to be higher.

They wanted to deal with truths in their studies and their lives, and found answers—truthful answers—were not forthcoming. Each student was different from the rest, each had his or her own particular truth to reveal, or perhaps I should say lesson to teach. I was impressed by a paper written by a young woman who told me that during her high school years she was class president, school vice president, and second in her class standing. She ran track, played soccer, and in her free time helped with tutoring. She was known as pretty and popular but underneath it all she was miserable:

> The pressure I had put on myself to achieve was really unhealthy. Setting my goals high, I was able to achieve the image I wanted but not to enjoy it. I have recently learned that getting a C on a paper is not the end of the world. I smile and laugh frequently and find that for the first time in my life I'm making decisions to better myself.

Good for her, I say, for true success, after all, comes only from within.

June (and I too) became very interested in the *mariposa monarca*, which every winter returns by the millions to the mild, humid mountain forests of Michoacán. We went to visit the region of Angangeo and Ocampo, the butterfly habitat, only to arrive before they did, and then we were obliged to leave for home. However, we learned that in the entire world no butterflies migrate like these Monarchs, traveling in masses of millions to the same winter roosts, often to the exact same trees. I was reminded of watching Monarchs, back East years before, feed on milkweed along the Appalachian Trail in autumn. They were preparing themselves for their long journey, but I had no idea of where they were headed, or that the butterfly migration compares in magnitude and meaning to the migration of birds, caribou, whales, and salmon. That is clearly the case, although exactly how their homing system works is an unsolved mystery, the answer known only to butterflies.

While still in Morelia, I had to take a couple of days off to fly back to the United States for a speech. It was in Asheville, North Carolina, which I had known and written about years before. In those days, it was an attractive resort town in the southern mountains, especially appealing for its clean air—that was why people went there. But now, as soon as I left the airport and wherever I went in Asheville, I felt the oppressive presence of yellowish-reddish-grayish haze, a dull, dispiriting layer of clouds that was virtually no different than the layer of haze I had left in Morelia.

That was only part of it. I was in Asheville to speak before a forum sponsored by the Western North Carolina Public Parks Task Force, a citizens group concerned with bureaucratic transformation of the Blue Ridge Parkway into a commercially oriented theme park. This was the very area, between Shenandoah and the Smokies, where I had begun my love affair with national parks many years before. The best I could tell my audience was that I had witnessed many changes in the national parks, some few for the better, but many highly damaging. I said these precious places were overused, misused, polluted, inadequately protected, and unmercifully exploited commercially and politically. It was good to see many people come to show their concern; the road to reclaim the park would not be easy, but I hoped that seeds properly planted and nurtured ultimately would bear fruit.

CHAPTER 24

John Oakes was gentle, but wrote with power – The old apartment buildings were
still there, seventy or so years later – An ancient city with narrow, winding cobbled
streets – Perle Hessing saw a cloud of insects with iridescent wings

.

Early in September 1997, I set out on my little pilgrimage, going home
to the Bronx, where I had not been for more than fifty years. I hoped to
show June my old neighborhoods and my high school, and also to visit
my parents' grave across the Hudson River in New Jersey. I wondered if
there was anything still remaining of the Zaleschiki Verein, the fraternal
society of the people who came from that town and that sponsored the
section of the cemetery where my parents were buried. Inquiries led me
to talk on the phone with Mrs. Shirley Bomze, who was indeed president
of the Verein or what was left of it into the second and third generations.
She still lived in the Bronx, and while growing up she and I had lived for a
time in the same neighborhood on Creston Avenue and attended Creston
Junior High, though I was a few years ahead of her. I asked if she had ever
been to Zaleschiki, the home village of her father and mine. No, but she
had been to Israel and related a particular happening there. "I went to the
Museum of the Diaspora," she said, "and as soon as I entered I suddenly
saw a reference on the wall to Zaleschiki and the total dissolution of the
Jewish community there. It was an eerie experience."

That made it a little eerie for me, too. The conversation kindled my
interest in Zaleschiki. It wasn't quite curiosity, but something more like
homing, a sense of searching for home, for roots from whence I came. But
maybe it wasn't exactly that either. I said to June, "How about after returning
from New York, we go to Europe, to Warsaw and my father's village in
Ukraine?" She was surprised, but responded without hesitation. "If that is
what you really want. But why?" It was difficult to explain. Maybe it was
for redemption: that I wanted to redeem myself in my father's eyes and my
mother's. But they were gone and would never know. At least I could honor

them and pay respect, honor and respect that I had denied them while they lived, and perhaps by doing so I could find redemption and make myself a more complete and peaceful person.

I did not spell out something to June that I could not fathom myself, but she understood without explanation. Strange that I should approach the home of my father and of his fathers, holding the hand of a *goy*, a *shiksa*, and an ordained Christian minister at that. Yet she knew my own Bible, the Old Testament, far better than I did. And so did my first wife, Thelma, who had blessed me, despite all that had come between us.

The first stop on our little pilgrimage was New York, the massive, vibrant, overpowering, ageless, and aging city that was my natal place. Although I had returned many times over the years, at least to Manhattan, on every visit I experienced a nostalgic twinge, an ache within, derived from recognition that both the city and I were older. Landmarks like Penn Station and Madison Square Garden were gone. Marvels of yesteryear that were new in my childhood, like the Daily News Building on 42nd Street and Rockefeller Center, had lost their sparkle with age. And yet, while buildings were changed or had been replaced, the streets and avenues were still in place, as they always had been, and might, for all I know, go on forever.

We stayed with friends who lived comfortably on 73rd Street, near the east side of Central Park in Manhattan. We spent a morning walking footpaths across the park in company with New Yorkers walking their dogs, baby carriages, spouses, and sweethearts, or sunning themselves on huge greenswards bordered by shrubs and trees that sheltered them from the city. Central Park has been pared around the edges and carries more lanes of noisy, polluting motor traffic than any park should be forced to accommodate, and yet it remains in place as William Cullen Bryant, the American poet and for fifty years editor of the *New York Evening Post*, envisioned it in 1844.

It was Bryant, the newspaper editor, who sparked the movement to establish the park that has since become the most valuable undeveloped parcel of real estate in America. They don't much do that any more, and yet on our very day in Central Park, June and I were invited and went to lunch with a particular hero of mine, John B. Oakes, one of the preeminent editorialists of the twentieth century, and his wife, Margery. We joined them at their apartment on Fifth Avenue in the 80s overlooking the park. Oakes had been editor of the editorial page of the *New York Times* for fifteen years starting in 1961, although he came into my life earlier, in the 1950s. At that time he was editor of the *Times*'s Review of the Week, but he also wrote a column titled "Conservation," which appeared in the travel section. I read it regularly as part of my work at the AAA. It intrigued me in 1956 to read about the introduction of the Wilderness Act and other environmental issues of that time, and it influenced me.

Later, when I started writing about these issues myself, I would meet John in Washington now and then, visit him in New York, and once we made a trip together in a group on the Colorado River through the Grand Canyon. One time, after he had retired, he allowed me to leaf through the scrapbooks of his editorials and op-ed columns. He wrote incisive pieces on a wide range—civil rights, the presidency, foreign affairs, politics, the environment, and protecting the integrity of Central Park. When I was through, I said something like, "These are great commentaries on our time and ought to be published in a book form." Margery heard me; she strongly concurred and hoped John would work on it, but that book never came to pass.

But then, while John Oakes wrote with power, he personally was gentle, modest, and soft-spoken. When we visited, he was eighty-four and hard of hearing; so was Margery. "We shout at each other all day," Margery said with a laugh. They loved June and invited us to come back and stay with them. Following his death at the age of eighty-seven in 2001, I sent Margery a note of sympathy and appreciation of John, to which she replied, "I hope you know how fully he reciprocated your feelings. It truly helps to hear from someone he valued as highly as he did you." I never felt up to such esteem, although knowing and associating with gifted people like John Oakes certainly enriched my life.

The next morning, we had breakfast with a friend at a coffee shop on Madison Avenue. When I mentioned that we were going to the Bronx for the day, he replied, "I never go north of 72nd Street." The Bronx for him was not another borough, but another country and not one to visit. New Yorkers can be that way, the most provincial of people. They know theater, restaurants, and world affairs, but little about their neighbors in the Bronx.

We took the subway to the station near my old high school at the edge of Van Cortlandt Park in the north end of the Bronx. The school was older, of course, but seemed smaller too. That often is the way: that what once was formidable to a child, to an adult has been reduced to the ordinary. Nevertheless, we found a huge, impressive banner above the main entrance proclaiming the DeWitt Clinton High School centennial, 1897 to 1997, and "100 Years of Excellence." The term had ended and school was out, although the auditorium was in use for a junior high school graduation. Students and their families appeared almost entirely black or Hispanic, reflecting the abundant changes in the neighborhood from my time until now. I wandered around looking for the office of the *Clinton News,* where I began in journalism. Someone said the paper did not have an office, that it had been discontinued for several years and had just resumed publication. How sad, I thought, considering that students need to learn to write and communicate and work together and read their names in print, either for what they had written or for their school activities.

From the school, we hired a taxicab to see the old neighborhoods and the apartment houses where I lived in the long ago. My parents had made a practice of moving virtually every other year. Thus, it was difficult to remember all the places we lived, but I did remember three: 2709 Webb Avenue, 2188 Creston Avenue, and 115 McClellan Place. Later, in reading Jonathon Kozol's book, *Amazing Grace,* a revelation of the impoverished and dispossessed, his reference to Featherbed Lane stirred my memory. When I was four years old, my family lived at 99 Featherbed Lane. Whatever it may have been then, it is definitely not a desirable address today.

The old buildings were still there, seventy or so years older than when we lived in them, presentable from the outside and occupied now by a new wave of black and Hispanic immigrants starting from the bottom with the same aspirations as those who came before. The most striking change to me was the graffiti, which I observed on almost every spare wall of subway structure, public building, or housing. Not crude scrawlings in chalk, although there were plenty of them, but meticulously designed and executed psychedelic murals in vibrant colors of subways, tenements, and spooks from space and the spirit world—people's art. Those lush colors were in markets on the shopping streets, where Caribbean and Latino people clearly came to find their favorite foods of home.

Returning to the Bronx, even for this brief time, stirred me to reflect on my time, when kids played stickball and roller hockey in the streets, and softball, handball, and basketball in the schoolyards, when I could easily walk from the family apartment on McClellan Street to the Yankee Stadium, and buy a ticket in the bleachers for fifty cents and a hot dog for a dime. The teams played on real grass and under natural sunlight, and starting pitchers stayed in the game for nine innings.

Another day of pilgrimage followed. We began by visiting the fur market. "This was the heart of it," I told June while we stood at the corner of Twenty-ninth Street and Seventh Avenue. We looked up at the old buildings and I wondered if much remained of the fur business that once thrived in the lofts. Animal rights groups had made women feel differently about the "luxury" of wearing fur. Then we sighted a banner hanging from the fifth or sixth floor windows of a building on Seventh Avenue:

WELCOME TO THE FUR MARKET
We Support Research for Cancer and AIDS
"A Responsible Industry That Cares!"

So there was that much left to the industry. But I felt relieved that my father was not around for it.

From the Port Authority Building on the west side, we rode the suburban bus for about an hour, through the Holland Tunnel under the Hudson River to Westwood, New Jersey. It was a pleasant place where my parents had lived for a time and my father had a fur shop. Neither of them had died there, yet the Beth-El Cemetery at the edge of Westwood was the chosen burial site of the Zaleschiki Verein, where my father and his landsmen and their wives came to rest.

We walked on landscaped paths through the cemetery. I thought, "Now I am older than my father when he died, older than my mother, and than my older brother, dead now for twenty years. I am old, but still the child and the last of the family." Presently we found the Verein section. A tall stone marker was inscribed with the names of the officers, headed by A. Fromm, my uncle Avroom, the ex-president, and at the base of it the inscription, "Organized 1906." All of them then were young and hopeful, speaking Yiddish at home, eating Yiddish food, reading Yiddish daily papers, and yet glad to be part of the great new world. June was first to find my parents' site. Both were buried under the same marker. It was ample and dignified. June picked up a small stone for me to place on top, the traditional testament of respect. I closed my eyes in prayer for us all and for a brief moment saw myself as the child of young parents in the Bronx.

Barely three weeks later, June and I left Bellingham again, this time for Warsaw and Ukraine, the second phase of my pilgrimage. I won't say that we deliberately managed things the hard way, but somehow our little brand of independent travel led to assorted obstacles and then to surprising adventurous and enriching solutions.

At the very outset, for example, I thought it would suffice to have a hotel room assured in Warsaw and to go on from there. With one or two days remaining before departure, however, our travel agent reported that Warsaw hotels were sold out. Oh dear—I hardly wanted to fly across the Atlantic Ocean and half of Europe only to start scouting for a place to sleep. Then a friend mentioned that a good fellow who worked at the university library in Bellingham was married to a woman from Warsaw, and that she had assorted contacts there. We telephoned Rick and Barbara Osen Sunday morning; we were scheduled to leave on Tuesday. "Come over at once," Barbara said, "and we will try." When we arrived she generously telephoned in our behalf four or five different hotels in Warsaw. All were completely booked with large conferences or conventions. Barbara was calm and collected. "Do not worry, " she said. "I will call my daughter, who is a physician in Warsaw. She will find a place for you. If she cannot, then you will stay with her and her family, husband and two children. And they will meet your plane at the airport."

Thus reassured, we set out. But when we arrived and went through customs and immigration, our hosts were nowhere to be found. After an hour, I panicked. I had their phone number and wanted to call. But what to use for a coin? Whom could I get to help? Just then they arrived, an attractive young couple, solicitous and apologetic. The problem was that the brakes in his car didn't work well and had needed emergency attention. We found the car was ancient, creaky, and questionable, an indicator of the Polish state of things.

Our host, tall, spectacled, and bearded, was cheery about the car and about life in general. He made his living writing and editing publications on Polish aviation. It could not have paid much, but that was his calling, derived from memory of the historic 1939 invasion when the Polish air force actually held off the feared Luftwaffe for a time, after which the Polish pilots flew again from England. Our hostess, the physician, apparently did not earn much either. Medical practice in Poland was not high up in the chain of professions, as in the United States, but low down, and she was thinking of switching to something else, like working for a travel agency.

The next evening, we went to dinner at their home, a very simple one-room house they shared with their two lively little blond children and the editor's aged mother. The house actually was the grandmother's, but they felt fortunate to have this much in post-Soviet Poland. Meanwhile, the doctor had arranged for us to stay at a Baptist guesthouse, which proved to be clean, congenial, inexpensive, and convenient to central Warsaw. One morning we walked for breakfast to a nearby four-star hotel, where tourists in huge groups stood in long lines waiting for cold breakfasts to eat in cavernous private dining rooms sheltered from the community they came to experience.

I had been in Warsaw once before, in 1946, one year after the end of World War II and after the German military forces had retreated, destroying almost everything as they left and leaving the city in ruins. Prewar Warsaw had held the second largest Jewish population in the world, second only to New York, but the Jews had long suffered from pogroms and anti-Semitism. Those who did not flee suffered again during the war when they were forced into a walled ghetto from which they staged a desperate, failed uprising. We visited that sad place and then, nearby, found a hopeful alternative: the headquarters of an optimistic new Jewish theater group.

When I had come to Warsaw fifty-one years before, one of the government ministers told me of plans to rebuild the core of the old town the Germans had leveled. Now we saw it in completion: the old houses, three or four stories, pastel-colored, with many windows facing the large square. It was authentic as a reconstruction of times past, many of the buildings now serving as cafes, bars, and restaurants. My impression was that Warsaw wanted to be a western city with western ways, and that it did not want to be an eastern, Soviet-type city any longer. Stores advertised Sony, Zerox, Microsoft, and other goodies of the West and Japan, and the latest movies from Hollywood, in contrast with the monumental Soviet-built Palace of Culture, twenty-five or thirty stories tall, gloomy, foreboding, overpowering, and unappealing.

We were readying for the one-hour flight to L'viv, the largest city in western Ukraine and what I assumed would be the gateway to Zaleschiki. I stopped in a Warsaw bank to buy some Ukraine currency. The teller smiled as though I had said something funny, then advised me the bank did not carry Ukrainian currency because it wasn't worth anything. "Why do you want to go there anyway? It's not safe." Yes, we probably were foolish to venture on our own into unknown territory, when we might have joined some tour group with everything planned and organized, but we were adventurous, spontaneous, trusting, and hanging-together kind of people. In Ukraine, we were received and treated well, and it was safe.

We hadn't counted on L'viv turning out as it did. Fortune was with us at the outset. We managed to locate a bright, lively, fairly upscale hotel situated above a landscaped park and the central city below. The ancient city had narrow, winding cobbled streets, all authentic and undisturbed by war, unlike the reconstruction of Warsaw. It wasn't Paris and it wasn't Prague, but L'viv had the character and quality of the past, and a lovely opera house, where on succeeding nights we saw credible performances of *Tosca* and *La Bohème*. L'viv was not a prosperous place; it was run-down around the edges, like most of the people we encountered there, and yet grand opera was plainly one of the staples of life, as it is everywhere in Europe, in contrast to the United States, where opera is expensive and considered elitist.

Few people spoke English, unlike in Paris or Prague, but then we were in a different culture, of the East rather than the West. Ukraine had been a large and significant component of the USSR. With the collapse of the Soviet Union, Ukraine in 1991 became a new country with many problems to resolve on its own. The most important, I suppose, was dealing with the aftermath of the 1986 fallout at the Chernobyl nuclear power plant, far to the east of us, which spread into the atmosphere ninety times more toxic waste than the American atomic bomb at Hiroshima.

We could not decipher the old Eastern Cyrillic-style writing. On Sunday morning, June wanted to attend church, which here meant Ukrainian Orthodox, or possibly Greek Catholic. She meant to arrive early, but the church was packed. She managed to find a seat while I stood outside with many others, listening to the strange chant of the choir and the response of the congregation, practicing religion as they wished after the long repression.

I consulted the travel agency in the lobby of our hotel about a tour to Zaleschiki. The manager spoke English and wanted to help. "We can arrange a one-day trip there and back, for $200, with car and driver," she said. But I had hoped to stay overnight. "There is no place to stay. If you prefer, you can go from here to Ternopol, which is closer, and try to make arrangements from there."

Perhaps we were foolhardy again, but we opted for Ternopol. The bus station from which we left in L'viv was ragged, worn, and old; so were the

bus we rode for three hours and the streets and the people—virtually everything in Ukraine. And it was raining. We arrived in Ternopol at twilight in
the rain. We couldn't speak Ukrainian, or even Russian, and nobody spoke
English or had time to stop while scurrying home at day's end in the rain.
It was discouraging.

Somehow we found a hotel; it was large, dark, and dimly lit. We were
greeted at the elevator on our assigned floor by a pleasant lady of middle
years, who escorted us to our room. She smiled, spoke a few words of
English and tried to be helpful. June and I played cards for a while, but I
kept asking myself, "Whatever do I do now? How could I have done this to
my wife?" At nine PM I was looking out the window at the rain and feeling
hopeless when the phone rang. I picked it up. "Yes?" I asked. "This is Nadia
and I will take you to Zaleschiki tomorrow. I will come at eight o'clock."

June would call it "the angels at work." Certainly Nadia Kuzmych
arrived as an angel in our lives. She was, in fact, the daughter of the pleasant
lady working on our hotel floor; her mother had phoned at home and told
her about us. Nadia was a nineteen-year-old second-year university student
focused on learning English and more than happy for the opportunity to
practice and to learn. She arrived in the morning as promised, with car and
driver. It would cost $100 for the driver and fuel, wholly reasonable and
acceptable. The driver was a pleasant, plump blonde of about forty, eager
to please as best she could. Owning a fairly modern car apparently was an
attainment in itself. She was married, but her husband worked as a waiter in
Greece—as was often the case in many countries in our time, when families
must separate in order to sustain hopes of ultimate togetherness.

For two or three hours, we drove through farmlands and vineyards
in what was once known as "the breadbasket of Europe," and was fought
over by diverse ruling powers and transferred back and forth, from Turkish
control, then Russian, Polish, Austro-Hungarian, and ultimately into a
World War I battlefield between Russians and Austrians. We passed an
occasional cart—two horses, the driver, and a crop I could not identify. I
wondered, "On which page of history did they belong?"

We came at last to Zaleschiki in the foothills of the Carpathian
Mountains. I could see why in its day it was a popular resort town. Most
houses were just one story high, of an old design plainly meant for the
provinces, many bordered by plants and flowers. The tree-lined central
plaza seemed full of stories and dreams, with a feel of history: on the town

hall was a cupola with a statue of a spear-holding Turkish soldier, dating from days when this part of Europe was overrun by the Turks. Best of all, we observed the Dniester River winding between forested cliffs in changing colors of early fall, resembling a scene somewhere in southern Appalachia.

This much I knew of Zaleschiki, the birthplace of my father. About the turn of the twentieth century, hostility toward Jews led many to emigrate to the United States. Early in World War I, after the Russians captured Zaleschiki, soldiers attacked the Jews, killing some, expelling others, looting, and destroying property and homes. Following the war, survivors returned and were generally well treated by their neighbors. By 1934, there were almost 2,500 Jews; five of sixteen members of the town council and the vice-mayor were Jews. The Germans captured Zaleschiki in July 1941 and initiated systematic persecution, sending one thousand Jews to ghettos, labor camps, and death camps. Others fled to Romania, a few miles to the south, hiding with Christians or in bunkers. In March 1944, after heavy fighting along the Dniester, the region was liberated by the Russians. A few dozen Jews returned, but only for a while, before departing for Israel and other countries.

The remains of war were manifest in a huge stone monument with photographs of Zaleschiki soldiers who were killed in action displayed at its base and in a Soviet tank standing in silent guard. Despite its attractive setting, there was a certain pathos or physical impoverishment, about the town. Here and there, we saw chickens, a goat, a turkey grazing unfettered in the grass. There seemed to be one restaurant, where we lunched well, but then when June wanted to buy a remembrance to take home, we found one store with the most meager merchandise. While we stood in the town square, I felt my father's presence. I had come in homage to him and my mother. "Remember that I left as a boy," he whispered, "and I never returned."

There is one more part to this story. When we returned, my niece Annette telephoned to commend a book to me, *A Mirror to My Life*, by Perle Hessing. Hessing was born in Zalezchiki in 1908 and lived the first years of her life there, when it was part of the Austro-Hungarian Empire. Later she lived in Australia and Europe. She took up painting and recorded her vivid memories of "this lovely little town and the countryside around it…of orange-colored rocks, green and golden trees, and the river Dniester with its soft yellow shores and water so clear that you could easily see the pebbles on the bottom." So I have this particular artistic record of my roots. The main strand of her painting derives from old Hasidic tales, mysticism, ancient ideas, and family life in central Europe. She painted *The Village Fid-dler, The Shtetl at Night, The Blacksmith, Jewish Wedding, An Ancient Synagogue,* pictures of narrow streets and flowers. She recounted how one evening as a child she looked out her window in early spring to watch the town prom-enading; she looked up beneath the street lamp and saw a magic array of blues, reds, purples, and greens—a cloud of insects with iridescent wings, buzzing noise, a strange sort of music. Her book was a spiritual autobiogra-phy in pictures that added depth and appreciation to my pilgrimage.

Nadia was in class at the university when we left Ternopol. Her mother had strongly urged us to steer clear of the rickety bus, but to take the train—better by far. She and Nadia's sister met us at the depot to make sure we got the right tickets, track, and train. They stood on the platform with umbrellas over their shoulders in the rain and sent us off with smiles and a wave. We went by train to Kraków in southern Poland. I won't go into it—at this point it would be anticlimactic—except to note that here was another classic city, like L'viv or Prague, spared wartime destruction, and that we enjoyed a festive time.

Maybe "festive" is not the right word, considering that we took a day tour by bus to Auschwitz, the notorious center for extermination of European Jews and the largest concentration camp for prisoners of various nationalities. I believe the Polish people suffered more than any other nationality; thus, to their credit, they have kept Auschwitz intact to interpret the profound crime and tragedy of the ages, reminding the world that, in the words of George Santayana inscribed on the wall, "The one who does not remember history is bound to live through it again."

That sounds right. I think that same idea has been expressed in differ-ent words at different times in history. Yet we were in a part of Europe that in a thousand years had gone from Turkish control to Russian, Polish, and Austro-Hungarian, and had been a battlefield in World War I and again in World War II. And the best they had to show for it were huge stone monu-ments to wars and warriors. My own country, the United States, was no better, except at building bigger and better monuments that glorify one war after another, and that perpetuate fear, hate, and violence on a global scale, despite the clear alternative that begins, "Blessed are the peacemakers."

CHAPTER 25

Walking on "stony ground" – Our balloon ride on Ascension Day – Introducing "warmth" and "verve" – Times to soak in foaming bubbles – And taste the best wine with a best friend

If I have given the idea that June and I lived in sheer serenity and harmony, I had better back up and confess that it wasn't all roses, not at the beginning, and not even ten years later. I don't know about other couples; maybe some get by being consistently and continually of one mind and one spirit, but I doubt it. In our case, I believe that love was constant and true, but we also had differences and misunderstandings. Perhaps, in looking back, they were part of the process, like hoops we had to go through to realize understanding and trust.

Reality arrived in mid-January 1995 after we returned from the honeymoon. I recognized that we both were walking on what might be called "stony ground," a condition rather than a surface that emerges in a relationship after living alone, without anyone to account to, or from living lonely even when not alone. June was a kingpin, or a queenpin, in her congregation, widely esteemed beyond the congregation, in demand for one thing and another, outgoing and on the go. I had friends, but needed quiet times, and probably was more reflective. We both were strong-willed and independent, with patterns that worked—for each as an individual focused on career, accustomed to making decisions, and having others perform assorted functions for us. Thus differences arose between us. They became challenging and at times distressing.

At the root of it, I'm sure, was fear. We both feared a change of lifestyle, feared moving out of a comfort zone to accommodate needs and desires of another person, feared surrendering possession of the past, both physical objects and mental images. Small matters tended to become issues. For instance, we ate different foods. A vegetarian stir-fry with tofu at home, with a glass of wine or whiskey, was good enough for me, while June liked eating out, found tofu alien to her taste, and rarely touched alcohol. We preferred different wake-up times; she wanted the blinds closed, I wanted them open—all kinds of little things on which you're afraid to give ground because you're afraid to lose face, or even worse to lose control, because you've always done it your way, which makes it the right way. In marriage, the new "partnership" works as long as you're senior partner. Yes, I'm talking of myself here, confessing that I could be demanding, unyielding and, as June complained, bossy. Of course, I didn't see it that way. At times, when she was angry, I didn't feel comfortable talking with her. The best I could say was, "Look, I don't want to regulate you; I don't want you to regulate me."

At first, early in marriage, we didn't even live together. We hadn't thought it through or discussed it. She was in Seattle and I was in Bellingham, eighty-five miles north. For the first few months, I would come down every weekend. It was easier for me, but she would come up when she could. Then she suggested we shop for a house in Seattle. I agreed, reluctantly. Bellingham was big enough for me. I loved my home at the end of the street at the edge of the woods and, after all my wandering, wanted to be rooted. I conceded that Seattle was a marvelous city, as cities go, where I always felt the nearness of water and mountains and of bright, lively people. A real estate agent showed us many houses. Those I liked were too expensive, twice or more what they would cost in Bellingham. Finally we found "the house on the hill." I told June I could be happy there and productive, and was ready to move. The price was right and Norma, the agent, called it "a steal," but June found assorted flaws, probably rightly, and we passed it up.

She came to spend two or three days in Bellingham leading to my birthday in May 1995. Friends had arranged a picnic celebration and a balloon ride over the Nooksack Valley for June and me. But she was terrified at the idea and didn't want to go. She was unhappy. She told me her friends in Seattle feared she was being absorbed into my world. She would recite moves from one city to another dictated by her former husband, and said that now she was trapped again. Bellingham was a honky-tonk town and my house was dingy, dark, run-down, and isolated at the end of the street. She didn't like the rain. "Every time I come here, I feel depressed and frustrated." The evening before my birthday, she sat at dinner without saying a word, except for an occasional moan. I was hurt and confused. I loved the house and the woods and rain as well, which fell from God's heaven to nourish

God's children. I needed somehow to affirm the good, so she knew that I cared. I asked myself, "What is love telling me to do?"

Then the next day everything changed. Without my saying or doing anything, all became right with the world. She had reconsidered, recollecting that it was now Ascension Day, forty days after Easter, the day when Jesus, following crucifixion and resurrection, rose into heaven. This was a message to her, for her ascension in the balloon. It proved a thoroughly enjoyable experience. My friends at the picnic had already met and loved June. She, in turn, set aside her apprehension and was her warm and wonderful best. When the balloon pilot showed up she climbed aboard without hesitation, while I, in truth, was terrified at entering that little woven basket, hardly large enough for the three of us. Away we went, in the cool and clear late afternoon, rising over the farmlands to one thousand or twelve hundred feet, drifting quietly, observing the rural landscape, bordered on the west by the San Juan Islands sprinkled in Pacific waters, and on the east by green forests rising to snow-covered peaks of the Cascades.

I might have learned that day that, if I would be patient and reassuring, giving her reason to be trusting, she would work things out in her own way and in her own time. I learned that with patience and a sense of humor, events always turned out better than feared or expected. From the outset love was constant and true. June showed that in many ways; by nature she was generous and kind. One day I mentioned that I was obliged to make a fixed monthly payment to my former wife, leading June to ask, "Does Thelma have enough?" She wanted me to consider increasing the monthly payment and suggested I leave more to my children. Another time she told me that she always felt she had enough and had turned down a raise from the congregation because she was privileged to serve and the Lord would care for her. Money was never an objective or issue.

Religion, however, was part of the problem between us. It was a much greater leap for her to marry outside her faith than for me to marry into it. She dearly hoped "we were both walking in His light." During the early period of tension, she wrote to me:

> It is almost as though long ago you made a strong decision to reject
> Christianity, and Judaism as well. Any institutional traditional
> faith or systematized theology was questionable and adversarial.
> Your way of handling it has been selective listening and tolerance.
> You "tune out"—detach and fall asleep or visit in the pews. That

is a way of distancing.

You speak of my preaching but I feel I have failed to truly deliver the impact of the text. It does not penetrate your wall of resistance. I question my own validity in the pulpit if on repeated occasions the word has not taken root. It would mean a lot to me if we were both walking in his light, but neither of us is godless. I wish I could share the vision and hope with you, but your faith takes a different direction. So I will share as I can in this life and place us both in the Holy Spirit's enlightenment—trusting that God knows our struggles and yearnings.

In response, I wrote that I respected her faith and belief system. Though I might not be a Lutheran, Protestant, Christian, or practicing Jew, I had my faith and belief. Curiously, at the conclusion of an article she had asked me to read, the author wrote, "Pluralism is a fact that we no longer dare deny," that the church of the future will need to become self-consciously variegated—in structure, content, and approach. I believed my approach was valid, it merited respect, and I was blessed:

I may be outside the pale, for not being baptized, but the Great Spirit, creator of us all, loves and protects me, no less than anyone else of any faith. My world is in conservation and wilderness. Yours is in the church and church-related. My hope is that we find convergence of worlds, developing common interest and activity to enjoy together. I hope that you find in me a loving mate. "Our belief at the beginning of a doubtful undertaking," wrote William James, "is the one thing that ensures the successful outcome of our venture." Believe and trust in our venture and it will succeed.

We both were committed and trying to make a go of it, recognizing that disagreements come with the territory in marriage; and yet belief and trust ultimately will prevail, at our age, or at any age. Our experience over time proved that to be so, as I can illustrate with the matter of churchgoing. June always welcomed me to go with her. It meant a lot to her and perhaps I should have gone more. Over the years, I accompanied her at special times, like Easter and Christmas, plus a few other Sundays. When it came time for communion I had the choice of remaining seated in place in the pew or going up to the communion rail with June but declining the bread and wine and asking only for a blessing. For a long time, I went up and simply asked for a blessing—at least we were together. Then one day June nodded to me to take the bread and wine. And I began to do that, bonding with my bride, and trusting that Jesus would allow and approve.

In the spring of 1995, I announced that I would retire from teaching at the end of the semester, fully expecting to relocate in Seattle. Then June announced that she would retire too and move to Bellingham. That was a major watershed in her life. She loved her congregation, her work, and the city, but now she felt it was time to concentrate on a new career, building a home together with me. So she cleaned out her apartment and moved north. On the appointed day, an entire squadron of her Seattle friends descended on my house in vans and cars and proceeded to unload furniture and furnishings—tables, chairs, cabinets, books, pictures. Where would it all go? In *my* house? Alongside all *my* good things? But she and the squadron took over, moving the bed and living room table, taking down and replacing pictures and posters.

That wasn't all; soon she announced her desire to introduce "warmth" and "verve" with the "feminine touch." This led to reupholstering sofa and chairs, redoing kitchen cabinets, painting one door green, and replacing the front door. My initial reaction was to question the importance or need for verve. In due course I reconsidered. Later, I wished we were in Seattle, not in Bellingham. I wished we didn't have any of *her* things or *my* things, but were starting with *our* things. I wished that instead of reupholstering furniture, we were doing it with new furniture. Now the best we could do was to negotiate and try somehow to accommodate each other. It wasn't easy. June vented frustration and anger. She would not talk to me for a day. When she did, she said I was manipulative, controlling, selfish. I made her feel compromised, demanding that our marriage take full priority and that her other commitments be dismissed. She certainly was out of her comfort zone. I also felt she somehow was striking back at her former husband, although she set me straight that this was not the case. Nine months into our marriage, she wrote to me, "I do not want the past to contaminate or cross over into our time and relationship. It doesn't belong there. Our challenge is in what we can learn from it in order to graduate into new depth and care. Even with love being strong and full of desire, there must be respect and hope. Communication between us and the essential third: God. My sweet darling, grow with me."

That was good enough for me. It was right to negotiate differences. I needed to share the home and work for mutual accord. I appreciated that she started at a disadvantage, giving up her career and its protective environment, and moving. I recognized that choosing upholstery together was a step in the right direction. Each of us should freely do things independently and still enjoy choice times together. We learned that different tastes are natural, to work things out and to ride them out, and to put up with each other's weaknesses as well as strengths. I learned that patience pays off every time.

She promised not to get angry, although she still would now and then, probably with reason. More important, she would say, " I intend to share my life with you. I want to bring you joy." She did that, one day after another, often expressing appreciation for little things I did for her. We enjoyed each other's company, travel, intimacy, affection, mutual goals, or parallel goals, in serving the human cause. When I think of the purpose of life, I venture it's not simply to live long but to achieve a life with purpose. The world is full of women and men, frustrated, frightened, and unfulfilled. And yet for June and me, every day together was a miracle.

In 1997 I had dental work and complained to June. It wasn't only the teeth that concerned me, but the pacemaker, deteriorating knee, prostate problem, high blood pressure, all those things. "I just want to be seventy-seven and enjoy life." "Come have a glass of wine on the deck," she said. It was late afternoon and the woods were filled with bird songs. I felt better. Then she went indoors and wrote me a note:

> I was thinking how rich it was to enter the last decades of one's life tasting the best wine with a best friend. His being seventy-seven made me feel young at sixty-five. He was leading me through the process. Things that all my life had been familiar—short walk, simple touches of affection, coins in my pocket for ice cream, early morning cuddles—appeared new in the fresh light of his lens....
>
> After all, these were the best of times, the times to soak in foaming bubbles, to watch the lights dance in crystal goblets, to read books and see movies you didn't get to enjoy before, and best of all to measure this against what all the other years had prepared you for: the treasure of finding someone who allows you to look around interior space and open mirrors into the core of your common substance.
>
> Weaknesses cause us to hide our real selves behind masks, but marriage is not a good place to hide.

For much of my life I would not remove the mask that I wore, or lower it, and thus allow anyone really close to me. It was my way to avoid hurt, but the real me was obscured and hidden. June taught me that marriage is not a place to hide. I certainly wanted to like myself and she showed me that it was all right to. I found the mirror of myself in June. I mean that when I saw her happy, then I could feel happy too. To say it another way, all through life, I was trying to prove something, never content with who, or where, I was. With June, I learned love is growth and change, work and play, decision, commitment, sometimes easy, other times hard. Love is learning, laughing, and crying. But love is constant and it doesn't go away.

June wanted to make a big thing of my eightieth birthday in May 2000, but I said, "No, let's just go away and be alone. At this stage of my life, I want to subtract numbers, not add to them." Nevertheless, the celebration began in the middle of the week and continued from there. On Wednesday, June brought out the first surprise present, a handmade bench, which she had painted brightly, meant for me to sit on the step just outside the front door. Next day, she produced the second present, a case of various, very nice wines, and just to make it official, we opened a bottle and toasted love and life together. On Friday, landscapers planted a flowering cherry tree in the backyard, where I would be able to see the blossoms of early spring from my desk. Then friends came, not a crowd, but a dozen or so, dropping by for lemon cake and champagne. It was humbling to hear those good people toast me with champagne and say more kind words than I deserved.

That was about the way it went from the beginning of our marriage. If it wasn't my birthday, then it was her birthday or the first day of summer, or Christmas, or our wedding anniversary on New Year's Eve, or St. Valentine's Day, or Easter. We went from one celebration to another. But there was a serious side to it. For one thing, she wanted me to be a Jew, to rediscover where I came from, and on several Fridays she took me to the synagogue in Bellingham and, if I had been agreeable, probably would have gone regularly. I was moved to hear the Hebrew words of my childhood, but not nearly enough to make it a weekly ritual.

It was the thought that counted. Material gifts meant little. I appreciated much more the gift of spirit that June gave. For my seventy-ninth birthday, she wrote me this letter:

> Sometimes the blue of your eyes shines as bright as the facets in
> the sapphire in my engagement ring. It is so precious and clear a

blue, it rivals the periwinkle flower or the sky over the bay on a sunlit afternoon. I do not see a man of seventy-nine. I get a glimpse of a young, aggressive reporter covering the story of the world with persistence and curiosity. Virile, energetic, and intuitive, a man with intention and integrity. Age has not dimmed that core or taken away the smell of your maleness. You attract me. You meet me at my level with a steady eye and a kind but firm stance. I do not intimidate you or frighten you away. Instead, you plant your feet and wait with the sure knowledge that we belong. We joke about the angels hearing our loneliness and steering us into proximity so that our deepest yearnings could be fulfilled. Yet, I do believe we are two strong personalities made stronger through our union. Somehow, our desires for companionship and love got attention from God.

I don't know how many more birthdays either of us will have or what the coming year holds. But I do know this very day God is birthing you again and life is here to claim.

Since we had an agreement that the birthday celebrant could decide where and how to celebrate, I had chosen Baja because I had been there in years past and wanted to share it with June. For me, Baja was a cosmos of wild desert gardens, lunar mountains, and blue lagoons—a fragment of the earth as God made it. Maybe I was first attracted to Baja on reading a report by Joseph Wood Krutch in the *New York Times* of February 22, 1959, in which he called it "one of the most nearly untouched areas of scenic beauty still left on the American continent." Later, in the 1970s, I was lucky enough to travel aboard and write about a naturalist cruise in the Sea of Cortez. Our small vessel, carrying but twenty passengers, journeyed gently through waters abundant with whales, porpoises, and sea lions, and below skies filled with high-flying frigate birds and red-billed tropic birds, nesting pelicans, grebes, and cormorants; we stopped at wild islands to observe vast colonies of gulls and terns, and boobies breeding in the cliffs. Another time, I flew to La Paz and then traveled overland to Bahia Magdalena, one of the winter breeding grounds of gray whales. Riding in a *panga*, a little rubber dinghy, I entered into whale waters. I tried to count them: there were easily two hundred or more, filling the bays and *bocas*, mothers and babies, unafraid, friendly, close enough to touch, an awesome spectacle.

So for my eightieth birthday, we went to La Paz. It was clearly changed since Krutch's day, and from my earlier visit. La Paz had grown, but was still inviting and congenial. The weather was hot, likely in the 90s, but tempered by a breeze. One day we parted—for a little while, we thought—to pursue separate interests along the ocean walk. But we managed to miss connections though waiting frantically across the street from each other. June feared I must be suffering a stroke while I envisioned her held hostage by drug bandits. I decided the best course of action was to return to our hotel and wait. That proved the wise choice, but when she arrived June didn't know whether to be angry with me or glad to see me alive. Then, a couple of nights later, we were robbed. We called it a minor misfortune and refused to hold it against Baja California. Instead, we joined a one-day boat cruise on which, even at my age, I was able to enjoy snorkeling among reefs and rocks.

In one way, that trip was pure play and pleasure, but there was more to it. As June and I continued our share of preaching, teaching, writing, and learning, I thought it obvious that one must love oneself in order to love others. I felt that while I still had strength, energy, and rational intellect, I should try to make a contribution, especially now, with the vicissitudes of earning a living behind me. I was blessed to have June, for one of the great adventures is to live in harmony with another person. It isn't easy, but the rewards make the effort worthwhile.

My favorite birthday came in 2001. Over months, or maybe years, June had shared her poems with me. I enjoyed and admired them, and urged her to put the best of the poems together and publish them. On the morning of my birthday, I received a surprise package with this inscription:

> I don't want to remember you in my will. I want to share my passion, thoughts, images and feelings while we are alive. This book is my legacy. It is a one-of-a-kind custom edition only for you of *Another 2nd Chance: Poetry and Photography by June Eastvold*. It is dedicated with love and deep appreciation to you, in honor of your eighty-first birthday. Thank you for being my creative, inspiring lover and mate.

In due course, she gave readings of her poetry here and there, sold several hundred copies of the book, and probably could have sold more. Her fans cheered, but if I can be selfish about it, the book was dedicated to me. I was proud and grateful. After all, in the twilight of my years, I had the pleasure of tasting the best wine with my best friend.

CHAPTER 26

Blackie was an outside dog – Brandy hardly weighed more than my laptop computer – Woods and water were ablaze – "Animals are footprints of God" – Terriers are earth dogs

I found it hard to believe, but on Friday, February 5, 1999, a doggie came to live with us. It was June's idea, of course. For weeks, or maybe months, she had kept saying, "Why don't we drive out to the animal shelter, just to see what's there?" Or, "Listen to this classified advertisement." She would read them aloud and circle advertisements offering a beautiful pooch or the best mannered kitty and leave them in front of my breakfast plate. I thought I had resisted effectively, even after June enlisted our children and friends to put the pressure on. "Don't we have enough to do," I argued, "without the responsibility of a pet? Who will care for it while we're away?" However, among those who joined June's campaign was Stewart Brandborg, "Brandy," one of my closest, dearest friends over a period of forty-plus years. He owned not only dogs, but a parrot and when we talked on the phone I could hear that bird cackle in the background, "Get a dog! Get a dog!" Thus, all my perfectly valid reasoning went for naught, as one friend and ally after another turned against me. I recognized it was only a matter of time. My only option would be to choose between a dog and cat.

In all my life I had had only one other pet, Blackie (short for Blackstone, which I bestowed as his proper name). Although he was a loyal friend and companion, I always had serious reservations about keeping pets, considering that many are cooped up all day, often in a small space, with nothing to do but turn off their intelligence and sleep, waiting for masters to feed them and walk them on a leash. That is not a dignified or natural way for creatures whose ancestors lived mostly under open sky with access to plenty of water and a variety of food.

But Blackie was an outside dog. He showed up at the house in suburban Virginia, outside Washington, before the children were school age and stayed with us until they were in college, a period of fourteen or fifteen years. I remember the day he walked down our driveway with a collar but no tag. Growing up in the apartment houses of New York, my brother and I had never had a family pet, beyond tropical fish and little painted turtles from the dime store. So Blackie stayed, but outside, with a pallet in the garage.

He was a mixture of species, middling to small in size, all black except for a white patch on his chest. Blackie was always there for us, as friend and companion. He would follow the children, Will and Michele, to the school bus stop every morning and be there to greet them when they came home. He taught me to understand why a dog is man's best friend, for he never complained and was grateful for all small favors.

Blackie definitely was an outside dog, a proud, tough little guy roaming unleashed in the woods beyond the house. Occasionally he'd be gone for days at a time. Will remembers it this way: "One day I received a letter from Mom saying that Blackie had left home and was considered lost in action. I bawled my eyes out. Three weeks later I received another letter saying that Blackie had come back." Sometimes he returned beaten and bloodstained, which I figured resulted from tangling with his peers over a female dog in heat.

Finally age and arthritis got to Blackie. He was hobbled and ailing and I took him to the vet, who dispatched him to Dog Heaven. In sorrow and pain, I vowed never, never to commit myself to another pet connection. And then in 1999, roughly thirty years later, June found the little terrier named Brandy. She had been to a morning meeting, after which, she said, the angels led her directly to the animal shelter. She walked through aisles of big barking dogs and was about to leave when the little one caught her eye and she applied for it.

"We don't have to take it and you can have veto power," she told me when she returned home, "but I thought you would like to know the name of the doggie. Her name is 'Brandy.'" That was the very name by which my close friend Stewart Brandborg was known. I had to concede that Brandy sounded about right for a pet. Besides, I had been writing for years about grizzlies and black bears, mountain lions, eagles, coyotes, wolves, and even a book for children, *The Varmints: Our Unwanted Wildlife*, and I made a habit of hanging out with wildlife experts like the Craighead twins, John and Frank, and Maurice Hornocker, and I was on the board of the organization Defenders of Wildlife. So I conceded that maybe it made sense to try owning a pet.

We brought Brandy home as the Valentine gift to each other. June drove while the doggie sat on my lap looking out the window as though she knew exactly where she was going. When we arrived she behaved as though this was the place she was meant to be, and that she approved, even of me. Now we were three. Brandy was a curly gray Norwich terrier that hardly weighed more than my laptop computer, with big brown loving, trusting eyes. June made a little bed for her in our bedroom, and once she was in it for the night we didn't hear from her till morning. She showed us that she knew her name, and on request would come, sit, roll over, stand on her two rear legs, and dance, and she added a rich dimension to our lives.

She was ten years old, by all odds too old for adoption, but she didn't know that, and as for June, that probably was the point of it. Brandy personified "Another 2nd Chance," the theme of the book of poetry she dedicated to me as a loving gift. And the poem "All Things Will Be Possible" leads from the animal shelter where we found Brandy to home and to Christmas:

> A creature small,
> Eight pounds in all,
> Feisty, proud, a terrier breed,
> "Brandy" registered her need.
>
> Her nubby tail and classic line,
> Her button nose, her silver shine,
> How could this star fall from grace
> Landing in that fearful place?
> Locked inside a metal cage,
> Abandoned at ten years of age?
>
> She gave us entrée to a mind
> Other than of humankind.
> She squealed as our spirits met,
> "There's lots of life in this old girl yet!"
>
> Now, at Christmas, she sits by our table,
> As steadfast animals who stood in the stable
> Together adoring the child with the key,
> To set all our captive spirits free.

Joy to the world! If a great wee dog
Can peer in faith through winter's fog,
And kick her legs in festive dance,
Will we too leap for a second chance?

Clearly she loved both of us, though June was the more gentle and affectionate. Brandy followed her around the house, up and down the steps, curled up in her lap, and stared into her eyes while June petted her. I think that doggie saw me as stern or preoccupied at times, but we both gave treats when the other wasn't looking.

Brandy and I shared together-time every morning when we walked in the hilly woods directly behind the house. We enjoyed those beautiful woods and so did the community. This explains why everybody in the neighborhood opposed the plans of a developer and the city's inept planning commission to cut down the trees and replace them with 172 houses. It reminded me of a column I had written in 1968, thirty years before, in *American Forests* magazine. In that piece, I described a protest walk I had joined from the campground of Worthington State Forest in New Jersey to the summit of Sunfish Pond on the Appalachian Trail. Sunfish Pond at that time was targeted for conversion into a pumped storage reservoir as part of a massive water development project. I walked a distance of 2.3 miles, through a forest of pine, hemlock, and oaks, landscaped with laurel and rhododendron, then wrote, "In the two-day weekend the total number counted reached 2,213—not counting pet dogs, of whom there seemed an appreciable number enjoying a romp. They too need the woodlands."

June and I loved to walk in nearby Whatcom Falls Park, which, with its lush Northwest woods and waters, may well have been the most enchanting spot in Bellingham. That changed, however, on June 10, 1999. On that day newspapers and national television recorded the grim and tragic story of the pipeline explosion in the park. The woods and water were ablaze and three innocent boys were killed. That was our neighborhood and, in a sense, everybody's neighborhood. At a memorial service after it was over, the words of one of the boys, Liam Wood, written months before, were recited—like an appeal of the dead to the living: "I value many things, life being the first and foremost. I value good, long-lasting friendships and courtesy. I value our wilderness areas and all creatures walking on the earth."

It is difficult to add to that, and yet the facts are that dogs don't watch senseless television shows and commercials, they don't build nuclear power plants, they don't buy and misuse handguns, and maybe the message of the dead is an appeal to the living to wake up and wise up while we still have the chance.

Our little dog came into our lives as a messenger. She introduced me to another world and taught me many lessons. "After all these years," wrote my friend Ted Williams (the outdoor writer, not the baseball player), "you have at last realized the importance of dogs." I became aware of many noteworthy expressions in behalf of pets and animals in general. One publication I read featured a wonderful interview with Paul McCartney, of the Beatles, about the devotion of his late wife Linda (and himself) to pet animals. Then another provided this quotation from Henry Beston, author of the classic *The Outermost House:*

> We need another and wiser and perhaps more mystical concept of animals. They are not brethren, they are not underlings, they are other nations, caught with ourselves in the net of life and time, fellow prisoners of the splendor and travail of the earth.[1]

I found another quotation from Martin Luther:

> Animals are footprints of God.... In a mouse we admire God's creation and craftwork. The same may be said about flies.... God is in all creatures, even in the smallest flower.[2]

There is strong convergence here between science and ethics, and religion, if you like. Considering that we share genes with every living thing, from bacteria to elephants, algae to sequoia trees—they are our kin. Maybe every once in a while I erred in getting anthropomorphic about Brandy, but, heck, she talked to me. She spurred me to learn a lot about the complexity of the lives of animals, of how smart and adaptable they are. Thus I think that foremost in any deliberations about other animals must be deep concern and respect for their lives and for the worlds in which they live. Whether for purposes of research, education, amusement, or food, we should err on the side of the animals. Expanding our circle of respect and understanding can help bring us all together. The animals "out there" need to become the animals "in here"—in our hearts.

Brandy, in truth, encouraged me to evoke a better vision for society, with more soul, reminding me: "Be sure to bring the concerns and interests of nonhuman animals into your moral gaze." Verily, I see people around me so preoccupied with careers, business affairs, civic missions, and assorted recreational comings and goings that they have little time or inclination for sentiment. Pets, I think, lead us off the stressful high-speed highway onto a slower trail where it is more possible to be considerate, gentle, and kind.

The doggie did that for June and me. Around the house she would devour all the favorite treats she could get and she was always ready for our walks, ever eager to attack big dogs that could easily swallow her whole for breakfast. At a summer street fair in Bellingham, I sat at a sidewalk café with Brandy while June and our friend Iris shopped the stalls. Presently Brandy became an attraction to people who stopped to say hello and to pet her. It struck me in due course that a good-looking little doggie free of guile, like our terrier, can make people smile and that children and dogs have an enviable way of communicating and understanding each other.

We took her on trips when we could and she enjoyed going with us. Once we went to Tofino, on the west coast of Vancouver Island in British Columbia, where we walked and walked on the sand beach, totally relaxed and breathing the zesty Pacific salt air. Sometimes, we had to leave her behind, luckily with wonderful dog sitters. When we flew to Cincinnati for a meeting we left her with neighbors Scott, Roseanne, and the three children. She seemed to have a super time playing with the children and feasting on treats. Brandy welcomed us home. She didn't exactly say that she missed us, except maybe in dog talk, but we did indeed miss her whenever we left her behind.

Early in June 2001, we drove east from Bellingham to spend two summer months in Milwaukee, June's old hometown, visiting with her family and friends and absorbing Midwest city life. Brandy proved a good traveler, as always. She didn't give signals of anything wrong and we didn't notice anything until we arrived in Milwaukee. Her right eye was coated with discharge; it looked enlarged and discolored. She was listless on her walks and seemed to lose her way. She was restless and did not sleep at night. She was hurting.

June thought it might be due to an eye infection. On Saturday, she had a poetry reading scheduled for late afternoon. But in midday, she declared with determination, "We need to find a vet to look at Brandy, and we need to do it now." We found the Animal Emergency Center, a modern, substantial facility in suburban Milwaukee, always open with a full complement of veterinarians and other personnel, and no appointment necessary. Sitting in the waiting room there, crowded with concerned pets and their owners on a sunny Saturday afternoon, I appreciated anew the deep, rich bonding between animals and humans. I saw all kinds of dogs and cats, and all kinds of people too. I can't imagine that anyone thought seriously about the cost—it was payback time, payback to pets for what they contribute to our lives.

The vets examined Brandy and elected to keep her overnight for tests. We went on to the poetry reading, but June could not bring herself to read "All Things Will Be Possible," the poem about Brandy. When we returned the next day and the veterinarian explained that our doggie was already blind in the right eye and suffering the intense pain that comes with glaucoma, I thought of our friend Betty back in Bellingham and Max, her big, old, and totally amiable dog. Max some time ago had been stricken with cancer. Betty faced a very difficult decision and I remember her and my pastor wife discussing "praying for the soul of a dog." Ultimately Max's cancerous leg was amputated and we had lately received an e-mail report sent to us in Milwaukee: "Max is doing very well and gets around amazingly. Long hikes wear him out, but after a little rest he is up and about. I washed his face this morning, and he growled at me. He hates water. But he looks pretty cute."

We prayed for Brandy, especially after the vets told us the diseased eye ought to be removed. I didn't want to believe it; I wanted a second opinion. They suggested that we go to the hospital of the University of Wisconsin Veterinary College at Madison, about two hours away from us at Milwaukee. I telephoned my friend Hugh Iltis at Madison for counsel. He was a botanist, not a veterinarian, but he knew all kinds of things and all kinds of people. "Yes, yes, it's a great place, the very best!" he said. "Bring the dog. I will alert my friend, who is a world-renowned animal pathologist."

Our doggie underwent surgery on Thursday, July 26. Drs. Miller and Diehl removed her right eye after deciding there was no other way. The pathology report showed it wasn't glaucoma, but histiocytosis, a rare disease similar to cancer in some ways. Everything went very well and everybody at the hospital loved her. We picked Brandy up the following day and felt she was more beautiful and lovable, if that is possible. She was no longer in pain.

Once again we heard from Betty. She was sorry to hear about Brandy's eye, little realizing how inspirational she and Max had been to me in the decision to have that eye removed. Then she reported:

Max has done well with the amputation, but, ... it looks like the cancer has spread to his lungs. We are taking him with us to Montana, because we don't want to leave him with anyone else for ten days. His time is limited, but you never know.

Time indeed is limited, and not only for Max, but somehow it all adds up and connects, in a world of spirit that transcends substance. I thought of the last stanza of June's poem:

Joy to the world! If a great wee dog
Can peer in faith through winter's fog,
And kick her legs in festive dance,
Will we too leap for a second chance?

With faith and hope, and the second chance, you never know. We started the drive home August 16, expecting to reach Bellingham August 24. Brandy still enjoyed going places with us and she looked pretty cute too, even with one eye.

Saturday, September 1, began with rain, like many, many mornings in the Pacific Northwest. I took the doggie out for her morning's morning, but she did not want to go. She piddled in the bushes next to the house and turned back to the door. I thought I was being considerate by calling things off and heading inside. I told June I would take her later when it quit raining.

But June observed that something was wrong. Brandy was banging into furniture and walls. She was in a blind frenzy because now she was blind in both eyes and didn't know where she was going. But perhaps she understood the worst. That little terrier always impressed me as intuitive and savvy. She had added a rich dimension to our lives, as though consciously filling her mission in life by doing so. Now it was our turn to do for her.

Our veterinarian was on duty and agreed to see us. She examined Brandy and advised that our dog was now blind in the left eye as well. She reviewed the pathology report from Wisconsin and the options available to us. We asked many questions, counseled together, and prayed. We asked for only what was right and best for Brandy. "You have chosen to act with love and kindness," Dr. Lucas told us. I held Brandy while the vet gave the lethal injection, and then our beloved pet and pal died in my arms. Later, on that same day, we dug a hole in a choice setting in the backyard that June chose and laid Brandy in. It all happened too fast to believe.

Thanks to Brandy, I learned a lot about dogs and people. I collected dog stories from friends. I read the words of John Calvin: "While we contemplate in all creatures, as in a mirror, those immense riches of His wisdom, justice, goodness and power, we should not merely run them over curiously, and, so to speak, with a fleeting glance, but we should ponder them at length, turn them over in our mind seriously and faithfully, and recollect them repeatedly."[3] But how could we do otherwise? That little doggie would be with us always. Best of all, however, was the note I received from my wife:

> My sweetheart, All the stories from so many different animal lovers expand the connections we have with each other and all the creatures God has made. You are such a sensitive loving man. How fortunate both Brandy and I have been as your "special females." You care for us so deeply and well. And I think you understand how much both of us care for you. Though physically gone, that spirit of caring still flows from the wee heart of our doggie. It is as close as the catalog of joyous memories and images she left for us. We can visit her anytime! I love you.

But that wasn't the end. June in her deep distress felt that she must do something more. She conceived the idea of writing and publishing a book as a lasting tribute to our doggie. She meant to have an artist friend illustrate it, but the friend was busy, leading June to prepare her own illustrations. At first I didn't care much for her black-and-white sketches, but they proved absolutely right for *Read My Tail: The Testimony of a Terrier Named Brandy.* It was a lovely little book that sold several hundred copies and could have sold many more, but that wasn't the point. Chapters with titles such as "The Children's Sermon," "Bobcats, Bears and Buttermilk Pancakes," "Escape Artiste Exceptionale," and "Helpless on the Freeway of Life," were written as though Brandy was recounting her adventures with us in her own words. The last chapter, "Earth Dog," ended as follows:

> I didn't go far. I came home in a box. We terriers are earth dogs. I am in the earth. I hear the creek, I smell the grass and feel My Man looking out the glass doors from his desk. My Lady smiles at me from the kitchen window and thinks of me every time she peels the carrots or cuts the banana. When you are in love you are never away.[4]

Chapter 27

Old pals and playmates were fallen or fading – A wheelchair would make things easier – Another magic moment, when total strangers appeared to help – The report was discouraging and frightening – An incredibly strong circle of support

Before going to the airport, we decided to call and order a wheelchair for me. It would make things considerably easier in getting from one terminal to another (on the other side of the airport, of course, or roughly half the distance between Seattle and Portland) and through customs, immigration, and security. It was the first time, early in 2003, that I needed and asked for help, an absolutely new and unwelcome experience. I was old enough, approaching eighty-three, and creaky and achy enough. But I hated it, believing that once you accept being old, you *are* old.

Growing into the early, middle, and then the late seventies, I recognized there were more years behind than ahead of me. Old pals and playmates were fallen or fading, from heart attack, stroke, Alzheimer's, diabetes, blindness, blood transfusions with bad blood or cancer; if it wasn't prostatectomy for men, then it was mastectomy for women. My age group became conscious of cataracts, diverticulitis, pancreatitis, phlebitis, and assorted other traditional and newly classified ailments. As I saw it, if you live long enough you grow older, and if you grow old enough, then you enter the dread zone of vulnerability, from which there is no escape—once in it, you're stuck in it. Or as Evelyn Grant, retired for many years from her job as executive editor of *Woman's Day*, put it when we visited in 1999, "I used to see one doctor for everything; now I have a Rolodex of them." Another friend said, "I used to carry a notebook full of restaurants. Now it's full of doctors." And another, "I'm not me. I don't know my body any more."

I thought I had taken pretty good care of myself most of my life. My father had heart problems, which made me aware that I may have inherited the same problems. Starting in my forties or early fifties, I began taking various medicines to keep my blood pressure under control and was smart enough to quit smoking, Thus, when I was sixty, in 1980, I looked more like fifty and spent considerable time hiking, backpacking, canoeing, and skiing in the parks and forests.

The first sign of physical problems arose early in 1981, while I was still living in northern Virginia with Thelma. During my annual examination my doctor told me the EKG showed that I had developed a "right branch bundle block." It was all new to me; it had something to do with the natural, internal electric system controlling the heartbeat. My doctor sent me to Johns Hopkins Medical Center in Baltimore for further evaluation and in the meantime, advised me to lay off physical exercise. I spent a day in Baltimore undergoing various tests that I did not understand. It ended with the physician in charge telling me, "Yes, you have a right branch bundle block, but otherwise your heart is fine; keep exercising as you wish."

That was the year my marriage fell apart and I left my home to spend a year at the Pinchot Institute for Conservation Studies. While visiting a dentist's office, the technician took my blood pressure and found it elevated—not seriously, but serious enough to do something about it. I found a doctor to work with and made changes in eating and drinking habits. I gave up salt, sugar, canned foods, fried food, preservatives, red meat, and hard whiskey, substituting grains, legumes, tofu, and herbal tea. I learned to practice abdominal breathing and systematic exercise, including long walks. I felt fine, but the secretaries at the Pinchot Institute thought I would die, especially without the benefit of meat to keep my blood red.

I kept up most of this routine through my year at Milford, four years at the University of Idaho at Moscow, and one year at Northland College in Wisconsin. When I came to Western Washington University in 1987, I was sixty-seven years old, living under the illusion that I was younger, maybe not ageless or indestructible but at least endowed with good health. Two years later, however, my doctor in Bellingham during the course of a . routine examination said that I was developing a left branch bundle block to go with the right branch bundle block, and that I might soon need a pacemaker. He didn't make it sound urgent and I went on my way.

Then, three weeks later, on a Saturday morning, I went for a run. I had just returned from a trip and felt the need of exercise. It couldn't be a long run, because I had an appointment to meet the dean at noon and then to talk to visiting parents of our students. I was running on the sidewalk about three or four blocks from my house when I felt light-headed and faint. I collapsed and passed out. When I came to I was lying on the ground, surrounded by half a dozen people. One was an off-duty policeman who called 911 on his cell phone. Another was an off-duty nurse who checked my vital signs, and a third was a high school gym teacher who lived in the house at hand and brought a blanket to cover me and keep me warm. I never saw any of those people before and did not know their names, but this was another of those magic moments in my life, when total strangers appeared from nowhere to help me. In the preface, I wrote that everyone comes into the world with love and trust and an innate desire to do good works and here now these people were living it out. The same for the two people who came to care for me in the ambulance. I told them I felt okay and wanted to go home, just up the hill, but they said, "Not a chance. We're taking you to the hospital," which led me to wonder what the dean would think when I failed to show up at noon.

The emergency room physician called in the cardiologist, and both stressed that it was time to implant a pacemaker, and without delay. As they explained, the arteries to the conduction system in my heart were blocked, slowing the heartbeat. That was why I fainted. The pacemaker implant would be relatively minor surgery: cutting an incision below the collarbone, inserting the pacemaker, a little computer or generator about an inch wide and half-inch deep, and connecting two wires from the pacemaker to veins into the heart. So I went through with it, drugged but conscious on the operating table, hearing the cardiologist complain aloud of trouble getting the wire into a vein and wishing that I could get up and get out. But that pacemaker worked for nine years, when the cardiologist inserted a newer model, the latest in medical technology.

That was the first of my serious surgical encounters associated with aging. The second came in July 1994. I was seventy-four, in good health, I thought, and courting June. Following a regular checkup, my physician advised me of a significant rise in my PSA over the past three years. At that point I knew nothing about PSA, or my prostate either. In looking back I think of the immortal words of the late George Sheehan, the literary running doctor, who said, "You go to a doctor for an exam you don't need and he tells you you have a disease you don't want."

Other than the questionable PSA there was no indication of problems, but my doctor thought it wise to check further. He referred me to a urologist, the first of three I would consult. The first told me the pathology report did indeed show signs of cancer, but the cancer was small and was detected early, and with the low PSA it was not likely at that time to spread beyond the prostate. That was encouraging; he added, however, there was no way of knowing that it would *not* spread. That was discouraging and frightening, since there was always the possibility that cancer would spread throughout the body. He outlined three principal options for me to consider. One was to do nothing, in light of my age and the likelihood of slow growth of the carcinoma. Another was radiation therapy, endeavoring to kill the cancer cells where they were. And the third was to remove the prostate through surgery, which he considered the best and surest way. He cited a fourth option, radioactive seed implantation, but dismissed it as unproven and insufficiently tested, with high recurrence rate and potential problems.

I needed a second opinion and maybe a third. The second doctor gave essentially the same response as the first and advocated surgery. "But, then," he said, "I'm a surgeon." The third doctor said much the same and recommended surgery. I could not be satisfied and sought other counsel and read a great deal. For one thing, I learned to appreciate the slow-growth factor in men my age and older and that I was not facing any immediate life-threatening crisis. In this period of casting about I learned about the positive side of radioactive seed implantation, not from a physician but from Patrick M. McGrady Jr. whom I had known years before as friend and colleague in the writing profession. He was chairman of the Professional Rights Committee of the American Society of Journalists and Authors at the time of my dismissal from *Field & Stream* and was my strongest advocate. His particular specialties as a writer were medicine, health, nutrition, and science. He was coauthor of *The Pritikin Program for Diet and Exercise,* a book that made a great deal of money and enabled him to leave New York and to buy a beautiful home overlooking the waters of Puget Sound near Seattle. Patrick's personal concerns led him to establish a unique cancer patient advisory service called CANHELP, keeping up on the latest, working with doctors, and counseling people with cancer all over the world.

He recommended I consult a group at Northwest Hospital in Seattle, known for its pioneering work in radioactive seed implantation. On examination the doctor there said my prostate felt perfectly normal. In the absence of other symptoms, he rechecked the data. "I can't feel anything, but you've got it." He reviewed the options—watching and waiting with no treatment, surgery, or radiation and seed implantation—and then concluded,

"There is no advantage to waiting."

Some type of action seemed the better part of wisdom. I had so much going that illness had no place in my life. Most important, I had just proposed marriage to a lovely, loving lady, so I faced new dimensions of shared happiness. June did not flinch a bit when I advised her of the prostate cancer, but pledged commitment and support. That helped immeasurably. Then I found significant reinforcement when I consulted a Seattle naturopath. At the outset, she said she could not hold out hope that naturopathy cures cancer, but explained the basic philosophy of healing from within and "Do no harm." That was what I wanted to hear and to connect with. She advised me to "gather information, feel what's right and what you can live with, and pray on it." She discussed with me different levels of healing—physical, emotional, and spiritual—and said that I was halfway there because I was not in denial and had the spiritual connection. Medical doctors don't much talk that way. She told me about her work with men with AIDS, with sick bodies but healthy spirits and who, when in love, benefited from a jump in T-cell count (relevant to the immune system). She talked to me about stimulating the immune system to build up my body and she helped with advice about nutrition, supplements, exercise, and love.

Plainly for me brachytherapy was the way to proceed, and I was blessed all the way through with a powerful support system, starting with June, my bride-to-be. My son wrote to me that "relaxing about it is an important part of the cure." My friend Sabin Robbins wrote, "The best possible cure for you will be marriage to a Lutheran minister! That gets you love, sex, companionship, and a straight pipeline to the boss upstairs! I will ask my gods—the trees, rocks, and water of the wilderness—to help out."

I underwent the seed implantation procedure as an outpatient, and it went well. In one month my PSA was lower and readings in subsequent years showed it lower still.

However, if you grow old enough, you enter the dread zone of vulnerability from which there is no escape—if it isn't one disease that comes to call, then it's another. In the spring of 1998, we were in Greece, and in the fall in Mexico. I did a lot of walking—a lot for me—to and from school twice a day, up and down the steps at school. Sometimes the left leg bothered most, sometimes the right. Examination showed the cartilage was gone from the outside of my left knee, probably the result of old surgery when I was a teenager. Now one bone rubbed against another. I limped and tilted to the left, no longer able to walk, hike, or do other exercises as I would have liked. The knee was collapsed, bent to the inside and I could not straighten the leg completely. In the meantime, something had gone wrong in the right leg that I could not understand: the strength had gone out of it, the right foot dragged or wobbled, and I was unable to fully raise it from the ground. One day in Greece I stumbled and fell. I began using a cane for hills and long walks.

When we returned home, my doctor talked to me about knee replacement surgery, which he strongly recommended. I consulted an orthopedic surgeon, who said that an operation would restore function and strength to the left knee, that it would be functional and flexible in six months, that I would be able to resume many, but not all, activities, depending on my exercise during recuperation. I would have to go from running to swimming. He asked if I had used an anti-inflammatory like ibuprofen. No, I said, I don't like to use those pills. They have side effects; one only leads to something stronger and then you're addicted.

I consulted a well-respected physical therapist, who suggested that I ask myself, Does the anti-inflammatory allow the increased activity level that I desire? But he also said I would probably need the surgery sooner or later because the knee was collapsed, with flexion contracture, which I think meant that I could not straighten the leg completely. My friend Runte said much the same: "You have no alternative. In three or four years your physical condition will decline and it will be worse." As for the right leg, the surgeon and my own doctor thought I might have had something like a small stroke. They decided I should have an MRI of the head, but it didn't show a thing.

I decided to go ahead with the surgery. It looked promising and led me to be hopeful. After it was over in December 1998, the surgeon said it went very well and three days later June brought me home. Soon I was walking with the aid of a walker and then crutches. I took pain pills as needed, exercised as prescribed, elevated the knee and iced it, and endeavored to be patient with recovery. At the end of six months, I told the surgeon I was still having problems, that the knee was stiff, sore, and swollen. He said that all the parts fit properly and it would likely take a year to recover fully. At the end of a year, the knee was still swollen. The surgeon gave me a cortisone injection, which helped for a while. Four years after the operation, I ventured to consult another surgeon for a second opinion. He recommended I use nonsteroidal anti-inflammatory pills. So I would now limp and tilt to the left, now with pain, no longer able to hike or do other exercises as I would like. The cane became a fixture with me.

My next serious encounter with aging began in February 2000. We had just returned from Mexico and were readying to fly to London for a British Airways banquet honoring winners of an environmental tourism contest of which I had been a judge. At the end of breakfast, I suddenly felt dizzy and lay down on the dining room floor. I rested a few minutes, and got up and went to the barbershop. In the barber's chair, I had another episode, feeling as though I was about to pass out. I sat still in my car, in front of the barber's, for a few minutes, recouping energy and confidence in my ability to drive home. Later in the afternoon, the same feeling of faintness hit me again. I believe I was cheerful through dinner, but when we were through I announced, "It is happening again. I have to lie down."

June spread a blanket over me and said something like"that's enough, I'm calling 911." I remember that they came quickly and in numbers—at least half a dozen big, brawny fellows. They went through preliminary tests, brought in the stretcher, moved me to the ambulance and to the emergency room. We were there for several hours, while the physician and staff did chest x-rays (to determine if the pacemaker was still wired properly and functioning), vascular tests in the neck, and an ultrasound. The doctor was a good fellow and we talked on and off of different things; I learned that he was a musician at heart, who played in the local symphony. Finally he reported the dizziness likely was caused by a clogged carotid artery.

That was a new word to June and me. He said that I probably had been through what was popularly known as a ministroke. The doctor felt the trip to London would be too great a risk. He prescribed rest for a week and a follow-up appointment with my own doctor (who found no signs or effects of a TIA, and thought the dizzy spells may have resulted from the long flight home from Mexico).

June wrote to our children:

He is drinking his tea, reading his publications, holding Brandy and at the moment feeling clear and grateful. We are lucky he didn't pass out while driving the car. We are lucky this happened here and not in the plane in the middle of the night in the middle of the ocean. We are lucky he has such a wonderful attitude and is basically so centered and secured in his being. It was a signal. He forgets he is almost eighty years old because his spirit, intellect, and interest in life are those of a much younger man. But the body wears out and he has been alerted of that.

That little episode turned out to be only for openers. In June 2002, dizzy spells struck again. I called my doctor, who immediately sent me for a Doppler ultrasound test, a system of checking the carotid arteries in the neck that control the flow of blood to the brain. Fortunately, one step led swiftly to another. Presently a vascular surgeon explained that the carotid artery on the left side of my neck was 90 percent blocked, cutting off oxygen-rich blood to the brain. With surgery, he said, I would face risk and possible complications. Without it, I faced a possible, or even likely, stroke. Some stroke victims have trouble walking. Others can't speak. In some cases, a stroke can kill. Two days later, I underwent heavy-duty surgery, called carotid endarterectomy. Going into it, June's personalized love therapy kept me in good cheer and I kept believing the best was yet to come. After I was wheeled into the operating room and June was left behind, the parish nurse of her church, Tisch Lynch, came to hold my hand, stroke my forehead, and say a prayer. I was never alone.

The surgery was successful, cleaning out the plaque, reopening and smoothing the carotid artery. One year later I returned for a checkup. The surgeon said the carotid artery on the left side was fine, but now the artery on the right side was more than 90 percent blocked. I didn't want to hear that, I didn't want to go through another surgery. But I had little choice. Once more it proved successful. The following year (two years after the first surgery) I went for another Doppler. Both arteries were clear and clean.

As I said earlier, if you live long enough you grow older, and if you grow old enough then you enter the dread zone of vulnerability. While there may be no escape from it, I was lifted and carried along by an incredibly strong circle of support. Going into one of my surgeries, I was in the anteroom to the operating room, overhearing a nurse prepare a chap in the next compartment. He was about to have radical prostatectomy, but he did not want anyone in his family to be advised. I felt for him. How terribly sad to go into such a procedure in loneliness. I was blessed by many hands visible and invisible holding mine and by many prayers, different kinds of prayers, on my behalf. Best of all, I had June. We went into this together and maybe she felt and shared the pain, reducing it to a minimum for me. We learned to celebrate every day, and to be of good cheer.

CHAPTER 28

Bellingham was on those magazine lists – Trees were coming down, subdivisions, shopping malls, and superstores going up – For me, it was the family that made the difference

We were well settled in Bellingham, I thought, although the town around us was changing, virtually every day. It wasn't really a town, but a city of sixty thousand, or maybe now it was seventy thousand and growing. Bellingham was on those magazine lists of "best places to live" or "best places to retire," and I could see why. It was sited at the edge of upper Puget Sound within view of the San Juan Islands and the Pacific Ocean stretching beyond to eternity. On the other side, to the east, it was within easy reach of the forested, snow-peaked mountains of the North Cascades, which, despite intrusive human efforts over the years, remained resistant to ruin. For big city pleasures, in little more than an hour we could drive south to Seattle or north to Vancouver. The weather usually was pleasant, rarely hot and rarely cold, although it rained a lot, especially between Thanksgiving and Easter. Then it was dark and gloomy, which made winter months a time to flee south, although many people managed to make it in good spirit by clustering in the coffee houses, community theater, the little artsy movie house, and cultural events at the university.

It wasn't always this way. In its earlier life, Bellingham was strictly a working town of loggers and logging mills and fishermen and the largest cannery in the world, and the university a modest state normal school. In due course, resources in the woods and the sea were exhausted and the factories closed. When I arrived in 1987, the town was just emerging from an economic low point. I found an ample apartment at a reasonable rate, pleasantly located at the edge of a beaver pond, with real beavers and abundant birds. I wanted a house to call my own and found a real estate agent, who told me I had come at the right time, in a buyer's market likely soon to change. After three weeks of looking, she brought me to the house on Bonanza Way next to the hilly woods.

It had just come on the market. "If you want it, you had best make an offer now. This house will go quickly," she said. I bought it for seventy-two thousand dollars, more than I had in mind, but that was what I paid.

June was not happy when she first moved to Bellingham in mid-1995. In time, however, I felt we became well settled. She introduced changes to modernize and brighten the house. She had an office at the opposite end of the lower level from mine, and now and then we would share tea together. She met with her Lutheran pastor colleagues in their weekly text study and occasionally substituted for one or another of them. On Sundays, she would walk about a mile each way to and from church. And three times a week, she went to a water aerobics class that was also a social club.

She made friends, kept busy, and we traveled. She sometimes complained about the time needed to go to Seattle to catch a flight and about missing the progressive environment of the Midwest, but those didn't much register with me. My theory was that contentment ought to be founded far more on inner feeling about oneself than on one's location. Theodore Roosevelt counseled, "Do the best you can, with what you've got, where you are," and that made sense to me. All three of June's children admired both our home and Bellingham. Carl, the youngest, would say, "You have the perfect place. Why *think* about a move?" But then we would be at social gatherings where our contemporaries talked of their grandchildren, of going places and doing things with them. While I had none of my own, June had three: Carl's daughters in Milwaukee. I felt her hurt at the separation from her grandchildren. At least we would go back once a year, but I recognized that it wasn't the same as being there or being close.

Bellingham meanwhile was changing, growing in all directions. Trees were coming down, subdivisions, shopping malls, and superstores going up, with new streets and highways to accommodate more cars and trucks. The city professed to be a progressive community, but that to me was sheer pose, illusion, and self-delusion. Air quality, water quality, soil stability, green space, and open space—in every respect the environment was daily degraded, in a process approved and encouraged by the city government.

I'm sure Bellingham was not unique; it represented the story of cities everywhere. As in most places, citizens complained, pleaded, and protested, to no avail. One wrote to the local paper: "Our city and county councils seem to get elected by vowing good intentions for the people and then allow the destruction of our neighborhoods by developers and their bulldozers." Another wrote of "planning that goes against all logic and experience, planning that cannot pass the commonsense test, planning that defies the public wishes." City planners and city government brushed off the private citizen as though he or she were a pest. Of fifty-two residential developments proposed for construction in a two-year period, not a single one was determined by the city to have any significant environmental impact. That didn't make sense except as a way to circumvent state environmental law and give developers what they wanted.

Then, in 1998, it struck close to home. My neighbors and I were confronted by a proposal for a massive 172-unit subdivision in a heavily forested area covering 89 acres. Because the former property owners had long allowed public access, the area called Park Ridge was well used by hikers and bicyclists, affording vistas on the trail and serenity along the creek headwaters. The draft environmental assessment prepared by the developer identified it as rich in forests, water, and wildlife habitat, with six wetlands areas and two creeks, providing habitat for eagles, hawks, owls, warblers, tanagers, song sparrows, and great blue heron that foraged for frogs and rodents around the creeks. The stream habitats were suitable for spawning and rearing of cutthroat and rainbow trout, and the lower reaches of the creek for anadromous salmon. It was a miracle to have such an asset available within the city limits. Students from Western Washington University completed a study that proposed preserving Park Ridge as an "Urban Natural Open Space." This made sense since it was clear that the site was fraught with obstacles to development, including two streams running the length of the property, extreme slopes and ridges, and limited traffic capacity.

Many in the neighborhood pointed this out in letters and at countless hearings. I felt the site should be acquired as a public preserve. Most neighbors, however, were not against all development, but wanted to safeguard the quality of life of the community. It didn't matter—all of our concerns were ignored. Consequently, we neighbors, as the Concerned Citizens of Park Ridge, were obliged to bring legal action with our own money against the very government we paid to serve us and protect our interests. We knocked on doors, held a public auction, and successfully raised more than $25,000 for legal fees. Unfortunately, the local judge ruled against us, holding that the city had adequately addressed the environmental impacts of the proposed development. However, the judge recommended further judicial consideration, declaring, "It needs review by an appeals court."

The appeals court also turned us down, declaring actual consideration of environmental impacts to be an unwieldy burden on the city. I thought this rendered the State Environmental Policy Act virtually useless—it denied citizens the right to participate fully in the process of decision-making, as I believed that law was meant to provide. But I was not a lawyer, and I was only one person. Many neighbors tired of the fight and quit. Some were intimidated by the threat of losing in court, which meant we would be responsible for the legal fees of our opponents, the developer, and the city government of Bellingham. We couldn't pay our lawyer and he quit.

Ultimately the pursuit of our cause came down to the president of the Concerned Citizens, Dr. Larry Moss, and me. At one point early in the fight, Larry said, "Michael, it's you and me against the world," and that's about what it amounted to. Citizens, I fear, are always disadvantaged, one way or another, when it comes to fighting city hall and moneyed interests. Still, I kept hoping for a break, especially after a young lawyer near Olympia offered to forgo a fee and enter an appeal for us before the state supreme court. It was risky, but I felt that we should not leave any door of hope unopened.

Many years ago, I was asked for advice by a group of concerned citizens in Memphis, when Overton Park, a lovely forest park in the middle of their city, was threatened by plans to run an interstate highway through the middle of it. It wasn't easy for them, but those people chose to stand and fight. Their case ultimately went before Congress, since federal highway funding was involved, and then before the United States Supreme Court. In the end, because good people who cared never gave up and never gave up hope, the natural treasure of their city is preserved and intact to this day.

I wanted the same outcome for Bellingham. Yes, it was my own backyard, but I believed that all of the city would benefit greatly and that it would leave a lasting legacy. True, it costs money to buy land in the public interest, but considerably less than underwriting the costs connected with development that communities are forced to bear. Perhaps some miracle had kept it natural and undeveloped, but now Park Ridge was ready to serve a growing community with green lungs, opportunities for outdoor recreation, and environmental education to complement classroom studies.

We didn't win. Early in 2003, the state supreme court handed down a ruling refusing to hear our appeal. The fight cost me more than $20,000.

That hurt, but it hurt even more to watch the future unfold. My $20,000 was small change in the big scheme of things. The first developer, who had paid one million dollars for the property, sold it to another developer for two million dollars. In a short while, bulldozers, trucks, and chain saws descended on Park Ridge to change its face forever. This was still my home. I was prepared to stay and watch it all happen; I was not going to be chased off. So I thought, but I did not have the foggiest notion of how life was soon to change for me.

The seeds of change were sown in mid-August 2003. We embarked, innocently, on the annual trip to the Midwest, to visit the three grandchildren and their parents in Milwaukee and then to Minneapolis to visit June's middle child, Kjersti. Normally we would drive, but this time we flew. Once in Milwaukee, we headquartered at our old favorite, the Knickerbocker, at the edge of city parks and boulevards bordering Lake Michigan.

We enjoyed a weekend with the family, followed by the fateful Monday. A friend, Daniel Grego, came to pick me up for lunch. Daniel was an educator who was dissatisfied with the established system and so was moved to set up his own network of alternative high schools catering to at-risk inner-city students; if they weren't in his schools, they likely would be in gangs on the street. On two or three previous visits I had met in classes with these students, mostly black and Hispanic. My experiences with them were revealing and rewarding—I met bright young people with potential for making something of themselves. Education in America, as I see it, is not truly meant to serve children of the poor and disenfranchised, but here in Milwaukee my friend was defying the rules and making *his* system work. So I welcomed my exchanges with him.

June, meanwhile, had walked into a real estate office in the lobby of the hotel and met a very nice young man named Jason who would take her out the next morning and show her several houses; as she saw it, there was no harm in looking, was there? "No," I said, "but remember we are scheduled to leave by two in our rental car." That would be no problem, no problem at all. She and Jason would skip possibilities in Milwaukee, because I didn't want to live in a city, and go directly to Cedarburg and Grafton, which were about thirty minutes north, not really suburbs, and meant for good living.

The next day they left early and did get back by two. I met Jason, listened politely to June's report on the houses she'd seen that were attractive but with steps too steep for me. The unusual house at Port Washington she loved, but it wouldn't do because even though it had space and light, it had only two rooms. We left and I thought that would be the end of it.

But it wasn't. The Port Washington house became an issue. June showed me the realtor's photographs: "Yes, it has only two rooms, but it's so contemporary, open and bright. Look at the lower floor, the bedroom, with that huge bathtub—that's a whirlpool built for two—it would be such fun. Look at the setting, surrounded by trees—exactly what you want—within view of Lake Michigan and yet right in town. And such a lovely town!" All this while we were driving from Milwaukee to Minneapolis. "Look," I said, "if you want, let's turn around right now and go back to pick up Jason and see the house." No, we couldn't do that because it was getting late and we had to see the Minnesota state fair, but we should call Jason. Okay, okay already.

I called Jason and offered to fly back to Milwaukee to see the house. No, he said, don't do it. There was a prior bid on the house from someone else and it might be sold. If that fell through he would phone me in a week. I felt relieved, and yet curious about the house and Port Washington, wondering whether it was time, after all, to leave Bellingham. I thought about it while we walked across the grounds of the Minnesota state fair, looking at prize pigs and horses, and the art show that included a striking photograph taken by Kjersti, June's daughter, my stepdaughter, of tulips in Skagit Valley near Bellingham, asking myself what the message in it was for me. Then that evening under a clear sky at the fairgrounds we heard a concert by Judy Collins and the Kingston Trio. I had never seen them before; I don't know why, but I never had. Now I was pleased to see and hear these were not only folk songs they were singing but also art songs, about good times, sad times, love, hope and healing, and maybe there was a message in the songs too.

I felt relieved when Jason did not call; I could put all that behind me. But then, in a few days, he did call. The prior bid had been withdrawn. If I flew into Milwaukee, he would meet me and show me the house. I went back early in September and saw the house twice, once with Jason on a Saturday, and then the next day, with Carl and his family. That house had a lot to commend it. It was on a tree-covered bluff within view of Lake Michigan, thirty miles north of Milwaukee. It would take rearranging, but I could see a special place for myself to work, quiet, free of distraction except for the woods outside and the books on my shelves. I looked out on big trees and ferns along the creek and sometimes two or three deer came by. I was writing at the same big table I had used for more than thirty years. June wanted to get me a new one, but the table was my old friend and a reminder of past accomplishments; it told me that I wasn't through and would do it again. For many years, I used the same typewriter (which was used when I bought it); I hated to give it up, and it took a long time to accept the way of the word processor.

Once you are set in your ways, change is difficult. Now it was the family that made the difference. They liked the house but, even more important, all of them, including the four-year-old, wanted what was best for me. June would be close to her family, but it was my family too.

When I returned home, June had surprising second thoughts. She woke me up in the middle of one night and said, "If you don't want to go, I'm willing to stay right here." Maybe we should have stayed. Maybe at my age, I ought to have been free to choose where to live, and not feel obligated to live any other place. Or maybe I should have been looking into retirement homes. Or maybe it was time to pick up the pieces, clean out the stale air, and ride the winds of change. When I called Dan Grego for his counsel, he said, "You have friends here. We will help you."

The owner of the house in Port Washington wanted $219,000. I offered $210,000, which he accepted. But I still had to sell my house in Bellingham. A realtor held an open house and a fellow came by, a retired professor from Colorado wanting to be near *his* grandchildren, and offered $210,000. I didn't get it all, but it was nearly three times what I paid for it. Maybe it was inflated, but I never, ever thought I would actually sell or buy a house costing that much money.

June and I gave away a lot of treasured items, books, paintings, outdoors equipment, clothing, and furniture. Boxes of correspondence I sent to the archives at the University of Idaho Library for its collection on conservation. I sold on consignment a few boots, backpacks, and my waxing wood skis made in Norway to ReSort, a cooperative secondhand store, which told me later the fellow who bought the skis was thrilled and vowed to learn waxing, the old-fashioned way. Friends came to help us pack, bringing order into chaos, and then held our hands through teary moments at a farewell reception. June and I were a couple of overgrown kids adventuring through life. It was a great run in the Northwest for us both, and now we were uprooting from one wonderful part of our country to resettle in another.

It wasn't easy, but it happened so fast it was hard to tell. I had flown out early in September to look at the house and before the end of October we were living in it—or at least living out of the boxes waiting to be unpacked. My routine was thoroughly disrupted. I wanted to get back to work on my book, *this* book, but I had to dig out reference materials and set myself up somewhere until we got organized. And what would I do for my support network—doctor, dentist, pacemaker check, tax accountant, computer guru, and personal friends to turn to when I needed them?

Late one afternoon I felt overwhelmed and sorry for myself. Maybe now, finally, I was able to understand June's feeling when she gave up her home in Seattle to move to Bellingham. My own little malaise didn't last. June called me out on the deck to watch a flight of geese in formation high above the woods and lake. For the next several days, I observed flight after flight of them, marveling at their uncanny communal structure. They *knew* their way and purpose. They knew it intuitively. And they were sheer inspiration to know mine and keep on course.

CHAPTER 29

Faith: churches sing patriotic songs as though they were hymns – Muir's entire life was a pilgrimage – It isn't easy to speak truth to power from the pulpit – Dorothy Day was in jail many times

The Koran opens with a clear proclamation that there is only one god, namely Allah. Jews believe they have been singled out as "God's chosen people." Christian churches and many (if not most) Christians are convinced that if you haven't been baptized in their faith you don't stand a chance of salvation or entry into heaven.

They may all be right, but none of it adds up for me. I think God, the really real God, does or ought to love all His children, or perhaps I should say all Her children. And by *all*, I mean man children and woman children, red children, black children, yellow children, white children, straight children and gay children, poor children and rich children, and all of them equally. But I don't see much of that happening, for if that code truly prevailed among the professedly religious of all faiths, the rich would share their wealth with the poor and I don't mean simply "alms for the poor," as in the common practice.

There would not be anything called "war" either. I mean, there might be a quarrel once in a while among kin, but to actually kill a brother or sister, or, even worse, to exterminate thousands with bombs and bullets and land mines and chemicals would be unthinkable within the family of God. Yet many churches sing patriotic songs like *God Bless America* as though they were hymns and wave the flag as though it was meant to rally the Christian soldiers onward against the anti-Christ foe. I daresay that militarism as U.S. policy can only be sustained as long as the mass of churches support it. But that is true everywhere and not only in this country. In the Middle East, Muslims conduct the holy war as though war is ever holy. Religious rhetoric and terminology are common from government leaders, who use the most popular religion in their nations to stir patriotism and to influence or manipulate public opinion, even when the tenets of the religion are diametrically opposed to the government's policies. The German Lutheran theologian Dietrich Bonhoeffer denounced Hitler and Nazism and suffered for it because of the compromise by his church leaders and their "cheap grace."

I did not read or know much of the Bible before meeting June. From the beginning of our courtship and then marriage, we had many discussions about faith and religion. I respected her beliefs and when she continually quoted the Bible to support them, I thought I should examine it for myself. I started with Genesis and kept going, reading many tender, gentle, and memorable passages. But I noted also the accounts of wars and violence, of slayings by the thousands in the interest of righteousness. Being in the Bible, I concluded, does not necessarily make it right, or a way of life to follow.

It is not only a question of war and peace. Nineteenth-century churchmen in the United States quoted the Bible to make a pro-slavery or pro-war case, depending on whether they were in the South or North, although few churches actually were anti-slavery. "What to the Slave is the Fourth of July?" asked Frederick Douglass in a speech he delivered in 1852. The church, he said, has

> shamelessly given the sanction of religion to the whole slave system. They have taught that man may, properly, be a slave; that the relation of master and slave is ordained of God; that to send back an escaped bondman is clearly the duty of all the followers of the Lord Jesus Christ; and this horrible blasphemy is palmed off upon the world for Christianity.[1]

Horace Greeley had a word for it, too. As founder and editor of the *New York Tribune*, Greeley in the midcentury was the most influential journalist in America. Following Lee's surrender at Appomattox, Greeley wrote a friend in Vermont:

> I have not usually believed that we should win, because I could not believe that we *deserved* to win. We are a pro-slavery people today. In the great city of Philadelphia, which gave Lincoln nearly 10,000 majority in '60 and again in '64, a black Union soldier is not allowed to ride the street-cars. I tried to pilot through a most respected colored clergyman, but was obliged to give it up. By all ordinary roles, we ought to have been beaten in this fight and the more consistent and straight-forward worshippers of Satan

triumph. Our great triumph is God's answer to the prayers of the Colored People; it is not *our* victory, and the result will show it....

I am becoming still more alienated from the religion which passes among us for Orthodox and Christian. Its teachers and professors are loudest in the cry for bloodshed and vengeance as against the prostrate Rebels. They want to erect the gallows all over the South and hang the baffled traitors whom we have not killed in battle. I am sure Jesus of Nazareth is not truly represented in this spirit.

As for me, I want as many Rebels as possible to live and see the South rejuvenated and transformed by the influence of Free Labor.... I see great trouble in the future growing out of our partial, tardy, enforced conversion to the Gospel of Equal Rights. I fear more calamity is needed to convert us to the true faith that wrong done to the humblest, most despised is an injury and peril to all.[2]

I feel, as Greeley did, "that wrong done to the humblest, most despised is an injury and peril to all." Compassion and caring must be at the root of values to make them valuable. True enough, people go to houses of worship to find compassion and caring, but those qualities need to be extended outward to embrace others as well. I don't see much of that in structured religions; buildings variously called churches, mosques, and synagogues seem more designed to divide people than to bring them together. This feeling doesn't mean that I'm without belief or faith. It only means that I follow a different system of belief. Ralph Waldo Emerson believed that evil is not a law but a sickness, that humanity essentially is good, and that the human soul is capable of transcending the physical and material to reach the universal truths, and that unspoiled nature, what we now call wilderness, is the sanctuary of universal truths. "Here," he wrote, "we find nature to be the circumstance which dwarfs every other circumstance, and judges like a god all men who come to her."[3]

The same holds for Emerson's friend and contemporary, Henry David Thoreau, of whom his biographer, Joseph Wood Krutch, wrote: "He did not believe, as some do today, that man was a failure beyond redemption, he believed only that his contemporaries were failures because the true way had been lost a long time ago." Krutch explained Thoreau's well-known term "In Wildness is the preservation of the World": "Every tree sends its fibers forth in search of the Wild. The cities import it at any price. From the forests come the tonics and barks which brace mankind." To which Krutch added on his own: "Nature is, after all, the great reservoir of energy, confidence, and endless hope, and of that joy not wholly subdued by the pale cast of thought that seems to be disappearing from our human world."[4]

John Muir was estranged from Christianity by his strict Presbyterian upbringing, but he was not estranged from religion. Like Emerson, he found it in nature, and in wilderness an expression of God. Where Jesus spent forty days in the wilderness, Muir's entire life was a pilgrimage. Once I followed his path to Glacier Bay in southeast Alaska while rereading his account of his exploration. He went in 1879, the first white man to enter that wilderness, then full of foreboding and mystery. He went in a dugout canoe with three Indians and a missionary. It was near the end of October, when the mountains were mantled with fresh snow from peaks and ridges down to the level of the sea. The Indians lost heart in howling storms, but Muir assured them they need not fear, that the sun would shine again, and that only the brave could look for Heaven's care. And so it came true. Sunshine soon streamed through luminous fringes of the clouds, falling on the green waters of the fjord, the crystal bluffs of glaciers, and fields of ice. Muir was overcome by what he called "icy wilderness, unspeakably pure and sublime."

Call it transcendentalism or pantheism or whatever. I think it was best summed up for me by Alan Watts on the dedicatory page of *Nature, Man and Woman,* one of the best books I know:

> To the beloved company of the stars, the moon, and the sun;
> to ocean, air, and the silence of space;
> to jungle, glacier, and desert,
> soft earth, clear water, and fire on my hearth.
> To a certain waterfall in a high forest;
> to night rain upon the roof and the wide leaves,
> grass in the wind, tumult of sparrows in a bush,
> and eyes which give light to the day.

I don't mean to quarrel with houses of worship. After all, I was married in one to a woman who for much of her life has been a pillar of the church. Organized, structured religion provides one approach to the mystery beyond all mysteries, and I hope that June and her fellow believers can be mindful of the admonition of C. S. Lewis to "be kind to those who have chosen different doors and to those who are still in the hall."

While we are all still in the hall together, I will acknowledge another side of religion as I see it. Shortly after we returned from Poland in October 1998, June went off again, to Columbus, Georgia, joining the vigil to close the School of the Americas. She stood in front of the Fort Benning Military Reservation along with several thousand others (nuns, priests, pastors, and everyday people) holding aloft banners demanding "Close the U.S. Army School of the Americas—Stop U.S. Funding of Torture and Oppression" and "Close the School of the Assassins." One sign in bold red and black read "Creator, Forgive Us, Forgive Our Country," and another, "To Promote Democracy Teach Democracy—To Promote Peace Teach Peace."

We don't do that in America. We do not teach or promote peace. June and many, many others were arrested for standing up for peace at the gates of Fort Benning. When the records are read and compared, the performance of the United States in undermining democratic governments in Central America and South America is on a par with the performance of Nazi Germany in Europe or of Saddam Hussein in the Middle East. Our schoolbooks don't tell it that way. Neither do most of our churches, nor do most of our churchmen and churchwomen. But some do, more like a few as compared with the many, but they do. Some of the most outspoken, committed, and courageous advocates of peace, human rights, and social justice have been ministers of one faith or another who follow their conscience and their religion as they see it.

It isn't easy to speak truth to power from the pulpit, since most houses of worship accommodate to power. June is one who does speak truth, without fear or favor, every chance she gets. On Sunday, September 23, 2001, less than two weeks after the World Trade Center disaster in New York, she was called on to preach at Our Saviour's Lutheran Church in Bellingham (as a substitute for the regular pastor, who was away). "The Gospel's message this week is clear," she began. "You cannot serve God and wealth. But a lot of Americans would ask, 'Why not? Isn't prosperity the same as godliness?'" Then she continued:

> Passengers who called from phones on the airplanes about to crash didn't call their lawyers, or check with the stockbrokers, or try to cancel appointments at the office. In the last moments, they tried to tell those closest to them that they loved them. In the final analysis, that is what mattered most. . . .

How we conduct our business, how we distribute our wealth, how we act as stewards of the environment, how we respect and honor diversity, how we humble ourselves and take responsibility as temporary managers of God's affairs on earth is how we define our relationship to the true riches of eternal value.

If we were as ingenious in our efforts to distribute wealth as we are in competing to acquire it and hold it; if we saw all the children—not just our little dumplings—as in need of affection, food, housing and clothing...if we admitted to the corruption of our corporate and military systems and confessed that we have been cooperators in consuming far more than our share, if we agreed to forgive the debts of so many poor nations in the world who are struggling just to come up with part of the interest on overwhelming loans on failed projects introduced by the World Bank; if we could apply our technology to shape a future without violence and war, ours would be a very different world.

We are not to buy the poor for silver, to trample and bomb the needy, or clamor to open the market so we can once again build up our stock in trade. We are all children of one God. We are here for a very short time. We take nothing with us. That's what the people on the plane called back to say....

At the end, it was love that mattered. If they, on a hijacked airplane headed toward death asked to be remembered in love, should we, who will soon follow them, not honor that legacy by living as they died? By living in love? You cannot serve both God and wealth. Choose while it is yet day. Amen.

I'm not sure she was invited back, but she met her obligation to her belief. And others too are ready to stand up to risk. Reverend Joseph Ellwanger began his Lutheran ministry in Birmingham in 1958, when, as he recalls, "it was probably the most segregated, the most racist city in the South," earning the nickname "Bombingham." He was already a civil rights activist in 1964 when a KKK bomb killed four black girls in the 16th Street Baptist Church in Birmingham. At the funeral service that followed, the church was packed, with thousands outside. Ellwanger, a white pastor in a black church, did a reading, then Martin Luther King preached the funeral sermon. The next year, 1965, Ellwanger led the Concerned White Citizens of Alabama on a 1965 demonstration in Selma for black voting rights.

"How did it happen," he asked years later, "in a city where there were so many churches and so many good people? The answer was that good people who are silent and do not participate in the public forum and do not take responsibility for seeing that things change when they need to be changed permit this sort of thing to happen. Not only in 1963, but right up to the present." The present then was 2004 in Milwaukee. He was seventy, recently retired from a multiracial, inner-city church, and volunteering for WISDOM, an affiliation of seven faith-based groups focused on the many economic, racial, and social disparities in Milwaukee. His wife, Joyce, meanwhile had lately returned from a federal penitentiary where she spent six months for her role in protest at the School of the Americas.

I'm sure that Dorothy Day was in jail many times. When I think of the outspoken, committed, and courageous who follow their conscience and their religion, her name and work come to the front. That may be because she started as a journalist, as I did. In 1932, she reported the Hunger March to Washington, which the popular press brushed off as a ragtag parade of dangerous radicals, ignoring its proposals for jobs, housing, and health care. So the next year she started the *Catholic Worker*. The purpose was not to report news but to create news. She wrote a column, "On Pilgrimage," defending the poor and the outcast for thirty-plus years until the month of her death in 1980. It was her way, she explained, of not separating Jesus from his cross.

Daniel Berrigan, in the introduction to the 1981 edition of Dorothy Day's autobiography, *The Long Loneliness*, stated that Day wrote about and stood with cotton pickers, *braceros*, prisoners, ex-prisoners, families of every condition, monks, alcoholics, addicts, slum folks, auto workers, and coal miners, and many others.

> She had long ago recovered from the malaise of her profession [journalism], which she described more properly as its curse: the inability to sort things out, the reeling head, the condensed brain, the eye that sees everything, sees nothing. She became, that is, a reporter with a conscience—a phenomenon that daily grows rarer.

The problem is that journalism is more than a profession, it is a business. So are religion and education. All of them are business institutions with bureaucracies that breed conformity and discourage individuality.

Reporters, preachers, and teachers may all be endowed with conscience, but risk-taking among them is rare.

In 1909, Ray Stannard Baker, one of the principal muckrakers early in the twentieth century, wrote a penetrating work about religion. He made strong points about the churches of New York.

> They help the poor child and give no thought to the causes which have made him poor. They have no vision of social justice: they have no message for the common people.... Human touch, not money, is required. There must be personal self-sacrifice. It was not until Francis of Assisi stripped himself naked that "he won for himself a secret sympathy in many souls."... Men who are willing to sacrifice most, never do it for salaries. And there is never any lack of men to go through fire and tempt death if only they are aflame with a great purpose.[5]

It's that flame of purpose that has grown rare and needs rekindling. Thoreau and Krutch would say the true way was lost a long time ago, and that energy, confidence, hope, and joy have diminished in our human world with loss of the great reservoir of nature. That must be at least a very large part of it.

In the mid-1960s, when I was researching my book on the Great Smoky Mountains, I was introduced to the Eastern Band of Cherokee, composed of the descendants of a remnant group of an Indian nation, most of whom were driven out of the southern mountains to make way for greedy whites searching for gold. I learned that the uncivilized Cherokee followed quite a different religion than the civilized whites who forced them to move west on the Trail of Tears. Like most Indians of the Americas and most primitive peoples across the world, they worshipped more than one god. This made them "pagans," who must be dealt with in a stern and serious way.

But the controlling force in the lives of the Cherokee was a natural religion. Every animal, stone, and tree was believed to have its own spirit and a particular reason for being. Ceremonials were devoted to fulfillment of the human role in the grand design of the universe. The Green Corn Dance, was a two-week thanksgiving celebration held in the seventh moon, when the first corn ripened and became fit to eat. Enemies were forgiven, fires extinguished, and new fire kindled by the shaman; then fires were lit on each family hearth. The first fruits were deposited in the council house for the poor who might otherwise have no corn for winter. On the main day, no voices were heard until nightfall, when the whole town assembled to watch the shaman sacrifice the new fruit, express thanks for the beneficence of earth, and pray for the spirits to bless the corn and meat during the year. Those people could feel the rhythms, cycles, and continuum between the hours of their lives and centuries of time. Rituals, dances, lustrations, and ceremonial hunts bound the generations with all living things.

It wasn't only Cherokee who found gods or goddesses in sky, trees, rocks, wind, and water. On the Northwest Coast, where June and I lived, native people for centuries sought the giant cedar, hemlock, and Douglas fir of the cold rain forest, not simply for canoes and longhouses, but as source of a sacred state of mind where magic and beauty were everywhere. In the Southwest, one Navajo ceremonial, the Blessing Way, is a ritual of legends, songs, and prayers concerned with creation and placement of earth and sky, sun and moon, sacred mountains, vegetation, control of he-rains and she-rains, dark clouds and mist, and life phenomena that brought blessing and happiness.

In 1832, however, when George Catlin rode the first steamer up the Missouri River into the Mandan country of the Dakotas, he saw a different scene. Catlin had quit his law career to become an artist, drawing inspiration from Indians living as God made them. He watched prairie dogs chirping from the tops of their mounds and buffalo running in flight. He observed Indians camped near Fort Pierre slaughtering buffalo to trade for whiskey, and realized the extinction of both Indian and buffalo was imminent "before the deadly axe and desolating hands of cultivating man." It was that way everywhere in the West. In the Sioux country, the military crushed the Sun Dance with armed force. Then Christian missionaries influenced the Indian Service to impose regulations against all pagan ceremonies. They cracked down on the Navajo sings, the vigils in the Pueblo kivas, and on keepers of the visions in the Mojave. Preachers and teachers came to Alaska, where they denounced Tlingit and Haida artwork records of clan and tribe as pagan idols and induced the people to destroy them.

The principle of the Navajo religion was to create harmonious living in the universe. Even in the twentieth century, while living in poverty with desert sage and jackrabbits, the Blessing Way for them was the means of restoring and strengthening harmony. In 1966, however, the federal government announced a program called the Central Arizona Project (CAP) to construct a system of massive coal-fired steam and electric generating plants in the desert, where clean air was a primary asset for many years. Interior Secretary Stewart L. Udall, one of the main advocates of this project, pledged it would be an absolute model of pollution control. As it happens, I knew Stewart Udall in Washington. He wanted to be identified as a conservation leader and wrote a popular book, *The Quiet Crisis*. I also knew his brother, Morris (Mo), who served in Congress and was chairman of the House Interior Committee. Both meant well, but when the chips were down, Stewart and Mo played politics with natural resources of Arizona, their home state. They were strong and aggressive advocates of the CAP. Mo said, "I am convinced that the net impact of this project on man's environment will be one of enhancement," while Stewart claimed the Hopi and Navajo Indians of the region would greatly benefit from exploitation of "their underutilized coal resources."

But it didn't turn out that way. The skies over the Southwest desert have been clouded, smoggy, and smoky with fly ash, sulfur oxide, and nitrogen oxide and the Native Americans haven't benefited at all. The CAP cost almost $3.5 billion more than anticipated and its victory left an ambiguous legacy. The plant at Page, Arizona, resulted in huge strip mines that scarred the Hopi and Navajo reservations

> Emissions from the plant created air pollution in the pristine Four Corners area that added to the buildup of greenhouse gasses in the atmosphere. The plant transformed the reservations into an energy colony for the benefit of whites while the Native Americans received a fraction of the market value for their coal and, in exchange for the plant, waived their claim to 50,000 acre-feet of water that had been apportioned to them in 1946. . . .
>
> The CAP spigot was turned on in Tucson in 1992. It delivered CAP water to 85,000 homes, but the tap was turned off in September 1994 because of outcries that the water was so full of minerals it corroded water pipes and poured out bad-tasting, foul-smelling, murky water. The city began pumping groundwater again. At the start of the twenty-first century, the city was still looking for a way to use CAP water. Without it, city officials said, the water table would continue to drop, sinkholes would develop, and the quality of water would diminish.[6]

The longer-term consequences may not become apparent for years.

Ultimately Stewart Udall conceded the CAP, which he had vigorously promoted, was an example of bad planning and bad economics. But the damage was done, devastating Navajo and Hopi Indian cultures and degrading national parks of the Southwest.

In her sermon in Bellingham on Sunday, September 23, 2001, June began by warning the congregation that one cannot serve two masters. That was precisely what the Udall brothers tried and failed to do. Better is to heed June's plea to act as stewards of the environment, to respect and honor diversity, and to take responsibility as temporary managers of God's affairs on earth. That isn't always easy, but it impresses me as the way to live in faith.

CHAPTER 30

My Texas advisor – Arriving like a prairie falcon with talons bared – The reporter's report and the editor's edit are never, ever, objective – The irreverent, independent reporter pays the price – Thomas Merton's true tidings

While I was with *Field & Stream* early in the 1970s, a reader in Texas wrote me a kind and thoughtful letter, which included a few words of advice: "If you lower your voice and make factual suggestions, you can do a service for all of us." It impressed me to the point that I saved the letter from then until now. And many times I wondered whether my writing shouted too loud or demanded too much to really be effective. But who can tell?

I recall also in this period listening to a radio interview with Marian Anderson. Inevitably the dialogue turned to the racial discrimination to which the great singer had been subjected in her career. How had she handled it? She replied that her mother had taught her to be free of hate, and "never abuse people who abuse you. Bear them no malice and theirs will disappear." That also registered with me and I hope that I too may have been free of hate, and that I dealt with issues rather than personalities. Oscar Wilde expressed the idea a little differently: "Always forgive your enemies. Nothing annoys them so much."

Still, one day when I was in New York having lunch with Clare Conley, the editor of *Field & Stream*, he cited a recent conversation with our colleague Ted Trueblood, who had said, "Get Mike to write it—he writes *mean*." I did not want to write mean; I wanted to make factual suggestions, as my Texas correspondent had counseled me to, though I wanted those suggestions founded on the truth as I saw it, and this was not always easy. In late September 1970, I addressed the annual Tallgrass Prairie Conference at Elmdale, Kansas, in the heart of the Flint Hills, which citizen conservationists hoped to preserve as a national park. Ray Heady, in the *Kansas City Star* (October 1, 1970), began his report by citing the annual migration of Monarch butterflies, which coincided with the conference. He wrote that

the Monarchs added a shimmering layer of black and orange wings to a
land of wind, grass, and sky, and continued:

> Michael Frome of Washington did not arrive like a fluttering but-
> terfly; he came in like a prairie falcon with all talons bared. . . .
>
> "The United States should have four, not one, grassland
> parks," Frome said—"one each in Kansas, the Dakotas, Texas,
> and Oklahoma. The National Park Service knows this but drags
> its feet."
>
> The Park Service has lost its vigor, Frome said, and is now
> a tame critter with a record that ranges from disappointing to
> dismal. "It's up to the people to raise the banner now."

Heady did indeed provide an accurate representation of my remarks. I felt
that I ought to tell it like it is; I didn't mind being equated to a prairie falcon,
not at all.

Over the years, in speaking and writing, I pursued a course of
advocacy aimed at making a difference in my own life and in the life of the
planet. As a journalist, I did not follow the code of "objectivity," believing
the reporter's report and the editor's edit are never, ever, objective. In my
book, advocacy journalism *is* journalism, and no place for propaganda. It is
the most honest journalism, and most enriching for the journalist.

Much traditional writing, like much of traditional scientific research,
tends to be narrowly focused, impersonal, free of "value judgments" that
might impair scrupulous objectivity, free of imagination and sense of
person. As John Muir once noted, however, "Dry words and dry facts will
not fire hearts. In drying plants, botanists often dry themselves." Perhaps
the chronic dryness is no accident. Institutions and professions of our time
tend to be conformist and conservative, breeding young talent to play it
safe, careful not to rock the boat. The media ought to be different, the one
institution of society that watchdogs all the others and keeps them honest.

I doubt that in the long run the *Washington Post*, where I began, would
have been a happy, satisfying place to spend my working career, but then,
the pinnacles of prestige are not always what they appear to be. Katherine
Graham's *Personal History* was in its way an honest and outstanding
autobiography, but it raised serious, disturbing questions about the *Post*
as an exemplar of journalism and social responsibility. Graham wrote of
detesting the Newspaper Guild and of smashing the printers union. She

ridiculed Ben Bagdikian, a former *Post* editor, "who since leaving the paper has made a cottage industry of attacking us." She was especially irked by an article he wrote in *Washington Monthly* entitled "Maximizing Profits at the *Washington Post*." In the same pages, she described in detail how she had indeed maximized profits. Besides, Bagdikian really did not need to make a cottage industry out of attacking the *Post*. He wrote a seminal work, *The Media Monopoly*, and later became dean of the graduate school of journalism at the University of California–Berkeley.

Her book is about the power of privilege, the privilege of power, exuding with names of pundits and presidents, crowned heads of Europe, cabinet members, the U.S. Supreme Court, White House, heads of state, the dinner party world, the network of the establishment, with a publisher woven into the midst of it. It reminds me of a passage from *Lords of the Press*, written by George Seldes in 1938:

> At some time in his experience every man should rub shoulders with his fellows; experience the excitement of a metropolis' nervous activity; live close to the great, the distinguished, the famous, and the merely notorious—if for no other reason than because only so can he learn properly to discount them.

And referring to Oliver K. Bovard, managing editor of the *St. Louis Post-Dispatch*, Seldes wrote:

> He saw fellow editors joining clubs, flitting about in society, he saw a noted columnist playing polo, he found a noted colleague giving more attention to his Wall Street investments than his editorial page, and it made him more determined than ever to steer clear of entangling alliances.[1]

The *Washington Post* under Philip Graham was a mass of entangling alliances. "These exchanges [between her husband and Lyndon B. Johnson]," wrote Katherine Graham, "reflect a relationship in which the press is closer to government than journalists ought to be."[2] Plainly they used each other and the *Post* supported Johnson in the Vietnam war. But Philip Graham and others of the *Post* had already had the same kind of relationship with John F. Kennedy. They knew of Kennedy's philandering, but kept quiet—in contrast to later crucifying Bill Clinton over his affair with Monica Lewinsky. It wasn't only the *Washington Post*, it was the best of the media at its worst. Washington pundits felt to expose Kennedy would have been keyhole journalism and declined to muckrake the president.

The same was true during the Persian Gulf War of 1990 through 1991. While reporting endlessly on the chemical weapon threat from Iraq—which never materialized—correspondents showed little interest in America's fearsome weapons, like napalm, used for the first time since Vietnam. That war was about Saddam Hussein, depicted as the power-hungry madman, not about Kuwait's insistence on lowering oil prices. People watched and read the news, but the more they watched and read, the less they knew. The media failed to be objective, communicating views to support the administration policy and playing down views that did not. In the name of "military security," they kept data from the public rather than enhance debate and risk disturbing audiences with discomforting information.

Philip Graham, that likeable fellow who had married the boss's daughter and started at the top, before he went off the deep end and committed suicide allied himself with the business and real estate community of Washington. He founded the Federal City Council, a glorified chamber of commerce, promoting a freeway system that would have destroyed whole neighborhoods. He delivered an address to the Washington Building Congress, but neither he nor the *Washington Post* really addressed the concerns of poor people living in Washington.

In the February 1977 issue of the *Washingtonian* magazine, I wrote an article entitled "Ten Environmental Emergencies." I cited issues the *Washington Post* had not covered or barely touched.

In what was "a city of trees," the trees are vanishing, either uprooted or choking in concrete and noxious automobile fumes. Crystal City, Rosslyn, and L'Enfant Plaza are examples of the look-alike high rises that box people into purely synthetic environments. Beyond the Beltway, a once-lovely countryside is afflicted with the blight called suburban sprawl....

I look at Washington and shudder because there is no significant reversal of the course of congestion, uglification, contamination. I fear that we don't know the worst of the environmental condition—experts may know, but they keep things to themselves. They withhold the facts of the case from the public....

The best of them [changes to cheer the spirit], I'd say, was the defeat of the Three Sisters Bridge, a clear declaration that the center of Washington should be for people and not automobiles, despite the contrary desires of the highway lobby and the *Washington Post*.

The Georgetown waterfront, according to the *Washington Post*, represents one of the "hottest areas" for development, which is one way of looking at this oldest part of the oldest part of Washington. The Citizens Association of Georgetown views it otherwise....

The *Washington Post* in the late 1960s and 1970s editorialized on conservation in distant places, such as the Grand Canyon, Alaska, and the redwood country of California, but on the home front, showed itself as part of the establishment strongly supporting commercial growth. Sam Smith, an advocate for the inner city, declared:

As a local power, the *Post* has not only been conservative, it has been dangerously reactionary, serving the economic interests of the most greedy and powerful. Urban renewal, freeways, convention centers, the multi-billion dollar subway fiasco, all owe a deep debt to the long loyalty of the *Washington Post*. To the city, the *Post* is Big Business first and journalism second.[3]

Editors did not assign reporters to expose zoning scandals, regulation violations, votes taken at 2:00 AM after the citizens had gone home, the conflicts of interest, or industry-caused air pollution and water pollution. Their "stories" were of murder and violence, not the pall of smoke, poisons in soil and water, vanishing open space, or overpopulation. The news copy in the weekly real estate section was little more than puffery designed to dignify the advertisements. The presentation of news presumably was the paper's basic function, but there was no weekly section on human rights or on natural resource conservation. But, of course, news came neatly packaged by industry and government PR people, while concerned citizens were considered by the editors to be kooks and crackpots.

Looking back on my career, I made my full share of mistakes. I did what in my heart I felt was right and tried to learn from mistakes. In September 1994, I was surprised to receive a note, out of the blue, from Ben W. Gilbert, the city editor under whom I had worked as a cub reporter almost fifty years before at the *Washington Post*. He was living in Tacoma, in western Washington: "It has been a long time since you did a stint as a reporter on the *Post*," he wrote. "I have noted your existence from quotes here and there, but did not know you had made the trek west as I did ten years ago." He hoped that we might meet, then concluded: "The news business lost a very promising person when you left, but I think you are doing more good monitoring the environment." So it turned out right over the long run.

But there is more to this phase of my life and story. I knew nothing about it when it was going on. I became aware of it in 1998—more than twenty-five years after the fact—while visiting with my friend Alfred Runte. He had been doing research at the Forest History Society in Durham, North Carolina, where he had read the text of an extensive interview with William E. Towell, the former executive vice president of the American Forestry Association, conducted by Harold K. Steen of the history society.

I obtained a typescript of that interview (which ran over forty-six pages) and found a lot more to it than that. Towell laid it on Jim Craig, the editor, even more than on me. He said Craig was basically a newspaper reporter, who "was hot on any subject that made news." And here are highlights of Towell's side of the story:

> And he loved controversy. This was why Mike Frome was so dear to Jim Craig. Jim Craig thought Mike Frome was the greatest thing that ever lived because he created controversy with every column he wrote. Challenged the Forest Service, the trade associations, and he evoked lots of response, lots of letters. Jim thought this was just great, and he was really encouraging Mike to say things that he knew would be controversial. I can remember one of Mike's columns that ended up on my desk before Jim saw it, and attached to it was a note from Mike Frome to Jim, "This ought to keep the pot boiling for a while." It had a statement in there that "the forests of this country are too precious to entrust to professional foresters."

Then Towell referred to an article titled "Mineral King: A Golden Opportunity," about the embattled Mineral King Valley (now part of Sequoia-Kings Canyon National Park):

> I thought it was a great opportunity when Disney proposed to establish that beautiful ski area in a valley which has already been desecrated by mining, by grazing, by roads, and allow nobody in except by tramway with a parking lot miles below. With Disney's

reputation for quality, I thought it was great. And in the same issue Mike Frome's column was against it. Completely opposite viewpoints.[4]

Towell explained that the AFA board had given him authority to set policy, to act on his own best judgment:

> The magazine did not and wasn't intended to, at that time, by Jim at least, reflect the positions or policy too much by AFA. It was a news magazine of interest to anybody in the forestry environmental field. Jim somewhat resented the fact that we would question anything he would want to put in there. Mike Frome was not the only question. I said, "Jim, I don't want to be a super editor, I don't want to review any articles that go in that magazine before I see it in print, but I expect you to reflect the philosophy, the policies that are established by AFA."
>
> We came to forks in the road shortly after I came there [in 1967], and it culminated in the Mike Frome problem. We reached the point where AFA was either going to take this wide open swing with the environmental movement and join the bandwagon, or we were going to stick to our guns and stand up for professionalism, for management, for wise use, as contrasted to preservation. The preservation movement is pretty much against everything. They're for more refuges, all wilderness, no cutting. Let me give you an example. A member, Gordon Robinson, was a forester with the Sierra Club.
>
> He came into the AFA offices and went to Jim Craig. Jim reported the conversation. The Sierra Club has saved about all the rivers it could, created about all the national parks, and we feel the urge for national park quality, now we're going after the national forests. We're going to take the national forests away from the Forest Service. We're going to make parks and wilderness out of these national forests, because we don't like the way the Forest Service is managing them. Mike Frome was following the same line of reasoning. The forests of this nation are too valuable to be entrusted to foresters. They're a public trust. AFA had to make a decision at that point, whether we were going to go along with the groundswell of environmental emotionalism or whether we

were going to stand up for the principles we believed in. This is what the whole Mike Frome affair was about. Of course Jim loved it because it made news.

Mike Frome is a product of the Forest Service. There's a great story about Mike Frome. He's a New York Jewish boy with a great disfigurement over half his face.

Enormous birthmark. Small of stature, with a deep ingrained inferiority complex.

He was a poor boy and, as I recall, he did not have much education, but he's one hell of a good writer. And Mike got interested in nature, in forestry, and Bill Huber of the Forest Service [an associate of Clint Davis in Information and Education] kind of took Mike under his wing and taught him, carried him around to a lot of the places and showed him what the Forest Service was doing. He wrote very knowingly of forestry and the Forest Service for quite a long time, and was a product very much of their creation, but a beautiful writer. Then he began to exhibit some of his anti-establishment views, and the column that gave him the most exposure, the best exposure he had—his books (he wrote several, even before he was a columnist for *American Forests*) didn't give him the exposure. The public following that *American Forests* did, and that was his great vehicle. But then he began to bite the hand that fed him, so to speak. ..."[5]

Towell was asked if I was technically Jim's employee. He replied:

He was a paid columnist. He wasn't on the staff. He was paid the paltry sum of $250 a column, which at that time was our highest paid article, highest pay we made for a contributor. My mistake was in trying to force Jim to control Mike. Finally I put it in writing in a way that backfired.[6]

The American Forestry Association lost members following my dismissal. It sold its building close to the White House and bought another elsewhere in Washington. Then it sold that one and continued losing membership. It still exists, focusing on urban forestry and tree planting. And now *American Forests* is published only as a quarterly.

As for me, the older I grew, the more I loved my work and the subjects I wrote about, I found pleasure in digging deeper and in learning through research and reading, and in working with editors, who almost always wanted only that I improve my writing and that it come through as mine. I observed the mainstream media provide plenty of information, packaged as facts, more than anyone could absorb or digest, but mostly bland, shallow, unquestioning; and the irreverent, independent reporter was apt to pay the price of a complaint to the editor for that unforgivable sin: "losing objectivity."

I explored works of Mary Austin, Paul Brooks, Rachel Carson, Bernard DeVoto, Joseph Wood Krutch, Aldo Leopold, John Muir, Sigurd Olson, Wallace Stegner, Edward Abbey, and others in the library of environmental literature. I found quotable passages where I least expected them, as in Thomas Merton's *Raids on the Unspeakable*:

> News becomes merely a new noise in the mind, briefly replacing the noise that went before it and yielding to the noise that comes after it, so that eventually everything blends into the same monotonous and meaningless rumor. News? There is so much news that there is no room left for the true tidings, the "Good News," The Great Joy. Hence The Great Joy is announced, after all, in silences, loneliness, and darkness.[7]

I endeavored in my own way to spread The Great Joy manifest in the preservation of nature within designated wilderness. Americans could be proud of the 106 million acres safeguarded by the Wilderness Act, for wilderness preservation treats ecology as the economics of nature, in a manner directly related to the economics of humankind. Keeping biotic diversity alive is the surest means of keeping humanity alive. But conservation transcends economics—it illuminates the human condition by refusing to put a price tag on the priceless.

In 1994, I was inducted into the Circle of Chiefs, a select group of conservation writers who belong to the Outdoor Writers Association of America. The OWAA to a large degree was made up of "hook-and-bullet" writers focused on the catch and kill, while the Chiefs, even within the ranks, had a broader, less consumptive vision of the outdoors. I owed my nomination to Ted Williams (absolutely no relation to the Boston baseball slugger of the same name), whom I met when he was starting his career as editor of *Massachusetts Wildlife*, the state fish and game magazine, and writing in protest to my dismissal from *Field & Stream*. He was talented, full of ideas, and successful in writing for outdoor magazines, as well as for *Audubon* and other environmental periodicals. I was glad Ted was with me at the OWAA convention where I became a Chief. One of the other Chiefs, Joel Vance, introduced me:

> He has been a leader in conservation writing for more than thirty years. He's what all good conservation communicators should be, a gadfly to some, an inspiration to others. You can't, as the old saying goes, make an omelet without breaking some eggs, and our new Chief has cracked more than a few vulnerable shells in his career.

A few years later, I was selected as an OWAA "living legend." When asked whom I would like to write a profile of me in *Outdoors Unlimited*, the OWAA journal, I immediately chose Ted Williams. His article appeared in the February 2002 issue. He wrote:

> My definition of a "legend" is someone who makes a difference, and to make a difference you have to be different yourself. You have to question, probe, and nag. Never can you be content with the status quo. You can't run out of fuel. You can't worry about who you might offend. You punch only with the truth; and, while you never "pull" the truth, you also never bully. Unless you're protecting a source or someone vulnerable to retribution, you need to name names in most cases; but you remember that the people you are naming have feelings, friends, and families just like you.
>
> I'm happy to report that Mike Frome, at 81, still follows the high standards he has set for himself and us, still is making a difference. He continues to speak, write, and gallivant around the world. I get tired just hearing what he's doing.

That recognition was welcome, but Jack Samson was also a member of OWAA. When he read the newsletter, he exploded in wrath and was ready to fire me anew from *Field & Stream*, all these years later. In a letter to the editor, he wrote:

> Frome was anything but objective in 1972 when I became editor in chief of *Field & Stream*, of that fine old outdoor magazine. His columns were politically motivated, not conservation-oriented. He spent most of his time in Washington, not out in the field.

His friends were from his political side of the fence. His enemies were from the opposing party. His Rate Your Candidate series in the magazine rated as "good" his political cronies and allies; he constantly rated as "poor" those whose political beliefs contrasted with those of his own.

I did not believe then, nor do I believe now, that a writer should use a national magazine as a springboard to advance his/ her own political agenda (unless the writer works for a political magazine or is an editorial writer). Frome was neither.

Ted Williams, who wrote the glowing tribute to Frome, is, by his own admission, an acolyte of Frome and has certainly followed his footsteps.... Williams, like his hero Frome, before him, writes editorials. They may be disguised as conservation editors in outdoor magazines, but they both are first and foremost *political* writers.

That sounded silly to me. I was willing to let it go, but Michael Furtman of Duluth, Minnesota, another Chief, dispatched this rejoinder to the OWAA editor:

> I thought Samson was kidding because his next-to-last paragraph is darn funny. In berating Williams, Samson wrote, "His columns are liberally sprinkled with attacks against politicians whose policies and politics are diametrically opposed to his own."
>
> Do you see the humor? Williams is a committed conservationist. Of course he should be skewering land-grabbers and other resource rapists whose politics are diametrically opposed to conservation.
>
> Anything less would be pabulum. But then, that's the strong suit of most outdoor magazines.

Humorous perhaps, but sad as well, that pabulum should be the strong suit of outdoor magazines, and not only of them, but of the mass or mainstream media, or whatever name we choose to call it.

I heard soon after from Sam Stavisky, my old friend of the *Washington Post* days. He had been a mentor when I was breaking in and we had corresponded through World War II and later. He had left the *Post* to start a public relations and lobbying firm. "You raised the flag, led and demonstrated the path to nature journalism," he wrote to me. "And I think that you not only were—and are—an inspiring guide to wannabe environmental writers, but also you made it clear to the disciples who will follow your banner that it's not all clover out there. Straight-shooting journalists have to deal with corrupting and competing influences in every area of reporting the news." I was pleased to be in touch with Sam over the years and doubly so that he would think well of my work. If you don't mind my saying so, I feel pleased and a little proud for having survived without bitterness or complaint, and for showing that it can be done.

CHAPTER 31

Walking uphill – The penny asked me to bend down and listen – Cephalus looked past the dark forebodings – Learning to speak from the heart – June blessed the greyhound nation – Saving the best for last

On a sunny summer Saturday morning, I was walking up the hill toward home, thinking that now I was past eighty-five and on the way to being eighty-six, if fate allowed or enabled me to make it through another year. June and I had walked downtown for breakfast at a favorite Port Washington restaurant, as we did on Saturdays, and now she was on to other errands. Walking was not exactly easy for me on my problematical legs, but the cane helped, and whenever I completed the half-mile or so uphill to home, I felt pleased and energized. I walked alone with my thoughts, which shortly turned to the ultimate end of my life on earth, whenever and however that would come. First came recollections of Sigurd Olson and of how he had lived and died. He was robust in his youth, working as a teacher and as a guide in the Boundary Waters Wilderness of Minnesota before becoming a professional writer and vigorous wilderness advocate. In 1980, he underwent a cancer operation; he was pretty weak for a while and walked with a cane. His days of rough woodsmanship were gone, though he recovered some of his strength. On a bright January morning in 1982, he went to his desk and began typing, "A new adventure is coming up and I'm sure it will be a good one," and then went snowshoeing near his home at Ely, Minnesota. He suffered a heart attack, collapsed in the snow, and died soon after at the age of eighty-two.

Now I was more than three years older, and plainly vulnerable. As Cephalus said in his dialogue with Socrates:

> When a man thinks himself to be near death, fears and cares enter his mind which he never had before; the tales of a world below and the punishment which is exacted there of deeds done here were once a laughing matter to him, but now he is tormented with

the thought that they may be true; either from weakness of age, or because he is now drawing nearer to that other place, he has a clearer view of these things; suspicions and alarms crowd thickly upon him, and he begins to reflect and consider what wrongs he has done to others. And when he finds that the sum of his transgressions is great he will many a time like a child start up in his sleep for fear, and he is filled with dark forebodings.[1]

But I was not fearful, tormented, or filled with dark forebodings— nothing like it. My life even in the advanced years was filled with wonderful things going on all around me. As I walked toward home, I looked down and saw a penny, a plain brown copper penny that asked me to bend down and look closely. The penny wasn't new or shiny, yet it wanted me to take it, examine both sides of it, and heed it as a talisman of things to come. That little penny told me how fortunate I was, and that I had saved the best for last in my life. It assured me that dying was no cause for worry or concern, reminding me of the words of my old hero, John Muir.

But let children walk with Nature, let them see the beautiful blend- ings and communions of death and life, their joyous inseparable unity, as taught in woods and meadows, plains and mountains and streams of our blessed star, and they will learn that death is stingless indeed and as beautiful as life, and that the grave has no victory, for it never fights. All is divine harmony.[2]

That penny might also have been a messenger of Cephalus and Socrates. Cephalus looked past the dark forebodings and said:

But to him who is conscious of no sin, sweet hope, as Pindar charm- ingly says, is the kind nurse of his age: "Hope," he says, "cherishes the soul of him who lives in justice and holiness and is the nurse of his age and the companion of his journey—hope which is the mightiest to sway the restless soul of man."[3]

So I felt encouraged to anticipate sweet hope as the kind nurse of my own aging. I couldn't say that I spent my life solely in justice and holiness, though I tried as best I could. Perhaps now I might prove good company for the nurse, for, as Socrates said:

The makers of fortunes have a second love of money as a creation of their own, resembling the affection of authors for their own poems, or of parents for their children, besides their natural love of it for the sake of use and profit which is common to them and all men. And hence they are very bad company, for they can talk of nothing but the praise of wealth.[4]

I never talked in praise of wealth, never loved money for its own sake, never envied those who had more than I had.

The more I thought about it, the more my little brown penny freed me from external matters and helped in my search for inner truth. I recalled how in 1975, I went to speak at the dedication of the Sipsey Wilderness, a part of the Bankhead National Forest in Alabama. The Sipsey was a chain of deep gorges threaded with streams and waterfalls, which citizens had labored to protect. Before the ceremony and speeches, a young woman who worked for the Alabama Conservancy and thought I was some kind of celebrity hung at my elbow. Finally I told her I needed time alone to work on notes for my speech. "No, you don't," she said, "Get up and speak from the heart."

That was *her* lesson and gift to me, one I remembered and treasured, like the little penny. I tried always to prepare, but always to speak from the heart. I think that many scholars and educators would insist on speaking objectively with scientific rationale. But Aldo Leopold, even though equipped with the proper education and credentials, demonstrated emotion and aesthetic sensitivity as wholly compatible with science. Leopold wrote, "We can be ethical only in relation to something we can see, feel, understand, love, or otherwise have faith in." William Faulkner, in accepting the 1949 Nobel Prize for Literature, expressed a thought closely akin: "The young man or woman writing today has forgotten the problems of the human heart in conflict with itself which alone can make good writing because only that is worth writing about, worth the agony and the sweat."[5]

My wife, June, has been the greatest support to me in saving the best for last. It isn't simply what she has done for me but how she leads her own life. One Sunday in September 2003, about one month before we moved from Bellingham to Port Washington, she had been invited by an affiliation of greyhound owners in British Columbia and Washington State to bless them and their pets in a rally at the Peace Arch that marks the boundary between Canada and the United States. Such groups and June have an uncanny way of finding each other. She told the owners,

Perhaps it is the recognition of our common plight that stirs us to relate to the greyhound, a species suited by nature and training to run in high-speed races, even as we humans train to compete on the fast track of business, finance, politics, and athletics. When a greyhound isn't winning, the glory train stops and she or he is pulled off the track to be abandoned at a strange and bleak new station in life. No money, no future. Just as companies that start to lose profits choose bankruptcy, closures, and cutback in benefits and jobs for employees. And who is there to slow down, get out of the fast lane, and have compassion for the unemployed, be that the noble greyhound or the marginalized worker? Who in this competitive society, where the creed is greed, is selfless enough to rescue another creature from the indignities of rejection and the threat of death? It is that person who can cross borders, transcend human language, and communicate instinctively with fellow beings caught in the common net of this time and place.

In sharing life with June, every day has given cause to celebrate; I have been blessed daily. I have a great deal to be thankful for, and no cause for complaint. Writing this book has done much to help avoid the trap of wailing about growing old. In the process, I learned the value of an old Hasidic blessing: "For the unlearned old age is winter. For the learned it is the season of harvest." My season of harvest has stimulated alertness, remembrance, and a new, comprehensive way of viewing life and continuing to learn. At the same time, I recognize that I can't move as fast as a young generation two or three times removed from mine. I can't keep up with the jargon they speak, write, and sing or with the technology they understand and use as second nature, and there is no point in trying.

Now and then I feel ready for my share of divine harmony—but the feeling passes. Most of my old pals and playmates are gone. They've done their time here and moved on. I don't know that they're waiting for me, but I miss them. And it hurts, deep down. In August 2002, I heard from a voice out of the past, of long long ago.

Hey Mike—While idly Googling or Yahooing—I forget which— on the Net, I indulged my weakness of typing in the names of old friends, perchance to peel away years of separation. It's usu- ally futile, but not when I pecked out Michael Frome. That one perchanced out like crazy. …

I'll just posit City College Summer Session using the *Main Events* typewriters to try to bang out potboilers for the detective story mags. We got no bites, but we did get paid for ghostwriting somebody's degree thesis on literature. If all this still hasn't conjured up the name Howard Silverberg, don't sweat it. Anyway, at age 85 I'm still here, none the worse except for a painful lower back. In any case, I would enjoy an occasional conversation with you to reminisce, discuss or perhaps argue—even about windmills, since they're now a gripping new energy alternative. With fond greetings, Howie.

I was thrilled to hear from my old pal and partner and answered at once. We exchanged e-mails. He brought me up to date on himself. He had been a merchant seaman in World War II, then an organizer for the National Maritime Union, a steelworker at the Bethlehem Steel Sparrows Point plant in Baltimore, and a life insurance agent. After his first wife's death of cancer in 1984, he remarried a retired parole and probation officer "who functioned like a concerned social worker, not like a cop." In retirement he worked as a part-time "legal courier" (a messenger for attorneys). He wrote, "As I tell my wife each time she asks me to quit, the job keeps my batteries recharged and, I firmly believe, accounts for my still being around. I've seen too many contemporaries sit still waiting to die, and not having to wait long."

He was still a deeply committed communist. He wrote a political column for a local community newspaper until it folded, reports and commentary for the *Peoples Weekly World*, and letters to the establishment and the alternative press. He had developed an e-mail mailing list of more than 160 activists to whom he sent weekly clips of articles from the *Peoples Weekly World, New York Times, Baltimore Sun,* and progressive material from the Internet. He added me to the mailing list. The materials he disseminated were well chosen and useful, and besides, they served as a bridge to connect with my old friend.

Once he e-mailed to especially recommend an article in *Mother Jones* written by Ted Williams on the timber industry influence on our national forests, as abetted by the George W. Bush administration. We talked on the phone and exchanged recollections. I mentioned that my daughter lived in Silver Spring, Maryland, a suburb of Washington DC, and that the next time I came East to visit her, I surely would come to Baltimore to see him.

When I wrote him that I still had copies of three of the detective stories we had written together, he replied by asking, What might have happened had that summer been longer? Isn't that often the question? What if that summer had been longer? Or shorter? Or spent somewhere else? But there is no answer beyond the given time and given place, to make the most of, or at least to accept, without pondering, what if?

Early in 2003, I asked Howard if he would read part of this book as I was writing it. He agreed and in March I sent him the first ten chapters. I appreciated his review and comments. He recalled details for me about our time at City College and people we had known there, and he raised issues for me to consider. In mid-April I sent him the second ten chapters. In response, he wrote me a handwritten scribbled letter dated May 8, 2003.

> This is being written from a hospital bed where I landed last week due to a disabling shortness of breath. The problem stems from pneumonia, but that's the least of it. The pneumonia is due to aspiration, which means what is intended for my belly goes into my lungs.
>
> The cause is my swallowing mechanism, which has broken down. I'm being fed by means of a thin tube into my stomach through my nose, for which a bunch of eager young university hospital doctors scramble to find a solution. I'm on oxygen, and completely comfortable, but not overjoyed at the possible outcome—as ... [illegible] into my stomach for feeding.
>
> Anyway, I can still function, so let me thank you for sending the new material. I'll give it my close attention and try to produce some pearls of criticism.
>
> With anticipation, Howard

That was the last communication from him. A few days later his wife, Jeanne, called to advise that he had died in the hospital. When people are in the mideighties, they're likely to do that, from one cause or another. I was saddened and empty inside, berating myself for not getting to see him, and asking, What if? when there really was no answer.

The June 4, 2003, *Baltimore City Paper* ran a very nice review, written by Anna Ditkoff, of a memorial service to my old friend.

On the afternoon of Saturday, May 31, the horseshoe bar atop the

Captain James Landing restaurant in Canton was packed with activists, communists, and residents of Southeast Baltimore's Washington Hill community. Standing against the walls and sitting on the floor, children, their parents, and grandparents sang protest songs and toasted the life of a man of whose unwavering belief in economic and racial equality and his commitment to fighting for them had inspired them all.

Howard Silverberg, a labor organizer, founding member of several community organizations, and member of the Communist Party of Maryland, died May 27 of complications from pneumonia. He was 86 years old.

He was born in Winston-Salem, NC, moved with his parents to New York as a child. Soon after Pearl Harbor, he enlisted in the merchant marine and become a member of the National Maritime Union. After the war he moved to Baltimore, worked in the ship-yards at Sparrows Point, and became involved in social issues.

He joined the Communist Party during the 1930s and was active in Maryland. He was called before the House Un-American Activities Committee, took the Fifth Amendment, was expelled from the National Maritime Union, and lost several jobs, but never expressed regret or self-pity. In 1971, his neighborhood, Washington Hill, was so run down and the houses in such poor condition, the city planned to demolish most of it. Silverberg, along with other residents, formed the Citizens for Washington Hill, successfully fought the city's plan, and revitalized the neighborhood.

He donated his body to science and did not want a funeral. So family and friends gathered at Captain James Landing. And while tears were shed, there was frequent laughter. People joked about Silverberg's love of bad puns, his enthusiastic dancing, his intimidating stature, and his gentle nature. "We have big shoes to fill. Howard had big feet."

The farewell party, tendered with tears and laughter to my friend Howard at Captain James Landing, brings me back to Socrates, the old sage.

My counsel is that we hold fast ever to the heavenly way and follow after justice and virtue always, considering that the soul is immortal and able to endure every sort of evil. Thus shall we live dear to one another and to the gods, both while remaining here and when, like conquerors in the games who go round to gather gifts, we receive our reward. And it shall be well with us both in this life and in the pilgrimage of a thousand years which we have been describing.[6]

There are different ways of expressing this idea, as the psalmist did in declaring: "I believe that I shall see the goodness of the Lord in the land of the living" (Ps. 27:13). To add a word of my own: Have faith, I say, and remember—if you haven't been lost, you haven't navigated. Furthermore, I'm glad I saved the best for last.

Notes

Preface

1. Dietrich Bonhoeffer, *Letters and Papers from Prison* (London: Fontana Books, 1960), 69.
2. C. S. Lewis, *Surprised by Joy: The Shape of My Early Life* (New York: Harcourt, Brace, & World, 1955), 157.
3. I. F. Stone, "Notes on Closing, But Not in Farewell," in the final issue of *I.F. Stone's Weekly*, December 1971. Stone called himself "a flickering flame in a naughty world."
4. Marcus Aurelius *Meditations* 2.5, quoted in Rex Warner, *The Greek Philosophers* (New York: American Library, 1958), 183.

Chapter 1

1. Michael Gold, *Jews Without Money* (1930; repr., New York: Carroll & Graf, 1990), 306.
2. William E. Towell, interview by Harold K. Steen, November 1988, transcribed by the Forest History Society, Durham, NC, 1989. Quote from p. 45 of transcript.
3. Helen Keller, quoted in Dorothy Herrmann, *Helen Keller: A Life* (New York: Knopf, 1998), 337.
4. Will Eisner, "The Early Years" (www.willeisner.com/biography/1_early_years).
5. James Baldwin and Sol Stein, *Native Sons: A Friendship that Created One of the Greatest Works of the 20th Century* (New York: One World, 2004), 3–4.

Chapter 2

1. Lincoln Steffens. *Autobiography of Lincoln Steffens* (New York: Harcourt, Brace, and World, 1931), 169.
2. Dorothy Day, *The Long Loneliness: The Autobiography of Dorothy Day,* with an introduction by Daniel Berrigan (San Francisco: Harper & Row, 1981), 29, 39.
3. Day, *The Long Loneliness,* 93.
4. Letter from John Kieran, April 29, 1941, on *New York Times* letterhead. A photocopy of the letter was reproduced on page 1 of the first issue of Pulse, "the choice creative artistic and literary effort of the four city colleges [Brooklyn, CCNY, Hunter, Queens]," which was published in June 1941. Authors personal files.

Chapter 3

1. Muir left with a heavy heart: "I gained a last wistful lingering view of the beautiful University grounds and buildings where I had spent so many hungry and hopeful days. There with streaming eyes I bad my blessed Alma Mater farewell.

But I was only leaving one University for another, The Wisconsin University for the University of the Wilderness." Linnie Marsh Wolfe, *Son of the Wilderness: The Life of John Muir* (Madison: University of Wisconsin Press, 1973), 5, 87.

2. Theodore Dreiser, *A Book About Myself* (New York: Boni & Liveright, 1922), 382.

3. Dreiser, *A Book About Myself*, 388.

4. Dreiser, *A Book About Myself*, 385.

5. John Strohmeyer, *Crisis in Bethlehem* (New York: Viking Penguin, 1987), 24.

6. Dreiser, *A Book About Myself*, 382–83.

7. Author's transcription of speech.

8. Author's transcription of speech.

9. "Democrats Sweep Election," *Union Press*, Aliquippa, PA, November 3, 1937.

10. "Victory" (editorial), *Union Press*, Aliquippa, PA, November 3, 1937.

CHAPTER 7

1. Plato *Republic,* trans. Benjamin Jowett (New York: Vintage Books, n.d.), 8.567, "The way of the tyrant." (transl. Jowett) There is more to it, Socrates continued: "And if any of them [his subjects] are suspected by him of having any notions of freedom, and of resistance to his authority, he will have a good pretext for destroying them by placing them at the mercy of the enemy; and for all these reasons, the tyrant must always be getting up a war."

2. Eisenhower, "Speech: Ottawa, Canada, January 10, 1946" (www.westpointgrads againstthewar.org).

3. Plato *Republic* 8.529–30.

CHAPTER 8

1. William Harlan Hale, *Horace Greeley: Voice of the People* (New York: Collier, 1961), 79.

2. Katherine Graham, *Personal History* (New York: Knopf, 1997), 131, 183.

3. Graham, *Personal History,* 571.

4. *Chapel Post* (a publication of *The Washington Post* during World War II), August 1945, 1.

5. Graham, *Personal History,* 148.

6. Ben Gilbert, "A Recollection: Lifting the Veil from the 'Secret City'—The *Washington Post* and the Racial Revolution" (unpublished paper, 1993), 1.

7. Gilbert, "A Recollection," 29.

8. Ralph Waldo Emerson, *Essays and English Traits* (New York: Collier, 1937), 9. In his celebrated speech to the Phi Beta Kappa society at Cambridge (August 31, 1837), Emerson declared, "This [the active soul] every man is entitled to; this every man contains within him, although, in almost all men, obstructed and as yet unborn. The soul active sees absolute truth; and utters truth."

CHAPTER 9

1. Robert Penn Warren, *All the King's Men* (New York: Harcourt, 2001), 3

2. Marjorie Kinnan Rawlings, *The Yearling* (New York: Scribner, 1967), 88.

3. George Seldes, *Lords of the Press* (New York: Julian Messner, 1938), 180.

CHAPTER 13

1. My column became a popular feature, generating assorted letters—both supportive and critical—in the Forest Forum section of *American Forests*. Criticisms became more frequent after my June 1970 column, which began: "The tide of disaffection with the management of our national forests grows stronger and deeper...."

CHAPTER 15

1. The Udall/Stansbury column was issued for release August 7–8, 1971.

2. American Society of Journalists and Authors, "White Paper on the Firing of a Journalist, May 1975," by McGrady and Samson, 2. In the Summary of Findings, Patrick M. McGrady Jr., chairman of the Professional Rights Committee, wrote: "We journalists and authors are especially concerned that our right-to-tell and the public's right-to-know are being increasingly suppressed as heavy-handed, secretive conglomerates aggrandize their power. We are fully aware that this is a complex problem with no easy solutions. We do not desire to impoverish or weaken any medium, but rather to strengthen the media generally by protecting our intellectual and expressive freedoms." Ibid., 6.

3. "Pollen Profiles as Indicators in the History of Lake Filling," *Ecology* 37, no. 3 (July 1956): 476–83.

4. Mary Evelyn Jergen, "Seeing Through Peaceful Eyes," *Fellowship* (November 1987): 26–28.

CHAPTER 16

1. Mary Hunter Austin, *The Land of Little Rain* (Charlottesville: University of Virginia Library, 1995), 7 [electronic resource transcribed from 1971 Ballantine Books edition].

CHAPTER 17

1. Sigurd Olson, "From the Friday Afternoon Discussion," address in *Wilderness and the Quality of Life: Proceedings of the Tenth Biennial Sierra Club Wilderness Conference,* April 7–9, 1967, San Francisco, ed. Maxine E. McCloskey and James P. Gilligan (San Francisco: Sierra Club, 1969), 88–90.

CHAPTER 19

1. Myles Horton, *We Make the Road by Walking: Conversations on Education and Social Change* (Philadelphia: Temple University Press, 1990), 102.

CHAPTER 21

1. Charles Darwin, *Journal of Researches into the Natural History and Geology of the Countries Visited During the Voyage of the HMS Beagle Round the World Under the Command of Capt. Fitz Roy, R.N.* (New York: Harper & Brothers, 1846), 1:145.

2. *Green Mansions: A Romance of the Tropical Forest* is the title of a popular novel

by W. H. Hudson first published in 1904. The title may derive from the biblical quotation, "In my Father's house are many mansions," implying the pristine forest is a sacred, natural cathedral.

Chapter 22

1. Theodore C. Blegen. *Norwegian Migration to America: The American Transition* (Northfield, MN: Norwegian-American Historical Association, 1940), 1–19.

Chapter 26

1. Henry Beston, *The Outermost House: A Year of Life on the Great Beach of Cape Cod* (New York: Owl Books/Henry Holt, 2003), 25.
2. Luther wrote this in his commentary on Genesis 1:22. See Martin Luther, *Luther's Works*, ed. Jaroslav Pelikan, vol. 1 (Saint Louis: Concordia, 1958).
3. John Calvin, *Institutes of the Christian Religion*, trans. and ed. Ford Lewis Battles (Philadelphia: Westminster, 1960), 1:180.
4. June Eastvold Nilson, *Read My Tail: The Testimony of a Terrier Named Brandy* (Bellingham, WA: GAM, 2000), 72.

Chapter 29

1. Frederick Douglass, "What to the Slave Is the Fourth of July?" 5 July 1852.
2. Horace Greeley to Mrs. Rebekah Whipple (Vermont), quoted in Hale, *Horace Greeley*, 299.
3. Emerson, "Nature," in *Essays and English Traits*, 233.
4. Joseph Wood Krutch, "Wilderness as a Tonic," *Saturday Review*, June 8, 1963.
5. Ray Stannard Baker, *The Spiritual Unrest* (New York: Frederick A. Stokes, 1910), 97, 98, 100.
6. Donald W. Carson and James W. Johnson, *The Life and Times of Morris K. Udall*, (Tucson: University of Arizona Press, 2001), 134.

Chapter 30

1. Seldes, *Lords of the Press*, 269.
2. Graham, *Personal History*, 234.
3. Sam Smith, interview with the author, January 1977. Sam Smith was the founder and editor of the *DC Gazette*, an early version of alternative weeklies that later spread widely to U.S. cities.
4. William E. Towell, interview transcript, 32.
5. William E. Towell, interview transcript, 33, 45.
6. William E. Towell, interview transcript, 46.
7. Thomas Merton, *Raids on the Unspeakable* (New York: New Directions, 1964), 67.

Chapter 31

1. Plato *Republic* 1.331.
2. Quoted in Wolfe, *Son of the Wilderness*, 112. In the course of his "thousand mile

walk to the sea," Muir camped one night in the Bonaventure Cemetery in Savannah, Georgia. Wolfe wrote: "The peace of his surroundings, 'where graves are powerless in such a depth of life,' inspired one of his most notable utterances upon Death." Ibid., 112–13.

3. Plato *Republic* 1.331.

4. Plato *Republic* 1.330.

5. Aldo Leopold, *A Sand County Almanac* (New York: Oxford University Press, 1987), 214; and William Faulkner, "Banquet Speech" (Speech at Nobel Banquet at the City Hall in Stockholm, December 10, 1950, available online at nobelprize. org/nobel_prizes/literature/laureates/1949/faulkner-speech).

6. Plato *Republic* 10.621.

ACKNOWLEDGMENTS

I began serious work on this book early in 2003 when my wife June and I rented an apartment for six weeks at Zihuatanejo, Mexico. We set aside one room as an office where I was able to work undisturbed through a mass of materials I had brought along. This led to a first draft and in time through three revisions.

Perhaps the most helpful comments and critique in the early stages came to me from Donald Edward Davis, professor at Dalton State College, Georgia (author of *Where There Are Mountains: An Environmental History of the Southern Mountains*), who showed me how to take myself more seriously as an environmental advocate. My close friend Alfred Runte, historian and author, gave significant encouragement from the very beginning until ultimate publication. Other academics and scholars who reviewed the work at one stage or another, or provided helpful input, include Ben Bagdikian, former dean of journalism, University of California at Berkeley; Richard Behan, professor emeritus and former dean of forestry, Northern Arizona University; Scot Danforth, University of Tennessee Press; James R. Fazio, professor of natural resources, University of Idaho; Hugh Iltis, professor emeritus, University of Wisconsin; and Carl Reidel, professor emeritus, University of Vermont.

Many friends and colleagues in the environmental field helped me considerably, notably Stewart Brandborg, former executive director of the Wilderness Society; Brock Evans, former executive director and now president of the Endangered Species Coalition; Paul Pritchard, president of the National Park Trust; Mack Prichard, chief naturalist of Tennessee; Mark Peterson, executive director of the Minnesota Audubon Society; Scott Silver, director of Wild Wilderness; and Ted Williams, editor-at-large of *Audubon* magazine.

My niece, Annette Fromm, folklorist and museum director, and her brother, Peter Fromm, keeper of the family photo archive, helped in recapping early years. The late Howard Silverberg and his wife, Jeanne Dresser, helped with recollection of college days (and nights). With reference to my wife's early years, I was aided by her sister, Audrey Light, and her husband, Robert

Light. I received important help from my children, William C. Frome and Michele L. Frome, and from June's children, Fjaere Nilssen-Mooney, Kjersti Nilssen, and Carl Nilssen.

I am grateful to Glenn Walters of Port Washington, Wisconsin, my friend and technical advisor, for guidance in the use of my computer; Lisa Friend, of Bellingham, Washington, who has indexed my books with care and concern for the past twenty years, and to the staff of Truman State University Press for personal and professional interest in making this book happen. I wrote in the preface that academic presses are staffed with competent, conscientious people, and they care. Truman State University Press has been the exemplar.

Above all, I am indebted to my wife, June Eastvold, who held my hand and cheered me on the way and *all* the way.

INDEX